Teacher's
Weather Sourcebook

Teacher's Weather Sourcebook

By
Tom Konvicka

1999
Teacher Ideas Press
A Division of
Libraries Unlimited, Inc.
Englewood, Colorado

TEACHER IDEAS PRESS
A Division of
Libraries Unlimited, Inc.
P.O. Box 6633
Englewood, CO 80155-6633
1-800-237-6124
www.lu.com/tip

Library of Congress Cataloging-in-Publication Data

Konvicka, Tom.
    Teacher's weather sourcebook / by Tom Konvicka.
    xvi, 321 p. 22x28 cm.
    Includes bibliographical references and index.
    ISBN 1-56308-488-0
    1. Atmosphere--Study and teaching. 2. Meteorology--Study and teaching. I. Title.
QC869.K66 1999
551.5'071'2--dc21
                                       99-13551
                                         CIP

Contents

The dew on the grass glistens in the oblique rays of the early morning sun. A small boy walks briskly through the ankle-high grass, dampening his shoes and the cuffs of his pants. He thinks about the origin of such strange water. Did it come from the sky or from the ground? Later, after the dew is gone, the boy lies on his back, staring at the patchwork of clouds in the sky, imagining them to be pieces of a grand jigsaw puzzle. He stands and feels the wind, wondering about the invisible force moving through his thick, dark-brown hair.

A great storm comes in the evening, prompting him to question how such a tranquil morning could give way to such a violent spectacle. Ah! But this is his kind of weather, and as long as it's safe he locks his eyes on the storm, awed by the fickle power of nature. Crash!! Lightning strikes nearby, and it's time to seek refuge. Safely inside, he reads about tornadoes and hail while stealing peeks out a nearby window.

Night comes and the boy dreams about the life experiences of the day, punctuating them with the weather events that he saw, heard, and felt. The boy continues his love affair with the weather in college. The university professor sloppily writes a slew of equations on the board and, somehow, the young man is able to connect his childhood observations to the mathematical mess in front of him. He was learning. Then, at the tender age of 26, he assumed his duties as chief meteorologist for one of the nation's highest-rated network affiliates. The introverted little boy had come full circle, the completion of a childhood dream. This is his book, intended for teachers so they, too, can capture a taste of his passion for weather and pass it along to their students.

The study of Earth's atmosphere is challenging and exhilarating. The challenge is to comprehend its phenomena and processes, to predict its behavior, and to understand the profound influence it exerts on each of us. Exhilaration arrives as a fresh breeze loaded with the distinctive scent of rain, the awesome fury of a hurricane, or the rude invasion of a crashing thunderbolt into the neighborhood.

I am frequently asked to visit the classroom and to speak with students about the weather. After speaking to thousands of students in hundreds of diverse classroom settings, I have one recurring thought: The need for *Teacher's Weather Sourcebook* is overwhelming. I see teachers who have the desire to teach the weather unit, but do not have the resources needed to accomplish that task. The scope and quality of instructional materials must increase, for we need not be illiterate about something that's a part of our everyday life.

A mission statement is "to assist teachers with their preparation for the weather unit and to stimulate thoughts on ways to deliver the information to students." Thus, the *Sourcebook* does not try to tell teachers how to teach the weather unit but allows them the freedom to interface uniquely with each class and student. In short, the *Sourcebook* stands as an equipping mechanism, a ready reference for factual information and an aid for facilitating the learning process.

In creating this book, I have kept the following points foremost in mind:

- Those who teach the weather unit must be better prepared.

- Much of the current resource material is clearly outdated, causing teachers and students to miss the exciting advances currently being made in atmospheric science.

- The emphasis is on "teacher power." Unfortunately, teachers bear most of the blame for the present shortcomings in our educational system, especially in math and science. Rather than berate teachers, the goal is to give them what they need to guide the students better.

- Teachers must be allowed to "do it themselves" by taking the material presented and using their creativity, formal education, and professional experience to interact with students. Hence, this book is an attempt to mesh the teacher's expertise with the resources of a professional meteorologist.

- In practice, the problems that confront scientists rarely fit into a nice, neat box that one can paste a label on. This "science without walls" approach treats meteorology as a topic free of unyielding boundaries, that is, an interdisciplinary science.

- There is less emphasis placed on memorization of facts and theories. Instead, there is more concentration on vital concepts and critical thinking through application and inference for older grade levels.

- The depth of material is much greater than other similar publications. The latest standardized test scores imply that all subjects in the curriculum must be taught at a deeper level, instead of superficially touching upon a topic.

- The American statesman and weather observer Benjamin Franklin wrote in the February 1735 issue of *Poor Richard's Almanack:* "Some are weatherwise, some are otherwise." The overwhelming mission of the *Sourcebook* is for all who use it to become more weatherwise.

Introduction

The vast majority of school districts in the United States include a "weather unit" in their curriculum. Two reasons for this trend exist. First, weather affects almost all aspects of life. It determines how we dress, what we eat, and it regulates the pulse of business and industry. At times weather prompts us to make life-or-death decisions. The nation's educators realize that we must not be illiterate about something that exerts such a profound influence on society.

A second reason for the precollege study of weather is the academic value of the topic. Atmospheric science, the scientific examination of Earth's atmosphere, is recognized by many educators and scientists as an ideal interdisciplinary science. It offers a unique opportunity to generate a young person's interest in other technical fields and promotes the appreciation of other scientific disciplines. The subject matter of atmospheric science can be melded in many ways and applied to a variety of scientific and technical problems. Therefore, through their study of our weather, students undergo a learning experience that they can transfer to any other field of science.

This book consists of two parts. Part I covers practically every major topic in atmospheric science. Chapter 1 introduces the scope of atmospheric science as viewed in a modern context. Chapter 2 explains several important components of the Earth-sun relationship. The chemical composition and vertical structure of Earth's atmosphere are discussed in chapter 3. The ingredients of weather—temperature, moisture, and pressure—are detailed in chapter 4. Next, in chapter 5, the reader is challenged to understand the complex movement of the atmosphere. Chapter 6 reviews instruments, equipment, and observations. More basic material follows in chapters 7, 8, and 9 with the precipitation process, weather systems, and weather forecasting, respectively. Finally, chapter 10 covers weather sights and sounds.

Part II, chapters 11 through 19, provides extensive treatment of Earth's climate system and the most notable manifestations of the atmosphere: thunderstorms, tornadoes, hurricanes, blizzards and snowstorms, floods and drought, and temperature extremes. These phenomena demand immediate, decisive action regarding life and property. For these reasons part II strives to give the reader a volume of material focused on education, awareness, and preparedness.

Part II also presents the important contemporary issues confronting our global community. These "hot" topics are air pollution, global warming, ozone loss, and acid deposition. The approach to these controversial issues is balanced, nonalarmist, and thorough. Again, the emphasis is that through proper education, awareness and preparedness are achieved.

Each chapter in each part begins with a body of factual material. This is intended as the main learning agent for teachers, as it provides them with the factual knowledge necessary for teaching the weather unit. The content is interrupted occasionally by a segment called "Teacher's Extra," tidbits of information related to the topic under discussion that teachers may find interesting, practical, or be questioned about by students.

A second major division of each chapter is "The Process of Scientific Thought." This may be thought of as the "practical" component of instruction (as opposed to the "theory" of the previous section). In its most complete sense, this section represents application, through activities, of the concepts and knowledge learned from previous material in the chapter. In short, the *Sourcebook* recognizes that students learn best through experimentation. "The Process of Scientific Thought" section follows concepts of developmental psychology and cognitive science. The primary goal is to instill and develop a student's ability to think critically and independently, that is, to think "scientifically." In professional practice, however, "thinking scientifically" is rarely adequate to solve the problem; one must also think creatively. The *Sourcebook* attempts to encourage teachers to spark students' creativity.

Several other items are contained at the end of each chapter. In "Ideas for Science Fair Projects," well over 100 viable suggestions are available for the teacher and student to choose from. I recommend these projects be carried out under the supervision of an adult mentor, preferably a science professional from the local community. "School's Out!" focuses on learning through social interaction. Students are encouraged to take what they have learned in the classroom and apply it at home, in the community, or just for something to do when they are bored.

Finally, the *Sourcebook* contains several appendixes. Appendix A gives the record high and low temperatures for all 50 states. Appendix B presents information on the climates of many cities in the United States. Appendix C contains a climatological profile for selected international cities. Appendix D is a summary of several different types of available resources, including books, periodicals, software, and videos. Appendix E is a unique feature of the *Sourcebook*, as it allows teachers and students to cruise the "information superhighway" via the Internet. Use of appendix E should greatly expand the information available to both students and teachers, as it allows them to search for interesting tidbits that previously were not available to the general public.

PART I

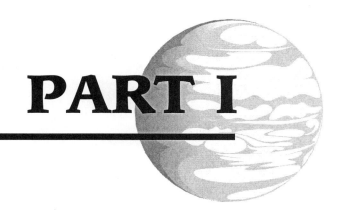

AN INVITATION
TO ATMOSPHERIC
SCIENCE

Chapter 1

The Scope of Atmospheric Science

When two Englishmen meet, their first talk is of the weather.
Samuel Johnson

Weather holds the fascination and imagination of humankind. Why? Probably no single correct answer exists. Some are spellbound by the singular beauty of a rainbow. To others the effects of weather are a brutal reality—a tornado, for instance, that destroys a home or severs a relationship. Still others concentrate on the economic aspects—an industry counts the profit from favorable weather or counts the losses from unfavorable conditions. Finally, there is the scientist who marvels at the magnificent and complex interplay of forces evident in the atmosphere and attempts to equationize, theorize, and predict. Perhaps we can accurately misquote Samuel Johnson, the English author and lexicographer, who uttered the above statement more than 200 years ago: "When two people meet, they will eventually talk about the weather."

Weather, Meteorology, and Atmospheric Science

The study of Earth's atmosphere has motivated and humbled scientists since antiquity. Scientists are challenged by their existence on a planet whose nature is so intricate that it almost defies comprehension. And scientists are humbled by the fact that, no matter how diligently they may labor and no matter what technology may evolve, they will never know everything about Earth and its atmosphere. The inquisitive human mind prevails, however, and scientists will continue to investigate and experiment. One feature of all scientific endeavor is that the more we know, the more significant that field of science becomes and the more cherished is our role as participants.

In order to progress to subsequent chapters, several important terms need clarification. The first of these is *weather*. A concise definition of weather might be: Weather is the short-term state of the atmosphere. This definition represents and includes two main components: 1) the state of the atmosphere commonly implies existence of its qualities at a particular time and location, and 2) the state of the atmosphere also represents and includes the way it manifests its existence, including what we see, hear, and feel. Thus, weather is that unique experience one has with the atmosphere at any given time and place.

A second important term is *meteorology*. In its purest sense, meteorology means "the study of phenomena in the sky." The word derives from the Greek *meteoron* ("phenomenon in the sky") and *logia* ("study"). The first record we have of a scientific study of meteorology is from Aristotle, the eminent Greek scholar and philosopher, whose book *De Meteorologia*, written more than 2,000 years ago, details some of the same topics covered in modern books on meteorology. Rooted in these beginnings, the modern connotation of meteorology is "the study of Earth's atmosphere and its phenomena."

To most the phrase "atmospheric science" is new. It is a modern attempt to further define what the study of Earth's atmosphere involves. In its most complete sense atmospheric science means the integrated, scientific examination of the atmosphere, including its composition, structure, behavior, phenomena, prediction, and effects. Hence, atmospheric science is interdisciplinary, employing the methods and ideas of other sciences. In the *Sourcebook atmospheric science* is used interchangeably with *meteorology*, but the former is preferred.

Teacher's Extra

What Is a Meteorologist?

One of the most common questions students ask is stated above. Probably the most common answer is the "weatherperson" who appears on the local TV station or on a cable channel. But these descriptions are oversimplified and, in many cases, incorrect.

The word *meteorologist* was coined in 1621 by the English author Robert Burton in *The Anatomy of Melancholy:* "Whirlewinds . . . and . . . storms; which our meteorologists generally refer to natural causes." Today, a meteorologist is a scientist who specializes in the study of the atmosphere or its phenomena.

What qualifies one to hold the title of meteorologist? The title is earned through a combination of formal education and practical employment experience. According to the American Meteorological Society, the professional organization of some 12,000 meteorologists in the United States, the formal education must include a bachelor's or higher degree in meteorology or a closely allied science such as physics, oceanography, or mathematics. A minimum of 24 semester-hours in meteorology is required. Employment must be on a full-time basis and in a legitimate professional setting, defined as one that applies the methods and concepts learned in the formal education process and one that furthers the cause of the science.

The Framework of Atmospheric Science

As we might surmise, there is more to "weather" than previously thought. This section brings the framework of atmospheric science into clear view.

Atmospheric science comprises some 27 subfields of specialization. In figure 1.1 we see a beaker labeled "Atmospheric Science," from which the individual elements emerge, each able to stand alone as a scientific discipline. A discussion of a few of the better-known specializations follows.

The best-known branch of atmospheric science is weather analysis and forecasting. Most meteorologists in the world are engaged in this subfield, working in the public and private sectors.

Another important subfield of specialization is severe local storms. Meteorologists with expertise in this area study tornadoes and thunderstorms. Much of their effort goes into learning more about storms and alleviating the effects of such storms through education and preparedness. Many severe storms meteorologists are also involved in prediction.

Some atmospheric scientists focus their attention on the tropical regions of Earth and the phenomena that primarily occur there. They understand the processes operating in the tropical atmosphere and in the structure, evolution, and prediction of tropical cyclones.

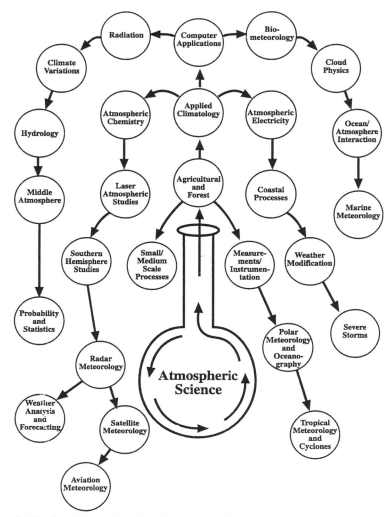

Fig 1.1. Atmospheric science contains many subfields.

The pursuit of many atmospheric scientists is in climate and climate change. They deal with the global climate system, its changes, and effects. This is an emerging field within the atmospheric sciences as consciousness of global climate change and human activity increases.

Computers are an indispensable resource in atmospheric science, and many meteorologists choose to combine their knowledge of meteorology with their computer skills to develop solutions to a huge array of problems. They write computer software that simulates many common atmospheric processes such as airflow within a thunderstorm, the movement of a hurricane, or the future evolution of wind patterns.

A few other specializations are worth noting. Satellite meteorologists interpret pictures taken by weather satellites, and apply their conclusions to problems concerning the atmosphere and oceans. Cloud and precipitation meteorologists study all aspects of the complex precipitation process. Bio-meteorologists understand how weather affects the human body physically and emotionally. A radar meteorologist designs and operates weather radar systems, and is able to interpret data gleaned from the radar. An atmospheric chemist knows the chemical makeup of Earth's atmosphere and applies that knowledge to solve a variety of problems. Others choose to focus on atmospheric electricity, with the lightning process and Earth's electric properties their chief research avenues. Finally, some meteorologists design and test instruments for use in field study or in the laboratory.

Clearly, the scope of atmospheric science is wide, and the *Sourcebook* will help teachers and students learn more about it.

Careers in the Atmospheric Sciences

One purpose in establishing the framework of atmospheric science is to make students and teachers aware of the diversified career opportunities available. The profession offers an intellectual challenge to even the most gifted persons and adequate compensation. The opportunities, rewards, and job description are determined by the discipline that the student enters, his or her level of education and motivation, and the economic philosophy of the employer. Job prospects are expected to keep pace with future demand.

Most meteorologists in the United States work for the government, where the chief employer is the National Weather Service (NWS). Their main job function is as a forecaster. Starting annual salaries are in the $20,000 to $30,000 range. Experienced forecasters, called "lead forecasters," draw $50,000 to $70,000 per year. Top administrators generally make more than $70,000.

A significant number of meteorologists prefer to work in the military, with the Air Force offering the most positions. Although salaries are not as high as in civilian jobs, the military benefits can, to some, compensate for the lower pay scale.

Broadcasting continues to offer on-camera and off-camera positions to meteorologists. The pay scale is highly variable, with some starting salaries as low as $12,000 to $15,000 per year. However, the goal of many broadcast meteorologists is to reach the top markets where salaries may be as high as $200,000 to $500,000. A top job with a network such as ABC, NBC, or CBS will pay even more. Most meteorologists who appear during weekday prime time in small and medium markets earn $35,000 to $75,000.

Private industry is hiring an increasing number of meteorologists as the demand for more accurate and specialized weather information grows. The gas/electric utilities, agriculture, and transportation industries need information that is not routinely supplied by the NWS. This has prompted many in the private sector to either hire meteorologists for staff positions or purchase the expertise from a private consulting firm.

Another major use for meteorologists in private industry is in air pollution control. With more stringent requirements on pollutant emissions, companies hire meteorologists to analyze their pollution output and its effect on the environment, and to ensure compliance with federal and state pollution standards. The pay scale in the private sector is similar to that of the NWS.

A small number of experienced meteorologists go into private, independent work as consultants. Clients call in these professionals when their expertise is needed on a particular problem. For example, an electric utility company may hire a consulting meteorologist to help determine the effect weather conditions have on daily operation and load demand. Consulting meteorologists may also give advice in forensic matters. The consultant is hired by a law firm or an insurance company to investigate weather's role in the contested matter. They may also serve as expert witnesses in court. Pay rates vary, with the person setting his or her own fee schedule. Most experienced consultants command $50 to $200 per hour for their services.

Atmospheric science offers rewarding and challenging careers. If you would like more information, seek a meteorologist in your area and talk with him or her about how he or she got into the field, likes and dislikes, and educational and professional requirements. The American Meteorological Society (AMS) in Boston publishes a guide for college-bound students that outlines coursework and degree programs across the country. The number is (617) 227-2425.

The Process of Scientific Thought

Activity #1

Title: The Many Hats of Weather Professionals

Objective: To illustrate the scope of atmospheric science

Procedure: Have students clip stories about weather from the newspaper or search for them in the school or public library in one of the following periodicals: *Time, Newsweek, Reader's Digest, National Geographic, Scientific American, Discover, Weatherwise, Science News, Smithsonian, Science,* or *Nature.* The *New York Times* carries a science section on Thursday.

Elementary

- Let students classify each clipping according to the subfield of atmospheric science that it pertains to. Some may fall into more than one category. For fun, make hats labeled with the specialization and have students wear them.

- Encourage free discussion.

- Ask students to compare the subject of their clipping to that of another student. How are they different? How are they the same?

- Students can practice their organization skills by sequencing the events in time, grouping by location, and locating on a map or globe.

- Do any of the clipping topics appear related?

Secondary

- Ask students if they see any patterns. Can they state any physical law governing what is happening in their clippings? What is their hypothesis?

- How likely is something like this in the future? Can anything be done to influence the event or minimize its effect on life or property? Can they make predictions about when and where something like this might happen again?

- Ask about the technological aspects. What technology was used to detect and report this? Can current technology affect this happening? Can expected future technologies affect it?

Ideas for Science Fair Projects

1. How is a TV weathercast prepared and delivered to viewers?

2. How does the weather affect utility (gas, water, electric) bills?

3. Aristotle: brilliant or bogus? (Research Aristotle's contributions to science and make up your own mind.)

School's Out!

1. Encourage students to write creatively—a poem or a story about weather. Use a story line where the hero is in conflict with some natural force or where the weather is central to an aspect of the plot.

2. List times when the weather influenced decisions, either at school or at home.

3. Poll the class to see which subfield of atmospheric science is: a) most rewarding, b) most popular, c) most difficult, and d) most stressful.

4. Have students read a book about weather to a younger sibling or to a kindergarten class.

Chapter 2

Earth's Place in the Sun

Humanity considers our incandescent "neighbor" in space to be the ruler of the sky. Some ancient cultures transferred the qualities of deity to the sun, for its brilliance and benefits were powerful and dramatic.

Indeed no astronomical phenomenon is more important than the position Earth occupies in the sun's rays. Practically all of the energy needed to drive the circulation of the atmosphere and oceans comes from the sun. The living Earth flourishes in the continual bath of light and heat provided by the sun. Without the sun Earth is doomed to a cold, dark, and lifeless existence.

Centerpiece of the Solar System

The sun occupies the center in a series of celestial bodies called the *solar system*. The sun is a *star*, a gaseous concentration of matter bound together by its own gravitational field. Astronomers believe the sun is a star of average size, but compared to Earth it is massive. The diameter of the sun is about 865,000 miles, or 109 times the diameter of Earth. The surface temperature of the sun is 10,000° F, but the interior burns at an incredible 30 million degrees F! The sun emits light and heat energy through interior nuclear fusion reactions. The energy production process involves the transformation of hydrogen into helium. Each second the sun converts 597 million tons of hydrogen to 593 million tons of helium. The 4 million tons of lost mass becomes the radiant output of the sun. This staggering amount of energy is equivalent to many billions of atomic bombs such as those dropped on Hiroshima and Nagasaki, Japan, at the end of WWII. Fortunately, Earth intercepts only about one two-billionth of the sun's total radiant energy. However, that amount of energy is sufficient to move oceans, serve as a catalyst for weather, and sustain life. Truly, the sun is not only the centerpiece of the solar system by virtue of its position, but also by its role as the light and heat source for the solar system.

Earth's Orbit and Rotation

Scientists once thought that Earth occupied the center of the solar system and the sun moved around Earth. When scientists established a theory contrary to that mistaken notion, they endured ridicule from peers and disapproval from religious leaders. We now know that Earth does indeed move around the sun. This motion is termed Earth's *orbit*.

Teacher's Extra

What's in a Year?

One of the most convenient methods for keeping track of time is based on Earth's orbit around the sun. Each complete trip Earth makes around the sun is called a year. Technically, however, it should be referred to as a "tropical year." The tropical year has a length of 365 days, 5 hours, 48 minutes, and 46 seconds, or 365.242 days. But the calendar says the year is exactly 365.000 days long. This means we "lose" about 6 hours every year. In order to correct this problem, 1 day every 4 years is added to the calendar. We call this "leap day," February 29. This procedure was decreed by Julius Caesar in 46 B.C., and it largely compensates for the one-quarter day excess per calendar year. Still, the problem is not solved. Caesar's original decree made the calendar year 11 minutes, 14 seconds too long. What now? In 1582 Pope Gregory XIII, on the advice of the astronomer Clavius, instituted the Gregorian calendar, which is used today. According to the Gregorian calendar every year evenly divisible by 4 is a leap year, except century years, which are considered leap years only if they are evenly divisible by 400. Confused? Well, 1800 was not a leap year but 2000 will be. OK. The problem is finally solved, right? Wrong!! Because of Earth's imperfect shape and gravitational interaction with other celestial bodies, the Gregorian calendar accumulates an error at the rate of about 1 day every 6,000 years. What can we do now? Well, how do you feel about a 363-day year?

The average distance from Earth to the sun is 93 million miles. An interesting feature of Earth's orbit is that it is not exactly circular; its true shape is slightly elliptical, or egg-shaped. The point where Earth is farthest from the sun is *aphelion,* and Earth's closest approach to the sun is *perihelion.* At aphelion Earth moves 1.5 million miles farther away from the sun, resulting in a distance of 94.5 million miles. At perihelion Earth travels 1.5 million miles closer to the sun, resulting in a distance of 91.5 million miles.

Two amusing facts about this arrangement are apparent. First, when Earth is at aphelion, it is summer in the Northern Hemisphere. Thus, summer in the United States occurs when we are farthest from the sun. Second, research indicates a 96,000-year cycle in this array. Hence, U.S. winters in the distant future will occur at aphelion. This scenario is expected to cause colder winters and cooler summers in the Northern Hemisphere.

Earth spins on an imaginary axis as it orbits the sun. This motion is called *rotation.* The importance of this simple fact cannot be overstated, for Earth's rotation regulates the biosphere and climate by bringing day and night in an orderly and predictable fashion.

Earth's rotation can be described as counterclockwise or west-to-east, depending on the frame of reference. An observer looking down on top of the world sees Earth's motion as being counterclockwise while an observer looking at the equator sees a west-to-east motion. This is why the sun and moon rise in the east and set in the west.

The speed of Earth's rotation is not constant. Since 1900 sensitive instruments and detailed investigations prove that Earth's rotation is slowing at the rate of 1.7 seconds per year. In the distant past the planet's spin was much faster. Fossils of marine organisms indicate that about 350 million years ago the year was 400 to 410 days long. The slowing of Earth's rotation is caused by tidal friction between the ocean floor and the water in the ocean basins. Since the moon is the primary cause of the tides, the energy lost by Earth in the tidal drag (which causes Earth's spin to slow) is gained by the moon. Eventually this process will result in the moon moving farther away from Earth!

The Tilted Earth and the Round Earth

Planet Earth is not oriented along a perfectly vertical line; it is displaced off an imaginary vertical axis by 23.5 degrees. In short, Earth is tilted. Combined with Earth's orbit, the tilt accounts for the observed seasons on the planet (see fig. 2.1). A *season* is defined as the regular and distinct shift of circulation patterns in the atmosphere. The four seasons are winter, spring, summer, and autumn. Winter in the Northern Hemisphere begins on December 21 or 22, a date referred to as the *winter solstice* (literally, "winter sun stance"). It marks the time when the sun's orb is lowest on the horizon, or the farthest south. The parallel of latitude corresponding to that point is the Tropic of Capricorn, located at 23.5° S. The Northern Hemisphere is tilted away from the more direct rays of sunlight. This creates a more diffuse pattern of incoming sunlight. Also, of lesser importance is the fact that the sunlight coming in at a lower angle must pass through a greater depth of atmosphere, resulting in a loss of energy through scattering. At the winter solstice locations from 66.5° N (the Arctic Circle) to 90° N (the North Pole) experience a 24-hour period of darkness because the sun's orb remains below the horizon for the entire day.

The *vernal equinox* occurs on March 20 or 21. At this time the sun's orb is passing over the equator on its northward journey. All locations on Earth experience a 12-hour day and a 12-hour night. People living in San Francisco, Denver, St. Louis, and Washington, D.C., have gained 3 hours of daylight since the winter solstice. Above the Arctic Circle the sun rises for the first time since the previous September.

As Earth continues orbiting the sun, the season progresses to the *summer solstice*, which occurs on June 20 or 21. The sun's orb is highest above the horizon, representing the northernmost point of its journey. That parallel of latitude is the Tropic of Cancer, located at 23.5° N. San Francisco, Denver, St. Louis, and Washington, D.C., now experience more than 15 hours of daylight, which is 6 hours more than at the winter solstice. Regions above the Arctic Circle receive 24 hours of illumination, resulting in no true darkness at night.

The *autumnal equinox*, on September 22 or 23, marks the time when the sun's orb crosses the equator on its trek southward. Again, each point on Earth's surface experiences a 12-hour day and a 12-hour night. Above the Arctic Circle the sun disappears until the next spring.

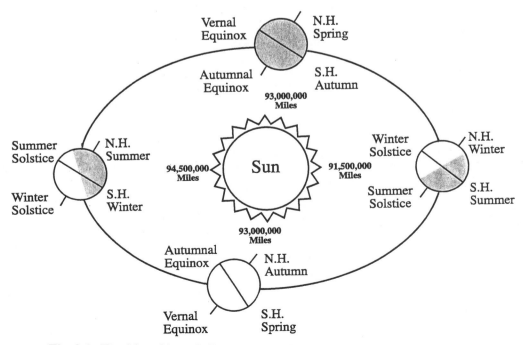

Fig. 2.1. Earth's orbit and tilt are primarily responsible for our seasons.

The amount of Earth's tilt varies over time. A cycle of 41,000 years is evident where the magnitude of Earth's tilt varies from 22.1° to 24.5°. The last trend in this cycle was 9,000 years ago with a tilt of 24.5°. Therefore, at present, the amount of Earth's tilt is decreasing and, in about 32,000 years, will be near 22.5°. Although this change is small, amounting to less than 5%, it can trigger significant climate alterations. A tilt of 24.5° brings hotter summers and colder winters to the Northern Hemisphere, along with a possible increase in storminess.

As stated earlier, Earth's place in the sun's rays assures us a generous supply of light and heat energy. However, all points on Earth's surface do not receive the same amount of sunlight. This aspect of the Earth-sun relationship dictates the observed array of world climates.

Earth is not a perfect sphere; it bulges a bit at the equator and is slightly flattened at the poles. According to the best estimates, Earth's polar circumference is about 27 miles less than its equatorial circumference. Earth's rotation is responsible for distorting the planet's form and figure.

The round Earth distributes solar energy unevenly, resulting in temperature differences across its surface. The sun's rays fall more directly on the equator and are less intense at the poles. Thus, the temperature pattern of Earth is characterized by a net surplus of heat in equatorial regions and a net deficit of heat in the polar areas.

The Radiation Budget

We know how tough it can be to design and implement a family budget—it's not easy keeping track of what comes in and what goes out. Planet Earth accomplishes that task with the energy it receives from the sun. The income we receive from employment is analogous to the incoming solar radiation (termed insolation) Earth gets from the sun. That portion of the income we spend relates to the insolation Earth loses and uses. This process is called the radiation budget.

Figure 2.2 and table 2.1 show how Earth earns and spends solar energy.

A Brief History of the Round Earth

Modern scientists know Earth is spherical but, for the ancient scholar, the goal of discerning Earth's shape was elusive. Near 247 B.C. the first scientifically sound approximation of Earth's circumference was made by Eratosthenes, librarian at Alexandria, Egypt. His calculation was within 10% of the modern accepted value.

Many years later suspicion surfaced and cast doubt on the idea that Earth's shape was a "perfect" sphere. The discovery occurred, like many scientific breakthroughs, by accident. In 1671 King Louis XIV sent a French astronomer named Jean Richer to the island of Cayenne, located at latitude 5° N. Richer's responsibility was to make certain astronomical observations. One of the instruments he took was a highly accurate clock whose pendulum was just the right length necessary to beat seconds in Paris, France (located near latitude 50° N). Richer noticed that the clock lost 2.5 minutes per day on the island. Upon his return to Paris, Richer shared his observations with the European scientific community. Much discussion arose, but the correct explanation was not given until 1686 when Isaac Newton stated that Earth was an oblate ellipsoid, meaning that it is slightly flattened at the poles and bulges just a little at the equator. Newton's hypothesis was not verified until the 18th century.

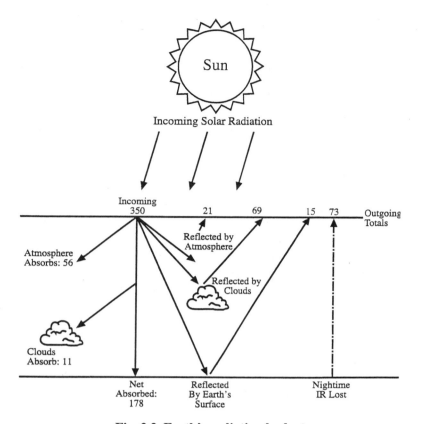

Fig. 2.2. Earth's radiation budget.

	Gains	**Losses**
TOTAL INCOMING SOLAR RADIATION	350	
Absorbed by the atmosphere		56
Absorbed by clouds		11
Reflected by the atmosphere		21
Reflected by the clouds		69
Reflected by Earth's surface		15
TOTAL INCOMING SOLAR RADIATION ABSORBED BY EARTH	178	
TOTAL RADIATION LOST BY EARTH AT NIGHT		73
NET RADIATION OF THE EARTH'S SURFACE	+105	

Table 2.1. The Radiation Budget of Earth's Surface: A Balance Sheet
(All units are in watts per square meter.)

Several important conclusions are apparent from figure 2.2 and table 2.1. First, Earth receives 350 watts per square meter of energy from the sun—enough to power nearly six 60-watt lightbulbs. Of that amount, 157 watts per square meter never reach Earth's surface because of absorption and scattering by the atmosphere and clouds. As a result, 193 watts per square meter actually reach Earth's surface. Of that amount, 15 watts per square meter are immediately reflected by the surface, thus leaving 178 watts per square meter that are eventually absorbed by Earth's surface. Finally, 73 watts per square meter are radiated back into space by Earth (remember, Earth "shines," or emits radiation). The bottom line is a surplus of 105 watts per square meter. This is the "net radiation received at Earth's surface." In other words, this is what Earth gets to spend. It turns out that Earth uses its surplus of energy wisely. The 105 watts per square meter fund the following major projects:

- the Energy Cycle, where the sun's energy is moved through and used by Earth's biosphere and returned to the environment

- the circulation of the oceans

- the circulation of the atmosphere

Despite the surplus of energy received at Earth's surface, the total global radiation budget is balanced because of the processes just mentioned. If this were not true, the temperature of Earth's surface would increase dramatically while the temperature of the upper atmosphere would decrease. This scenario is not compatible with life.

The Process of Scientific Thought

Activity #1

Title: Earth's Seasons

Objective: To illustrate the cause of the seasons we experience

Materials Needed: globe, large flashlight

Procedure: Make sure the globe is tilted 23.5° from the vertical like the real Earth. Divide students into five groups. There are five roles to play:

1. The sun

2. Earth during the Northern Hemisphere winter

3. Earth during the Northern Hemisphere spring

4. Earth during the Northern Hemisphere summer

5. Earth during the Northern Hemisphere autumn

Refer to figure 2.1 for help in positioning students around the sun. Darken the room some. The student or group of students playing the role of the sun will hold a strong flashlight. Let the student(s) representing Earth during the Northern Hemisphere winter hold the globe first, then have them pass it to the group representing spring, then summer, and finally autumn. This simulates Earth's orbit during the year.

Elementary

• Have students communicate (oral, written, pictures) what happens to the intensity of the light during their season.

• It's important for students to compare the amount of light received during each season. Which seasons have an equal amount? The least? The most?

• In order to expand their relational thinking skills have students vary the distance to the sun. Vary the tilt angle of Earth. Allow them to discuss informally and freely what it might be like with a different set of Earth-sun relationship parameters.

Secondary

• Have students develop a model of the Earth-sun relationship (it should resemble figure 2.1).

• Again consider the discussion of varying the parameters of the Earth-sun model. What would it be like if Earth were 120 million miles from the sun? What if Earth were only 70 million miles from the sun? What if the tilt angle were different, say 26° or 18°? Look at various combinations of Earth's tilt and distance from the sun. Is the combination we have the best?

• Let the students choose a city in the United States. Have them research the present climate of that city. Next, ask them to predict the changes in climate associated with a tilt angle of 22.1°. (In most cases, there would be less seasonal variation with milder winters and cooler summers.) What about 24.5°? (In most cases, the seasonal changes would be sharper, with colder winters and hotter summers.) What are the implications for humanity in each scenario?

Activity #2

Title: The Spinning Earth—Understanding Day and Night

Objective: To show that Earth's rotation causes day and night

Materials Needed: globe, large flashlight

Procedure: Let students choose a city in the world. Darken the room. Shine the flashlight on the globe and ask each student if his or her chosen city is experiencing day or night. Then rotate the globe 180°. Now ask if it is day or night in the city.

Elementary

- Have students communicate orally about what they've seen. They could draw a picture of the daytime or nighttime sky of their chosen world city. You may need to help them locate a picture of their city in an encyclopedia, CD-ROM, or some other source.

- Compare their feelings about the day and night. Which time do they like best? Why?

- Consider animals. Students could classify animals as mainly daytime or nighttime dwellers. Make a list of these.

- Use the list to explain why these animals prefer day or night. Is it because of feeding, prey, mating, etc.?

Secondary

- Use the list of animals. Ask if they know any natural laws that dictate the behavior of these animals. What are the main characteristics of the animals that prefer daytime? How about those that prefer the night? Watch for patterns.

- Create a fictitious animal or use one that's extinct. See if students can perform the above analysis in that situation.

Activity #3

Title: Unequal Sunlight

Objective: To demonstrate how Earth's shape distributes sunlight

Materials Needed: flashlight, graph paper

Procedure: Have students pair up. Let one student hold a flashlight vertically about 6 inches above a piece of graph paper. The other student draws the outline of the light on the paper. Count the number of squares present in the traced-out area. Repeat with the flashlight held at an angle. Again, note the number of squares in the traced-out area.

Elementary

- Attempt a number of trials using different flashlight angles. In each case note the number of squares illuminated.

- Build a table. Can they come up with a hypothesis that relates the number of squares illuminated to the angle of the flashlight?

Secondary

- Have students state a general conclusion. What physical laws are at work?

- Can they develop a simple mathematical expression that will predict the relationship between the flashlight angle and the number of squares illuminated? Let them use a computer if they want.

Activity #4

Title: The Sun Stimulates Life

Objective: To see how important the sun is to Earth's life-forms

Materials Needed: water weed or other green plant, a large jar

Procedure: Place several shoots of water weed or some other green plant in a large jar about three-quarters full of water. Place it in a dark area for a while. Look at the jar and you will see little activity (few bubbles). Then move the jar into the sunshine. The bubbles will increase.

Elementary

- Have students draw a picture of the jar and its contents before and after placement in the sun.

- They can compare and discuss the pictures they drew.

- Perform several trials using different plants and amounts of sunlight and darkness. Look for relationships in the data. Is the number of bubbles related to plant type, the intensity of sunlight, or both? Does the degree of darkness prior to the activity have an effect? Make a simple graph.

Secondary

- Explain the life processes of green plants and the sun's role in those processes. Try to make predictive statements based on data obtained thus far.

Activity #5

Title: The Sun Supplies Energy for Earth

Objective: To prove that Earth receives solar energy

Materials Needed: magnifying glass, piece of paper

Procedure: In this activity we draw upon an old experiment, probably one that most students have already done at home but, in this case, it's presented scientifically instead of informally.

Place a magnifying glass in direct sunlight; then put a piece of paper under the glass. Focus the sunlight with the magnifying glass on the paper. The paper will burn.

Elementary

- For preschoolers the sense of taste is added to the experience (in addition to letting them hear the paper sear, seeing the smoke, and smelling the smoke) by making "sun tea." Fill a large glass container with water and put two to three tea bags in the water. Close the jar. When it's ready (after 2 to 4 hours) they can taste the tea made by the sun (tea made by a "star").

- Communication skills can be expanded by drawing a picture of what they see. They can also write a brief report or summary on what happened to go with their picture. Some may prefer to write a poem.

- Repeat the experiment using different substances such as wood, plastic, cardboard, etc. Time how long it takes for each substance to melt, smoke, or burn (some may not do anything). Use different magnifying glasses.

- Construct a graph of substance vs. burn time, or diameter (or thickness) of magnifying glass vs. burn time. What, if any, relationships exist? Write a summary.

Secondary

- Research alternative solar-powered energy sources. Consider solar-powered homes, automobiles, and instruments. How feasible is each one? Write a report on a specific type of energy source or technology.

Ideas for Science Fair Projects

1. Investigate how to set up a Foucault pendulum experiment to prove Earth's rotation.

2. Science fair project ideas concerning sunspots abound. Here are some that aren't worn out.

   a) Do sunspots affect the number of Atlantic hurricanes?

   b) Do sunspots affect the number or severity of tornadoes?

   c) Is there any relationship between sunspots and global temperature?

3. Investigate the sun's role in communications on Earth. How do sunspots and solar flares affect modern communications, electric power grids, and computers?

4. What is the solar wind and how does it affect Earth?

5. What kind of star is our sun? Compare and contrast it with other known stars in the universe.

6. Find out how to make a sundial, an instrument that shows the time of day by the shadow cast by a gnomon on a horizontal plate of a cylindrical surface. (A *gnomon* is an object that serves as an indicator of the hour of the day by the position or length of its shadow.)

7. Use a prism to separate the colors of sunlight (the solar spectrum) and be able to explain the natural laws operating.

8. Research the medical/psychological aspects of the sun. For example, the sun's ultraviolet (UV) output damages biological tissue. This is a medical application. Another example: Lack of sunlight for extended periods of time can contribute to depression. Talk to a psychologist or psychiatrist.

9. Study solar and lunar eclipses with the aid of diagrams and models.

10. Here's a project title: "Nuclear Fusion: Powering the Sun." Find out about the process of nuclear fusion and more details about how it operates in the sun's interior. Will nuclear fusion ever be feasible on Earth?

School's Out!

1. Read a book about the sun, moon, or solar system to a younger child.

2. Join or found an astronomy club.

3. Go to a local Head Start program, day care facility, or early childhood enrichment program and teach the children about a topic you've chosen from the material in this chapter.

4. Prepare a list of questions for an adult to help you find answers to.

5. Take a science fair project to a local service organization and present it to its members.

Chapter 3

The Composition and Vertical Structure of Earth's Atmosphere

The unique importance of Earth's atmosphere cannot be understated—we breathe its contents every few seconds. It affords Earth's biosphere the breath of life. But what are we inhaling? The answer serves as the content of this chapter.

At this early point in our journey through the grand tour of atmospheric science, the atmosphere is defined as an envelope of air that surrounds Earth's surface. Technically, the atmosphere is a series of envelopes, or "shells," and a study of that detailed structure comes later in this chapter.

Function and Importance of the Atmosphere

The atmosphere is bound to Earth by the planet's gravitational field. If Earth's gravitational pull was too weak, then the atmosphere would escape, and life would perish. Such is the case with Earth's lifeless moon. Our blanket of air is vital for several reasons. First, it shields earth's lifeforms from the harmful effects of ultraviolet (UV) radiation from the sun. If Earth had no atmosphere, then practically all life would be bombarded by large doses of UV radiation, and eventually, life would cease.

A second benefit is protection from almost constant meteor strikes. Although objects occasionally impact Earth, the frequency would be much greater if there was no atmosphere. Essentially, the action of friction causes these objects to "burn up" as they move at very high speeds through the atmosphere.

The atmosphere also regulates global temperature. If Earth had no atmosphere, the surface temperature would reach 200° F during the day and would fall to -200° F at night. There would be no wind and no precipitation. Of course, this type of environment cannot support life.

Finally, one often overlooked facet of the atmosphere is its role in facilitating communication. The temperature and moisture structure of the atmosphere allows long-range movement of radio waves, microwaves, and other transmission mechanisms. Hence, the atmosphere is a communication medium, allowing one part of the world access to another.

Gases and Aerosols

We've stated that the atmosphere is an envelope of air. But what is air? An accurate and concise definition is this: Air is a mixture of gases and aerosols. A gas is a physical state of matter characterized by molecules that are widely spaced. Aerosols are liquid and solid particles of matter that are suspended in the atmosphere and tend to remain there for a certain period of time. These particles are normally too small to be seen without magnification. Aerosols and gases are placed in the atmosphere by natural and anthropogenic (of human origin) processes and activities.

In the atmosphere the number of aerosols is staggering. In general, smaller particles are more numerous than larger particles. Some smaller aerosols may occur in a concentration of 100,000 per cubic inch. The largest particles may be as scarce as less than 1 per cubic inch. As one might suspect, the major supplier of aerosols is the oceans. Salt from ocean spray becomes airborne and rides the wind through the atmosphere. About 83% of Earth's naturally occurring aerosols originate from the oceans. Natural sources account for 93% of all airborne material in the atmosphere, an amount that far outweighs the anthropogenic contribution.

Teacher's Extra

Earth's Previous Atmospheres

Earth has not always been endowed with a life-sustaining atmosphere. In fact, a principal component of the planet's history is the emergence of the modern atmosphere, generally thought to be the fourth stage in a continually evolving process.

Earth's first atmosphere, the primordial atmosphere, is believed to have existed during the first 600 million years of the planet's existence, or between 4.6 and 4.0 billion years ago. The main constituents of the primordial atmosphere were water vapor, hydrogen cyanide, ammonia, methane, and sulfur. Many of these products are poisonous, thus the primordial atmosphere was incapable of sustaining life.

Next came the evolutionary atmosphere between 4.0 and 3.3 billion years ago. This atmosphere comprised water vapor, carbon dioxide, a small amount of nitrogen, and little or no oxygen. Earth, shrouded in clouds, was very warm, and water began accumulating on the surface. Also, a process called outgassing (referring to the release of trapped gases from beneath Earth's surface through cracks, fissures, and volcanoes) contributed significantly to the content of the evolutionary atmosphere. Sometime near 3.6 billion years ago, this environment was able to sustain Earth's first life-form—bacteria that used chemical energy to synthesize organic compounds.

The third stage, the living atmosphere, existed over a much longer time span than its predecessors, covering 2.7 billion years from 3.3 billion years ago to 600 million years ago. The living atmosphere, at about 3.0 billion years ago, contained 70% carbon dioxide, 20% water vapor, 10% nitrogen, and less than 1% oxygen. The living atmosphere witnessed the first organism to perform photosynthesis—*Cyanobacteria* (blue-green algae) in the shallow oceans of some 3.3 billion years ago. Earth remained warm and heavy global rains helped fill the ocean basins. Outgassing continued and the continents began to break apart near the end of this period. The stage was set for the explosion of life that would take place as the modern atmosphere gradually developed.

The above discussion presents the views of many scientists regarding the long process of chemical evolution required to arrive at our modern atmosphere, under whose thin veil life flourishes. Many of these scientists contend that Earth's fifth atmosphere may be evolving.

Fixed and Variable Constituents

Earth's atmosphere contains fixed and variable constituents. This fact is notable because not only is the chemical makeup of the atmosphere important, but so is the distribution, amount, and staying power of each constituent.

Table 3.1 lists the principal fixed gases present in the atmosphere. The presence of a fixed gas is basically constant over the entire Earth, both horizontally and vertically. The term also implies that these gases exist in relatively unchanged amounts through lengthy time periods, especially when compared to human life expectancy.

Constituent	% of Atmosphere by Volume	Sources	Importance
Nitrogen	78.084	Decaying Agricultural Debris Animal Matter Volcanic Eruptions	Essential for All Life Most Abundant Constituent
Oxygen	20.946	Photosynthetic Growth of Vegetation	Necessary for Virtually All Forms of Animal Life
Argon	0.934	Radioactive Decay of the Potassium Isotope	Most Abundant Chemically Inactive Gas Uses: Incandescent Lamps, Arc Welding and Fluorescent Lamps
Neon	0.00182	Radioactive Decay of Terrestrial Materials	Used Commercially in Electric Signs and Lights Used in High-Energy Physics Research
Helium	0.000524	Radioactive Decay of Terrestrial Materials	Used Commercially for Inflatable Flight
Methane	0.00015	Decay of Organic Matter Escape from Oil Wells	Poisonous Underrated "Greenhouse" Gas
Krypton	0.000114	Radioactive Decay of Terrestrial Materials	Used in Electric Lamps "Planet" of Superman
Hydrogen	0.00005	Diffusive Separation	Lightest and Most Abundant Element in the Universe

Table 3.1. Primary Fixed Gases Comprising the Atmosphere

Almost all of Earth's atmosphere comprises fixed gases. Nitrogen, the most abundant gas, occupies nearly 78% of the atmosphere. Nitrogen is the basis for many chemical compounds, and is therefore essential for life. The main sources of nitrogen in the atmosphere are decaying agricultural debris, animal matter, and volcanic eruptions.

Oxygen, the second most prevalent constituent, makes up almost 21% of the atmosphere. Together, nitrogen and oxygen contribute to 99% of the chemical composition of Earth's modern atmosphere. Oxygen finds its way into the atmosphere through the photosynthesis process occurring in green plants and is necessary for virtually all life-forms. It's instructive to note that life on Earth did not flourish until the amount of oxygen in the atmosphere increased.

The remaining 1% of the atmosphere is made up of argon, neon, helium, methane, krypton, and hydrogen. Most of these gases are present in the atmosphere because of radioactive decay of terrestrial materials. Despite their meager presence, these "trace" gases, as they are called, are important. Several, such as neon, argon, and krypton (Superman's "planet") are used commercially in the electric sign industry. Methane is a highly efficient regulator of global temperature and an underrated "greenhouse" gas, a topic discussed in part II. Hydrogen is the lightest and most abundant element in the universe, and could easily supply humanity with a clean and endless energy source if nuclear fusion wasn't such a difficult and expensive technological obstacle.

Although the fixed gases account for the vast majority of atmospheric chemistry, there are other gases present that are significant. These are called variable gases and are outlined in table 3.2. As the name implies, these gases vary considerably throughout the atmosphere, both horizontally and vertically. They vary over time frames that are

short when compared to the human life span. One of the most important variable gases is water vapor. By volume, water vapor occupies from near 0% to near 5%, but it serves as the raw material for the precipitation process. Water vapor is also a "greenhouse" gas, and exerts some control on global temperature.

Another primary variable gas is carbon dioxide (CO_2). This gas is fundamental in the respiration of plants and animals. It reigns as the most famous of all "greenhouse" gases, and is widely cited as the chief contributor to global warming. Ozone is another important variable gas in the atmosphere. It is present in minute quantities and is well known for shielding Earth from harmful UV radiation from the sun. More on ozone follows in part II.

Constituent	% of Atmosphere by Volume	Sources	Importance
Water Vapor	near 0 to 5	Evaporation of Terrestrial Water	"Raw" Material for Precipitation Vehicle for Energy Transfer
Carbon Dioxide	increasing	Decay of Plant Material Burning of Fossil Fuels like Coal, Oil, Natural Gas Volcanic Eruptions	Helps Regulate Global Temperature Carbon Is Essential for Life
Carbon Monoxide	trace	Inefficient Burning of Fossil Fuels (largely automobiles)	Colorless, Odorless, and Very Toxic!
Sulfur Dioxide	trace	Industrial Combustion Volcanic Eruptions	One Contributor to Increased Acidity of Precipitation
Nitrogen Dioxide	trace	Industrial Combustion Volcanic Eruptions	Another Contributor to Increased Acidity of Precipitation
Ozone	trace	Chemical Reactions involving Sunlight and Oxygen	Absorbs Harmful UV Radiation

Table 3.2. Important Variable Gases in the Atmosphere

Earlier we learned that the constituents of Earth's atmosphere are produced by natural processes and human activities. In a similar manner, they are also removed from the atmosphere by these methods. For example, nitrogen is removed by biological processes involving the oceans and vegetation. Of less significance is lightning, which converts nitrogen gas to compounds of nitrogen

that are easily washed out of the atmosphere by precipitation, a process called "nitrogen fixation." Oxygen is taken out by the respiratory processes of humans and animals. We inhale oxygen and exhale carbon dioxide. The plant kingdom uses carbon dioxide in its life processes and discharges oxygen as a waste product. The oceans also consume CO_2. Ozone is destroyed by chemical reactions involving certain synthetic chemicals (see part II).

The Vertical Structure of Earth's Atmosphere

Figure 3.1 is a simple depiction of Earth's atmosphere. Clearly, the atmosphere surrounds Earth the way an envelope encloses a letter. The depth of the atmosphere is greater over equatorial regions than over the poles. Earth's imperfect shape provides a slightly stronger field of gravity over the equator than over polar areas, thus a greater depth of atmosphere can be held in place.

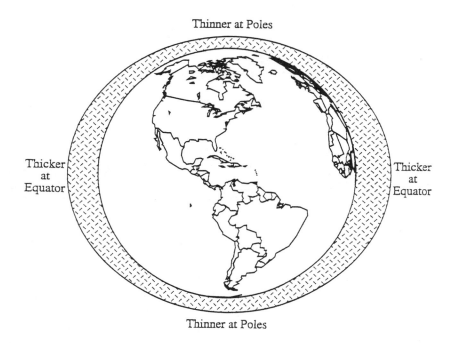

Fig. 3.1. A simple illustration of Earth's atmosphere.

The Layers of the Atmosphere

The vertical structure of Earth's atmosphere consists of several layers and each layer contributes to the function and importance of the whole. Figure 3.2 illustrates the detailed vertical structure of the atmosphere. It is important to note that figure 3.2 shows globally averaged atmospheric conditions. The actual vertical and horizontal structure of the atmosphere can be substantially altered at any time and at any location.

Troposphere

The lowest layer of the atmosphere is the troposphere. It is the air in the troposphere that we breathe and is therefore the single most important layer of our atmosphere. The troposphere extends from Earth's surface to 5 miles high over the polar regions and to about 8 miles high over equatorial regions. The troposphere contains 80% of the mass of the entire atmosphere. Also, almost all of what is considered "weather-related" phenomena such as clouds, storms, and precipitation occur in the troposphere.

In the troposphere the temperature profile decreases with increasing height. The average rate of decrease, or lapse rate, is 17° F per mile. Of course, there is considerable daily and seasonal variation on this general theme. One final note concerns the tropopause, the upper limit, or top of the troposphere. As such the tropopause marks the vertical boundary between the troposphere and the stratosphere.

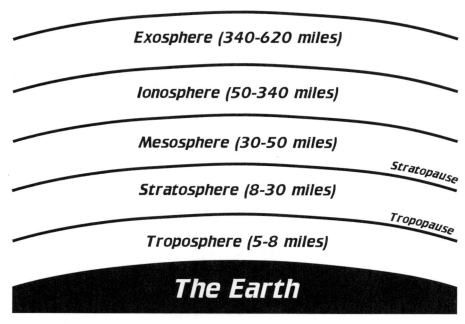

Fig. 3.2. The layers of Earth's atmosphere.

Stratosphere

The next layer of the atmosphere, the stratosphere, extends from the tropopause upward to about 19 miles. The temperature profile of the stratosphere is nearly constant, or isothermal, for the lowest 6 miles. This layer is overlain by a region of temperature increase called an inversion. This temperature increase with height is caused by the direct absorption of solar radiation by oxygen and ozone. One of the most important attributes of the stratosphere is that it contains the "ozone layer" at an altitude of 9 to 19 miles. Because of the observed temperature profile, the stratosphere is sterile to active weather development. However, aerosols can persist in the stratosphere for several years, especially sulfate particles from volcanic eruptions. As a final note, the top of the stratosphere is called the stratopause.

Mesosphere

The mesosphere is located above the stratosphere. It begins around 19 miles high and extends upward to nearly 50 miles altitude. The entire mesosphere is characterized by decreasing temperature with increasing height at the rate of 12° F per mile. The temperature of the mesosphere can reach -150° F, among the lowest anywhere in the atmosphere. The main reason for such low temperature readings in the mesosphere is the lack of oxygen and ozone, which are responsible for the very high temperature in portions of the stratosphere.

Ionosphere

Above the mesosphere is the ionosphere. It begins at about 50 miles high and extends to nearly 340 miles high. It is characterized by rising temperatures up to about 190 miles high and then a constant temperature profile up to 340 miles. The ionosphere is also where ionized (electrically charged) molecules and atoms are dominant. Helium and hydrogen are found in the ionosphere. These elements are exposed to the complete spectrum of solar radiation, including extreme UV and X-rays. These harsh forms of radiation dissociate and ionize molecules. Because of this process, temperatures above 190 miles high fluctuate wildly, ranging up to 2,000° F during the day and "cooling" to 600° F at night.

Another interesting feature of the ionosphere is a global circulation of 150 to 450 miles per hour.

The ionosphere also plays a role in communications and is the home of the famous aurora phenomenon.

Exosphere

That portion of the atmosphere above 340 miles is the exosphere. Not much is known except that it is practically empty, as Earth's gravity is not sufficient to hold even the light hydrogen atoms, thus allowing them to escape. Above the exosphere Earth's atmosphere and the "solar wind" (the flow of charged particles from the sun) merge.

The Cruel Air

You're cruising at 35,000 feet in a luxury aircraft. You look out the window and the clearest shade of blue that you've ever seen washes the sky. It seems to beckon you for a momentary rendezvous. But wait! Have you forgotten how cruel the air can be?

High altitudes affect humans adversely. Without protective measures humans begin suffering from reduced oxygen pressure at altitudes near 10,000 feet. Some of the symptoms of this "thin air" ailment include labored breathing, very high heart rate, headaches, nausea, vomiting, and general malaise. Unfortunately, our knowledge of the cruel air "up there" has been based on a number of deaths of balloonists in the 19th century. These adventurous (and ignorant) folks ascended to heights above 20,000 feet, only to die for their efforts. The nature of this type of disaster was described well by French balloonist M. Lortet, who ascended to an altitude estimated near 30,000 feet in the mid-1800s.

"Towards 7,500 meters," Lortet reported, "the numbness one experiences is extraordinary, the body and mind weaken little by little, gradually, unconsciously, without one's knowledge. One becomes indifferent, one no longer thinks of the perilous situation or of the danger; one rises and is happy to rise. Vertigo of lofty regions is not a vain word. But as far as I can judge by my personal impressions, this vertigo appears at the last moment; it immediately precedes annihilation, sudden, unexpected, irresistible."

Lortet carried two companions to their deaths on that ill-fated journey. On a brighter note, the world record for altitude in a manned open-basket balloon is 53,000 feet by Chauncey Dunn of the United States on August 1, 1979. He must have realized how cruel the air can be—he wore a pressure suit!

The Process of Scientific Thought

Activity #1

Title: The Mystery of Air

Objective: To illustrate the behavior of a gas

Materials Needed: soft drink bottle, balloon, bowl of hot water

Procedure: Snap a balloon over the neck of an empty soft drink bottle. The balloon will hang limp. Then partially immerse the bottle in a bowl of hot water. The balloon will inflate as if someone were blowing into it.

Elementary

- Ask students to communicate what happened, using verbal, written, and pictoral methods. Scientists would say that the air inside the bottle expanded when the bottle was heated by its contact with the hot water. As the air in the bottle expanded, it pushed its way up into the bottle. This activity demonstrates a fundamental property of all gases: A gas has no definite shape and will react to temperature changes and any constraints or boundaries placed upon it.

- Run a number of trials varying the water temperature, bottle size, and balloon size. Record the time it takes for the balloon to begin expanding in each case.

- Make a list of the combinations that led to the fastest expansion rate of the balloon.

- Using the list just completed, draw a graph or construct a table to show relationships evident from the trials.

Secondary

- Explain the natural laws at work. Make predictions and then do some extra trials to verify the predictions.

Activity #2

Title: To Catch an Aerosol

Objective: To prove that aerosols exist

Materials Needed: microscope slide, piece of damp white cloth, microscope

Procedure: Obtain a microscope slide and a piece of damp white cloth. Place them outside at the beginning of the school day. When class meets, bring the slide and the cloth inside. Analyze the cloth visually and put the slide under a microscope.

Elementary

- Communicate orally, in writing, or through pictures about what's happening.

- Note the different size, shape, and type of aerosols caught. Make comparisons.

- Gather data and classify the aerosols in terms of size, shape, and type.

- Make a graph of size vs. number and size vs. type. Is there a pattern?

Secondary

- Ask the following: Why are aerosols of different sizes? Why are the small ones more numerous?

- Analyze the sources of aerosols (see table 3.1). It may be instructive to repeat this activity over a period of several days. Did the size, number, or types of aerosols change? Why? What are the implications?

Activity #3

Title: Where Is Air?

Objective: To show that air is present in unexpected places

Materials Needed: two jars of water, one bowl of water, lump of soil, a brick

Procedure: Place a lump of soil in a jar of water and observe. You will see bubbles, caused by air from the lump of soil. Next, fill another jar with water and let it stand in a warm place for several hours. Check the container and you will see tiny bubbles. Last, put a brick in a large bowl of water. Again, air bubbles will be present.

Elementary

- Ask students to describe what's happening orally, in writing, or through pictures.

- This activity implies that air is present just about everywhere: in soil, in water, and even in solid materials such as bricks. How did air get there?

Secondary

- Develop a theory about how Earth's atmosphere evolved. Two important concepts that should be mentioned are outgassing and the appearance of water on a global scale. Also, there appears to be a feedback mechanism involving the biosphere; the presence of life sustains life (see Teacher's Extra earlier in this chapter).

Activity #4

Title: Air Has Weight

Objective: To demonstrate that air has mass (weight)

Materials Needed: thin cheap yardstick, thin nail, two drinking glasses, large balloon, hammer

Procedure: Hammer the thin nail through the exact center of the yardstick. Balance it between two drinking glasses. Attach a large empty balloon to one side of the yardstick and balance it with counterweights on the other end. Pay attention to where the balloon was, remove it, and blow it up. Then reattach it exactly where you took it from. The balance that existed previously is destroyed because of the extra weight of the air.

Elementary

- As in previous activities, elementary students can improve their communication skills by discussing the activity orally, by drawing a picture, or by writing a one-paragraph summary of the experiment.

- Explain why air has mass (weight). (Answer: It is matter—a mixture of gases and aerosols.)

Secondary

- See if students can weigh the air in the balloon by balancing it exactly with a known counter-weight. See if they can calculate the weight of the air inside the classroom.

Activity #5

Title: Air Is Strong

Objective: To show that air has weight

Materials Needed: clean tin can with a cap, one cup of water, a heat source

Procedure: This activity is another proof that air has mass. Obtain a clean tin can with a cap. Take the cap off and pour about one cup of water into the can. Place the open can over a heat source until the water inside boils. Quickly remove the can from the heat source and put the cap on tightly. Place it in water or run water from an open tap over the can. The can will crumple.

Note: Be careful handling the hot can. Also, do not use the heat source to "blow" the can back up again. Use an air pump or just let it rebound slowly on its own.

Elementary

- Draw a picture of the can before and after this experiment. What caused the can to crumple?

- This activity can be repeated if you have several tin cans or if you have enough time to reinflate the used one. Use different water temperatures for immersion. Use containers of other materials. Vary the heat intensity. How long does it take the can to crumple in each case? Record the data in a table.

Secondary

- What natural laws are at work? Are there any patterns? Can any generalizations be made? What predictive statements can students make?

Activity #6

Title: Air Occupies Space

Objective: To show that air occupies space because it is matter

Materials Needed: handkerchief, tall glass of water, bowl of water

Procedure: Place a small handkerchief firmly into the bottom of a tall glass. Immerse it upside down into a bowl of water. The handkerchief does not get wet because the air located between it and the water takes up space and does not allow the water to move upward. Eventually, the handkerchief will get wet if you keep pushing the glass into the water.

Elementary

- Draw a picture of the situation or explain it orally.

- Write a story entitled "The Magic of Air."

Secondary

- Discuss technology that uses the "weight of the air" as a principle of operation.

Activity #7

Title: The Structured Atmosphere

Objective: To understand the temperature profile of the atmosphere

Materials Needed: hot plate, thermometer

Procedure: Turn a hot plate on low heat. Place a thermometer above the plate at vertical intervals of several inches each. Read the thermometer and note that the temperature decreases with height, just like in the troposphere.

Elementary

- Draw a picture. Have students write one paragraph on what they saw or have them explain what happened. Compare the observed temperatures at the various levels. Where is the highest temperature located? The lowest? Present this data in the form of a graph or a table. What would happen if the hot plate were turned to a lower setting? A higher setting?

Secondary

- Repeat the activity using the hot plate on a very low setting and on a high setting. Record the results and construct a table or a graph. State any generalizations that appear evident. Explain results. Compare the results with the known structure of the troposphere. Can students develop an equation that describes the temperature profile of the activity? How does it compare to the real atmosphere?

Ideas for Science Fair Projects

1. Recall that one subfield of atmospheric science is atmospheric chemistry. Develop a science fair project with the title "The Beneficial Chemistry of Earth's Atmosphere." Outline the constituents present, their importance, their sources and sinks, and their effect on the biosphere.

2. Choose a constituent from table 3.1 or table 3.2. Perform in-depth research on it and bring out the information in a science fair project.

3. "Aerosols in the Atmosphere" is another working title for a project. Trace their origin, importance, and role in the precipitation process.

4. "The Evolution of Earth's Atmosphere" is another original idea. Trace the beginnings of Earth's primordial atmosphere through the modern atmosphere. Tie it in with the explosion of life that occurred during the living atmosphere and the modern atmosphere stages. Which atmosphere is best?

5. Several of the activities outlined earlier in this chapter are good science fair projects, especially activities #1, 2, 3, 5, and 6.

6. Research the concept of cycling as it applies to the Earth-atmosphere system. Important cycles are the oxygen cycle, the nitrogen cycle, the carbon cycle, and the hydrologic cycle. Tell how each represents the natural recycling of vital substances by the Earth-atmosphere system and how they relate to and affect life.

7. Research modern communications. How do we broadcast live reports on TV and radio from foreign countries? Your main topic will be artificial satellites.

8. Research communication methods of the past. Before satellites, the propagation of radio waves through the ionosphere was the only way to communicate live. Center your discussion on WWII or the Korean Conflict.

9. Prepare a science fair project on what's called the "Standard Atmosphere." The Standard Atmosphere is a globally averaged model of the typical temperature and pressure distribution of the vertical atmosphere. More details on this can be found in a meteorology textbook or in an encyclopedia.

School's Out!

1. Tour an environmental laboratory.

2. Find out more about atoms and molecules.

3. Interview a chemist.

4. Read a book about air to a younger child.

5. Take the science fair project to a civic organization.

Chapter 4

The Ingredients of Weather

The weather is where you're standing.
Ed Dombrowsky

Chapter 1 presented a working definition of weather. Here, we inquire in more detail about the elements or qualities that describe the state of the atmosphere at any given time and at any given location. In short, our goal is to know the basic building blocks of weather so we can portray our unique experience with the atmosphere.

It is generally accepted that there are four main elements which, if taken collectively, completely describe the state of the atmosphere at any particular time and at any given point. The essence of weather is the ingredients that combine uniquely to produce what we experience from the atmosphere. A helpful analogy to draw is that of a recipe. The ingredients discussed in this chapter form a recipe for weather. These four basic ingredients are temperature, moisture, pressure, and motion. Figure 4.1 illustrates this analogy.

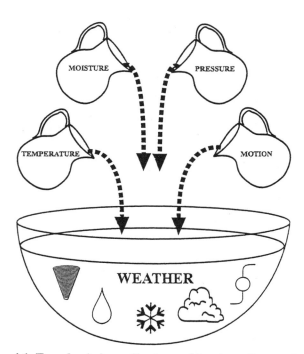

Fig. 4.1. Four basic ingredients combine to make weather.

33

Temperature

Temperature is simply the numerical indication of hotness or coldness. Taken further, this definition involves the atoms and molecules of air. These molecules are in constant motion. They travel in different directions at various speeds. In a given sample of air the number of molecules is huge (6.0×10^{23}, called Avogadro's number) and, therefore, collisions are frequent. Thus, temperature is a numerical measure of the average collision rate of air molecules with a thermometer sensor. Faster movement yields a higher temperature; slower movement gives lower temperature.

An interesting aspect of temperature involves extremes. Specifically, are there limits for temperature extremes in the universe? The lower limit for temperature is called "absolute zero," which corresponds to -460° F. The concept of a lower bound for temperature is important theoretically for it represents a point where all motion at the molecular level stops. In special laboratory settings, scientists have attained temperatures within one-millionth of a degree of absolute zero, although absolute zero itself is unattainable.

The question of an upper limit on temperature in the universe is not so easily answered. It's believed that the universe began in a burst of heat of at least 1 trillion degrees. Although no maximum temperature limit is known, it's difficult to imagine a higher temperature than at the moment of creation.

Teacher's Extra

The Origin of Temperature Scales

A scientist drives to work on a cold morning. He passes the bank and glances at the temperature display. It reads 20°. He arrives at his laboratory and sheds his coat. The laboratory thermometer also reads 20°. What's happening? The paradox is explained by the fact that the two thermometers are using different temperature scales. The bank thermometer used the Fahrenheit scale, while the reading on the laboratory thermometer was in Celsius (sometimes called Centigrade).

The Fahrenheit and Celsius scales were devised in the early part of the 18th century. One of the first men to turn his attention to the subject was Gabriel Daniel Fahrenheit, a maker of meteorological instruments who emigrated to Amsterdam, Holland, from his birthplace in Danzig (now Gdansk), Poland, early in his life. In 1724 he set out to develop a temperature scale that would not include negative numbers. He assigned the value of 0° to the lowest temperature that he could obtain in his laboratory by using a mixture of ice water and salt. He chose as the upper reference point normal human body temperature (which he set at 96°). He later adjusted the scale to make the temperature of pure boiling water (212°) the upper limit. The Fahrenheit scale was adopted in the Netherlands and in Great Britain soon after it was announced. It remains in use in the United States.

The Celsius scale was developed in the early 1740s by Anders Celsius, a Swedish astronomer who divided the difference between the freezing (32°) and boiling points of pure water into 100 equal increments. He placed the freezing point at 0° and the boiling point at 100°. The Celsius scale is used by most of the world's population.

One goal of science is to have the ability to move from one scale to another. Fortunately, the conversion is straightforward. If you need to convert Celsius to Fahrenheit, multiply the Celsius temperature you are given by 1.8 and then add 32. In order to convert Fahrenheit to Celsius, subtract 32 from the given Fahrenheit reading and then multiply by 0.556. Finally it may be helpful to remember that a 5° change on the Celsius scale corresponds to a 9° change on the Fahrenheit scale.

Moisture

The second ingredient of weather is moisture, generally defined as the presence of the water substance in the atmosphere. In the context of weather, moisture means the amount of water vapor in a given sample of air. Scientists now recognize two fundamental functions of water vapor in the atmosphere. The first, and best-known, role of water vapor is that it serves as the raw material in the precipitation process. Lesser known is that water vapor is a highly efficient greenhouse gas, allowing sunlight to pass through the atmosphere to Earth's surface but effectively acting as a blanket for outgoing radiation. The net result is an increase in global temperature. Hence, water vapor regulates global temperature.

Two primary indications of water vapor content in a given sample of air are *relative humidity* and *dewpoint*. The best-known expression is relative humidity, which relates the moisture present in a sample of air to the maximum amount possible at a certain temperature. Put another way, the relative humidity is simply a ratio expressed as a percentage. For example, if a weather broadcast says the relative humidity is 50%, then the air is holding one-half the amount of water vapor that is possible at that temperature.

Another expression for the amount of water vapor present in a sample of air is the dewpoint temperature. This is defined as the temperature that a sample of air must be cooled to in order for the relative humidity to reach 100%, a state called saturation. A higher dewpoint temperature means a greater amount of water vapor is present. Dewpoint is preferred by meteorologists because it is not as temperature dependent as relative humidity.

The content of water vapor is expressed in grams per kilogram, or g/kg. This represents a mixture of water vapor and "dry" air and is termed the mixing ratio. The largest amount of water vapor possible in a given volume of air at a certain temperature is the saturation mixing ratio. As an example, suppose the mixing ratio is 10 g/kg and the saturation mixing ratio is 20 g/kg. The relative humidity is 50% (10 g/kg divided by 20 g/kg).

Phase Change Processes

One prime mechanism of Earth's climate and weather is transformations involving the water substance. These energy transformations, caused by phase changes of water in the atmosphere, help supply the fuel needed for atmospheric processes and phenomena. Thus, phase change processes represent some of the most important of all physical mechanisms occurring in the Earth-atmosphere system. Water exists in three phases: solid (ice), liquid, and gas (vapor). There are six basic phase change operations in the atmosphere: evaporation, condensation, melting, freezing, sublimation, and deposition. Figure 4.2 illustrates these processes and how they relate.

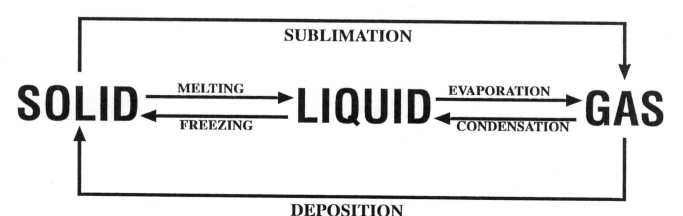

Fig. 4.2. Important phase change processes involving water and their relationship.

Evaporation/Condensation

The first set of phase change processes that we will discuss is evaporation/condensation. Evaporation is the transformation of water from a liquid to a gas. The presence of water vapor in the atmosphere results from evaporation of ocean water. The secret of evaporation is evident at the molecular level. In the liquid state water molecules are bound by forces of attraction. Heating the liquid loosens the bonding forces, eventually to the point where they move freely. On earth the two most important evaporative agents are insolation and wind.

Condensation is the opposite of evaporation. The condensation process transforms water vapor into liquid. At the molecular level condensation strengthens bonding forces, thereby leading to tighter organization and increased order. Condensation is instrumental in the precipitation process.

Melting/Freezing

Two more vital processes involving the water substance are melting and freezing. These are some of the best known of all thermodynamic processes. Melting involves changing water from the solid state (ice) to its liquid state. At the molecular level melting loosens the very tight bonds that hold the ice together and results in a decrease in the order of the structure.

Freezing is the opposite of melting. In this process water is changed from the liquid state to its solid state. Freezing tightens the bonding forces within the substance, resulting in a tighter structure and increased molecular order.

Sublimation/Deposition

The third set of transformation processes involving water is sublimation/deposition. These are probably the least-known set of phase change processes. Sublimation and deposition are interesting because their effects can be fascinating. As a child I was baffled one winter day because the snow on the ground disappeared, yet the temperature was 20° F! I later learned that the snow sublimated, moving directly to the vapor state without melting. Sublimation also fools folks when they want to save large hailstones. Some people, unaware of sublimation, will place hailstones directly in the freezer, only to find that, at a later time, the stones have mysteriously shrunk. What happened? Sublimation took its toll on the hailstone.

Deposition is the opposite of sublimation. It involves bringing water from a gaseous state to a solid state. We see deposition at work on automobile windshields on cold mornings. The frost on the windshield was deposited there, as water vapor in the surrounding air contacted the freezing windshield. Frost is not, as many believe, frozen dew.

Pressure

The third fundamental ingredient in the recipe for weather is pressure, defined as the force per unit of area that is exerted by matter. In this section pressure is discussed as it relates to weather. Is it really possible that something as invisible and tenuous as air can exert a physical force? As we've already discovered, the atmosphere has mass because air is matter. Atmospheric pressure is significant, amounting to 14.7 pounds per square inch. If you live in a house with an area of 2,000 square feet, the atmosphere is exerting a pressure of over 2,100 tons on your home. If you are an adult of average size, then the atmosphere is exerting a total force of several tons on you. Why doesn't this force crush our house or our bodies? First, the pressure is distributed evenly. Second, in the case of our homes, the pressure inside the home is equal to the pressure outside because of leakage through windows and doors. In the case of our bodies, however, the balance of forces is accomplished by internal fluids, principally the circulatory system.

What Determines Air Pressure?

The above question arises frequently. In order to provide a satisfactory answer it is necessary to consider a hypothetical column of air extending upward through the troposphere. Imagine this column positioned over an instrument that measures air pressure (called a barometer) as shown in figure 4.3. The actual reading the barometer gives, as well as the tendency of air pressure, is governed by temperature, moisture, and dynamic effects caused by the moving atmosphere. In this section we consider only how temperature and moisture affect our imaginary air column. The dynamic influence comes in chapter 5.

Temperature/Pressure Relationships

Temperature and pressure are related. It is common knowledge that cold air is heavier than warm air. This simple but vital fact allows us to state that cold air is capable of exerting greater pressure than warm air. Thus, one way high pressure occurs in our imaginary column is through the movement of colder air into it. Conversely, warm air is lighter and able to exert less pressure. With a net influx of warmer air into the column, lower pressure is favored.

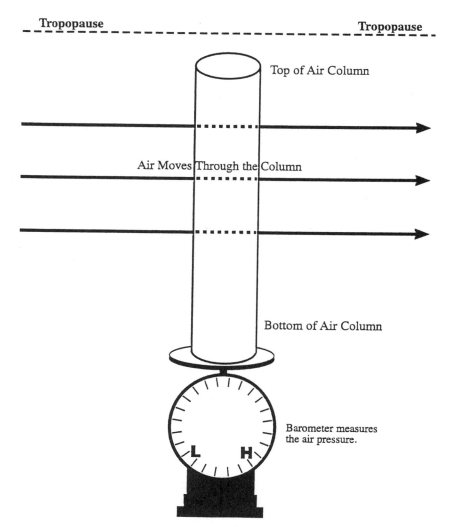

Fig. 4.3. Air pressure can be understood by imagining a column of air positioned over a barometer.

Moisture/Pressure Relationships

Moisture and pressure are also related. The effects of moisture on air pressure are not as well known by laypersons as the effects caused by temperature. The moisture/pressure relationships are dictated by the presence of water vapor in our imaginary column. The key statement concerning the moisture/pressure relationship is that moist air is lighter than dry air. As the amount of water vapor in the column increases, the air becomes lighter and exerts less pressure. If the net result is to move moister air through the column, the pressure is apt to be low or the tendency is expected to fall. If drier air moves through the column, the pressure is expected to be higher or the tendency is most likely to rise.

Temperature/Moisture/Pressure Relationships

In the atmosphere various combinations of temperature, moisture, and pressure exist. Some of these relationships are straightforward. For example, very high pressure or a rapidly rising trend results from a net influx of colder, drier air into our imaginary column. Likewise, it's easy to see how very low pressure or a rapidly falling trend results from a net influx of warmer, wetter air into the column.

What happens with less obvious cases? Suppose colder, wetter air circulates through the column or warmer, drier air moves in? The picture is less clear in these cases. One important fact, however, is that the net characteristics of the air in the lower one-fourth of the column are mostly responsible for dictating the pressure value and its trend. Finally, dynamic effects caused by the movement of the atmosphere can change the above scenarios dramatically.

Motion

The fourth ingredient of weather is motion. The movement of the atmosphere is extremely complex and its significance in weather paramount. For these reasons and others, the discussion of Earth's restless atmosphere will come in chapter 5.

The Process of Scientific Thought

Activity #1

Title: Straw Magic

Objective: To demonstrate that air exerts pressure

Materials Needed: straw, jar of colored water

Procedure: Hold one finger over the end of a straw and dip the other end into the jar of colored water. Remove your finger and watch what happens. Then put your finger back on top of the straw and lift the straw from the jar. The colored water stays in the straw.

Elementary

- Have students communicate their thoughts on why the colored water moved up into the straw the first time. Why did the water stay in the straw when it was lifted from the jar? Use pictures, write, or talk about what happened.

Secondary

- Perform several trials using different amounts of water and straws of varying lengths. Does this change the overall result of the experiment?

- Those seeking a mathematical challenge can try to calculate the pressure per square inch that the atmosphere exerts at any one point. (Answer: 14.7 pounds.)

Activity #2

Title: Water in Limbo

Objective: To illustrate air pressure

Materials Needed: small to medium-sized glass, note card

Procedure: Fill the glass with water until it overflows. Lay a postcard or a note card on top. Support the card with one hand, turn the glass upside down, and remove your hand from the card. It remains on the glass, and the water doesn't escape (at least not at first).

Elementary

- Have students write a one-paragraph explanation of what happened and why it happened. They could also draw a picture or explain orally to a classmate.

Secondary

- Repeat using different glass sizes and different materials. The results may change. For example, a tall drinking glass may prevent the experiment from working properly. Different materials may not support the weight of the water, etc.

- Can any generalizations or predictive statements be made using results from these different trials?

Activity #3

Title: The Origin of Atmospheric Moisture, Part I

Objective: To show that one source of atmospheric moisture is the soil

Materials Needed: scale, pot of soil

Procedure: Fill a container with moist soil and weigh the container. Weigh it again the next day. If you've weighed carefully both times, you should see that the container has lost weight. The weight loss occurred because moisture in the soil evaporated into the air. This is one way moisture gets into the atmosphere.

Activity #4

Title: The Origin of Atmospheric Moisture, Part II

Objective: To show that the plant kingdom is another source of moisture in the atmosphere

Materials Needed: cellophane bag, some fresh moist leaves

Procedure: Place some fresh, moist leaves into a bag and seal it. Wait awhile and observe what's happened. Evidence of moisture should be present in the bag.

Activity #5

Title: The Origin of Atmospheric Moisture, Part III

Objective: To show that the animal kingdom serves as a source of atmospheric moisture

Materials Needed: a glass

Procedure: Place a glass in the refrigerator for a few minutes to cool it. Take the glass out and breathe on it. Moisture will appear on the glass.

Activities #3, 4, and 5 show that atmospheric moisture comes from a variety of sources. Of course, the primary source is Earth's oceans.

Elementary

- Write a one-page summary of these experiments. Can anyone write a poem about how moisture gets into the air?

- How are these three activities similar? How are they different?

- All of these activities are done at room temperature. How would the results be changed if the activities were conducted in a colder environment? A warmer environment?

Secondary

- Are there any patterns?

- What physical laws are at work?

Activity #6

Title: Water Appears

Objective: To illustrate the process of condensation

Materials Needed: ice, water, a tin can or a glass

Procedure: Mix some ice and water in a tin can or in a glass. After a while observe the outside of the can or glass. Unless the air is very dry, you will see tiny beads or droplets of water collect on the outside of the can or glass. If the air is really humid, it won't take long for droplets to appear. Note how long it took for water to collect on the outside of the can or glass.

Elementary

- Allow the children to feel the ice, water, and container. Have them write a brief statement about what happened and why it happened. Have them draw a picture.

- Have one student pose as a reporter. Have the reporter interview other students about the experiment and ask them to tell what they saw and what they think happened.

- Do another trial using water only. Compare how this affects the time it takes for condensate to form on the container. (It should take longer.)

- Do another trial using ice, no water. Compare how this affects the results.

- Summarize results in a table and look for patterns.

Secondary

- State the physical law of condensation.

- State a generalization evident from the data of several trials.

Activity #7

Title: Water Disappears

Objective: To show how most water vapor reaches the atmosphere

Materials Needed: water, eyedropper, aluminum foil

Procedure: Use an eyedropper to place five drops of water on each of two sheets of aluminum foil. Put one sheet in the sun and leave the other sheet in the shade. The drops placed in the direct sunlight will disappear sooner.

Elementary

- Draw a picture of the scene in shade and in sunlight. Talk about the difference.

- Apply the "reporter" role playing used in activity #6 to this situation.

- Repeat the activity but instead of putting one sheet of aluminum in the sun, place it in front of a fan to simulate wind action. Which sheet loses more water?

Secondary

- Obtain four sheets of aluminum and use the dropper to put five drops of water on each sheet. Put one sheet in the sun, one in the shade, one in the shade in front of a fan, and the fourth in the sun and in front of a fan.

- In which of the above four cases did the most water disappear? It's likely to be the sheet placed in the sun and in front of a fan. This illustrates the physical concept of evaporation. On Earth, the two primary evaporative agents are the sun and the wind.

- State the physical law of evaporation.

Activity #8

Title: Dewpoint

Objective: To measure the dewpoint temperature simply

Materials Needed: drinking glass, thermometer, ice

Procedure: Mix water and ice in a glass. Put a thermometer into the mixture. Watch closely and feel the outside of the glass for condensate. When you feel the outside of the glass getting wet, immediately read the thermometer. This gives you an estimate of the dewpoint temperature. If the air is very humid, the condensate will form quickly. Also, if the air is very dry, the condensate may not even form. *Note:* For best results do this activity outside in a shaded area.

Elementary

- Let each student touch the glass and describe how it feels.

- Use different containers. Does the material the container is made of make a difference in the results?

- Use water only and then ice only. Does this make a difference?

Secondary

- Call the nearest airport, National Weather Service office, or TV station and ask what the latest dewpoint is. Compare your result with that. If it's far off (like 10°) try to think of ways to improve the accuracy of this experiment. Change containers, use water or ice only, etc.

Activity #9

Title: Frosty

Objective: To illustrate sublimation and deposition

Materials Needed: glass, freezer

Procedure: Put a drinking glass into the freezer for 30 minutes. Remove the glass and let it stand for 30 seconds. Watch for a cloudy formation on the outside of the glass. This is not frozen dew—it's frost, which has been deposited on the glass. Place an ice cube in the freezer without protective wrapping. Look at it several days later. It will be a little smaller. Why? Because some of it sublimated.

Elementary

- As before, let students touch the containers and talk about what they feel.

- Use different containers. Does that make a difference?

- If you're demonstrating sublimation, weigh the ice cube before placing it in the freezer. Weigh it again when you take it out. It should be slightly lighter. Where did the lost weight go? (Answer: It went into the air as a gas, or vapor.)

Secondary

- State the laws of deposition and sublimation.

- If you weigh the ice cube before and after its trip to the freezer, can you calculate the percentage of weight lost?

Ideas for Science Fair Projects

1. Conduct the class outdoors. Did this affect mood, performance, etc.?

2. Visit a local TV station to see how a weathercast is done, and design a science fair project.

3. Get to know the three phases of water better. You can get to know ice better if you make a snow cone. For water in the liquid state, get a cookbook and see the role water plays in cooking. For water vapor, make a "vapor chamber" by boiling water in a small enclosed space and see how its presence changes the way the air feels.

4. Research how dewpoint and relative humidity are used in practical applications. The moisture content of the air, as measured by dewpoint and relative humidity, is vital information to nurseries, various industrial processes, woodcrafts, cooking, and is even used for instrument making and in wine cellars, which must have a controlled environment.

5. Research the medical aspects of temperature (the heat index, heatstroke, heat cramps, and heat exhaustion), pressure (aches and pains), and moisture (the heat index and the other heat-related ailments mentioned). How sound is the medical basis for these complaints?

6. Research the psychological aspects of weather, temperature, pressure, and moisture. What combinations of conditions are best for our mental health and best for a positive outlook? When are we apt to be more depressed?

7. Find out how temperature, pressure, and moisture affect the animal kingdom. Choose a favorite animal or a species and develop a report and project.

8. Find out how the ingredients of weather affect the plant kingdom. Select one specific plant or a species and write a report and develop a project.

9. Research crops and their relationship to temperature and moisture.

10. Talk to the manager or owner of a local business and see how weather, temperature, and moisture affect the business. Some ideas: retailers, restaurants, construction, farmers, timber, industry in general, and utilities. Is business better when the temperature is high or low? When it rains or is dry?

11. Find out how weather, temperature, pressure, and moisture affect sporting events and athletes. Talk to coaches, doctors, groundskeepers, and athletes.

12. Research the emerging field of cryogenics, the study of the behavior of substances, materials, and gases at extremely low temperatures. The phenomenon of superconductivity, wherein a material loses all resistance to the flow of electricity, is an example in this field of science.

School's Out!

1. Read a book about weather, temperature, moisture, water, or air to a younger sibling or friend.

2. Teach preschoolers at a local day care, Head Start, or early childhood enrichment program about temperature, moisture, or pressure.

3. Prepare a list of questions and ask your favorite adult for help in finding the answers.

Chapter 5

The Atmosphere in Motion

The trees bow as it passes by. It refreshes those who labor in the sweltering heat and it nourishes the reproductive freedom of the plant kingdom. It is the wind, a symptom of our restless atmosphere. The movement of our atmosphere is complex and can be represented by charts, graphs, equations, and computer simulations. This body of knowledge is called the theory of atmospheric motion, and although this theory is a creation of human intellect, scientists believe that it mirrors nature's design. As such, we can reach for, and perhaps even touch, some of the truth hidden in nature's intricate plan.

The aim of chapter 5 is twofold. The first goal is to present a factual basis for how and why the atmosphere moves. The second intention is to provide a rational foundation upon which to predict future patterns of atmospheric motion.

The Cause of Atmospheric Motion

We can accomplish the first goal by asking, What causes the atmosphere to move? How are the winds born and how do they die? Ultimately, it is the unequal distribution of sunlight caused by Earth's shape that gives life to the wind. Figure 5.1 shows the annual net radiation of the Earth-atmosphere system. This data is based on eight years of satellite observations. The conclusion from the data presented in figure 5.1 is that the net radiation of the Earth-atmosphere system is positive at latitudes equatorward of about 40° and negative poleward of 40°. The highest positive values of solar energy are evident over Earth's vast oceans, especially over the Indian Ocean with a surplus of nearly 90 watts per square meter and over the equatorial Pacific where anomalies exceed 80 watts per square meter. A lower net positive amount of solar energy is noted over the tropical Atlantic between South America and Africa.

Global Wind Patterns

Some have wondered why the excess of energy in equatorial regions fails to produce unbearably high temperatures and why the deficit of energy at the poles doesn't lead to drastically low temperatures. The answer is that global wind patterns develop in response to the equator-to-pole temperature difference. At this time in Earth's history, the basic global wind patterns shown in figure 5.2 are observed. These zones represent areas where there is a distinct shift in the prevailing wind direction. The primary wind belts of Earth are the trades, the doldrums, the prevailing westerlies, and the polar easterlies.

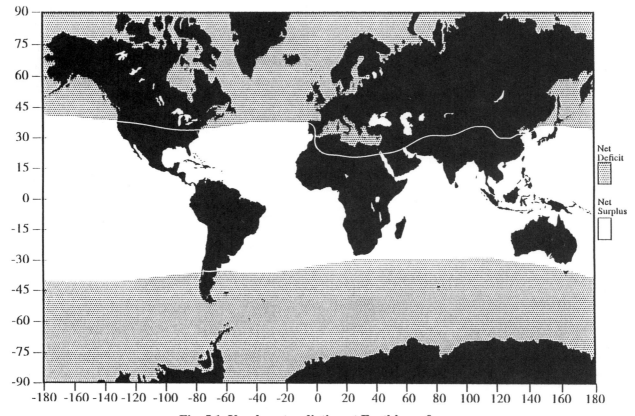

Fig. 5.1. Yearly net radiation at Earth's surface.

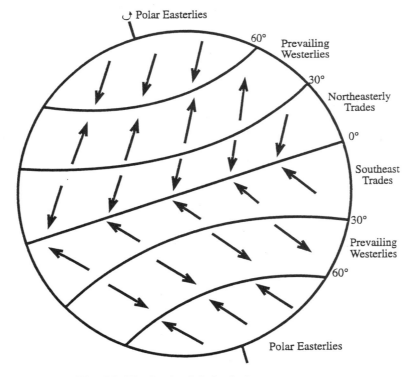

Fig. 5.2. The basic global wind patterns.

The Trade Winds

The dominant winds across Earth between latitudes 30° N and 30° S are the trade winds, or simply the trades. Used in this context the word *trade* means "straight course" or "common course," not the commercial connotation. The trade wind belts result from Earth's attempt to balance the excess radiation received there with the lower radiation received to the north and to the south. Because of the persistent radiation imbalances that drive the trades, they are quite reliable. Some areas in the trade wind zone have surface winds that blow from the same direction 80% of the time.

The Doldrums

The trades from each hemisphere converge in a narrow zone near the equator known traditionally as the *doldrums*, a term coined in 1811 by sailors. The doldrums are an area of light and variable winds and unsettled weather. The great sailing vessels of old could be stranded in the doldrums for weeks at a time.

A more modern description of the doldrums is the Intertropical Convergence Zone, or the ITCZ. Meteorologists know the ITCZ as a zone where the trades from each hemisphere converge. Hence, the squally weather and the chaotic wind pattern. The presence of the ITCZ is marked by almost constant cloud cover and intermittent clusters of showers and thunderstorms. The ITCZ is usually located near 5° N latitude but can extend to 10° N latitude during the summer. The ITCZ favors the Northern Hemisphere in summer because it has more landmass, which promotes higher average temperatures.

The Prevailing Westerlies

The third wind belt is the prevailing westerlies, located in each hemisphere between 30° and 60°. The nature of the prevailing westerlies is more unreliable than the trades. The westerlies change dramatically daily and seasonally.

One interesting area near 30° latitude in each hemisphere is a transition zone between the trades and the westerlies called the Horse Latitudes. Generally, the Horse Latitudes are dry with few clouds. Indeed, many of the world's deserts are located on or near the 30th parallel. The region got its name in colonial times when vessels carrying horses from Europe to the West Indies were sometimes becalmed so long that the horse's feed and water were used up and the animals had to be thrown overboard.

The Polar Easterlies

Like all of the other wind belts of Earth, the polar easterlies represent an attempt to balance radiation differences. Because of this, the winds in polar regions favor an easterly direction, although there is marked variation from time to time. The easterlies are more common and persistent over the South Pole than the North Pole.

A Vertical Look at Earth's Winds

At the equator converging and rising motion dominates, which explains the persistent cloudiness and showery precipitation. Diverging and sinking motion occurs near 30° latitude in each hemisphere, which leads to a general lack of cloud cover and a deficit of precipitation. Finally, sinking motion occurs again at the poles. This giant circulation is called the Hadley cell after the man who first adequately explained its existence in 1735.

The Monsoon

In many parts of the world the basic wind patterns just outlined undergo distinct and significant changes. Perhaps the best-known and most dramatic example of this seasonal shift in wind patterns occurs in southern and eastern Asia. Here, winter winds drain dry air from the massive Asian continent, causing a 6-month-long "dry season." During the summer the pattern reverses, and moisture-laden winds push northward into the continent. This seasonally reversing wind pattern is called a *monsoon*, from the Arabic *mausin*, meaning "season."

The Three Fundamental Components of Atmospheric Motion

Earth's wind patterns arise as a magnificent attempt to balance temperature differences. But what are the details of this arrangement? We now know that all atmospheric motion is governed by three fundamental components: horizontal, vertical, and rotational. In this section we discuss the basic forces controlling our dynamic atmosphere.

Horizontal Motion

The analysis of horizontal motion in the atmosphere begins with Newton's Second Law of Motion. This basic tenet of science states that the sum of all forces acting on a piece of matter is equal to the mass of the matter multiplied by any acceleration it experiences. Here is Newton's Second Law in a more compact form:

The sum of the forces = mass times acceleration
OR, using symbols:
$$F_{sum} = ma \quad (5.1)$$

What does equation 5.1 have to do with the weather? One of the most important conclusions from chapter 3 was our realization that air has mass, and therefore is considered matter. In fact, meteorologists use equation 5.1 as the foundation upon which the theory of atmospheric motion exists. Here, we will use it to construct a framework of the horizontal component of atmospheric motion.

Horizontal motion in the atmosphere is controlled by a sum of four forces: the pressure gradient force, the Coriolis Force, gravity, and friction.

We can now state what meteorologists call the equation of horizontal motion:
The horizontal acceleration (or movement) of air = Coriolis Force + Pressure Gradient Force + Gravity + Friction.

OR, using symbols,
$$A_h = CF + (PGF)_h + G + F \quad (5.2)$$
where the subscript "h" denotes the horizontal direction.

Equation 5.2 can be simplified. Research indicates that the value of gravity varies only about 0.3% throughout most of the troposphere. Thus, the contribution of gravity in equation 5.2 can be removed and we have:

$$A_h = CF + (PGF)_h + F \quad (5.3)$$
where "h" again refers to the horizontal direction.

The Coriolis Force

Now let's discuss the individual members of equation 5.3 and their contribution to the horizontal component of atmospheric motion. The first term in equation 5.3 is the *Coriolis Force*. Because we live on a rotating planet, horizontal air motion is "deflected" by Earth's spin. This causes a state of continuous acceleration for a parcel of air, much like a vehicle moving around in a circle. Essentially, the Coriolis Force acts to pull a parcel of air at a 90° angle to the right in the Northern Hemisphere and at a 90° angle to the left in the Southern Hemisphere.

The Pressure Gradient Force

The pressure gradient force arises from a difference in air pressure across a certain horizontal distance. It is always directed from areas of higher pressure to areas of lower pressure, and its magnitude is proportional to the distance through which it operates.

Friction

The concept of friction is elusive. It is a fact that no scientist has been able to develop an accepted theory of friction from first principles. Despite its difficulty we can understand friction from a practical standpoint. Consider an automobile traveling too fast on an icy or wet road surface. The vehicle cannot be stopped as soon as it could if the surface were dry. Why? Friction between the road surface and the tires is greatest when the road is dry. As another example, rub your finger briskly on a coarse fabric. Soon, your finger gets uncomfortably hot. Again, it's the practical experience with friction. The key to understanding friction is looking at it from a molecular viewpoint. A nontechnical explanation of friction involves knowing that it results from a molecular exchange between two substances. In the atmosphere, the wind experiences friction with Earth's surface. The important conclusion is that friction always acts to slow air motion.

In summary, three forces determine the horizontal component of atmospheric movement. They combine in unique ways to bring the observed patterns of winds we desperately try to predict. Figure 5.3 sketches the relationship of these three basic forces. The direction of the actual wind is displaced about 45° to the right because the Coriolis Force dominates friction.

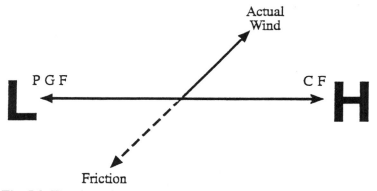

Fig. 5.3. The three fundamental forces that contribute to our wind.

Vertical Motion

Vertical motion represents another basic component of the moving atmosphere. As one might expect, the same forces that dictate horizontal motion also affect vertical motion. This type of motion in the atmosphere has a special name: convection. In considering vertical motion, we begin by using a restated version of equation 5.1:

$$A_v = CF + (PGF)_v + G + F \quad (5.4)$$

where the subscript "v" is used to indicate that we're considering only the vertical component of motion. In this case the contributions of the Coriolis Force and friction are negligible; therefore, equation 5.4 quickly reduces to:

$$A_v = (PGF)_v - G \quad (5.5)$$

where "v" implies that we're only considering vertical air motion, and the negative sign in front of the gravity term is used to denote a downward force, or one that counteracts the upwardly directed pressure gradient.

Rotational Motion

Consider a snowflake on its gentle journey to Earth. Suddenly, it spins uncontrollably. Then, as quickly as it began, the snowflake stops spinning and resumes its flutter Earthward. Dust whirls, tornadoes, and hurricanes represent some of the better-known examples of rotation in the atmosphere. Rotational motion in the atmosphere serves the vital function of alleviating temperature contrasts, as it's been shown by mechanical engineers that the most efficient way to mix fluids is through rotation. Thus, the many examples of rotation we see in the atmosphere make our planet more habitable by efficiently preventing deadly temperature extremes.

The rotational component of motion results from two sources. First, physical forces can impart spin to air. Second, a parcel of air can obtain vorticity from Earth's rotation.

Deformation Forces

In addition to the forces already mentioned, the horizontal pattern of atmospheric motion creates forces that distort air. Most often, either convergence or divergence results from the pattern of horizontal motion.

Divergence

If the horizontal pattern of atmospheric motion spreads out, then the flow is said to be divergent, such as indicated in the top sketch in figure 5.4. An imaginary pancake of air is distorted by the divergent flow around it, and it begins to spread out. Because of this, the area occupied by our pancake of air increases. However, since air is matter and cannot be destroyed, the increase in area must be compensated for by a corresponding decrease in its vertical extent as shown in figure 5.5. This illustrates a fundamental physical theory called the Law of Conservation of Mass. In the final analysis, divergence leads to horizontal stretching and a vertical compression of our pancake of air.

Convergence

Convergence is the opposite of divergence. The bottom sketch in figure 5.4 illustrates the effect a horizontally convergent flow pattern would have on a pancake of air. In this case the area of the pancake decreases, but the Law of Conservation of Mass dictates that the loss of area must be compensated for by a gain in vertical extent as shown in Figure 5.5. In conclusion, convergence compresses our pancake of air horizontally and stretches it vertically.

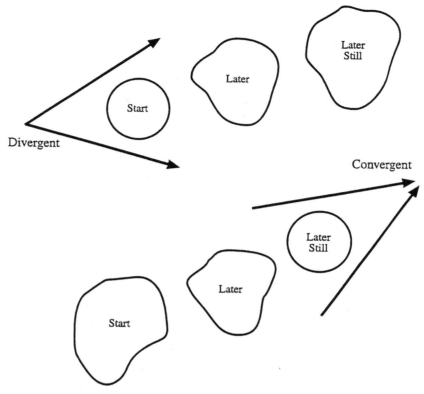

Fig. 5.4. The effect of horizontal divergence and convergence.

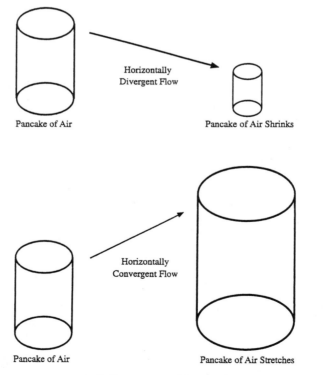

Fig. 5.5. How convergence and divergence affect an imaginary pancake of air.

Convergence, Divergence, and Vorticity

Convergence and divergence also impact the vorticity of our imaginary pancake of air. Figure 5.6 illustrates these relationships. In the case of convergent flow, the increase in areal coverage of our pancake of air dictates the column stretch. The laws of physics say that the spin associated with that stretching process will increase. Thus, the important conclusion is that horizontal convergence leads to increased vorticity. In a similar manner, the shrinking column associated with divergence allows for less vorticity. These observations are vital in the development of weather systems.

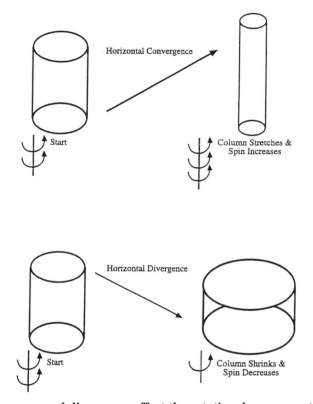

Fig. 5.6. Convergence and divergence affect the rotational component of air motion.

The Jetstream

During WWII American pilots flying missions across the Pacific Ocean encountered terrific headwinds and a tremendous tailwind. At the time it was known theoretically that zones of fast-moving, high-altitude winds existed, yet WWII provided the first practical encounter of the phenomena called the *jetstream*.

By definition, the jetstream is a relatively narrow, fast-moving zone of air aloft. It is like a river of air flowing through an ocean of atmosphere. The jetstream is normally located at heights of 20,000 to 40,000 feet. Windspeeds in these high-altitude jetstreams can reach 250 mph and represent a manifestation of the global circulation. Temperature differences across Earth's surface supply the energy needed to maintain the jetstream. The position of the jetstream meanders north and south, presumably driven by the complex processes controlling Earth's radiation budget. The jetstream acts as an efficient transportation mechanism for moving vast quantities of warm air northward and huge amounts of cool air southward. The United States is affected primarily by three types of jetstreams: the polar jetstream, the subtropical jetstream, and the low-level jetstream. A brief discussion of each type of jetstream follows.

The Polar Jetstream

The high-altitude jetstream just described is commonly called the polar jetstream. An important aspect of the polar jetstream is the polar front, the surface reflection of the polar jetstream's position. The polar front marks the boundary between the mid-latitude westerlies and the high-latitude polar easterlies. As such, the movement of the polar jetstream brings important weather changes to the United States. When the polar jetstream bends southward, outbreaks of cold air follow in winter.

During the summer, pleasantly cool air follows the polar jetstream southward. A northward shift in its position brings mild to warm weather in the winter and can bring spells of oppressive heat in the summer. Inherently, the polar jetstream is responsible for steering weather systems. In fact, the connection is so close that the average position of the polar jetstream is commonly called the "storm track" by weather forecasters.

The Subtropical Jetstream

What is termed the subtropical jetstream is commonly a branch of the polar jetstream that is displaced southward. During the winter the subtropical jetstream is an important weather-maker in the southern United States as it snakes from Baja, California, and northern Mexico. Strong, wet

disturbances embedded in the subtropical jetstream bring episodes of flooding and severe storms to the southern United States periodically. During the summer, the subtropical jetstream normally disappears.

The Low-Level Jetstream

The Low-Level Jetstream (LLJ) is another important phenomenon in the United States. The LLJ is evident at heights of 1,000 to 5,000 feet above the surface. A strong LLJ may blow at speeds of 50 to 100 mph. It is driven by the large pressure gradient associated with strong weather systems. It also develops at night (when it's called the nocturnal jet)

in response to the surface elevation increase as one moves southeast to northwest toward the Rocky Mountains. The LLJ occurs anywhere in the United States but the nocturnal jet is usually only found between the Mississippi River and the Rocky Mountains. Both the LLJ and the nocturnal jet are important agents in outbreaks of severe storms.

The Dynamic Contribution to Air Pressure

Earlier, in chapter 4, the relationship between temperature, moisture, and pressure was presented. At this point, it is appropriate to touch on the dynamic contribution to air pressure. Once again, as in chapter 4, we consider an imaginary column of air sitting over a barometer and extending upward to the tropopause. Figure 5.7 illustrates the presence of a jetstream aloft and the corresponding effect on surface pressure. The pressure is likely to fall because the rapidly moving band of air flowing through the column results in a net removal of air, which leads to less weight and therefore lower pressure.

The jetstream is frequently a region where deformation forces such as convergence and divergence occur. In fact, the presence of the jetstream is one of the major causes of convergence and divergence in the pattern of horizontal motion. But what influence do these deformation forces have on the pressure at the surface? Essentially, falling pressure occurs if there is divergence at the top of the air column, convergence at its base, or both. If there is divergence at the column's summit, mass will be depleted and must be replaced by rising air from the bottom of the column. This results in a net loss of air volume and, consequently, a likely fall in pressure at the surface.

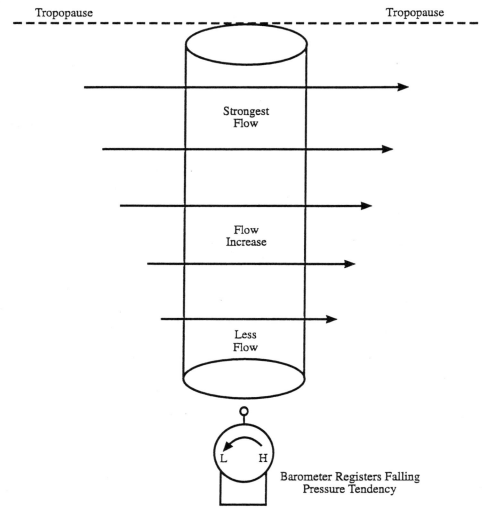

Fig. 5.7. The presence of a jetstream aloft causes surface pressure to fall.

Convergence at the base of the column also causes the pressure to fall. In this case, the convergent air is forced upward (it can't go through the ground), resulting in a deficit of air in the lower levels. This leads to a net loss of volume in the column and a pressure fall is likely. Ideally, in the real atmosphere, it is common to have low-level convergence and upper-level divergence. This arrangement assures rising motion in the column, a net loss of air volume, and a corresponding fall in surface pressure. Figure 5.8 illustrates this principle.

The converse of the scenarios presented above is also true. Divergence at the base of the column or convergence at the top of the column causes a net sinking motion, a net increase in air volume, and a rise in surface pressure. In the atmosphere it is common to see low-level divergence and high-level convergence. Figure 5.9 depicts this situation.

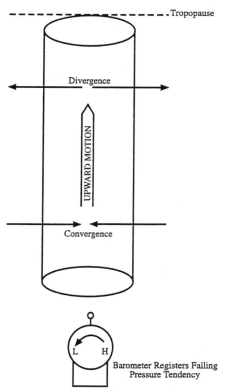

Fig. 5.8. Low-level convergence and high-level divergence cause rising motion and a resulting surface pressure drop.

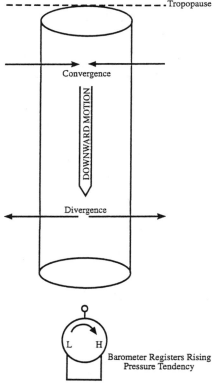

Fig. 5.9. Low-level divergence and high-level convergence cause sinking motion and a resulting surface pressure rise.

The Concept of Advection

You may have noticed how weather seems to move from one place to another. Meteorologists call this *advection*, defined as the horizontal transport of atmospheric properties or phenomena from one location to another. Temperature, moisture, pollution, storms, and even insect populations can be advected. The concept was realized long ago and motivated the saying "The wind brings the weather." In the United States a south wind usually advects warm air northward. Conversely, a north wind is known for transporting colder air southward. West winds are noted for their dryness while an east wind heralds foul weather.

The Semipermanent Pressure Areas of the Northern Hemisphere

Earth's surface is characterized by several persistent regions of high and low pressure. Figure 5.10 represents the normal summer and winter pressure distribution of the world.

The solid line meandering across the equator depicts the position of the ITCZ. Included in this classification are the subtropical and subpolar highs and the subpolar low-pressure belt.

Subtropical and Subpolar Highs

The subtropical high-pressure belt extends across the Northern Hemisphere and includes the Bermuda-Azores High and the Pacific High. The Bermuda-Azores High is located over the North Atlantic Ocean. When displaced over the western part of the North Atlantic it is called the Bermuda High. When displaced over the eastern part of the North Atlantic it is known as the Azores High. This feature affects the United States. In summer, periods of warm and humid weather invade the eastern United States under the influence of the Bermuda-Azores High.

The Pacific High is located over the North Pacific Ocean and centered, on the average, at 30° to 40° N latitude and around 140° to 150° W longitude. It is generally a summer feature with an average central pressure near 30.30 inches. During the winter, this high weakens and moves southeastward.

The North American High covers much of the interior sections of North America during the winter with average sea-level central pressure on the order of 30.25 inches. The North American High disappears during the summer.

The final feature of the high-pressure belt is the Siberian High. This high forms over northeastern Asia during the winter. It is normally centered over Siberia, hence the name. Mountains surrounding Siberia keep the cold air from draining off and, as a result, sea level pressure readings are very high, usually exceeding 30.50 inches.

The Subpolar Low-Pressure Belt

The subpolar low-pressure belt consists of the Aleutian Low and the Icelandic Low. In the winter these features become very persistent and intense. Both are located between 50° and 70° N latitude and have central sea level pressure readings near 29.40 inches. In the summer these features disappear.

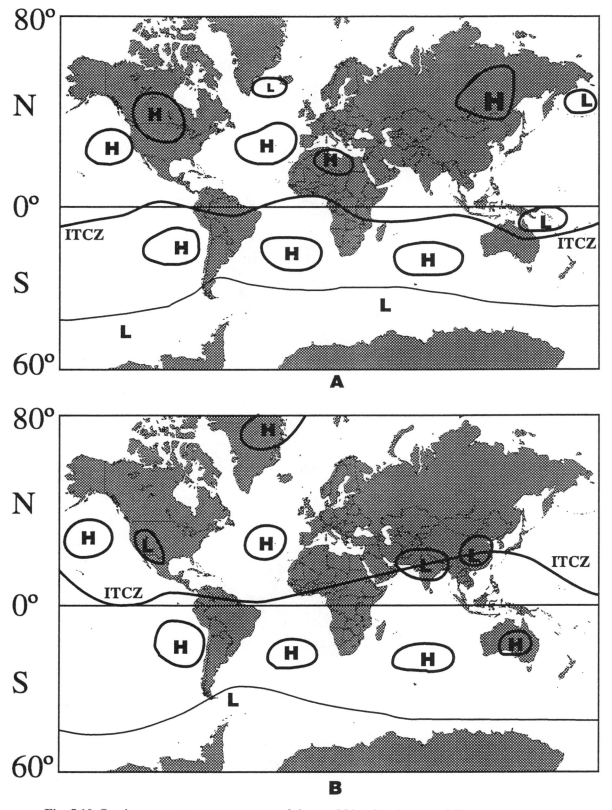

Fig. 5.10. Semipermanent pressure areas of the world in: A) winter and B) summer.

The Semipermanent Upper-Level Circulation

The normal global circulation pattern in winter is shown in figure 5.11. A strong low is present just west of Greenland. The upper low stretches across the North Pole into northeastern Asia. Because this low encompasses the polar regions, it is known as the "Circum Polar Vortex." It represents a circulating mass of cold air with the polar jetstream outlining its southern periphery and the polar front the southern extent of cold air penetration.

Another important aspect of figure 5.11 is the pattern of lines. These lines are called contours and represent the average temperature from the surface up to about 18,000 to 20,000 feet. Notice the packing of these lines, which implies a sharp north-south temperature difference.

In contrast to the winter pattern, summer brings a much weaker Circum Polar Vortex and a less compact contour structure. The implications are weaker jetstream flow and a less pronounced north-south temperature contrast. Figure 5.12 is a sketch of the normal summer circulation pattern.

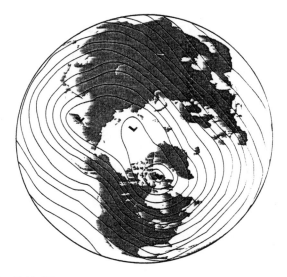

Fig. 5.11. The average general circulation during winter.

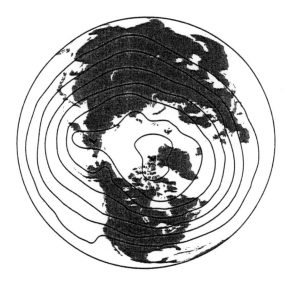

Fig. 5.12. The average general circulation during summer.

The Process of Scientific Thought

Activity #1

Title: How About a Lift?

Objective: To illustrate lift associated with moving air

Materials Needed: a piece of paper

Procedure: Take a piece of paper about 12 inches long and 1¾ inches wide and crease the paper about 1¼ inches from one end. Now hold the short end of the fold against your chin with the crease level with your lips. Blow hard across the top surface of the paper and observe what happens.

Elementary

- Draw a picture of the airstream as it moves over the paper. Try to capture the rising action of the paper.

- Write two or three sentences explaining what happened. (Answer: The air moving rapidly over the crease of the paper lifted it because of the difference in pressure created by the moving air.)

- Name some other examples of moving airstreams that create "dynamic lift." (Answer: Section of an airplane wing, a football spiraling upward, a baseball spinning as it moves up.)

- Compare a moving airstream to a moving stream of water. You'll notice they are similar.

Secondary

- This activity is an example of dynamic lift, a lift created by a moving airstream. Look into the role of dynamic lift in getting an airplane airborne.

- Study projectile motion (a branch of physics called ballistics) and note the importance of dynamic lift.

Activity #2

Title: The World in a Box

Objective: To show that temperature differences set air into motion

Materials Needed: a large box, small candle, two blocks of wood, paint, lamp

Procedure: Obtain a cardboard box about 12 inches long and two blocks of wood about 5 inches long each. Paint the top of one block black and paint the top of the other block white. Place them in the box so that they are about an inch apart. Now shine a heat lamp or a strong light on the blocks of wood. After a few minutes, light a small candle, blow it out, and put it between the blocks of wood. The smoke should drift gently toward the black block.

Elementary

- Draw a picture. How do you explain what you observed? Write two or three sentences. (Answer: The black block absorbs more heat and becomes warmer. This creates a miniature low-pressure area over the black block. Because air must flow from higher pressure to lower pressure, the slight movement of air toward the black block confirms what's happening.)

- Do you have a closet in your classroom that always seems too hot or too cold? If so, use it to demonstrate how temperature differences move air. Open the door slightly and use an extinguished candle to trace the movement of air currents around the opening at different levels above the floor.

Secondary

- Repeat the activity using a black block of wood and a tray of cool water. The smoke will again drift toward the black block. Later, try it again. There should come a time when the smoke drifts toward the water. This simulates a sea-breeze circulation—an onshore flow during the day and an offshore flow at night.

- Repeat using light of varying intensity. You may notice an increase in the movement of the smoke. If so, use that observation to make general statements about the pressure gradient force.

Activity #3

Title: Around and Around

Objective: To understand the Coriolis Force

Materials Needed: a rotating surface, black construction paper, chalk

Procedure: Use a rotating surface of some kind; a phonograph will work well. Cut a disc of construction paper about the size of the rotating surface. Punch a hole in the center. Place it on the turntable. Turn it on low speed. With the piece of chalk, draw a line from the center to the edge. Despite your best effort, the line will be curved, not straight.

Elementary

- In what direction does the curve move? (Answer: To the right.)

- Repeat the activity. On the other half of the paper, draw a line from the edge to the center. In what direction does that line curve? (Answer: To the left.)

- In which hemisphere does the Coriolis Force turn air motion to the right? (Answer: The Northern Hemisphere.)

- In which hemisphere does the Coriolis Force turn air motion to the left? (Answer: The Southern Hemisphere.)

- Fill a sink with water and undo the drain plug. It might help to add some food coloring to the water to make its motion more evident. Does the water spin clockwise or counterclockwise? Repeat several times. (Answer: You'll notice that the water spins in both directions, with no particular pattern evident. This means that your sink is on such a small scale as to not be affected significantly by the Coriolis Force.)

Secondary

- Here's a mathematical challenge. The amount of Coriolis effect depends on latitude and is given by the formula 2Wsinf, where W is the Coriolis constant and is equal to 7.3×10^{-5} and f is the latitude in degrees. Figure out the value of the Coriolis Force at the equator (0°), 20°, 40°, 60°, and at the North Pole (90°). You'll find that the Coriolis effect increases as one moves away from the equator. What is the meteorological significance of your results? (Answer: The Coriolis Force is an important factor governing global wind patterns.)

Activity #4

Title: The Dishpan Experiment

Objective: To simulate Earth's general circulation

Materials Needed: a 10- to 12-inch metal pan, glitter, heat source, ice, small glass

Procedure: This experiment may be hard to get right at first. Keep trying; the results will be well worth it. It will show students more about Earth's winds than any book! Fill a 10- to 12-inch round metal pan, preferably with a handle, with about 4 inches of water. Set a small glass of ice water in the center. Find a heat source such as a Bunsen burner, hot plate, or stove burner. Use whatever source you think would be easiest and safest to work with. Sprinkle a generous supply of glitter over the surface of the water. Arrange the pan so that only the edge is heated. Rotate the pan slowly, about one revolution every 6 seconds. After a while the glitter traces the existence of wavelike patterns in the pan, which is analogous to the general circulation of Earth's atmosphere. The fluid in the metal pan crudely represents one hemisphere of Earth and the rim of the pan represents the equator. The small glass of ice water represents the polar region.

Elementary

- Draw a picture of the experiment and write a paragraph to explain what happened.

- Why does the heated rim correspond to the equator? (Answer: The equator is Earth's heat source.)

- Why does the chilled water in the middle represent the equator? (Answer: The polar region is Earth's heat loss.)

Secondary

- Vary the rotation rate of the pan. How does rotation rate affect the circulation patterns?

- Vary the intensity of the heat source at the rim. How does it affect the circulation?

- Vary the amount of cooling in the center. Does this have any noticeable effect?

  (Answers: Stronger temperature differences should yield a more rapidly changing pattern. A slow rotation rate is best. Ideal: slow rotation with moderate temperature contrast.)

- This one really requires some original thought. Recall from earlier chapters that Earth's tilt varies over time. Can you make predictions about how the circulation would change in this future Earth? (Answer: A tilt of 24.5° would likely lead to stronger temperature contrasts and a more changeable pattern with hotter summers and colder winters for the United States. A tilt of 22.5° would likely give the opposite effect.) What about melting of the polar ice cap? (Repeat the experiment using tap water instead of ice water. Scientists believe this scenario would lead to a northward displacement of global circulation and milder winters and warmer summers for the United States.) What about in a time when glaciers advance? (Repeat using a much larger glass of ice water. Scientists believe that in glacial times the global circulation is displaced southward, leading to cold snowy winters and cool summers in the United States.)

Ideas for Science Fair Projects

1. Modern meteorologists have a good understanding of the basic framework of global wind patterns. But how did we learn what we know now? The historical development of our state of knowledge would make a good science fair project. The project could include some of the history given earlier in this chapter and any other information that is available. An important component of this project would be using replicas of old wind charts from previous centuries. These might be available in an encyclopedia, museum, or book. If you have a hard time finding such charts, enlist a local meteorologist or historian to help.

2. Monsoons make a good science fair topic. The world's most famous monsoon affects southern and Southeast Asia. In this region up to one-third of the world's population is affected by the monsoon. Research the cultural dependence on the monsoon in this region, its meteorological cause, and give a few statistics on the unbelievable amount of rain the monsoon can sometimes bring. A lesser-known monsoon affects the southwestern United States during the summer and early autumn. Under certain upper flow patterns, moist air moves into this area, triggering flash floods and spectacular thunderstorms.

3. Look into the large amount of financial and human resources being used to learn more about Earth's global circulation. Focus on the development of GCMs (Global Circulation Models) that are used to understand and predict possible human-induced climate changes. This information is readily available from the periodicals listed in chapter 1.

4. The jetstream makes a good science fair topic. Students should define it, touch on its discovery, and discuss its importance as an agent for moving weather patterns. It wouldn't hurt to outline the types of jetstreams that affect the United States, as mentioned in this chapter.

5. Present the dynamic contribution to pressure as outlined in this chapter. Many people don't know what surface pressure is and what causes it to rise or fall.

6. Research ocean currents that affect the United States. These include the Gulf Stream and the North Pacific Current that moves along the West Coast. How do they arise and what effect do they have on the weather and climate of nearby regions?

7. The El Niño is a very appropriate science fair topic. What is it? How does it develop? What are its effects? How long does it last? When does it appear? The answers to these questions will set the student in motion toward a very good project.

8. Any of the following are appropriate: Coriolis Force, gravity, and friction. Also, activity #2 could be done as a science fair project.

9. If the Dishpan Experiment is not done as a classroom activity, then encourage a student to do it as a science fair project. It won't be easy, but if the student can make it work, it's a sure winner.

School's Out!

1. Read a book about wind to a younger child.

2. See the wind in action—go fly a kite!

3. Think about making or buying an anemometer for home use.

4. Observe the wind and its effects carefully, and then try to estimate windspeed and direction.

5. Be sensitive to what the wind brings (advection). Does it bring the scent of distant rain? Did it move a storm in your direction? Or did it serve to move a swarm of insects nearby?

6. Look into the devastating personality of the wind. Watch a video on tornadoes or hurricanes.

Chapter 6

Probing the Atmosphere: Instruments, Equipment, and Observations

Toys of the Human Brainchild

Earth's weather machine runs constantly. It manifests itself in both the visible and the invisible. But how do we detect the unseen, and how do we analyze what we can see? The answers are by instruments, equipment, and observations.

The Basic Instruments

We begin with the most basic weather instruments. These instruments are readily available and can reveal a surprising amount of information about local meteorological conditions.

The Thermometer

The first historical record of a thermometer was Galileo's "air thermoscope," invented in 1593. This instrument consisted of a glass bulb containing air connected to a glass tube of small bore dipping into a colored liquid. In reality, this instrument sensed pressure changes, not the actual temperature.

Today, there are many different designs of thermometers. The liquid-in-glass thermometer (see figure 6.1) consists of a small reservoir of fluid (usually mercury or alcohol) at the bottom called the bulb. The level of this fluid rises or falls in the capillary tube as the temperature changes. The meniscus is the slightly curved upper portion of the fluid. The thermometer is read by looking at the scale notation corresponding to this level. Finally, the expansion chamber at the top is normally evacuated or filled with saturated vapor. This minimizes the instrument's sensitivity to pressure changes, and assures an accurate temperature reading. Liquid-in-glass thermometers are stable and are normally accurate to within 2° F. Inexpensive mercury thermometers can be purchased for less than $10. Highly accurate ones for scientific use cost much more.

The dial thermometer has a round face on which a pointer indicates the current temperature. The bimetallic sensing element is made up of two bonded strips of different metals. As the temperature changes, each metal expands (for rising temperatures) and contracts (for falling temperatures) at a different amount. Thus, the curvature of the bi-metal strip changes. The bimetallic strip is generally arranged in a spiral form that produces rotation of a pointer located on the face of the thermometer. Bimetallic dial thermometers can easily be adapted for use as maximum-minimum thermometers by adding two additional pointers, one on each side of

65

the primary pointer. Dial thermometers are easy to read and many models cost less than $20. Highly accurate ones, however, will cost $100 or more.

The Six's thermometer (invented by James Six in England in 1782) may be the most functional of the four basic types since it provides current temperature and maximum-minimum temperatures. A typical Six's thermometer, shown in figure 6.2, consists of two fluids: a light oil considered the "working fluid" because it expands and contracts as the temperature changes; and the second fluid, mercury, which is the indicating system because it is more visible than the oil in the bulb. The end of the U-tube opposite the bulb is terminated in a closed glass cylinder that is only half full of oil; the top part of this cylinder is filled with air.

It is important to note that the scales on the Six's thermometer are inverted. The scale on the right is read for the maximum temperature while the scale on the left reads the minimum temperature. The indices are reset by sliding a small magnet down the tube or by pushing a button located near the center of the instrument.

Despite its functional design, the Six's thermometer has several drawbacks. First, some people find the inverted temperature scales confusing while others forget whether they should read the bottom or the top of the index. Second, the small reset magnet is easily lost or misplaced. Third, the working fluid eventually "wets" the glass and creeps around the mercury column, making resetting the thermometer difficult and causing calibration problems.

On the positive side, in addition to its functionality, the Six's thermometer is an excellent tool to learn interpretation and measurement skills. Also, Six's thermometers tend to be quite accurate, with errors generally of 1.5° F or less. Many Six's thermometers are inexpensive, with costs less than $30 common.

Finally, there is the digital thermometer. In this type of thermometer, the sensor probe is connected to the physical unit by a small cable, the electrical properties of which change as the temperature

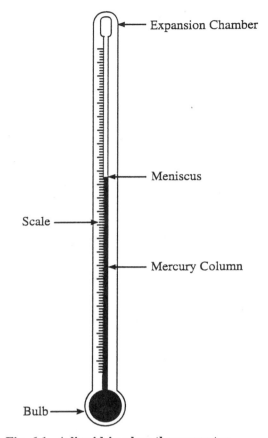

Fig. 6.1. A liquid-in-glass thermometer.

changes. This information is sent through the cable to the physical unit, which is equipped with additional circuitry that converts the sensor output into a digital display. It also contains an electronic chip that "remembers" the highest and lowest temperatures sensed by the probe since last reset. An electronic readout appears as the appropriate function is executed.

Digital thermometers offer several advantages. They are economical, easy to use, and easy to read. Also, the temperature is displayed to the nearest one-tenth of a degree, a feature not available with other designs. Many simple digital thermometers are available commercially at reasonable prices (generally $20 to $35) and offer an acceptable level of accuracy (usually within 2° F).

The Barometer

Barometers are made in two basic designs: liquid-in-tube and aneroid ("containing no liquid"). The first liquid-in-tube barometer was used in 1643 by Evangelista Torricelli, who had been an assistant to Galileo. The utility of this instrument was quickly recognized and it came into wide use during the early 18th century. A variety of designs for liquid-in-tube barometers have been developed over the years.

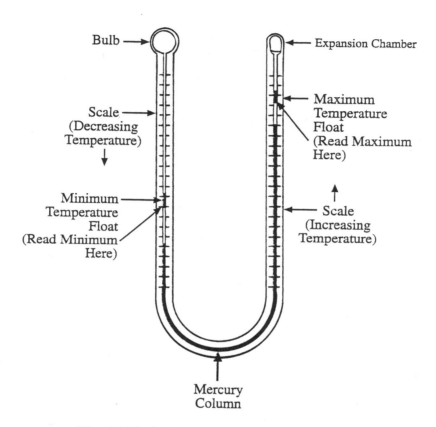

Fig. 6.2. The basic design of a Six's thermometer.

In a cistern barometer the weight of the atmosphere rests on the surface of the working fluid and is balanced exactly by the pressure of the column of fluid in the tube. If the pressure rises, fluid flows from the cistern into the tube; if the pressure falls, fluid flows from the tube into the cistern. Thus, the height of the column of fluid is controlled by the pressure of the atmosphere. Mercury, the fluid most used in a cistern barometer, is known for its extreme accuracy.

The first practical aneroid barometer was developed and patented by the Frenchman Lucien Vidie in 1844. The concept dates back to 1698, with ideas expressed by Gottfried Leibniz; however, the technology in the 17th century precluded actual construction of the instrument.

See figure 6.3. The weight of the atmosphere rests on a flexible, partially evacuated chamber. This chamber generally is in the form of a thin disk. The pressure on the chamber is balanced by the action of a spring and the air remaining in the chamber. The spring may either be inside or outside of the chamber, and prevents the chamber from collapsing under the weight of the atmosphere. Today, many aneroid barometers are equipped with a clockwork mechanism carrying a paper chart. This allows a continuous record of atmospheric pressure to be kept at the location. These recording instruments are called barographs.

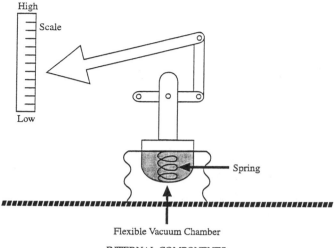

Fig. 6.3. Two views of an aneroid barometer.

Teacher's Extra

Under Pressure

The measurement of atmospheric pressure at a location is termed the station pressure. Because the pressure in the atmosphere decreases with increasing height, station altitude is a principal determining factor in station pressure. Because elevation varies greatly from place to place, meteorologists eliminate the effect of elevation from each reading by using "mean sea level" as a standard. This is the pressure value that would exist if the station were located at mean sea level (or 0 feet elevation).

The long-term average value of mean sea level pressure is 1013.25 millibars (mb), which is equivalent to 29.92 inches of mercury. This means that the pressure exerts enough force to support a column of mercury 29.92 inches high. Put another way, normal sea level pressure is worth about 14.7 pounds per square inch. The normal range of sea level pressure is 970 mb to 1040 mb, or 29.00 to 30.50 inches of mercury. Occasionally, extreme values outside this range are observed. The lowest barometric pressure readings are associated with tropical cyclones and tornadoes. The world record for lowest sea level pressure is 25.70 inches in Typhoon Tip near the Philippines on October 12, 1979. Pressure readings in strong tornadoes are undoubtedly lower, but have never been directly measured. Extremely high pressure values are associated with very cold air over continental polar locations. The world record for highest pressure is 32.01 inches on December 31, 1968, in Agata, Siberia.

The Wind Vane and Anemometer

It's believed that the earliest attempts to measure wind were done by observing the effects it had on familiar objects. The first wind instrument was the wind vane, a device that indicates wind direction. Since its invention, the basic design of the wind vane has changed very little. The typical vane consists of an ornamental top, a horizontal shaft supporting a tail at one end and a counterweight at the other end, directionals, and a mount or clutch base. The assembly turns on a bearing about a vertical mast through the balance point of the horizontal shaft, allowing the instrument to always point into the wind.

In addition to wind direction, windspeed is measured by anemometers. Several different styles of anemometers exist today. One popular type is a cup anemometer, which consists of a wheel of small cups arranged to rotate about a vertical axis. The open face of the cups catches the moving air and, in response to this force, the wheel of cups turns. Faster turn rates correspond to higher windspeeds.

A propeller anemometer consists of a propeller arranged so that it will spin on a horizontal shaft. The windspeed is obtained by determining the rotation rate of the propeller and converted by an electrical signal to output that is shown on a digital display.

Some anemometers are based on pressure effects. These instruments rely on pressure differences induced by air moving past an orifice in the end or on the side wall of a tube. In some cases pressure anemometers offer the advantage of limited maintenance.

The Hygrometer

The hygrometer measures atmospheric humidity. The first hygrometer was invented by Leonardo da Vinci around 1500 and was based on the principle that certain substances have an affinity for water vapor and absorb it readily. Leonardo's hygrometer measured the humidity by weighing a ball of wool, which absorbed varying amounts of water vapor. In 1783, Horace Benedict de Saussure described a hygrometer that used a clean strand of human hair. As the humidity increased, the hair lengthened. When the humidity decreased, the hair became shorter. This is the so-called hair hygrometer, which remains in use today. In 1802, C. W. Boeckmann made measurements of humidity by comparing two thermometers, one with a dry bulb and the other with a piece of wet material wrapped around the bulb. The closer the readings, the higher the humidity. As a final development, in 1845, Henri Victor Regnault succeeded in measuring the dewpoint. He used a highly polished silver cylinder, cooled it until dew formed on it, and then measured the temperature of the cylinder.

There are three types of hygrometers currently used to measure humidity. Digital instruments involve a sensor that changes its electrical properties based on changes in atmospheric moisture, and is converted electronically to a digital display.

Dial-type instruments use a de-oiled human hair or a synthetic hygroscopic material that expands or contracts based on humidity. Through a mechanical linkage, this expansion and contraction turns an indicating needle. Research indicates that the length of a human hair increases by about 2.5% as the relative humidity rises from 0% to 100%. In a hair hygrometer, the relative humidity is actually obtained directly as a function of the change in the length of the hair.

A wet/dry thermometer system is a third common design for modern hygrometers. These instruments consist of two identical thermometers mounted on a frame with wet wicking covering the bulb of one thermometer. This type of instrument is known as a psychrometer, and is basically the same as Boeckmann's hygrometer of nearly 200 years ago.

The Rain Gauge

The measurement of rainfall is defined as the depth of water that crosses a horizontal surface during a specified time period. The earliest known concept of a rain gauge was described in writings from India around the 4th century B.C. and was nothing more than a large bowl. Simple rain gauges were used in Europe in the early 17th century. At present, rainfall depth, or the liquid equivalent of frozen forms of precipitation, is expressed in centimeters (cm), millimeters (mm), or inches.

Rain gauges come in a variety of designs, but the simplest is a nonrecording tube gauge. In a tube gauge, rainwater is accumulated until the gauge is read by an observer. Tube gauges are further classified as direct-read or indirect-read, a distinction based on the way the depth of rain is determined from the accumulated rainwater. In a direct-read tube gauge the tube is transparent and has a measuring scale so the depth of rainfall can be read directly. The dipstick gauge has a measuring stick inserted into the tube. The depth of the rain is determined from a measurement on the wetted length of the rod. Dipstick gauges of 8 inches diameter are standard at many National Weather Service offices.

It is important to note that all rain gauges are subject to measurement errors, characterized as either overcatch or undercatch. Overcatch leads to an overestimate of rainfall depth resulting from splash-in, either by water rebounding from the rain gauge structure, the collection of spray, or both. Undercatch results from splash-out, evaporation, and wind. Splash-out is caused by raindrops impacting within the gauge and causing smaller drops to be ejected. Unless the gauge is read soon after the rain ends, evaporation will take its toll on the sample. Finally, airflow around the physical structure of the rain gauge is perhaps the most serious problem facing accurate rainfall measurement. As smaller drops move in the wind, some of them that would ordinarily have fallen in the gauge are swept past the orifice. Research indicates that for sustained windspeeds over 25 mph, catch errors may reach 50%.

Advanced Instruments and Equipment

The basic instruments give us instant data; however, in meteorology, data must be obtained from locations that are not easily accessible. For example, measurements taken at 40,000 feet high are important for diagnosing flow patterns and characteristics in the upper atmosphere. It's also necessary for meteorologists to look inside a thunderstorm and decide whether it is a threat to life and property.

The rawindsonde is one of such instruments using a radiosonde that measures wind as well as temperature, pressure, and humidity. A radiosonde is an array of instruments attached to a balloon that ascends and sends back the data by radio signals, allowing for a vertical profile of data in the atmosphere, called a sounding. Today, there are about 100 rawindsondes in the United States, located at an average spacing of 250 miles. Observations are normally taken twice daily, once in the early morning and another in the evening. Special rawindsonde observations are taken during potential severe weather situations. Information from rawindsondes worldwide serves to develop forecast models and analyze data to produce a three-dimensional snapshot of the atmosphere. Although the data from rawindsondes is invaluable, there are several distinct disadvantages. The chief shortcoming is the sparse coverage of the rawindsonde network. Other faults include measurement errors, transmission errors, and expense.

Use of satellites began on April 1, 1960, when the first meteorological satellite, TIROS-I (*T*elevision *I*nfra*R*ed *O*bservational *S*atellite), was launched. The second quantum leap came later in the 1960s with the development of the Geostationary satellites, or GOES (*G*eostationary *O*perational *E*nvironment *S*atellite). The advantage of these satellites is that they move with Earth, and stay positioned over the same point at all times. The GOES program was developed primarily for the tracking and analysis of severe local storms and hurricanes.

Radar, an acronym for *RA*dio *D*etection *A*nd *R*anging, works by using electromagnetic energy to detect and locate reflecting objects called targets.

Radar operates by transmitting an electromagnetic signal and comparing the returned signal (called an echo) with the transmitted signal. During the 1990s the conventional weather radar network across the United States was phased out and replaced with an array of Doppler weather radars. The Doppler principle was discovered in 1842 by an Austrian physicist named Christian Johann Doppler. It is defined as the apparent change in wavelength of radiation emitted by a moving object. The effect is noticeable when the source is moving toward or away from an observer. An often-cited example of the Doppler effect is the change in pitch of a train whistle as the train approaches and then recedes from an observer. Astronomers use the Doppler principle to estimate the motion and direction of celestial bodies.

Recent technology has allowed the development of portable Doppler radar units. These portable units are providing severe storms intercept teams with vital information on windspeeds and flow characteristics. The first successful deployment of portable Doppler radar was on April 26, 1991. On that date a tornado intercept team used a portable Doppler radar to measure the fastest winds ever clocked—287 mph inside a tornado just north of Red Rock, Oklahoma.

The Wind Profiler

Another outgrowth of Doppler technology is the wind profiler, a vertically pointing Doppler radar. It is designed to measure wind velocity above its location. The antenna is a grid of wires resembling bedsprings laid on the ground. It measures the wind profile through the troposphere and even up into the lower stratosphere. The data is provided hourly, but can be given at 6-minute intervals if necessary. This data also serves as input for computer forecast models. Currently, a network of 30 wind profilers exists as an experiment by the U.S. government to fill voids in the rawindsonde network. The wind profiler has met with overwhelming success thus far. Current plans are to add profilers that will sense temperature and moisture, thereby complementing the wind-sensing profilers. The establishment of a complete wind profiler network will translate into better warnings and forecasts.

Lightning Detection Systems

For many years the only lightning detection device was the human eye. Then, in 1976, the first research was published that established principles for lightning detection and outlined the type of equipment necessary to detect it. Later, in 1984, the initial development of a national lightning detection network began with the establishment of a small regional network in the Northeast. The apex of the lightning detection effort came during summer 1987 with the formation of the National Lightning Detection Network (NLDN). The NLDN covers the entire contiguous United States with 115 magnetic lightning finders.

How does lightning location work? Research indicates that the electric and magnetic fields radiated by a lightning stroke have signatures that can be detected by certain equipment containing radio receivers. All lightning locators within the NLDN operate on the principle of magnetic direction finding. The lightning finders have a 70% to 80% efficiency rate at distances of less than 250 miles. The lightning detectors consist of two antennas, one that detects the magnetic emission from the lightning stroke and the other that uses an electric field to remove any ambiguity of location. They are also equipped with the associated electronics that process the incoming signals radiated by the lightning discharge.

Automatic Weather Stations

Almost all meteorologists agree that the network of surface weather observations needs to be more dense. In order to satisfy this important demand, the U.S. government is deploying Automated Surface Observing Systems (ASOS) as part of the NWS modernization effort, replacing, to some extent, human weather observations at busy airports and in data-sparse regions. Plans are to install at least 868 ASOS units by the year 2000.

ASOS is designed to handle routine weather observations and record-keeping functions, thus reducing the need for human input. The ASOS offers distinct advantages of greater density and fre-quency of observations, but has drawbacks as well. The installation of ASOS has led to the displace-ment of some human observers and their families. Also, the units are prone to erroneous readings, such as reporting rain when none has fallen, and failing to report important changes in visibility, winds, and temperature.

Observations in the Classroom

One of the most valuable learning vehicles for weather is to make your own weather observations, and ultimately build a weather station in your class-room. The following guidelines will help you in setting up a weather observation center.

Observation of Temperature

The observation of temperature is probably the most common of all weather observations. For school use, the following recommendations are made:

- Purchase a liquid-in-glass thermometer for use in determining current temperature for older elementary through secondary levels and a dial face thermometer with large, bold numerals for younger elementary ages. Both of these types of thermometers are widely available and cost only a few dollars.

- If you choose to observe maximum and minimum temperatures, you can use a digital thermometer, but be sure the students can read and interpret other types before you do this. Good-quality digital max/min ther-mometers are widely available for $20 to $35.

- Keep the thermometer out of direct sunlight. This causes the thermometer to overheat by direct absorption of solar radiation thus your readings will be too high.

- To ensure that the temperature observed is representative of the free air circulating about the area, it is necessary that the bulb be ventilated. This can be accomplished natu-rally by choosing a location where wind moves freely or by artificial ventilation pro-vided by a fan.

- The thermometer should be located over a surface that is level and covered by soil or grass that is considered natural for the re-gion. Avoid locations where water tends to stand.

- Locate the thermometer away from build-ings and roofs.

- Standard height is 5 feet above ground level.

- Teachers must realize that the ideal site may not be available at school. Choose the loca-tion that seems best suited.

- An instrument shelter is recommended. The shelter is a naturally ventilated, louvered wooden box that ensures a representative sample of environmental air. See activity #4.

Observation of Pressure

Observation of atmospheric pressure is one of the most technical and difficult of all weather observations. However, the suggestions listed below should prove helpful:

- An aneroid barometer is recommended for school use. It contains no toxic substances, requires no corrections, is easy to read, and is portable. Aneroid barometers are widely available commercially, with costs ranging from under $100 to nearly $500 for a high-quality instrument.

- Consider making your own barometer. See activities #9 to #12.

Observation of Surface Wind

Although many different types of wind instruments are available commercially, the *Sourcebook* recommends the class construct simpler tools from readily available materials. See activities #14 to #17. In order to arrive at an accurate measurement of wind velocity, the following advice is given:

- The surroundings should be free of obstacles such as buildings and trees. If obstructions are present, locate the instrument at a

- If funding is available, a barograph is a very useful classroom instrument. The barograph is a barometer that "writes" a trace of the pressure changes on special paper. With a barograph, students can see daily pressure fluctuations and can document events such as frontal passages or storms. A "cheap" barograph costs around $300 while a high-quality one costs $1,250 or more. There are also recurring expenses for charts and ink.

- Barometers are generally indoor instruments and should be mounted on a sturdy wall or placed on a piece of well-constructed, substantial furniture. Ideally, extremes of temperature should be avoided.

distance of four times the height of the obstruction from the obstruction.

- Measurements should be taken 33 feet high. If this is not possible, then 20 feet is acceptable.

- Rooftops are to be avoided unless no other appropriate site is available. If the instrument is located on top of a roof, then it should be located at a level that is 1.5 times the height of the building.

Observation of Atmospheric Moisture

As with the other instruments, choosing a hygrometer for school use involves several decisions. Cost, educational value, and ease of use are three of the most important considerations. Commercially available digital and dial hygrometers are normally expensive, with prices exceeding $100. Sling psychrometers sell for around $100 but come with recurring costs for wicks. A less expensive alternative is a Mason's hygrometer, consisting of two identical alcohol thermometers mounted on each side of a water reservoir. This instrument

costs less than $50. Digital hygrometers offer less of an educational experience by decreasing student involvement in the process of siting the instrument, and reading and interpreting scales. If you choose to buy a hygrometer, the *Sourcebook* recommends either a dial type or a Mason's design. Of course, the best alternative for your class may be to build your own instrument. Several activities offer suggestions for building a hygrometer.

Siting guidelines for hygrometers are the same as those outlined earlier for thermometers.

Observation of Rainfall

Many commercial rain gauges are available, with costs under $10 common. Any of these are suitable for school use. Of course, you can construct a simple rain gauge in class.

The best rain gauge in the world will not perform unless it is located in the proper setting. The siting guidelines presented here will minimize gauge catch problems mentioned earlier. These suggestions are outlined below:

- Locate the rain gauge over a grassy area to prevent splash-in and spray.

- The height of the orifice should be 1 to 5 feet above ground level.

- The gauge should be located in an open area so that obstacles such as trees and buildings do not interfere with the measurement. The distance between the gauge and any obstruction should be at least four times the height of the obstruction, if possible.

- Gauges mounted on posts should extend above the top of the post by several inches. A 2-inch-by-4-inch landscaping timber makes a good mount for a rain gauge.

- The orifice should be level. A small carpenter's level placed across the orifice will tell if the gauge is properly leveled.

- Be sure to mount the gauge securely so that it will not be disturbed by strong wind or very heavy rainfall.

- In areas where strong winds are common, a wind shield should be used.

The Process of Scientific Thought

Activity #1

Title: Rising Pitch, Falling Pitch

Objective: To demonstrate the Doppler principle

Materials Needed: a tuning fork or some other source of sound

Procedure: Obtain a tuning fork or some other source of sound capable of generating a continuous level of sound. Have a student hold the tuning fork and walk toward stationary observers. The pitch will increase as the sound source approaches and the pitch will fall as the tuning fork moves away.

Elementary

- Draw a picture of sound waves coming from the tuning fork. Picture them as being bunched up as the tuning fork approaches and dispersed as the tuning fork recedes.

- Record feelings about the sound. Is it harsh or pleasant? Do students prefer higher-pitched sounds or lower-pitched sounds?

- Try to get students to explain, in one short paragraph, what the Doppler principle is.

Secondary

- Develop another application of the Doppler effect. Hint: The Doppler principle applies to light waves. As a moving source of light approaches a stationary observer, the light waves "pile up," resulting in a higher frequency and a bluish color shift called a "blue shift." As the source of light moves away, the light waves disperse, causing a lower frequency and a reddish color shift called a "red shift." Research the application of these concepts in cosmology, which is the scientific study of the origin, evolution, structure, and fate of the universe.

- A second example involving sound waves is the sonic boom. Find out more.

Activity #2

Title: Temperature: The Human Touch

Objective: To understand why we need thermometers

Materials Needed: three bowls of water

Procedure: Place three bowls of water on a table. Put cold water in one, lukewarm in another, and hot (slightly above body temperature) in the third bowl. First, have students place their right hand in the bowl of hot water. Then have them place the same hand in the bowl of lukewarm water. They may describe it as being "cool" or even "cold."

Next, have them place their left hand in the bowl of cold water and then in the bowl of lukewarm water. They might describe it as being "hot."

Elementary

- Draw a picture of the three bowls of water. Label each one as hot, warm, or cold.

- Place a thermometer in each bowl. Put the temperature of the water on the picture.

- Do humans make very good thermometers? (Answer: No, because each person perceives temperature differently and humans are not equipped to give an objective, numerical indication of the temperature.)

Secondary

- Replace the bowl of lukewarm water with a bowl of ice water. Place your right hand in the bowl of hot water for 30 seconds. Then place your right hand in the bowl of ice water. The temperature change you sense will be sharp. Next, start by placing your left hand in the bowl of cold water for 30 seconds. Then, put your left hand in the bowl of ice water. The change won't feel nearly as abrupt. Why? The answer is acclimation. Earth's living organisms are equipped with the ability to acclimate to their environment. Study this important trait.

Activity #3

Title: The Chirping Thermometer

Objective: To measure the temperature by using a cricket

Materials Needed: a willing cricket

Procedure: It's been said that if you count the number of chirps that a cricket makes in 14 seconds and add 40, you will have the temperature of the cricket's location.

Elementary and Secondary

- Try to verify this claim. Use a stopwatch to count 14 seconds. A student will need to count cricket chirps. After you've calculated the temperature given by the cricket, verify it with a thermometer. If possible, repeat in several different environments. Keep your data in a table. For upper and secondary grades, calculate the percentage of difference between the chirping thermometer and the "real" thermometer.

Building Your Own Weather Station

Activities #4 through #21 focus on building basic instruments for school use.

Activity #4

Title: A Sheltered Environment

Objective: To build a small instrument shelter

Materials Needed: wood, paint, woodworking talent

Procedure: The design, fabrication, and testing of an instrument shelter is an excellent joint project between a science class and a shop class. Here are some general guidelines for constructing a small instrument shelter suitable for mounting on a north-facing wall or post:

- Clear pine wood is normally used as the construction material.

- Dimensions: inside (16.5 inches L by 8 inches W by 5 inches D); outside (23 inches L by 11 inches W by 8.25 inches D).

- Use a good-quality flat or low-gloss white paint (two coats).
- All sides of the shelter should be louvered and the bottom should be vented.
- A double roof is recommended. It should slope from front to back. The roof should not be louvered.
- There should be a front door that can swing open.

When the shelter is finished:

- Follow the siting guidelines for temperature to select a location.
- Place the shelter so that the door opens to the north.
- Place the thermometer and hygrometer at least 4 inches from any wall.

Note: Instrument shelters can be bought. Small ones cost $100 to $150.

Activity #5

Title: When Is It the Hottest? Coldest?

Objective: To determine the daily temperature variation

Materials Needed: your weather station as constructed thus far

Procedure: Assign one team of students (group 1) the duty of observing temperature and assign another group of students (group 2) the task of recording the information. Let each student in group 1 go out and read the thermometer every hour. Ideally, this should be done all day, from the time school begins until school is over. In fact, because the teacher is usually one of the first arrivals, he or she could take the first reading. By the end of the day you will have about six to eight temperature readings at hourly intervals.

Elementary

- Draw a picture of the sky at the time the thermometer was read. How does sky condition affect the temperature?
- Talk about how it felt when you went out to read the thermometer. How does what the thermometer say correspond to what you perceive the temperature to be?
- While walking to where the thermometer is located, try to make a guess as to what the temperature is. How close were you?
- Make some simple statements that appear evident from several days' worth of data.

Secondary

- Construct a graph of temperature vs. time of day for each day this activity is done.
- Compare and contrast the graphs. Draw generalizations that appear evident from the data.
- Try to make predictions about what the temperature profile for the next day will look like. Were you close? Why or why not?
- Enter the information into a data file and use a computer to plot and analyze the data.
- You might notice the maximum temperature lags behind local noon by 2 to 4 hours. Why? (Answer: There is a cumulative effect in daytime heating.)

Activity #6

Title: That Variable Temperature

Objective: To show how temperature varies from point to point

Materials Needed: several liquid-in-glass thermometers of the same type, PVC pipe, black paint, aluminum foil, several soda straws

Procedure: Obtain several liquid-in-glass thermometers like the one you're using for your official school weather station. Next, you will need to construct a simple thermometer shield to ensure accurate readings. To do this, take a piece of thin-walled PVC pipe about 8 inches long and 1 inch in diameter. Spray the interior with a flat black paint and cover the exterior with aluminum foil. Make a small plug with the soda straws and place this plug in one end to support the thermometer. Be sure the plug doesn't obstruct the flow of air through the shield. Insert the thermometer through the plug so that the bulb is suspended in the middle of the shielding tube. Repeat this procedure for as many observation points as you desire. Be sure to place your instruments in different environments (grass, on trees, on poles, over parking lots or streets, or over puddles). Take three readings at each site; one at the beginning of the school day, another around lunchtime, and the third near the end of the day.

Elementary

* Draw a picture of the environment where each thermometer is located. Put the temperature on the picture.
* Discuss the importance of the environment in determining temperature.
* Make some simple statements that are evident from the data collected. Which environment was warmest? Coolest?

Secondary

* Construct a graph of temperature vs. type of environment. What do you find? Explain.
* Make another graph of temperature range vs. type of environment. What are your findings? Explain.
* Make predictions about how the temperature will behave prior to taking readings.
* Use a computer to plot and analyze the data.

Activity #7

Title: Temperatures, High and Low

Objective: To investigate the vertical temperature profile

Materials Needed: same as those in activity #6

Procedure: Here's another application using the equipment you made for activity #6. Arrange your thermometers vertically on a 6-foot thermometer stand at the following heights: 1 inch, 1.5 feet, 3 feet, 4.5 feet, and 6 feet. Take readings three times per day as in activity #6 at any site you choose.

Elementary

- Draw a picture of the thermometer stand with the temperature for each height noted.
- Talk about the results.

Secondary

- Construct a graph and compare the data.
- Develop a hypothesis that explains the observed vertical temperature profile. (Answer: The atmosphere is heated from below.)
- Look into micrometeorology, a subfield of atmospheric science that covers the near-ground behavior of temperature.

Activity #8

Title: The Soil Gives Life

Objective: To relate soil temperature and seed germination

Materials Needed: a liquid-in-glass thermometer

Procedure: A liquid-in-glass thermometer can be used to obtain the soil temperature at various depths. Normally, the depth taken as being significant to agriculture is 4 inches. Do this activity near the time your local growing season begins. Take the reading early in the morning and keep track of the data for at least a month.

Elementary

- Plant some seeds near where you take the soil temperature readings. Watch for them to germinate as you read the soil temperature.
- What was the soil temperature when the seeds germinated?
- Consult a gardening book and compare your results with normal conditions. Did your seeds start growing early, late, or on time?
- Find out more about the process of seed germination.

Secondary

- Keep a 10-day running average of the soil temperature.
- Talk to farmers in your area who raise different crops such as corn, soybeans, wheat, or cotton. Stay in touch with them to determine at what temperature the seeds for their crop germinated. Discuss with them the factors other than soil temperature that help determine seed germination.
- Talk to gardeners who grow ornamental plants or vegetables and relate the progress of their germination to your soil temperature.
- Find out if soil temperature is taken by another local source. Compare your reading to theirs. Explain differences.

    Note: At this point the class should begin keeping a weather log and making an entry for temperature. As each section on basic instruments is completed, the class will add that entry to this log.

Activity #9

Title: Air Pressure

Objective: To make a Cape Cod-style barometer

Materials Needed: eyedropper, ink bottle, colored water, gallon jug, cork

Procedure: Fill an ink bottle about two-thirds full of colored water. Cut the rubber bulb off the eyedropper and insert it in the ink bottle. Be sure to keep your finger over the top of the eyedropper while it is being inserted. This keeps air from moving in and ruining the accuracy of your instrument. With the tip of the eyedropper located above the bottom of the ink bottle (about one-half to one-third of the bottle's height), colored water should rise about two-thirds of the way up the eyedropper. At this point it might be a good idea to call the nearest NWS office or TV station to get the latest barometric pressure reading. Then compare this to what's considered high, low, or normal (see Teacher's Extra). This should help you design a scale, which you can tape to the exposed portion of the eyedropper. Now place the apparatus in the center of a corked gallon jug using a wire or a string.

Activity #10

Title: The "Chicken Feeder" Barometer

Objective: To construct a very simple cistern-style barometer

Materials Needed: an empty soft drink bottle, pan of water

Procedure: Obtain a soft drink bottle and fill it half full of colored water. Now fill a bowl one-quarter full of colored water. Invert the soft drink bottle with its neck under the surface of water in the bowl. Construct a scale by calling for a reading from the NWS or TV station and placing it on the soft drink bottle. This is the device used as a chicken feeder, but it also represents how a cistern barometer works. Variations in air pressure can be seen as the fluid level in the bottle rises and falls.

Activity #11

Title: The Spaghetti Barometer

Objective: To build an aneroid barometer

Materials Needed: large Tupperware container, small cork, index card, thumbtack, one strand of uncooked spaghetti, some glue

Procedure: This activity constructs a simple aneroid barometer using a sealed Tupperware container and a strand of raw spaghetti. The Tupperware container should be large because the sensitivity of this instrument depends in part upon the area of the flat surface on which the pointer is mounted. Place the lid on the Tupperware container and "burp" excess air from the inside by pressing down on the middle of the lid with one hand and opening the lid slightly with the other hand. You should hear air being expelled from inside the container. This partial vacuum inside the Tupperware will ensure accurate results also. Glue a small rubber cork to the top of the Tupperware between the center and the rim. Cut a slot in the cork and glue a strand of uncooked spaghetti in the slot. This is your pointer or indicator. A ruled card can be devised that provides a scale to infer pressure changes.

Activity #12

Title: Balancing Act

Objective: To build a balance barometer

Materials Needed: two large Tupperware containers, a balance scale

Procedure: Burp one of the Tupperware containers. It will serve as a reference specimen of air. Leave the lid slightly ajar on the other container so air can freely enter. Balance them carefully on a balance scale. Place the apparatus under a large box to shield it from drafts caused by people moving or by the air-conditioning or heating. After a while, check the balance. Do this for several days and notice the shifting balance. In times of high pressure, the reference container will be balanced higher than the partially open container (because the open container is taking in heavier air, thus it outweighs the lighter reference container). The opposite line of reasoning applies for low pressure.

After building the barometer of your choice, have students do the following.

Elementary

- Have students draw a picture of the instrument and label its components. They should be able to state briefly the importance of each part.

- Have students explain the overall principle of operation.

- Compare pressure readings from your barometer with those from another school.

- Add pressure data to your weather log—the actual reading and the tendency. Your weather log should now have three entries: temperature, pressure, and pressure tendency.

Secondary

- Here's a mathematical challenge: Figure the weight of the air pressing down on you, your house, your school, and Earth. (Answer: 5,600 trillion tons!)

- See if the class can write a computer program that would calculate the weight of the air over any size surface.

- Here's a way students can understand the horizontal variation in air pressure, but it takes a sensitive barometer capable of measuring the pressure to within 0.1 inch of mercury. Call a TV station or an NWS office that is located more than 200 miles to the west and call another located more than 200 miles to the east. Compare their readings to your reading. Differences will exist because of traveling areas of high and low pressure.

- Here's a way students can understand the vertical difference in pressure, but again it takes a barometer capable of measuring to within 0.1 inch of mercury. Read the barometer and then take it to the top of a tall building. Near sea level, an ascent of five or six stories (assuming 10 feet for each floor) should show a pressure change of about 0.17 to 0.21 inch of mercury.

- Calculate the horizontal and vertical pressure difference from the data collected above. To do this, divide the pressure change by the distance between the two observing points. You'll find that the vertical pressure gradient is much greater.

- Try to correlate pressure changes to medical complaints, mental attitude, employee productivity, and the behavior of animals and birds.

> *Note:* Be sure to add pressure data to your weather log. You'll have two new entries: pressure and pressure tendency. At this point, your weather log should have three entries: temperature, pressure, and pressure change.

Activity #13

Title: How Strong Is the Wind?

Objective: To learn how to estimate windspeed and direction without instruments

Materials Needed: a copy of the Beaufort Wind Chart

Procedure: See below.

Elementary

Lay out some reference points using familiar surroundings. This will help you estimate wind direction. As an alternative you might consider using a compass. Estimate the windspeed using the scale below (the Beaufort scale may be too difficult):

LIGHT—smoke drifts and is felt slightly on face

MODERATE—raises loose dust and papers

STRONG—large tree branches move

HIGH—the entire tree moves, twigs broken

• Have students make their observations independently and compare their estimates.

• Repeat the following day. Has the wind changed? Why?

Secondary

This age group can use the Beaufort Wind Chart included in this section (table 6.1).

• Have students make their observations independently and compare their results.

• Call the nearest NWS office or TV station and ask them for the current windspeed and direction. How accurate is your estimate? (Don't get too discouraged if your estimate is far off. Wind, like all other weather elements, varies considerably from point to point.)

• Can the students make statements regarding the daily variation of the wind? (The answer has to do with weather systems—a topic coming up in chapter 8.)

BEAUFORT NUMBER	WIND SPEED	WIND DESCRIPTION	OBSERVED EFFECTS ON LAND
0	L1	Calm	Smoke rises vertically; not felt on face; instrument cannot measure
1	1-3	Light Air	Smoke drifts slowly in direction of wind; slight leaf movement
2	4-7	Light Breeze	Wind felt on face; leaves rustle; wind vanes moving
3	8-12	Gentle Breeze	Leaves and twigs move; small flags and banners extended
4	13-18	Moderate Breeze	Small branches move; large flags extended; dust raised; dead leaves and paper blow about
5	19-24	Fresh Breeze	Small trees in leaf sway; crested wavelets form on lakes and rivers; small branches move constantly
6	25-31	Strong Breeze	Large branches move constantly; wind howls around eaves; wires whistle; umbrella used with difficulty
7	32-38	Near Gale	Entire trees move; walking against wind is inconvenient
8	39-46	Gale	Twigs and a few small branches break off trees, difficult to walk against wind; moving automobiles forced to drift or veer
9	47-54	Strong Gale	A few larger branches break off trees; ground littered with twigs and smaller branches; a few shingles may be blown off roof
10	55-63	Storm	Ground littered with broken branches; some trees snapped or uprooted; signs damaged; damage to roofs and chimneys likely
11	64-73	Severe Storm	Extent of damage increased
12	74 Or Higher	Hurricane/Tornado	Damage potential increases exponentially; see scales for hurricanes and tornadoes in Part II.

Table 6.1. The Beaufort Wind Chart

From *The Teacher's Weather Sourcebook*. © 1999 Frank T. Konvicka. Teacher Ideas Press. (800) 237-6124

Activity #14

Title: A Feather in the Wind

Objective: To build a simple feather wind vane

Materials Needed: feather, 4-inch x 4-inch x 1-inch block of wood, small nail, 3-inch finishing nail, a one-hole eyedropper

Procedure: Drive the finishing nail through the block of wood just far enough for it to be secure. Slip the glass from an eyedropper over the finishing nail so that it is about one-third lower than the nail. Pierce a hole in the top or bottom of the stopper and set it over the eyedropper. Position the stopper so the hole is near the top, then insert the feather and nail on opposite sides of the stopper. Secure them with glue if needed. Label the base N, E, S, and W. The feather plays the role of the tail of the vane so that the balancing nail points into the wind.

Activity #15

Title: Pointing to the Wind

Objective: To make a more complicated wind vane from wood

Materials Needed: a piece of soft wood 10 inches long and .5 inch square, another piece of soft wood about 36 inches long, saw, small nail, file, medicine dropper, a 4-inch x 4-inch x 1-inch block of wood

Procedure: Secure a piece of soft wood about 10 inches long and .5 inch square (call this piece 1). With a saw, cut a slot about 2.5 inches deep in the center of each end of piece 1. Next, select a thin piece of wood about 4 inches wide that will fit tightly into these slots you just cut. From this piece cut two sections, one like the head of an arrow and the other like the tail of an arrow. Push the head and tail sections into the slots and secure them with glue or with small nails. (Is this getting too complicated? Well, call in the shop class again!)

Balance piece 1 on a knife blade and mark the place where it balances. Secure the glass part of a medicine dropper and close the small end by rotating it in a flame. At the place where piece 1 balanced, drill a hole just slightly larger than the medicine dropper tube about three-fourths of the way through piece 1. Put the small end of the tube up in the hole and fasten it securely with glue.

To make a supporting rod for your wind vane select a piece of soft wood about 36 inches long and drive a small nail in the top. With a file sharpen the end of the nail to a point. Place the medicine dropper over the nail. Mount the assembly on the 4-inch x 4-inch x 1-inch block of wood and mark the directions N, E, S, and W on the base. Place the assembly in an appropriate location and start getting accurate wind direction information.

Activity #16

Title: A Sock in the Wind

Objective: To use a wind sock as a wind direction indicator

Materials Needed: a 36-inch x 24-inch piece of heavy cloth, four 10-inch-long pieces of wire, a wire coat hanger, a 36-inch-long piece of wood, large nail, wooden spool

Procedure: Form the wire hanger into a loop about 9 inches in diameter. Attach the four wires to the loop at four equidistant points. Cut the cloth into a sleeve. Sew the sides together, making a cone. Sew the wide end of the cone to the loop. Twist the exposed ends of the wires around the spool. Place the nail through the spool and hammer the nail into the end of the 36-inch piece of wood so that the spool can pivot freely around the nail. Nail the assembly to a tall object away from obstructions. Air blows into the larger end of the cloth and extends it in the direction from which the wind is blowing.

Activity #17

Title: Windspeed

Objective: To construct a simple cup anemometer

Materials Needed: two pieces of light wood about 20 inches long and .5 inch square, medicine dropper, saw, five nails, file, four small plastic cups

Procedure: Select two pieces of light wood about 20 inches long and .5 inch square. Cut a notch .5 inch wide and .25 inch deep at the exact center of each piece. Fit the two pieces together at the notches to form a cross arm. Obtain the glass tube from a medicine dropper and close the small end by rotating it in a flame. At the exact center of the cross arms drill a hole about three-quarters of the way through the wood and set the medicine dropper tube securely in the hole with glue or putty. Secure four small plastic cups to the ends of the cross arms by fastening them with small nails. Be sure the cups are all facing in the same direction. Prepare a mounting stick and base in exactly the same way as described in activity #14. Locate the assembly next to the wind vane you made.

The anemometer will spin in the wind. You can get a rough idea of the windspeed in miles per hour by counting the number of turns it makes in 30 seconds and dividing by 5.

Here is the process of scientific thought for activities #13 to #17.

Elementary

- As always, students can communicate orally, in writing, or through art.
- Make several wind socks and place them around the school. Have students observe and record their wind observations and compare them to those made by other students.
- Mount several wind socks or simple anemometers on obstacles such as buildings and trees. How does this affect the wind?

Note: Be sure to add wind information to your weather log. You should enter wind direction and windspeed. Up until this point, your weather log should have entries for the following: temperature, pressure, pressure tendency, wind direction, and windspeed.

Secondary

- Compare your measured windspeeds using the anemometer you made to estimates using the Beaufort scale.
- After you've observed wind direction for one month, construct a wind rose. A wind rose is a circular diagram that shows the distribution of wind direction over a specified time period. The most common form has 16 radial lines emanating from its center toward each cardinal point of the compass (i.e., S, SSW, SW, WSW, W, WNW, etc.). The length of each line is drawn in proportion to the frequency of wind from that direction.

• Many climatological publications contain wind roses for 30-year periods. Study these and note prevailing directions during each season.

   Note: Be sure to add your wind observations to your weather log. You should add entries for windspeed and wind direction. At this point, your weather log should have five entries: temperature, pressure, pressure tendency, wind direction, and windspeed.

Activity #18

Title: Pinecone Weather

Objective: To demonstrate a simple natural hygrometer

Materials Needed: a large dry pinecone, wooden base, sealing wax or glue, pin, straw

Procedure: Place a large, dry pinecone on a wooden base with sealing wax or glue. Stick a straight pin into one of the central scales and cover the pin with a straw. Put the cone near your thermometer. Protect it from rain. The pinecone closes as atmospheric moisture increases and opens as the air dries out. The straw will serve as a reference pointer as the pinecone expands and contracts.

Activity #19

Title: Wet and Dry

Objective: To build a simple Mason's hygrometer

Materials Needed: Two identical liquid-in-glass thermometers, a 4-inch x 10-inch board, linen cloth or muslin, fan

Procedure: Obtain two identical liquid-in-glass thermometers. Before using them in this activity, make a comparison between the two to see how closely they agree on temperature. Note any correction needed to reconcile their differences. Attach the two thermometers to the board about 4 inches apart so that their bulbs project below the bottom of the board. Tightly fasten a soaked sleeve made from linen cloth or muslin around the exposed bulb of the thermometer on the right side of the board (as you're facing it). Set up the assembly in front of a fan and wait 5 minutes. Then read both thermometers. The one on the right will read lower than the one on the left. The reading from the thermometer on the left is called the dry bulb temperature and the reading from the thermometer on the right is known as the wet bulb temperature. Look in table 6.2 to arrive at the relative humidity.

Dry-Bulb Temperatures (° F)

Wet-Bulb (° F)	56	58	60	62	64	66	68	70	71	72	73	74	75	76	77	78	79	80	82	84	86	88
38	7	2																				
40	15	11	7																			
42	25	19	14	9	7																	
44	34	29	22	17	13	8	4															
46	45	38	30	24	18	14	10	6	4	3	1											
48	55	47	40	33	26	21	16	12	10	9	7	5	4	3	1							
50	66	56	48	41	34	29	23	19	17	15	13	11	9	8	6	5	4	3				
52	77	67	57	50	43	36	31	25	23	21	19	17	15	13	12	10	9	7	5	3	1	
54	88	78	68	59	51	44	38	33	30	28	25	23	21	19	17	16	14	12	10	7	5	3
56		89	79	68	60	53	46	40	37	34	32	29	27	25	23	21	19	18	14	12	9	7
58			89	79	70	61	54	48	45	42	39	36	34	31	29	27	25	23	20	16	14	11
60				90	79	71	62	55	52	49	46	43	40	38	35	33	31	29	25	21	18	15
62					90	80	71	64	60	57	53	50	47	44	42	39	37	35	30	26	23	20
64						90	80	72	68	65	61	58	54	51	48	46	43	41	36	32	28	25
66							90	81	77	73	69	65	62	59	56	53	50	47	42	37	33	30
68								90	86	82	78	74	70	66	63	60	57	54	48	43	39	35
70									95	91	86	82	78	74	71	67	64	61	55	49	44	40
72											95	91	86	82	79	75	71	68	61	56	50	46
74													96	91	87	83	79	75	69	62	57	51
76															96	91	87	83	76	69	63	57
78																	96	91	84	76	70	64
80																			92	84	77	70
82																				92	84	77
84																					92	85
86																						92

Table 6.2. Wet Bulb/Dry Bulb Temperature Graph

Activity #20

Title: Hairy Humidity

Objective: To make a hair hygrometer

Materials Needed: a human (or horse) hair about 10 inches to 12 inches long, soda solution, a small weight, wooden stand, small spool, postcard, balsa wood

Procedure: Ask a student (or a horse) to volunteer to give one strand of hair about 10 inches to 12 inches long. Degrease the hair by using a diluted form of caustic soda solution. Fix one end of this hair to the upper end of a stand and stretch it with a 2-ounce weight. The hair should pass two or three times around a small spool fixed to an axle, which is free to rotate in bearings made from a piece of tin and fastened two-thirds of the way down the stand. Fix a light pointer of balsa wood to the axle and arrange a postcard as a scale. Be sure to locate the instrument near your thermometer. Changes in atmospheric moisture will affect the length of the hair and the position of the pointer.

Here is the process of scientific thought for activities #18 through #20.

Elementary

- As always, younger grades can draw pictures and discuss freely what they see.

- Explain in simple terms how instruments measure moisture present in the air.

- After you've taken several moisture readings, add descriptive words such as rain, dry, humid, and changeable to your scale. Can you rely on these indications?

- Compare your humidity readings with other schools and with professional sources.

   Note: It is now time to add humidity to your weather log. Depending on which instrument you use, your entry may be as simple as "dry" or "humid" or you might actually have a measure of the relative humidity (you'd have to use the Mason's hygrometer activity and table 6.2). By now, your weather log should have six entries: temperature, pressure, pressure tendency, wind direction, windspeed, and moisture.

Secondary

- Obtain a psychrometric slide rule or calculator and use it instead of tables. These normally cost less than $30.

   Note: Add humidity to your weather log. By now you should have the following: temperature, pressure, pressure tendency, wind direction, windspeed, and humidity.

- Have students think about the relationship between the entries in their weather log. As they write in their weather log daily, their awareness of the ingredients of weather should increase. Which wind brings moist air? Which wind brings dry air? What winds are associated with the highest and lowest temperatures? How are wind and pressure related? What about pressure and moisture? These are just a few of the questions they should seek answers to as they observe the weather using their school weather station.

Activity #21

Title: Rain Dipper

Objective: To construct a simple dipstick type of rain gauge

Materials Needed: large coffee can, a plastic or wooden ruler

Procedure: Place the coffee can in a suitable location (see siting guidelines) and wait for it to rain. When there is rain to measure, position the ruler vertically in the center of the can and hold it there steady for a couple of seconds. Then bring the ruler out by lifting it straight up. The ruler will be wetted at a level corresponding to the depth of the rain that fell.

Elementary

- Make several dip-style rain gauges from cans of various sizes. Set them about 5 feet apart. Compare the depth of rain caught by each can. What do you find? (Answer: The size and shape significantly affect the catch.)

- Identify one gauge as the "standard" and make several gauges of this type. Mount them at various heights. Locate one as close to ground level as possible, locate another 12 inches high, and a third as high as you can reach. Compare the results by drawing a graph. Which gauge caught the most? The least? (Your results will likely show that height affects the catch. Why? Wind and splash.)

- Place other standard gauges under trees, on roofs, and near buildings. Compare these results. (There will be large differences. Each of these catches will be adversely affected by the obstacle. Moral: Don't put rain gauges in these locations!)

Note: Add a column for rainfall amount in your weather log. You should now have the following information: temperature, pressure, pressure tendency, wind direction, windspeed, humidity, and rainfall amount.

Secondary

- Let each student have a standard rain gauge to take home. After a rain event, each student should measure the amount and note the beginning and ending time. Plot this data on a county (parish in Louisiana) or a city map. You will see differences. Note the character of the event. Was it light rain from low gray clouds or thundery weather? You'll see more variation in stormy situations because intense bursts of rain are usually localized.

- Pay attention to rainfall rate, the depth of rainfall per increment of time. What situations lead to the highest rainfall rates? (Answer: Usually those associated with thunderstorms.)

- Try to develop a more sophisticated rain gauge using an interior measuring tube.

Note: Be sure to add rainfall to the observation sheet. You should now have temperature, pressure, pressure change, wind direction, windspeed, humidity, and rainfall amount.

Building a School Weather Station: *Sourcebook* Recommendations

Two goals of this chapter are to share with teachers information on the observation of weather using the basic instruments and to expose teachers to a variety of these instruments that can be made safely and with little expense. However, the *Sourcebook* realizes that time is of the essence for teachers and many don't have time to make the more complicated instruments, or they may become confused by reading about so many different methods and types of instruments. Therefore, this section is devoted to those who like things simple and easy.

The *Sourcebook* recommendations for a school weather station are motivated by the combination of educational value and experience for the student, level of difficulty, expense, accuracy and usefulness of the readings, and the normal shortage of time that teachers have. Below, then, follow suggestions for the ideal school weather station:

- For the observation of temperature, a liquid-in-glass thermometer should be purchased. They are widely available, provide a useful level of accuracy, and are inexpensive. The *Sourcebook* considers the observation of maximum and minimum temperatures optional. If

the teacher chooses to incorporate max/min temperatures into the weather station, a simple dial-type thermometer with large numerals on its face can be purchased cheaply at a local discount store. Two indicators can easily be added that will be pushed by the pointer positions marking highest and lowest temperatures. You can also use a digital thermometer.

- For the observation of pressure, either the spaghetti barometer (activity #11) or the balance barometer (activity #12) will work. In this case, record your pressure observation as "high," "low," or "average." Record your pressure tendency as "lower than yesterday's reading," "higher than yesterday's reading," or "about the same as yesterday's reading."

- For the observation of surface wind, the wind sock works well as a measure of wind direction (activity #16). The windspeed is best given by activity #17. For younger ages, the simple descriptive words in activity #13 might be best.

- For the observation of humidity, the dewpoint is the best indicator of atmospheric moisture. Thus, use activity #8 from chapter 4. Be sure to do this near where your thermometer is located. As a second choice, use the Mason's hygrometer in activity #19.

- For the observation of rainfall amount, an inexpensive rain gauge should be bought at a local hardware or discount store. This way, a reliable measurement (usually within 0.10 of an inch per 1 inch of rainfall) is ensured; with the coffee can dipper, no measurement standard exists.

Recording Your Weather Observations

At this point the class has a weather station! The next step is to maintain a daily log of these observations. This will allow a convenient form of expression for all of the data gleaned from observing the basic instruments in the weather station. Table 6.3 is a recommended format for recording weather information. Attention to detail is necessary when recording weather observations. A systematic approach is helpful in minimizing errors. The following suggestions will help the class in their daily recording and observation of the weather:

- Take observations at the same time every day.

- Read each instrument twice to ensure accuracy.

- Record the information immediately following the observation.

- Be sure to reset instruments (if they need it) and empty the rain gauge.

- Take readings at eye level. Don't look up or down to read the instruments.

- Record the information in the weather log carefully. Be sure it is readable.

Ideas for Science Fair Projects

1. Any of the activities are suitable for a science fair project. Be sure to build the instrument, explain how it works, and what its usefulness is.

2. Choose any of the basic or advanced instruments and develop a project covering historical development, methods of use, importance to society, and explain why accurate readings are important.

   Note: Regarding 1 and 2 above, the most original ideas, and therefore the ones most remembered by judges, are outlined below.

3. Obtain two rain gauges that are exactly alike. Put one in your yard and another in your neighbor's yard. Be sure the siting guidelines are followed. Compare results. Are the readings as close as you thought? (Reasons for variation: Even a slight distance makes a difference—natural variability—and the same rain gauge can read differently.) Now place the rain gauges as close together as possible without having them interfere with each other. Compare the catch of each gauge. Even located side by side there will be differences. Do this for five rainfall events and present your results as a project.

4. Research the rawindsonde. Present its history, how it is used, importance of the data it gives, its accuracy, and pros and cons. Try to get one from the local NWS office.

5. Other project ideas: Repeat the tasks for #4 with weather satellites, conventional weather radar, Doppler weather radar, portable Doppler radar, and the wind profiler.

6. "Automatic Weather Stations: Help or Hinder?" is a title worth pursuing. The ASOS have come under fire lately because of inaccurate reporting and observations. The ASOS have replaced humans to some extent and represent a cost-cutting measure by the federal government.

Are they doing the job? Talk to NWS, airport officials, pilots, and humans who have been replaced.

7. Center on the modernization effort under way in the NWS. Present reorganization plans, cost, benefits, and reasons for modernization.

8. Research our national lightning detection system. How is lightning detected? Why the interest in lightning? Who controls the network? How much does it cost and who pays for it? What are the benefits to meteorologists and to society? Try to obtain some lightning footage from a local TV station and try to get some actual lightning data from the NWS.

School's Out!

1. Become a cooperative observer for the NWS. Call your nearest office. Don't take this lightly. The NWS will expect dedication, dependability, and accuracy. But you'll get a free rain gauge and max/min thermometer out of the deal.

2. Expand your weather log to include feelings.

3. Take your science fair project to a local civic organization.

4. Teach younger children about weather instruments.

5. Write a story or a poem about your favorite weather instrument.

6. Tour a TV station and concentrate on the technology of their "weather center."

7. Tour the NWS. They can show you Doppler radar, a rawindsonde, and professional-level basic instruments.

	Day 1	Day 2	Day 3	Day 4	Day 5	Day 6	Day 7
High Temperature							
Low Temperature							
Current Temperature							
Pressure							
Pressure Tendency							
Wind Direction							
Wind Speed							
Dewpoint or Humidity							
Rain Fall							

Table 6.3. A Suggested Format for Reading Weather Observations for One Week

From *The Teacher's Weather Sourcebook.* © 1999 Frank T. Konvicka. Teacher Ideas Press. (800) 237-6124

Chapter 7

The Precipitation Process

Rain isn't altogether wet.

At one time or another, we've all had our "perfect" outdoor plans spoiled by untimely precipitation. Most believe that the precipitation "came out of nowhere." In reality, however, it seldom happens that way. The precipitation process is complex, and certain details continue to elude scientists.

Precipitation physicists understand the basic mechanism for the process, but don't have all the answers. It seems there is a mystery lurking under each milestone that's uncovered. We sometimes even question whether rain is really wet!

The Hydrologic Cycle

It is possible that the same raindrops or snowflakes have fallen on you before. The reason for this surprising statement is an important phenomenon called the *hydrologic* (or water) *cycle*. First described by Leonardo da Vinci around 1500, the hydrologic cycle may be defined as the natural movement and recycling of Earth's water. The cycle works to change the complexion of the planet, regulates the heartbeat of weather and climate, and maintains the biosphere by providing a continual source of life-giving water.

The dimensions of Earth's water cycle are huge. It is estimated that the total amount of water available on Earth is 335 million cubic miles. Of this amount, about 127,000 cubic miles, or 0.04%, makes its way into the atmosphere annually through a process called *evapotranspiration*. The word is a combination of *evaporation* and *transpiration*. We've already discussed evaporation in

chapter 4. The other term, *transpiration*, refers to the moisture that finds its way into the atmosphere through the respiration processes of plants and animals. Together, evaporation and transpiration account for the water vapor in the atmosphere. Evaporation from the oceans is the primary vehicle for driving the hydrologic cycle, but transpiration may be more significant than one might think. For example, a birch tree gives off the equivalent of 70 gallons of water per day and a cornfield gives off the equivalent of 4,000 gallons of water per acre.

The movement of this 127,000 cubic miles of water constitutes the essence of Earth's water cycle. The average residence time of water from evaporation to return by runoff is 9 to 11 days. At any one time less than 1/100,000th of Earth's water is present in the atmosphere as water vapor. Figure 7.1 illustrates the hydrologic cycle using the analogy of a giant waterworks.

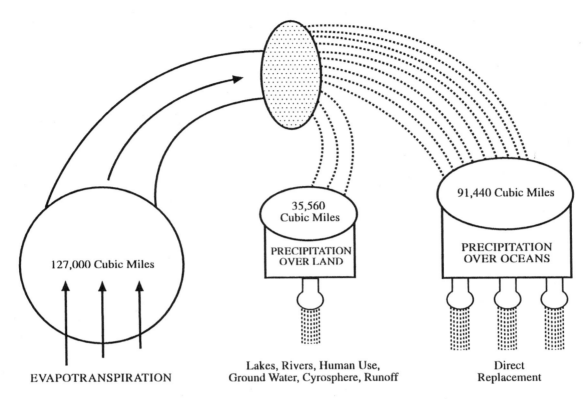

Fig. 7.1. The hydrologic cycle as a gigantic waterworks system.

Some 84% of all atmospheric moisture is evaporated from the oceans. Of that amount, 77% falls directly back over the oceans as precipitation, while the remaining 7% is carried over land by wind. This 7% combines with the 16% of water that evaporates from land areas. The result is that approximately 23% of all precipitation falls over land. Around the world this amounts to an average annual precipitation of 34 inches. For the United States the average annual precipitation is about 30 inches. This amounts to 4.3 trillion gallons of water per day! Of course, there is a large range in the amount of precipitation from one location to another.

Humans use only about 6% of the water available through precipitation. Of that amount, one-half is used for industrial purposes, 42% is used for irrigation, and the remaining 8% is used in urban areas.

The Precipitation Process

Precipitation occurs in a well-ordered sequence. At times, however, the formation of precipitation seems elusive. Indeed, the greatest challenge facing precipitation physicists is growing raindrops. In the *Sourcebook*, the precipitation process is outlined in four steps. First, we consider the clear and undisturbed atmosphere. Step 2 looks at how balance is disturbed as upward motion is initiated. Next, if upward motion continues and the supply of moisture is ample, a cloud forms. Finally, we actually grow raindrops in step 4.

STEP 1: The Clear and Balanced Atmosphere

The precipitation process begins with a clear and balanced atmosphere. Consider a parcel of air in the atmosphere. In step 1 of the precipitation process we imagine the forces acting on our air parcel to be in balance, or we could say that the parcel is in equilibrium with its environment. In chapter 5 we learned that there is an equation that states the sum of the vertical forces acting on an air parcel depends on the vertical pressure gradient and gravity:

$$A_v = (PGF)_v - G \quad (7.1)$$

Meteorologists call equation 7.1 the equation of vertical motion. It states that the vertical acceleration of the air parcel depends on the vertical pressure gradient force and the force of gravity. In step 1 of the precipitation process our air parcel is in equilibrium with its surroundings, so there is no acceleration. Thus equation 7.1 can be written as:

$$(PGF)_v = -G \quad (7.2)$$

The term (PGF) is positive because it is directed upward while gravity is negative because it is directed downward. At this stage in the precipitation process the vertically directed pressure gradient force and the downward directed force of gravity are in balance and there is no net vertical movement.

STEP 2: Equilibrium Is Destroyed

For the precipitation process to continue, the hydrostatic balance that exists must be destroyed. There are three results: the parcel can move sideways, upward, or downward. For our purpose we will neglect sideways motion and concentrate on upward and downward movement. Thus, we are left with a parcel that will either rise or fall, depending on the respective magnitude of the vertical pressure gradient force and the force of gravity.

What factors destroy hydrostatic equilibrium, thereby allowing us to move into the second stage of the precipitation process? It turns out that many natural processes operate in the atmosphere to disturb the environment of our air parcel. Disturbances traveling through the jetstream are a common phenomenon that can bring the air parcel out of balance. Fronts can cause the air parcel to move vertically. Even ordinary heating of Earth's surface by sunlight destroys balance. In the vast majority of cases, these factors combine to knock the air parcel out of balance.

The Concept of Stability

At this point it is necessary to digress a bit and discuss the concept of stability as it applies to the atmosphere. The degree of stability determines what happens to our air parcel. If the force of gravity dominates the vertical pressure gradient force, then the net motion of the air parcel is downward. Put another way, we could say that the tendency of the air parcel is to sink, and we would describe the atmosphere as being stable. On the other hand, if the vertical pressure gradient force is able to dominate gravity, then the air parcel has a tendency to rise, and we say that the atmosphere is unstable. Figure 7.2 illustrates these cases.

STEP 3: A Cloud Is Born

People look upon clouds with different attitudes. To the artist they bring the inspiration to place something new on canvas. The farmer may look upon clouds with anticipation that they will bring needed rain. Scientists see a topic of inquiry, one laced with intricate beauty, yet one that is a complex challenge.

A cloud is a collection of minute water and/or ice particles of sufficient number to be visible. But what does the phrase "of sufficient number to be visible" mean? It means that the cloud must be dense enough to be seen. Usually, the concentration of cloud droplets/ice particles is around 100 to 500 per cubic centimeter.

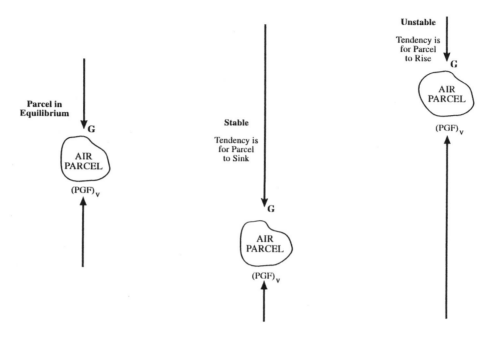

Fig. 7.2. The concept of stability as it applies to an imaginary parcel of air.

Types of Clouds

Cloud type depends on the temperature and moisture profile, the characteristics of the horizontal wind, and the strength of the vertical motion field. In any given situation these factors combine to produce the myriad sizes and shapes in the clouds we see.

Clouds are classified according to their visual appearance from the ground. This system was originally proposed by Luke Howard, a British pharmacist, in 1803. Howard's classification scheme recognizes four major cloud types:

- *cumulus* (clouds with vertical development), from the Latin for "to heap up"

- *cirrus* (fibrous or hair-like), from the Latin for "curled"

- *stratus* (clouds in flat layers), from the Latin for "layer"

- *nimbus* (rain clouds), from the Latin for "rainstorm"

Within these four basic cloud genres are the following 10 types: cirrus (Ci), cirrocumulus (Cc), cirrostratus (Cs), altocumulus (Ac), altostratus (As), nimbostratus (Ns), stratocumulus (Sc), stratus (St), cumulus (Cu), and cumulonimbus (Cb). In addition to these 10 types are 14 species dealing with the shape and structure of the cloud, nine varieties describing special characteristics of arrangement and transparency, and nine more describing supplementary features and accessary clouds. The 10 basic cloud types are sketched in figure 7.3.

The vast majority of clouds exist entirely within the troposphere. The exception is the cumulonimbus, which can penetrate into the lower stratosphere. However, most of the cumulonimbus resides in the troposphere and will be considered as a tropospheric cloud. Table 7.1 presents a summary of tropospheric clouds.

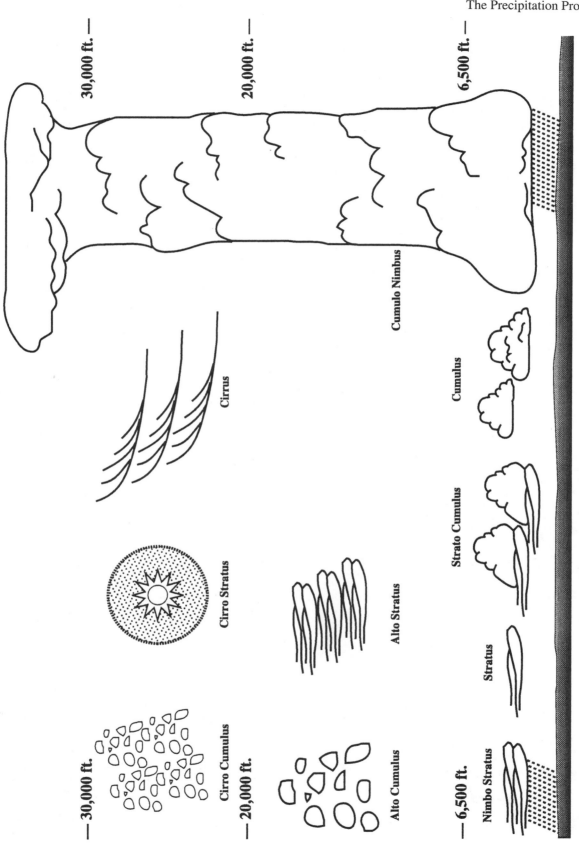

Fig. 7.3. The 10 principal cloud types.

CLASSIFICATION	CLOUD TYPES	HEIGHT	COMPOSITION	DESCRIPTION
HIGH CLOUDS	Cirrus	20-30,000 feet	supercooled water and ice	wispy, fibrous, color is usually white, feathery
	Cirrostratus	20-30,000 feet	primarily ice crystals	casts thin veil in the sky; halos common
	Cirrocumulus	20-30,000 feet	supercooled water and ice	tiny cumuliform shapes thin, white patchy
MIDDLE CLOUDS	Altocumulus	6500-15,000 feet	primarily water some ice crystals	white and/or gray color cumuliform arranged in layer or patch-like pattern w/ breaks
	Altostratus	6500-15,000 feet	ice/ water mix	gray/ bluish sheet or layer w/ no halo; covers the entire sky; can produce light precipitation
LOW CLOUDS	Stratocumulus	less than 6500 feet	small droplets	gray and/or whitish layer w/ some darker spots; rounded elements; roll-shaped
	Stratus	less than 6500 feet	usually water occasional ice	form is gray layer with a uniform base
	Nimbostratus	less than 6500 feet	usually water occasional ice	dark gray and thick, produces widespread and continuous forms of precipitation
CLOUDS OF VERTICAL DEVELOPMENT	Cumulus	varies	usually water ice (rare)	usually white; rounded tops and flat bases can produce showers
	Cumulonimbus	varies, but can extend to 70,000 feet in height	all forms of the water substance	white w/ dark bases, exceptionally dense top can spread out in an anvil shape produces showery precipitation lightning is common "thundercloud" "thunderhead"

Table 7.1. Principal Cloud Types Seen in the Troposphere

From *The Teacher's Weather Sourcebook.* © 1999 Frank T. Konvicka. Teacher Ideas Press. (800) 237-6124

High Clouds

High clouds include Howard's *cirrus* variety. The three most common examples of high clouds are cirrus, cirrocumulus, and cirrostratus. These clouds are found at heights of 20,000 to 30,000 feet. At these altitudes the temperature is below freezing and the composition of high clouds is mainly ice crystals. However, owing to the fact that most atmospheric aerosols are in the lower troposphere, supercooled water also exists.

The appearance of high clouds varies. Cirrus appear to be mainly white, with a feathery or wispy shape. Cirrostratus usually have a thin, veil-like appearance in the sky. Haloes are common with cirrostratus. The Cs vary in thickness, ranging from extremely thin as to be hardly visible to thick enough to partially obscure the sun's orb. The appearance of cirrocumulus differs markedly from cirrus and cirrocumulus. The cirrocumulus usually exhibit a patch-like array of tiny cumuloform clouds.

Middle Clouds

The chief middle clouds are altocumulus and altostratus. These clouds form generally from 6,500 to 15,000 feet high. At this height the clouds may be composed of ice, supercooled water, or water. The altocumulus is colored white/gray and is arranged in layers or patches that have breaks between them. The altostratus is a grayish/bluish sheet or layer and rarely has breaks. No halo is cast because altostratus is usually too thick. The typical altostratus covers the entire sky and is capable of producing light forms of precipitation that reach the ground.

Low Clouds

Low clouds include stratus, stratocumulus, and nimbostratus. The low clouds are found below 6,500 feet and are normally composed of water, supercooled water, and ice, depending on the temperature profile. The stratocumulus forms a white or gray layer with embedded darker spots. The cloud elements are rounded or roll-like and can produce precipitation that reaches the ground. Typical stratus forms a gray layer with a uniform cloud base. Stratus is commonly seen with fog and produces drizzle, ice crystals, and snow grains. Nimbostratus resemble stratus but are thicker and produce heavier forms of precipitation than stratus.

Clouds of Vertical Development

Clouds of vertical development include cumulus and cumulonimbus. The typical cumulus cloud is white with a rounded top and a flat base. The composition varies with season and the cloud's vertical extent. For the most part the cumulus cloud is composed of water. Small cumulus ordinarily do not produce precipitation unless the environment is tropical. Larger cumulus, known as *cumulus congestus* ("swelling" cumulus), can produce showery forms of precipitation.

The cumulonimbus is the "king" of all clouds. Its appearance is usually white with a dark base. The cloud matter is exceptionally dense and typically spreads out in an anvil shape at its summit. The typical cumulonimbus extends to 25,000 to 40,000 feet high, with maximum heights of 70,000 feet inferred from weather radar. All forms of the water substance are included in the cloud material. The great vertical extent of the cumulonimbus results from strong upward movement of air, called an updraft. Heavy, showery forms of precipitation can occur. The cumulonimbus commonly produces lightning and is also known as a "thunderhead" or a "thundercloud."

The Lenticular Cloud

One final tropospheric cloud that really doesn't fit into any of the other categories is the lenticular cloud. This interesting type of cloud varies in altitude, from below 6,500 feet to above 20,000 feet. The lenticular clouds have a wavy appearance and a somewhat smooth lens or almond shape. They are associated with topographic features such as mountains and hills. As strong winds blow across these barriers, the flow of air is distorted and, if there is enough moisture, a lenticular cloud can form.

Another interesting characteristic of the lenticular cloud is that it remains nearly stationary with respect to the topographic feature causing it. The term "standing" lenticular is used frequently.

Nacreous Clouds and Noctilucent Clouds

There are two types of clouds that are seen but do not reside in the troposphere: nacreous and noctilucent clouds. *Nacreous clouds* are rarely seen and it is believed that they can be viewed only from certain regions. They have been observed mainly over Scotland and Scandinavia in winter. They have also been observed over Alaska. During the day nacreous clouds appear stationary and resemble pale cirrus. At sunset they increase in brilliance and exhibit all the colors of the solar spectrum. As the sun disappears below the horizon, the clouds become orange and then pink, which contrasts vividly against the darkening sky. The clouds then become gray. Two hours after sunset nacreous clouds can still be seen as a gray, tenuous foreground to the starry sky. If there is sufficient moonlight nacreous clouds can be seen all night. At sunrise, the same series of aspects appear, but in reverse order.

Nacreous clouds appear at heights of 10 to 20 miles where the temperature is normally between -60° F and -70° F. Thus, nacreous clouds are likely composed of minute ice crystals.

Noctilucent clouds appear at great heights. Measurements locate them 45 to 70 miles high, where the temperature can reach -120° F. The composition of these clouds is not known, but it is postulated that fine dust particles from meteoroids or volcanoes are capable of sublimating minuscule amounts of water vapor at such low temperatures.

Noctilucent clouds resemble thin cirrus, but usually with a bluish or silverish color, sometimes with an orange or reddish tint. These colors stand out against the darkening sky. Noctilucent clouds are extremely rare and are seen only at twilight. They have been observed only during the summer between latitudes 50° to 75° N and 40° to 60° S. They become visible after sunset as grayish clouds and become more brilliant as twilight progresses. The color finally becomes a bluish-white. It is thought that noctilucent clouds move very fast because of swift, high-altitude winds.

STEP 4: Raindrop Formation

At this point we've completed three steps in the precipitation process. The hydrostatic balance has been destroyed and we've been able to form a cloud. What remains is for us to actually grow raindrops.

Atmospheric Condensation Nuclei

Here is an interesting fact: Water droplets will not form in "pure" conditions until the relative humidity reaches 300% to 400%! The first reaction to this is probably one of surprise, for it's not common knowledge that the relative humidity can exceed 100%. However, these conditions can be produced in a laboratory setting. But what about in the real atmosphere? Do raindrops form under such strange conditions? The answer involves the aerosols we met in chapter 3.

Certain types of aerosols have an affinity for water vapor, a property called hygroscopic. These hygroscopic particles suspended in the gases of the atmosphere serve as condensation nuclei. The process by which water droplets condense on a condensation nucleus is called heterogeneous nucleation. The process of condensing water vapor in a pure, controlled laboratory environment is called homogeneous nucleation.

The atmosphere contains many different types of condensation nuclei. These particles are formed by the condensation of gases or by the disintegration of liquid or solid material. Examples of condensation nuclei are windblown dust, oceanic salt (resulting when sea spray evaporates in the air), human-created pollution (including sulfate and nitrate particles), and other natural aerosols. The largest condensation nuclei are sea-salt particles. One of the most hygroscopic materials is magnesium chloride, which becomes wetted at relative humidities of less than 70%.

Condensation nuclei come in a variety of shapes: spherical, fibers, crystals, or irregular fragments. These particles continually undergo many chemical and physical changes, including coagulation, condensation, washout, mixing, and dispersion. Research shows there is a large number of condensation nuclei in a small sample of the atmosphere. The typical condensation nucleus, with a diameter of 0.2 micrometer (mm), is estimated to have a concentration in the atmosphere of about 1 billion per square meter. It turns out that the larger the condensation nucleus, the fewer there are in the air. Giant condensation nuclei, defined as those having a diameter greater than 2 mm, are much less numerous. Some particles, such as sea-salt, dust, and combustion aerosols, have diameters greater than 10 mm. Smaller particles, less than 0.2 mm in diameter, are called Aitken particles, after a Scottish physicist of the 19th century who developed instruments for observing aerosols.

Concentrations of condensation nuclei vary in time and space. The highest values occur near the ground and near obvious sources such as cities, industrial sites, fires, and active volcanoes. A concentration of 100,000 per cubic centimeter is considered typical for these locations. Values near these sources can be 100 to 10,000 times greater than in "clean" air.

The Concept of Supersaturation

At this point in our journey through the precipitation process, we've been able to wet condensation nuclei. Put another way, we now have cloud droplets. A fundamental task in the precipitation process is growing raindrops from these tiny cloud droplets. In order to do this we must be familiar with the concept of supersaturation.

Recall from chapter 4 that saturation occurs when the relative humidity reaches 100%. In the atmosphere, however, a state of supersaturation can occur in growing clouds. Hence, the term *supersaturation* refers to an excess of relative humidity compared to saturation. Generally, the supersaturation is low, around 0.1 to 0.3, corresponding to a relative humidity of 100.1% to 100.3%. In clouds there are always enough nuclei present to keep the supersaturation from rising above 1%, which would mean a relative humidity of 101%. This is a vital characteristic of the atmosphere: that there are always enough condensation nuclei to provide for cloud formation when the relative humidity barely exceeds 100%. In this way the atmosphere makes it easier to grow raindrops.

The Process of Coalescence

At this point in our discussion of the precipitation process we've been able to form a cloud and we understand that some amount of supersaturation occurs in clouds. It's crucial to realize that the typical raindrop is 100 times the diameter of the typical cloud droplet. Even more striking is the fact that the volume of water in a typical raindrop is 1 million times that of the typical cloud droplet! This observation has always been a crucible for scientists studying the precipitation process: How can such a massive increase in water volume be achieved in 15 to 20 minutes, the time it takes for the precipitation process to operate? The other part of the answer, in addition to the concept of supersaturation, is the process of coalescence.

Coalescence derives from the Latin *coalescere*, meaning "to grow." The process of coalescence refers to the collision and merging of water droplets in a cloud. Coalescence becomes important only when some of the cloud drops grow to a radius of about 20 mm. Smaller drops are so tiny and fall so slowly that they have little chance of colliding with one another. It's been estimated that a typical raindrop of 1,000 mm radius may be the result of 100,000 collisions operating through coalescence.

It is thought that one 20 mm-sized particle in 100,000 can initiate the coalescence.

Scientific observations show that rain can develop through the coalescence process within 15 minutes after the cloud forms. It is common for this to occur in environments where the cloud top does not extend high enough in the atmosphere to penetrate the freezing level. Much of the rain that falls in tropical regions is the result of the coalescence process. Outside of the tropics, coalescence can produce rain in rare instances, so it is obvious that coalescence is not the only process that is capable of producing precipitation-sized particles. In order to explain the vast majority of precipitation that falls in the middle and higher latitudes, another process is necessary.

The Ice Crystal Process

A second method by which precipitation-sized particles are formed is the ice crystal process. It is also known as the "Bergeron-Findeisen Process," after the two men who developed the idea. Tor Bergeron was a Scandinavian meteorologist who pioneered the study in the early 1930s. His ideas were later extended by the German W. Findeisen in the late 1930s. This process rests on the following observational foundation: Almost all of the precipitation that falls in the middle and high latitudes is associated with clouds that penetrate well above the freezing level in the atmosphere. Thus, across most of the world, ice plays a central role in the precipitation process.

Atmospheric Ice Nuclei

If condensation depends on hygroscopic matter, then it is logical to assume that there are also substances that accelerate the freezing process, called ice nuclei. The study of ice nuclei is commonly done using cloud chambers. A sample of air is drawn into the chamber and cooled to a controlled temperature. Sufficient water vapor is added and a cloud forms. An optical system or some other means of ice detection is used to count the number of crystals that form.

A second method consists of collecting aerosols by drawing the air sample through filter paper with known pore sizes. The particulates trapped in the filters are then introduced into the environment that is suitable for ice crystal growth and observations are made of the number of crystals that form. These experimental methods indicate that the ice nucleus content of the atmosphere is highly variable.

Research indicates that ice nuclei are very rare when compared to the number of total aerosol particles. For example, under normal conditions, we see that one ice nucleus is active per 10 million particles!

Separating and identifying such rare particles is not easy but much evidence points to clay minerals as a major source of ice nuclei in the atmosphere. The primary clay minerals are kaolinite and montmorillonite, which nucleate at temperatures of $16°$ F and $3°$ F respectively. These clay minerals are placed in the air through the action of wind on the ground.

Another source of ice nuclei has been revealed by the discovery that the bacteria in decaying plant leaf material can be effective ice nucleants at temperatures warmer than those associated with clay minerals. Research shows that the bacterium *Pseudomonas syringae* serves as an ice nucleus at temperatures as warm as $29°$ F. The overall significance of such biogenic ice nuclei in the atmosphere has not been established and remains an exciting area for future research.

A third possible source of ice nuclei in the atmosphere is debris from meteoroids and meteorites. Some scientists claim there is a loose relationship between extreme rainfall events and meteor showers. It has also been observed that submicron-sized meteorites are effective ice nucleants.

The Process of Ice Multiplication

A perplexing problem facing scientists is to explain the vast discrepancies between observed ice crystal concentrations and measured concentrations of ice nuclei in the atmosphere. First, it is obvious that the initial ice to appear in a cloud must form on an ice nucleus. But since the actual number of ice nucleants is so small, there must be some way to increase the amount of ice in a cloud, thereby increasing its significance in the precipitation process. This is accomplished by the ice multiplication process. The process operates in two ways: by the fracture of existing ice crystals and the shattering and splintering of freezing drops. In conclusion, there is no doubt that the number of ice crystals in a cloud is greatly enhanced by ice multiplication, yet our understanding of these processes is limited.

Ice Crystal Growth by Accretion and Aggregadation

In common usage the word *accretion* is reserved for the capture of supercooled droplets by an ice-phase precipitation particle. *Aggregadation* is the clumping together of ice crystals to form snowflakes or other dendritic structures. We can draw parallels to droplet growth by coalescence because important concepts like terminal velocity and collection efficiency apply. The fastest falling ice particle is graupel, which are aggregates of frozen drops. Next would be crystals attached to drops, followed by dendritic forms.

Precipitation: The Bottom Line

For precipitation-sized particles to form in the time available it is necessary that the ice-crystal process and the coalescence process work together. However, coalescence is capable of producing precipitation-sized particles without the ice crystal process. Precipitation resulting from the ice crystal process alone is limited to drizzle or snow grains.

In summary, we can state that coalescence is the primary process of tropical rain and is sufficient to operate alone in the middle and high latitudes (but this is rare). The vast majority of precipitation of middle and high latitudes is formed by both processes operating together.

Types of Precipitation

This section outlines the most common forms of precipitation: rain, freezing rain, drizzle, snow, sleet, snow grains, and hail.

Rain is a liquid form of precipitation with a diameter greater than 0.5 mm. The intensity of rainfall is described as:

- very light, where drops do not completely wet an exposed surface

- light, defined as less than or equal to 0.10 inch per hour

- moderate, defined as a rate of 0.11 to 0.30 inch per hour

- heavy, defined as falling at a rate greater than 0.30 inch per hour

Light and very light rain is caused by gentle upward motion in the atmosphere and commonly occurs with stratus clouds. Heavier rain is caused by stronger upward motion.

Freezing rain falls in liquid form but freezes upon impact. It forms a coating of ice on the ground or on other exposed objects. In order for this to happen, the temperature of the exposed object must be at or below freezing and the raindrop must be supercooled before striking the object. This implies that the raindrop falls through a shallow layer of freezing temperatures just above ground level. In winter storms, the occurrence of freezing rain is commonly observed prior to sleet or snow. A widespread, heavy fall of freezing rain results in an ice storm. In an ice storm, damage to trees and other plant foliage results, as well as damage to power lines and utility poles.

Drizzle is a liquid form of precipitation where the drop diameter is less than 0.5 mm. This form of precipitation frequently appears to float, and normally falls from stratus clouds. Fog is commonly observed with drizzle. Freezing drizzle can also occur, resulting in thin, although dangerous, icing on highways.

Snow is a form of precipitation composed of white ice crystals, chiefly in complex forms of branched, hexagonal, dendritic structures. Like rain, snow can be characterized as:

- very light, where no accumulation occurs

- light, described as lowering visibility to no less than $\frac{5}{8}$ mile

- moderate, which lowers visibility to less than $\frac{5}{8}$ mile but not less than $\frac{5}{16}$ mile

- heavy, which lowers visibility to less than $\frac{5}{16}$ mile

Sleet, also known as ice pellets, is a frozen form of precipitation consisting of small (less than 5 mm) transparent or translucent pellets of ice. It is common to hear sleet impact objects such as automobiles and metal roofs, and to see it bounce upon hitting the ground. Sleet frequently occurs with freezing rain and contributes to causing icestorms. Sleet also causes hazardous travel conditions.

Snow grains are a form of frozen precipitation consisting of very small (less than 1 mm), white, opaque ice particles. They represent the frozen equivalent of drizzle.

Hail, or what is known as "true hail," is precipitation in the form of irregular or smooth lumps of ice. More information about hail is in part II.

Teacher's Extra

Rainmaking: Fact or Fiction?

Examples abound of how people have tried to modify the weather. Little progress was made, however, until 1946 when a remarkable experiment was carried out by Irving Langmuir and his colleagues at the General Electric Research Laboratory in Schenectady, New York. The Langmuir team discovered that dry ice could be used to produce ice crystals in supercooled clouds. Later, Bernard Vonnegut discovered that silver iodide and lead iodide are effective ice nuclei. Thus, the science of weather modification was born.

Most efforts of weather modification center on the precipitation process, although fog dissipation and hail suppression are also important goals. Specifically, in human intervention into the natural precipitation process, the goal is to increase the amount of rain or snow that falls. The growing demand for fresh water and the periodic occurrence of drought in agricultural areas have motivated a commercial interest in weather modification. There is a great amount of debate among scientists as to the feasibility of "rainmaking" or "snowmaking." Despite the potential economic benefit, these endeavors suffer from poorly designed experiments, lack of funding, inconclusive results, and legal ramifications. Efforts continue, however, and perhaps a new generation of "rainmakers" will yield the conclusive evidence that humankind can make rain.

The Process of Scientific Thought

Activity #1

Title: Clouds, Clouds Everywhere

Objective: To observe clouds and record what is seen

Materials Needed: a large sheet of construction paper (dark), cotton balls

Procedure: When you go out to read the instruments in your school weather station, read the sky also. Identify cloud type and try to estimate the amount of the sky covered by clouds. Use the 10 basic types of clouds for identification purposes. Record all genres of clouds that are visible. Use the following guidelines to estimate sky condition:

- CLR, meaning no clouds (clear)
- SCT, scattered clouds; one-half (or less) of the sky covered
- BKN, broken clouds; more than one-half of the sky covered
- OVC, overcast or cloudy; sky is covered with clouds
- X, meaning sky is obscured by fog or precipitation

Mark off a portion of the construction paper, beginning in the upper lefthand corner. In each section, put the day of the week, date, cloud type, and sky cover (shown in table 7.2). You can use cotton to picture the clouds or you may draw the clouds. Do this until you finish the weather unit or until the end of the school year. Combined with the observation form you did in chapter 6, you now have a complete weather log.

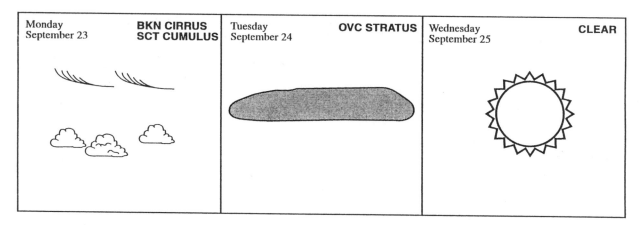

Table 7.2. A Sample Chart and Format for Recording Sky Observations

From *The Teacher's Weather Sourcebook.* © 1999 Frank T. Konvicka. Teacher Ideas Press. (800) 237-6124

Activity #2

Title: Moving Water

Objective: To illustrate the hydrologic cycle

Materials Needed: metal tray, cigar box (or shoe box), ice, heat source, teakettle or flask

Procedure: Place a cigar box or a shoe box of plant seedlings on a table. Secure a metal tray about 18 inches above the box of seedlings. Place chipped ice on top of the tray. Now put a teakettle or flask containing water over a heat source so that the steam will issue between the seedlings and the tray. It won't take long for water to drip from the bottom of the tray to the seedlings as rain.

Elementary

- Draw a picture showing the steam coming from the flask or kettle and rising to the bottom of the tray. Picture the water dripping from the bottom of the tray.

- Write a paragraph explaining how this experiment simulates Earth's own water cycle. (Answer: The teakettle or flask serves as Earth's source of water. It evaporates due to heating from the sun, rises up into the cooler atmosphere, and condenses. The condensed water then falls as rain.)

- Review the processes of evaporation, condensation, and precipitation.

- Study the box of seedlings with attention to runoff of the water. Moving water is responsible for erosion. Investigate these ideas in more detail.

Secondary

- Try to describe the hydrologic cycle quantitatively. At any given moment the total water vapor cycling through the atmosphere is equal to the difference between evaporation and precipitation. Try to do this by repeating the activity. Use a measured amount of water in the kettle or flask and, instead of catching the dripping water from the bottom of the tray with the box of seedlings, use a pan. After a few seconds, compare the amount of water caught in the pan with the amount in the flask or kettle. How do you explain your results? (Answer: The amount caught in the pan will be much less than what remains in the flask—just like the real water cycle.) Mathematical challenge: Express your results in percentage.

Activity #3

Title: Really Cool

Objective: To illustrate what "supercooled" means

Materials Needed: container of ice water, salt, and test tube

Procedure: Obtain a container of ice water. Put a generous amount of salt in the ice/water mixture. Fill a test tube about one-half full of water and place it in the middle of the container. Wait 15 minutes. Then carefully lift the test tube out of the container. Drop a sliver of ice into the test tube. The water will freeze.

Elementary

- Draw a picture accompanied by a brief explanation of what *supercooled* means.

- What would happen if the test tube were placed in a water and ice mixture without the salt added? (Answer: It would not reach a state of being supercooled. The salt added to the water and ice allows the mixture to exist well below the freezing point of water.)

Secondary

- Investigate the molecular structure of water (recall chapter 4) and explain how it contributes to the unique antics of water as it approaches the freezing point.

- Explain how the presence of impurities in the atmosphere affects the freezing of water.

Activity #4

Title: Big Drops, Little Drops, Part I

Objective: To understand cloud droplet growth by coalescence

Materials Needed: a smooth flat surface, water

Procedure: Sprinkle a generous supply of water droplets on a smooth flat surface such as a mirror or a piece of wax paper. If possible, try to put drops of different sizes on the surface. Tilt the surface vertically and watch the drops slide down the surface. Some of the drops should collide, just like in the natural process of coalescence.

Elementary

- Draw a picture of the drops merging.

- What happens when two drops merge? (Answer: The resulting drop is larger.)

- Repeat the experiment using fewer drops to begin with. How does this affect the results? (Answer: The number of collisions is lower.)

- Repeat using more drops to begin with. How does this affect the results? (Answer: The number of collisions should increase.)

- Which droplets tend to collide the most with others? (Answer: The larger ones.)

Secondary

- After doing everything in the elementary section, state general principles governing the experiment. (Answer: The two most important factors that determine coalescence are the initial concentration of drops and the number of "large" drops.)

- Which clouds are more likely to produce precipitation? (Answer: The larger clouds will because their concentration of drops is greater and the number of large drops is higher.)

Activity #5

Title: Big Drops, Little Drops, Part II

Objective: To study the fall speed of raindrops

Materials Needed: one small dropper and one large dropper, stopwatch

Procedure: Have a student stand on a stepstool or a small ladder, table, or chair (or perform the experiment in the stairwell). Have that student point a small dropper toward the floor. Squeeze gently and release one drop. When the drop leaves the dropper, the student should shout "Go!" and another student who is located near where the drop will fall should start the stopwatch. When the drop hits the floor, he or she should stop the watch and call out the time it took for the drop to fall. Repeat, using the larger dropper.

Elementary

- Draw a picture of the drops falling through the air. Picture them in a race.

- Repeat the activity several times for each dropper. Present data in the form of a table or graph.

- Can you make a general statement about which drop falls faster? (Answer: The larger drop should fall faster because it's heavier.)

Secondary

- Perform several trials and graph the results or put the data in a table.

- Measure the radius of the opening of each dropper (the radius is one-half the diameter).

- Use your results to develop a formula for the fall speed similar to the one given below:

$$U = kR^{1/2}$$

where U is the terminal fall speed, k is 2.0×10^{-3} cm/sec, and R is the dropper radius.

Activity #6

Title: Rainmaking

Objective: To understand the natural precipitation process

Materials Needed: a glass, a flask or beaker

Procedure: Run hot water into a drinking glass. Place cold water in a round flask or beaker. Put the flask on the glass at a 45° angle. The hot water will evaporate, condense on the cooler surface of the flask, and fall back into the glass as droplets.

Elementary

- Draw a picture of the drops falling from the bottom of the flask into the glass.

- Briefly explain what happens.

- Name the processes involved. (Answer: evaporation, condensation, and precipitation.)

Secondary

- Repeat, using water of the same temperature. How do you interpret the results? (Answer: The natural precipitation process depends on the vertical temperature contrast in the atmosphere. A temperature profile where cool air overlays warm air is unstable.)

Activity #7

Title: Easy Cloudmaking

Objective: To make clouds the easy way

Materials Needed: large glass bottle

Procedure: Place 1 inch of warm water in a large glass bottle and introduce some smoke from an extinguished match or candle. Stand with your back to the light and blow air into the bottle. A cloud should form.

Activity #8

Title: Professional Cloudmaking

Objective: To understand cloud formation

Materials Needed: large bottle with a rubber stopper, a 4-inch length of glass tubing, a piece of rubber tubing, an air pump

Procedure: Obtain a large glass bottle (juice bottle, milk bottle, water cooler) and fit it with a rubber stopper carrying a 4-inch length of glass tubing. Place about 1 inch of warm water in the bottle and introduce some chalk dust or smoke from an extinguished match or candle. Quickly place the stopper to close the bottle and connect the glass tube to an air pump (a bicycle pump works fine) with a piece of rubber tubing. Have a student pump air into the bottle by pumping the air pump several times. Wait a few seconds and then loosen the stopper to let cool air in. A cloud will form.

The process of scientific thought outlined below applies to activities #7 and #8.

Elementary

- Draw a picture and name the type of cloud that forms.

- Write a short paragraph explaining how the activity worked.

- What would happen if cold water were placed in the bottom of the bottle instead of warm water? (Answer: A cloud probably would not form since there needs to be ample water vapor present.)

Secondary

- In the real atmosphere air is commonly heated by compression and cooled by expansion. If the air remains unsaturated, the process is called *adiabatic* (meaning no heat is added) and the rate of temperature change is 5.5°F per 1,000 feet of ascent or descent. Solve the following problems:

1.   Suppose a parcel of air initially at 78° F rises from the surface to 5,000 feet high. What will its temperature be? (Answer: 50.5° F.)

2.   Suppose a parcel of air initially at 5,000 feet and a temperature of 50.5° F descends to the ground. What will its temperature be? (Answer: 78° F.)

• If the air parcel becomes saturated, the rate of temperature change is different. This is called the saturated adiabatic rate and is equal to 3.3° F per 1,000 feet of ascent. Solve the following problem:

1.   Suppose a parcel of air starts at the surface with a temperature of 80° F. It rises at the dry adiabatic rate to 3,000 feet high and then rises at the saturated rate to 20,000 feet high. What is its temperature? (Answer: 6.5° F.)

Ideas for Science Fair Projects

1.   After a snowstorm, measure the depth of the snow on a level surface with a ruler. Next, take a vertical sample of the snow using a piece of glass or plastic tubing 1 inch in diameter. Melt the snow and note the liquid equivalent. Do this several times over the course of the winter and present your results in a project entitled "Not All Snow Is Created Equal." Snow that is considered "wet" will have a snow depth to liquid water ratio of about 5:1, that is, 5 inches of snow equals 1 inch of liquid water. The ratio of 10:1 is considered average and fine, powdery snow may have a ratio of 20:1 or 30:1.

2.   Obtain a sample of rainwater. Compare it to ordinary tap water. Are they different chemically? How about salinity? Which is more acidic? Which freezes more quickly when placed in the freezer? There are several chemistry kits available commercially to help, and you might consider talking to a local chemist.

3.   The captioned quote at the beginning of this chapter makes an intriguing title for a science fair project. Explain why "rain isn't altogether wet." Discuss that some materials are hygroscopic. Present statistics on the concentrations and types of aerosols found in the atmosphere and their role as condensation and ice nuclei.

4.   The classification of clouds is another idea for a project. Provide answers to the following: How and why are clouds classified? What types of clouds are there? How do so many different types of clouds form? Use table 7.1 to answer some of these questions. Center your project on some of the more unusual cloud types such as lenticular, nacreous, and noctilucent. Try to get pictures—a good cloud chart or encyclopedia may have pictures.

5.   Do something on ice crystals in the atmosphere. Discuss the different shapes, conditions responsible for these shapes, and their role in the precipitation process.

6.   "Rainmaking." Research human intervention with the natural precipitation process. Talk about methods, results, legal issues, and current status. Alternatives: Center project on efforts to disperse fog at airports or in hail suppression.

7.   As always, the activities section brings out appropriate ideas for science fair projects.

School's Out!

1. Collect statistics for world, national, state, and local precipitation records. Put these in a book called "My Book of Science Records."

2. Write a short story where rain, snow, or clouds are central to the plot structure.

3. Paint a picture of clouds.

4. Compare your yard immediately before and after a precipitation event. For example, after a heavy rain you will see ponding of water, moving water, and the resulting erosion; you might notice more insects or birds, or you might hear more frogs croak.

5. Collect a cup of freshly fallen snow and make snow ice cream.

6. Read a book about rain, snow, or clouds to a younger child.

7. Volunteer to teach something about precipitation at a Head Start, day care, or early childhood enrichment program.

Chapter 8

Weather Systems

We shiver as we're caught in the icy teeth of an arctic blast. Two days later we bask in springlike warmth. Thunderstorms erupt with curtains of rain, followed by a raw chill. Why does the weather change? The answer involves weather systems.

A weather system is an atmospheric circulation entity comprised of air masses, fronts, a forcing agent aloft and its surface pressure reflections, and the attendant cloud shield and precipitation forms. Before proceeding any further with our discussion of weather systems, though, we must introduce air masses and fronts.

Air Masses

An air mass is a large, relatively homogeneous reservoir of air. The basic properties of an air mass are fairly constant through a large horizontal and vertical extent. We use the term "relatively," so our definition of an air mass can account for the local variation that is observed. It is not uncommon to have a difference of 10° F over an area of 10,000 square miles. We might describe a particular air mass as being cold and dry, with these being the basic characteristics of that body of air. Within the large geographical area covered by the air mass, pockets of air exist that are warmer, colder, drier, and wetter than the average for the air mass. These inhomogeneous qualities at the local scale are caused by topographic features, lakes and rivers, cities, vegetation, and soil.

Several different types of air masses exist and are classified according to the temperature and moisture characteristics of their source region. The source region is the geographic part of Earth where the air mass originates. The air mass stays in its source region for days, weeks, and even months at a time, thus taking on the attributes of that part of the world.

The unique topography of the United States allows several different types of air masses to affect the nation. These air masses and their source regions are outlined in figure 8.1.

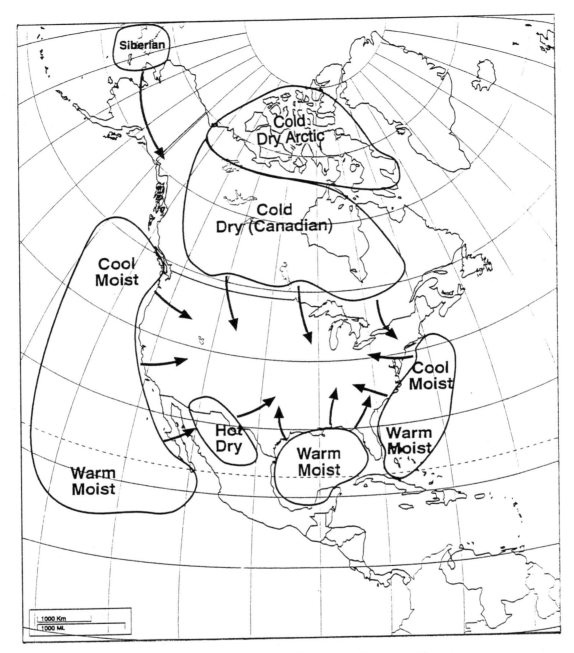

Fig. 8.1. Principal air masses that affect the United States.

Tropical Maritime Air Masses

Moisture-laden air masses that affect the United States originate over the warm waters of the Gulf of Mexico, the subtropical Atlantic Ocean, and the eastern Pacific Ocean off the Mexican coast. The origin points of these air masses establish the fact that they are inherently warm also. The level of moisture varies with the season, ranging from balmy during the winter to dangerously oppressive during the summer. Air masses from the Gulf of Mexico serve as the primary source of raw material for precipitation in the United States between the Appalachian and Rocky Mountain chains. The subtropical Atlantic usually provides moisture to the United States east of the Appalachians. Across the Southeast, however, both sources can supply moisture. The barrier presented by the Rockies normally prevents Gulf air masses from crossing over into the far western portions of the United States.

Moist air masses may also originate in the far eastern Pacific Ocean off the coasts of Baja and Mexico. Under certain circulation patterns aloft, these air masses from the eastern Pacific can be injected into the United States. This moisture can then be turned into precipitation that nourishes the parched lands of the southwestern United States. Satellite photos reveal that it is common for a plume of Pacific moisture in the middle and high levels of the atmosphere to move across Mexico and into the United States. Dangerous flood potential can exist when this Pacific moisture connection combines with rich, low-level Gulf moisture. Also, an occasional tropical system moves across Mexico and into the southern Plains (and sometimes into the Midwest and Great Lakes). This scenario often results in flood-producing rainfall for those regions.

Tropical Continental Air Masses

Warm and dry air affecting the United States originates over the continental deserts of the southwestern United States and the Chihuahuan desert of Mexico. The heat associated with this air mass can be blistering during the late spring through early autumn and can bring record high temperatures to the southwestern and south-central United States.

Polar Maritime Air Masses

Cool and moist air masses that affect the United States originate in the eastern Pacific Ocean in high temperate and subarctic latitudes. Invasions of these air masses serve as an important source of precipitation in the United States west of the Rockies, bringing heavy rainfall and snowfall. This air frequently comes during the October-April time period with fewer passages during the summer. Because of the rather high latitude of their source region, these air masses are also cool. Also, polar maritime air frequently is transformed into a continental air mass as it crosses the Rockies and moves into the Great Plains.

Polar Continental Air Masses

Polar continental air masses arise over the continental, high latitudes of North America south of the Arctic Circle. The properties of this air mass vary considerably with the season. During summer the air is refreshingly cool. During winter it brings very cold air. It is common to see subzero readings in the northern United States when this type of air mass is present, while the Deep South can experience widespread freezing temperatures. The air mass obtains its properties while sitting over snow-covered high latitudes for long periods of time.

Arctic Continental Air Masses

Arctic continental air is similar to polar continental air but due to its origin above the Arctic Circle, it is sometimes even colder. There are two source regions for arctic continental air that affects the United States. The first is over North America above the Arctic Circle, and the second is over Siberia. The North American variety is more common because the Siberian air mass moves into the United States under unusual upper-level flow regimes. An outbreak of this air from Siberia crosses the Bering Strait, moves into Alaska (where it can bring record low temperatures), and then travels through western Canada and eventually into the United States from North Dakota westward to Washington.

Fronts

A front is a boundary that separates two air masses with dissimilar properties. A front can be thought of as a transition zone between two different air masses. The term was brought into meteorology during WWI. At that time much of the military action occurred along battle "fronts." The analogy was extended into meteorology by realizing that fronts are often zones where air masses battle for superiority.

An interesting thought arises when one considers why fronts exist at all. The answer lies in the fact that air masses do not mix easily. For example, consider two air masses located next to one another. Along the front, the boundary where they are in contact, the tendency is for the air masses not to mix. Because of this, the properties of each air mass "pool" along a narrow zone where the air masses are in contact. This leads to an increasing temperature contrast along that boundary. As such the contrast across the front becomes larger than the contrast within each individual air mass. In this way a front is born. The birth of a front is called *frontogenesis*, and the demise of a front is called *frontolysis*.

Several types of fronts exist. The most common examples are cold, warm, stationary, occluded, and the dryline.

The Cold Front

A cold front is an advancing boundary that overtakes and replaces a warmer air mass. Thus cold fronts represent zones where colder and drier air is advancing and replacing warmer and wetter air. On a weather map a cold front is marked with a line containing triangles, which tell the direction in which the cold front is moving (see fig. 8.2).

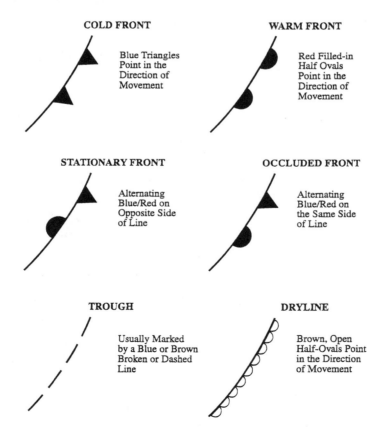

COLD FRONT

Blue Triangles Point in the Direction of Movement

WARM FRONT

Red Filled-in Half Ovals Point in the Direction of Movement

STATIONARY FRONT

Alternating Blue/Red on Opposite Side of Line

OCCLUDED FRONT

Alternating Blue/Red on the Same Side of Line

TROUGH

Usually Marked by a Blue or Brown Broken or Dashed Line

DRYLINE

Brown, Open Half-Ovals Point in the Direction of Movement

Fig. 8.2. Common representations of surface fronts used on a weather map.

Cold fronts bring a variety of weather phenomena and changes to the areas they cross. Obviously, the distinguishing characteristic of a cold frontal passage is a temperature drop. Sometimes a fall of 50° F occurs in less than three hours, but usually the temperature drop is less. The passage of a cold front is normally marked by a drop in atmospheric moisture content. The pressure rises, the wind veers in direction, usually anywhere from west to northeast. Prior to the frontal passage, showery forms of precipitation occur frequently. If the air mass ahead of the cold front is unstable enough, then severe thunderstorms can develop.

The Warm Front

A second major type of front is the warm front. The warm front is an advancing boundary that overtakes and replaces a colder air mass. At the surface, the horizontal position of a warm front is marked by a line containing half-oval shapes that tell the direction of frontal movement (fig. 8.2).

The warm front has a well-defined sequence of weather events associated with its passage. The first signal of an approaching warm front is the appearance of cirrus clouds that advance from the south or southwest. As time passes, the clouds lower and thicken, perhaps becoming altostratus. Finally, stratus or nimbostratus form and precipitation and fog ensue. Sometimes showers and thunderstorms are embedded within the cloud mass associated with the warm front. As the warm front passes, temperatures and moisture content rise, the pressure continues to fall, and the wind becomes southerly.

The Stationary Front

It is common to see no discernible movement of air masses; in this case the front is said to be stationary. Alternating ovals and triangles are used to depict a stationary front (see fig. 8.2).

The Occluded Front

The occluded front develops during the strongest point in the life of a weather system. At this time, the cold front sweeps around the weather system, thereby catching up with and replacing the warm front. The front is marked with alternating ovals and triangles on the same side of the line (fig. 8.2).

The Dryline

The dryline is a regional front with extreme importance to the regions where it resides. The dryline is a boundary that separates a dry air mass from a moist air mass. Under certain weather patterns, hot, dry air from the deserts of the southwestern United States and northern Mexico is advected into the Great Plains. The leading edge of this air mass represents the dryline.

The dryline's horizontal position is marked by a line with continuous half-ovals on the forward-moving side of the dryline (fig. 8.2). A frequent zone for dryline formation is in eastern New Mexico and far western Texas, but it can journey as far east as the Mississippi River. An average position is from near Amarillo, Texas, to just west of Midland to near Del Rio.

Daily movement of the dryline occurs when it is not interrupted by larger-scale features. The motion of the dryline is caused primarily by mixing of higher-level air into the lower levels. This process moves the dryline eastward during the day. During the evening, the eastward movement of the dryline stops and, at times, it may retrograde westward. A common trait of dryline motion is an eastward bulge. In most cases, this is caused by a middle- or upper-level jetstream moving over the dryline. Mountain waves may also contribute to dryline bulges.

The dryline is a major cause of thunderstorms in the central and southern Plains of the United States. These storms have a significant impact on human activity in the region. Several large cities are vulnerable to the tornadoes, hail, damaging wind, floods, and lightning that can be associated with dryline thunderstorms.

The passage of a well-defined dryline is unmistakable. The feel of the air changes quickly from oppressive humidity to parched dryness. It is common for temperatures behind the dryline to be higher than temperatures ahead of the feature. Surface winds usually rise following dryline passage, especially behind dryline bulges. Wind gusts to hurricane force sometimes occur behind the strongest drylines. Dust storms frequently result from the high winds associated with the dryline.

The Extratropical Weather System

Now we are ready to study the extratropical weather system in more detail, with two goals in mind. The first is to present the observed horizontal and vertical structure of an extratropical weather system, and the second is to discuss the evolution of an extratropical weather system.

The Observed Horizontal Structure

The observed horizontal structure of a well-developed, extratropical weather system is sketched in figure 8.3. At the surface, a center of low pressure draws air in from a large area in a convergent, swirling flow pattern. An area of high pressure located upstream brings a divergent flow of air. Because the weather system acts over a very large area, these winds are able to tap several different source regions of air masses. Colder air moves into the system from the north or northwest (the leading edge is the cold front), warmth and moisture respond from the south or southeast (the leading edge is the warm front), and dry air drives in from the southwest (representing the dryline). The clash of these contrasting air masses causes clouds and precipitation. Thunderstorms are favored ahead of the dryline while steady rain and fog are favored north of the warm front. Behind the cold front and dryline, the sky is usually clear or partly cloudy. There are, of course, many variations, but this is the basic picture.

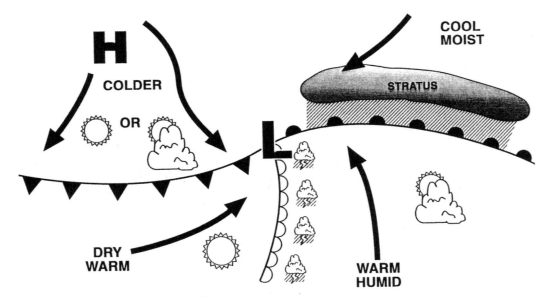

Fig. 8.3. The horizontal structure of a strong, extratropical weather system.
Note convergent winds into the low pressure area and divergent winds from the high pressure area.

The Observed Vertical Structure

The observed vertical structure of an extratropical weather system is sketched in figure 8.4. In the vertical, the main component of the extratropical weather system is some sort of dynamic forcing agent aloft. In figure 8.4, this forcing mechanism is pictured as a wavelike structure moving through the atmosphere at 20,000 feet. In reality, however, this "disturbance" can take many forms, among them a closed low and a speed maximum in the jet-stream. Whatever form it takes, the result is forced upward motion and the formation of surface reflections. Also of special note in figure 8.4 is the existence of divergent flow ahead of the wave axis and convergent flow behind it. This pattern of horizontal winds aloft plays a vital role in determining the development of the weather system at the surface.

The Evolution of an Extratropical Weather System

An extratropical weather system goes through a well-defined process of evolution. This orderly progression of events was first described by the Norwegian School over 70 years ago, and the basic framework of the theory remains. In what follows, the process of evolution for an extratropical weather system is outlined.

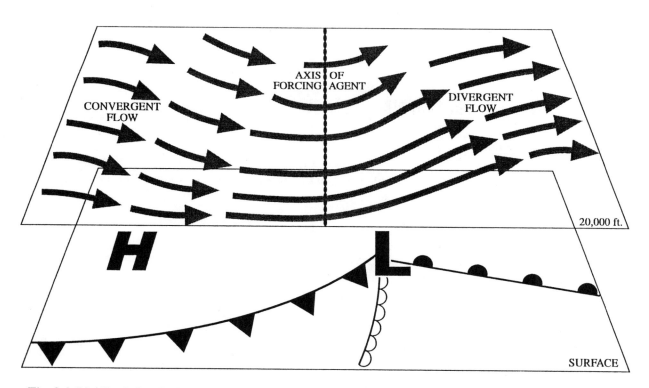

Fig. 8.4. Idealized sketch showing the vertical structure of a well-developed, extratropical weather system. Note convergent flow aloft behind the axis of the forcing agent and divergent flow aloft ahead of the axis.

STEP 1: A Temperature Contrast Exists

The initial stage is characterized by a horizontal temperature contrast. This first criterion is easy to meet, as temperature contrasts abound in the atmosphere. The most common scenario is to consider a north-south temperature contrast that exists along an east-west-oriented stationary front, as depicted in figure 8.5.

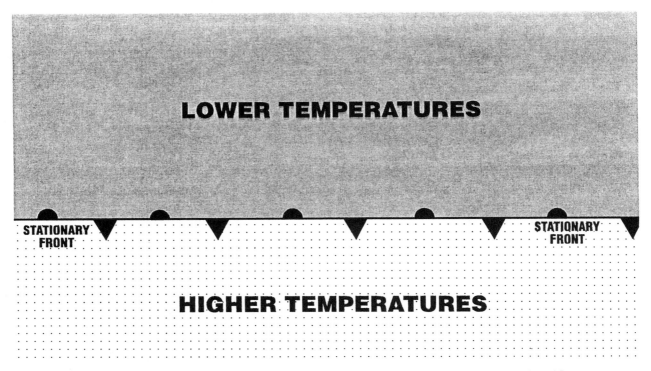

Fig. 8.5. Before an extratropical weather system develops, a temperature contrast is evident.

STEP 2: Dynamics Aloft Interact with the Situation

This may be the most difficult step in the evolution process to visualize, but at some point in time dynamics aloft interact with the horizontal temperature contrast along the stationary front. As mentioned before, this mechanism takes many forms and is commonly referred to under the general term of "disturbance." In the atmosphere a disturbance is any departure from straight west-east flow. Forms of disturbances include wavelike patterns of wind, closed lows, and speed maxima in the jetstream.

Why should these disturbances aloft have any effect at all on what happens on the surface? Recall the dynamic contributions to surface pressure tendency in chapter 5. Somewhere along the stationary front, perhaps where the temperature contrast is greatest or where the forcing is strongest, a "wave" develops. This open wave represents the embryonic weather system. It also represents the initial concentrated surface pressure fall associated with the forcing being felt from above.

In response to this initial surface pressure fall, colder air begins to slip southward and warmer air begins to inch northward, although there are no well-defined boundaries at this point (except for the stationary front). Figure 8.6 is a sketch showing this stage of development.

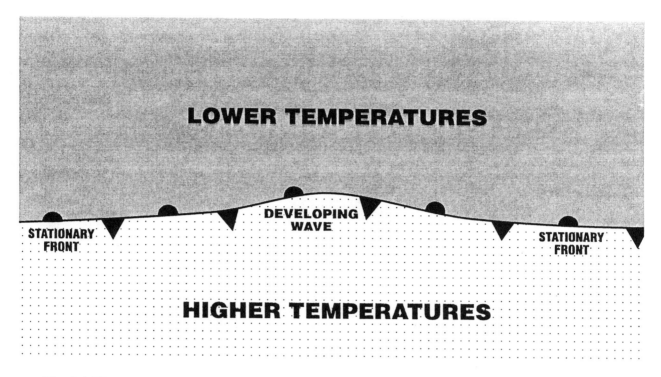

Fig. 8.6. The second stage in the development of an extratropical weather system is highlighted by a "wave" forming on the stationary front. This wave is a response to dynamic forcing aloft.

STEP 3: Adolescence

During adolescence, the wave develops into a closed center of low pressure and fronts begin to form (see fig. 8.7). This occurs in response to the forcing mechanism aloft moving closer, getting stronger, or both. The open wave develops into a closed center of low pressure by a combination of upper-level divergence and lower-level convergence. Recall from chapter 5 that this is the ideal way to increase the local spin of an air parcel. Imagine an air parcel located at the point where the open wave is. As this air parcel experiences low-level convergence and high-level divergence associated with the horizontal wind pattern of the dis-turbance aloft, the air parcel is forced to stretch. This increases the amount of spin that the air parcel experiences. This physical process is precisely how the open wave grows into a center of low pressure. In effect, we literally "spin up" the weather system in this manner (with an additional contribution from Earth's spin).

Remember that behind the forcing agent, the opposite is occurring and an area of high pressure develops. There is low-level divergence and upper-level convergence. This pattern of horizontal winds aloft decreases the spin on an air parcel and forces the development of high pressure at the surface.

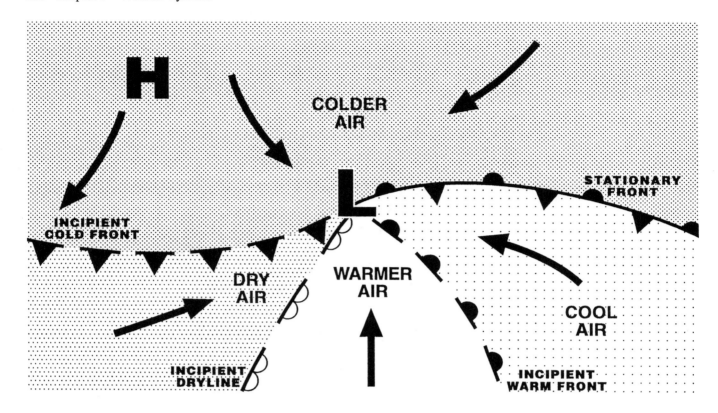

Fig. 8.7. An extratropical weather system in adolescence.
Dynamic forcing from aloft is increasing and frontogenesis occurs. The wave is amplified into a center
at low pressure and an area of high pressure develops upstream.

STEP 4: Maturity

As the forcing from upstairs increases, so does the strength of the weather system. At some point it reaches maturity. The low-pressure center deepens, the high-pressure area becomes stronger, and fronts are active and well defined. The same physical processes that brought the system to adolescence continue to operate and result in a system that increases in strength. During maturity, precipitation and clouds are widespread because of the upward motion associated with the dynamics and the supply of warm, moist air responding to the deepening low. Thus, at maturity, the system is being supplied energy by the vertical wind field and the horizontal temperature contrast; it will continue to grow. Figure 8.8 catches the weather system in maturity.

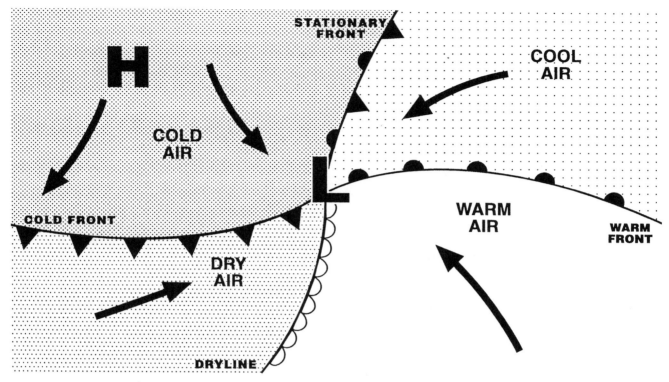

Fig. 8.8. The extratropical weather system reaches maturity. The surface low deepens, the area of high pressure acts stronger, and fronts intensify.

STEP 5: Occlusion

Occlusion represents the most vigorous point in the life of our weather system. The upper forcing mechanism has caught up with the system, and the system is vertically stacked. The system is so wound up that the surface cold front overtakes the warm front. An occluded weather system frequently is visible in satellite photos as a comma-shaped pattern of clouds.

The weather system is at its greatest vigor in all respects. The heaviest precipitation is falling, surface wind is greatest, the central pressure in the low bottoms out, and the high pressure behind the system is at its strongest (see fig. 8.9).

STEP 6: Decay

Following occlusion, a distinct change occurs. The high-level forcing has moved away or weakened, and the system "winds down" by the same physical processes that caused it to "spin up" into adolescence. Frontal contrast is not as sharp, precipitation decreases, and the western end of the cold front is now transformed into a warm front. Surface winds also decrease. At this point, however, the development of a new weather system can occur at point "X" if dynamics aloft once again interact with the situation. Figure 8.10 illustrates the dying weather system.

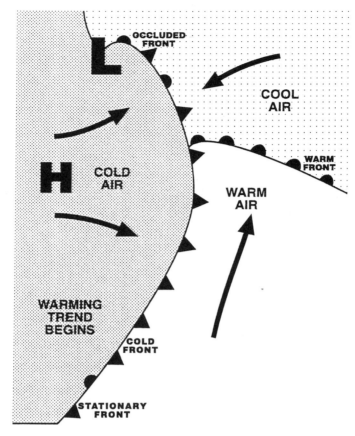

Fig. 8.9. The extratropical weather system reaches occlusion, its strongest point.

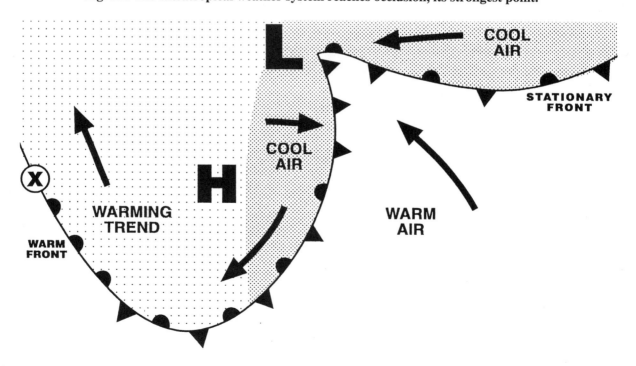

Fig. 8.10. The extratropical weather system enters retirement and eventually decays as the upper-level agent weakens or moves away. Another weather system could begin developing at point "X" if a new forcing mechanism aloft appears.

Weather Systems: A Summary

We've outlined the structure and evolution of a strong extratropical weather system; in effect, the modern, scientifically acceptable model has been presented. In this model, we see the extratropical weather system as being energized by temperature contrast and the vertical wind field. We see the system grow through the pattern of wind brought about by a disturbance of dynamic origin. And, finally, we see the system travel through the atmosphere, steered by the tropospheric winds. It is this model of the extratropical weather system that underpins the scientific approach to weather forecasting and that stands in stark contrast to the tropical weather system that we'll meet in part II.

The Process of Scientific Thought

Activity #1

Title: The Mystery of Fronts

Objective: To understand how fronts form

Materials Needed: glass aquarium or clear plastic shoe box, freezer bag, ice, red and blue food coloring, clothespin, straight pin

Procedure: Fill the aquarium or shoe box two-thirds full of warm water. Put several ice cubes in the freezer bag and use the straight pin to punch three small holes in the bottom of the bag. Place the bag at one end of the aquarium or shoe box and use the clothespin to clip it to the side. Add three drops of blue food coloring to the water directly in front of the bag. Now add three drops of red food coloring to the water at the opposite end of the container. Be sure to keep the container still so the food coloring can disperse naturally.

Elementary

- Draw a series of pictures illustrating how the colors move through the water.
- Write a paragraph explaining what you see. (Answer: The blue color seeps to the bottom of the container, driven by the dense, colder water seeping through the holes in the ice bag. The red color, in the lighter and warmer water, disperses on top of the blue.)
- What type of air mass does the blue represent? (Answer: cold.)
- What type of air mass does the red represent? (Answer: warm.)
- Which type of front marks the boundary between the red and the blue? (Answer: a cold front.)

Secondary

- In the real atmosphere fronts form due to the reluctance of air to mix readily. Instead, the air pools along narrow zones. Can you find out why? (Answer: Look at the molecular level. The air molecules spread out laterally.)
- Research the battle fronts of WWI and draw analogies to fronts in the atmosphere.

Ideas for Science Fair Projects

1. "Bubbles of Air." Demonstrate the inhomogeneous nature of an air mass. Use a month's worth of climatological data for your state. (Each state has a publication that summarizes temperatures and precipitation that is available from your local library if it is a government documents depository. Otherwise try the NWS or a local professional for the data.) As an alternative, check your local newspaper for the data; many newspapers include a summary of state or regional temperatures and precipitation on their weather pages. Plot the data on a map and offer explanations as to why differences exist. Your answer will include the fact that air masses contain wet, dry, warm, and cold "bubbles" of air. This natural tendency is also altered by topographic features (hills, valleys), bodies of water (lakes, rivers), cities, vegetation (especially forested areas), and soil type and color. In your project, you will

also need to explain how each of these factors influences the data. For example, cities are known for holding nighttime temperatures up, and the presence of a lake or river is known to hold daytime maximum temperatures down.

2. "Why Does the Weather Change?" Develop a project that focuses on the extratropical weather system. Draw the various components of the system on a large piece of construction paper. Your sketches should look like those in this chapter. Be sure you can tell the judges why each component exists and how the traveling weather system brings weather changes. Include historical context and evolution. It would help if you can obtain satellite photos of an occlusion and radar data.

3. Develop a project that centers on air masses that affect the United States (or your local area). As part of your project, you should use a map like figure 8.1. Explain what an air mass is and what a source region is. What determines the characteristics of each air mass?

4. Develop a project on fronts. Define a front, give a bit of history (WWI battle fronts), why fronts exist (activity #1 serves as an excellent demonstration of this concept), types of fronts, and weather changes associated with each front as it passes.

5. Here's an original idea: "The Dryline: Mysterious Rogue of the Plains." In your project you should define a dryline, tell where it occurs, and give its structure and its role in severe storms and associated weather changes.

School's Out!

1. Clip a series of weather maps from the newspaper. Follow the progress of fronts by making a notebook and pasting each newspaper weather map on a page. This will show you how weather systems and fronts move. Relate these movements to changes in your local weather.

2. Detail the passage of a front: record time, associated weather, type of front, and changes in temperature, pressure, wind, and moisture.

3. Think about the connection weather systems have to forecasting the weather.

4. Take your science fair project to a local service organization.

5. Read weather books to younger children.

6. Find out if fish really do bite better as a front approaches.

7. Find out if game really are more active prior to a front.

8. Make a list of air mass types affecting your hometown over a period of one month.

Chapter 9

Weather Forecasting

Never . . . will honest scientific men who have regard for their reputation venture to predict the weather.
François Arago (1783–1856)

How do meteorologists forecast the weather? What methods do they use to arrive at the conclusion that it will rain, or how can they tell what the low temperature will be three days into the future? Do they really know anything at all?

"Weather forecasting" has many connotations. Many people still believe that looking out the window qualifies as weather forecasting. Others view weather forecasters as being on a par with corrupt lawyers and shifty used-car dealers. A few folks would say that a weather forecast is nothing more than an "educated guess." Probably all of these interpretations contain a measure of truth. Forecasters can tell a gullible public that it surely won't rain on the homecoming parade—only to recall they said the same thing last year and were wrong. A weather forecast is nothing more than a "best guess" as to what future weather conditions will be like. The profession, however, has moved forward since the 18th century when François Arago uttered the famous statement above. Now, at the brink of the 21st century, thousands of dedicated professional meteorologists put their reputations on the line every day in service to public and private interests.

Weather forecasting is both an art and a science. It is a more formidable scientific and mathematical challenge than building a bridge or a skyscraper. But the science of weather forecasting still contains an artistic element as well. Perhaps one could even claim that weather prediction represents an apex where science and art meet. For all of the intellectual challenge it presents and for all of the human and technical resources that go into the forecasting process, the final decision on whether or not it will rain tomorrow is still subjective; it comes from the heart and emotion of its author.

Historical Background

How did weather forecasting begin? No person has been able to trace the origin of weather forecasting. It is safe to assume, though, that for as long as humans have lived on Earth, they have learned to correlate certain observations with common future occurrences, thereby applying that information in an attempt to predict.

Much of the early background of weather forecasting can be traced to the ancient Greeks. That culture had an intense desire to learn and believed fervently in the reliability of human intellect. These ancients were keen observers of nature. Thus, it was not surprising that they turned their attention to the study of the world around them and the sky

129

above them. The vigorous Greek civilization applied its knowledge of weather to human activities also. In this respect they inferred weather forecasts from the state of the sky and the behavior of animals and insects. Many familiar sayings come from Theophrastus's (ca. 373-286 B.C.) *Book of Signs*.

The state of weather forecasting stagnated for the next 1,800 years. In the interim, what passed as weather forecasting focused on the motions, positions, and phases of celestial bodies. A remnant of this almanac-type technique is still used today and is disseminated as reliable science.

Progress resumed during the 17th century. Leading the way was the development of simple instrumentation and data collection. Edmund Halley mapped wind patterns in tropical and subtropical latitudes in 1686. Thomas Jefferson initiated the first extensive series of weather observations in North America at Monticello in 1772. Other famous weather watchers of the colonial period included George Washington, Benjamin Franklin, and several of the colleges and universities of the Northeast. By 1800 there were volunteer weather stations in six states: Massachusetts, Pennsylvania, Connecticut, New York, North Carolina, and Virginia. Dr. James Tilton, surgeon general of the U.S. Army, was responsible for the first national weather observation network. On May 2, 1814, Dr. Tilton instructed army surgeons to keep weather diaries in order to investigate the influence of weather and climate on diseases.

A slow increase in meteorological knowledge continued through the early 18th century, but it took a technological advance to accelerate the pace of weather forecasting. This occurred in 1844 when Samuel B. Morse perfected the telegraph in the United States. In 1849, Joseph Henry, the secretary of the Smithsonian Institution in Washington, D.C., received the first weather report sent by telegraph in the United States. The invention of the telegraph put weather information at people's fingertips almost immediately; thus observations of weather conditions from diverse locations could be received quickly and collected together at one site in a short period of time. With this wonderful new technology available and the feeling that the public needed to know weather conditions into the future, a few "scientists" succumbed to the temptation to issue weather forecasts. Their lack of skill dismayed serious scientists and many divorced themselves from this great practical application of meteorological knowledge. It is ironic that, even today, weather forecasting is viewed by some as a "seat-of-the-pants" affair.

The next major event occurred in the United States in 1870, when the government made the commitment to stay in the weather business. The first government-sponsored weather entity became part of the Army Signal Corps. At that time some 100 stations around the United States were established as the first organized weather observation network. Congress organized the U.S. Weather Bureau with legislation in 1890, and the new weather agency began operation on July 1, 1891. This government support gave the fledgling science of weather forecasting the firm foundation that it needed to thrive.

Weather Observations and Maps

The accurate and timely observation of weather conditions forms the foundation upon which modern scientific methods of prediction are built. The volume of information available on weather conditions worldwide is staggering. Each hour, some 50,000 to 60,000 regular hourly reports are available. This does not count data from radar, satellite, wind profilers, lightning detection networks, and information from 12,000 cooperative weather observers nationwide. This additional information makes millions of pieces of data available to the meteorologist every hour of every day.

The two most common types of routine weather observations are hourly surface and upper air. The surface readings are taken hourly by trained personnel at civilian and military installations (unless they've been replaced by automatic stations). These observations are in support of commercial and military aviation and operations. If inclement weather is present or conditions are changing rapidly, then special observations are required. During these times, 5 to 15 of these "specials" might be required in less than one hour.

Observations of upper air conditions are not taken as frequently as the surface observations. They are taken two or three times daily, in the early morning, sometimes at noon, and in the evening. The data, obtained from rawindsondes (see chapter 6), serves as vital information to weather forecasters. Essentially, these upper air observations give meteorologists a three-dimensional snapshot of the atmosphere over a certain location at the time of observation.

The study of meteorological data collected at these surface and upper air sites, as well as the subsequent application of that information to weather analysis and forecasting, is termed *synoptic meteorology*. The word *synoptic* comes from the Greek *synoptikos,* meaning "to bring together" or "to see together." Thus, weather observations from around the world are seen together by the eyes of the meteorologist. Hence, weather forecasters have a picture of weather conditions both horizontally and vertically over a large geographic region.

The National Centers for Environmental Prediction (NCEP)

The massive volume of data requires an efficient communications effort of international scope; the nations of the world have shown greater cooperation in exchanging weather information than in any other activity. The international agency that assures weather information is able to cross natural and political boundaries is called the World Meteorological Organization (WMO). The WMO, an agency of the United Nations, serves as a sponsor of the World Weather Watch program. Through this program weather data is collected by more than 140 countries belonging to the WMO. The information is then distributed among the member nations by means of a worldwide communication network. The various meteorological agencies of the member nations provide the facilities for the program. In the United States, this role is fulfilled by the National Centers for Environmental Prediction (NCEP).

NCEP is a geographically dispersed organization with nine major components, with its core of four centers located in the World Weather Building in Camp Springs, Maryland. NCEP is the operating nerve center for weather information for the United

States and much of the rest of the world. It provides weather analysis, forecasts, and climate outlooks. NCEP also provides an increasing number of end products such as forecasts for domestic and international aviation, ocean analysis, marine interests, space environment needs, and precipitation for hydrologic and public services.

NCEP's products cover the entire globe, with most products covering the Northern Hemisphere and the tropical regions of the Southern Hemisphere. The WMO has designated NCEP as the analysis and forecast arm of the World Meteorological Center (WMC) with other similar centers in Moscow and Melbourne. NCEP is also a World Area Forecast Center (WAFC) under the International Civil Aviation Organization (ICAO) along with Bracknell, England.

These designations carry global responsibilities for the center in most meteorologic, oceanographic, and hydrologic activities, in international aviation, and in the cooperative effort known as the World Weather Watch. NCEP has a Central Operations, an Environmental Modeling Center, and seven service centers.

Central Operations

Central Operations (CO) is responsible for all aspects of NCEP's operations. It provides the management, procurement, development, installation, maintenance, and operation of all computing and communications-related services that link all of the NCEP centers. CO houses and runs the supercomputer complex that executes the various numerical

weather and climate prediction systems. It supports quality control, preparation, presentation, and distribution of atmospheric and oceanographic observations and generates the myriad products resulting from the numerical prediction systems. CO develops and tests various automated techniques for automated products, including automated graphics.

Environmental Modeling Center (EMC)

The EMC improves numerical weather, marine, and climate predictions through a broad program of data assimilation and computer modeling. In support of the NCEP operational forecasting mission, the EMC develops, adapts, improves, and monitors data assimilation systems and models of the atmosphere, ocean, and atmosphere/ocean system using advanced modeling techniques developed internally as well as cooperatively with scientists from universities, the international scientific community, National Oceanic and Atmospheric Administration (NOAA) laboratories, and other government agencies.

Hydrometeorological Prediction Center (HPC)

The HPC supports the hydrological forecast functions of the NWS. Its National Precipitation Prediction Unit incorporates the latest in technological support, maintaining up-to-the-minute monitoring of all precipitation-related events such as rain, snow, and ice across the contiguous United States. The HPC provides detailed quantitative precipitation forecasts to the NWS field offices in support of its heavy snow and flash flood watch/warning responsibilities. The HPC prepares forecast guidance products based mainly on the interpretation of numerical weather forecasts for periods of 12 to 72 hours in the short range and for 3 to 7 days in the medium range.

Marine Prediction Center (MPC)

The MPC produces and issues a wide variety of marine meteorological and oceanographic analysis, forecast, and warning products for a diverse user community including fisheries, merchant marines, and recreational boaters. The center provides warnings for gales, storms, and tropical systems (in coordination with the Tropical Prediction Center). MPC also forecasts and analyzes conditions such as wind, waves, fog, ice accretion, ocean boundary currents, and sea surface and subsurface temperatures.

Climate Prediction Center (CPC)

The CPC provides climate services to users in government, the research community, private industry, and the public. Services include operational prediction of climate variability, monitoring of the climate system, and development of databases for determining current climate anomalies and trends. The center makes forecasts on a 6- to 14-day basis, monthly, and seasonally. Long-range outlooks are made for the United States up to a year in advance.

Aviation Weather Center (AWC)

The AWC in Kansas City, Missouri, issues warnings, forecasts, and analysis of hazardous weather for aviation interests out to two days. Warnings include hazards such as turbulence, icing, low clouds, and reduced visibility up to 24,000 feet. Above 24,000 feet, the center provides warnings for dangerous wind shear, thunderstorms, turbulence, icing, and volcanic ash for the Northern Hemisphere from the Middle Pacific Ocean to the Middle Atlantic Ocean. Through international agreement, the center has the responsibility to back up other WAFCs with aviation products distributed through the World Area Forecast System.

Storm Prediction Center (SPC)

The SPC, located in Norman, Oklahoma, provides short-term guidance products for hazardous weather over the contiguous United States. The center coordinates with NWS field offices for short-term aspects of hazardous weather such as flash floods, thunderstorms, tornadoes, winter storms, blizzards, and freezing precipitation. The center collaborates with local, national, and international meteorological communities as well as various NOAA offices.

Tropical Prediction Center (TPC)

The TPC issues watches, warnings, forecasts, and analyses for tropical weather conditions to save lives and protect property. The National Hurricane Center (NHC) in Coral Gables, Florida, remains an integral part of the TPC, with the responsibility of tracking and forecasting tropical cyclones in the Atlantic Basin and the eastern North Pacific Ocean. Through international agreement, the center also has responsibility for tropical cyclone forecasts and warnings for many countries in the Caribbean and North, Central, and South America.

Space Environment Center (SEC)

The SEC is administratively attached to NCEP but remains part of the Office of Oceanic and Atmospheric Research. The center provides national and international forecasts, alerts, and warnings of extraordinary conditions in the global space environment such as solar radio noise, solar energetic particles, solar X-ray radiation, geomagnetic activity, and foreign body impacts. The SEC issues specific predictions of space weather for three days and more general predictions up to several weeks in advance, and provides monthly summaries of observed solar-terrestrial conditions.

In summary, these nine components of NCEP efficiently work together to monitor the ever-changing personality of the atmosphere and the oceans in order to serve the best interests of many diverse users.

NWS Field Office Organization

In addition to the National Forecast System outlined above, several types of field offices in the NWS fulfill vital duties on a more local or regional level. These community-oriented field offices include River Forecast Centers (RFCs) and Forecast Offices.

River Forecast Centers

A vital component of the NWS is the River Forecast Center (RFC). Currently there are 13 RFCs in the United States. These offices prepare river, flood, and water resources forecasts for a total of 3,500 locations. Flood forecasts include height of the expected crest as well as times when the river is expected to overflow its banks and when it will recede. At many points along larger streams and rivers such as the Columbia, Missouri, Red, Ohio, and Mississippi, daily forecasts of river stages are routinely prepared for navigation and for water management. Forecasts of seasonal flow are critical elements in the operation of dams, navigation systems, and irrigation systems.

Forecast Offices

At the regional level in the NWS is the Weather Service Forecast Office (WSFO). At this time, there are 52 WSFOs in the United States. States without a WSFO (Rhode Island, Connecticut, Vermont, and New Hampshire) are served by those in other states. There are two WSFOs each in Pennsylvania and in California. Texas, Alaska, and New York each have three WSFOs. These offices use information from all other organizations and issue public forecasts for time periods of 12 to 48 hours and for 3 to 5 days. They also give terminal and route forecasts for aviation. Forecasts of flash flood potential, high seas, and tsunamis (tidal waves generated by earthquakes) are also provided. The WSFOs give information to fire control agencies, agricultural interests, and marine interests. They also provide local warnings of flash floods and severe thunderstorms.

The most numerous exponent of the NWS is the Weather Service Office (WSO). At present, there are 206 such offices in the United States, representing the NWS at the local level. The WSOs have several important responsibilities. The most important duty is issuance of warnings to the public for severe local storms and flash floods. In addition, the WSO adapts forecast products from its parent WSFO for its local area of responsibility. Many WSOs now also issue forecasts of lake levels and river stages. Officials at WSOs and WSFOs work closely with 911 and other local emergency preparedness organizations to ensure public safety from severe storms and floods.

Weather Maps

A weather map is the most common element used in weather forecasting. There are many ways to chart weather observations and information. This representation captures the essence of a particular weather situation and is an important tool for weather forecasters. Weather maps are a convenient, shorthand method to put lots of information together in one place, so the forecaster can quickly capture the unfolding weather situation.

The surface analysis, or surface map, is one of two basic types of weather charts used by weather forecasters. The surface analysis provides a snapshot of weather conditions, pulling together a large amount of observations from diverse sites into one map. The surface chart employs a shorthand style of data plotting that describes in detail the state of the atmosphere at the observation site. Figure 9.1 is called a "station model," which is the format used to convey to forecasters the important information for each observation point.

Table 9.1 outlines the most commonly used symbols to describe present weather.

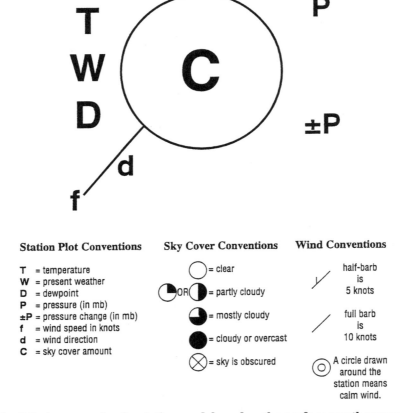

Fig. 9.1. An example of a station model used as the surface weather map.

From *The Teacher's Weather Sourcebook.* © 1999 Frank T. Konvicka. Teacher Ideas Press. (800) 237-6124

Symbol	Meaning on a Weather Map
••	Light Rain
⁖	Moderate Rain
⁘	Heavy Rain
**	Light Snow
̣	Moderate Snow
̣̣*	Heavy Snow
oo	Haze
=	Light Fog
≡	Heavy Fog
Δ	Sleet (ice pellets)
∇̇	Rain Shower
*∇	Snow Shower
))	Light Drizzle
)′)	Moderate Drizzle
)̣)	Heavy Drizzle
⌢̇～	Freezing Rain
⌢～	Freezing Drizzle
↟→	Blowing/lDrifting Snow
⦓	Distant Lightning
↖↘	Thunder
↖̇↘	Thunderstorm w/ Rain
*↖↘	Thunderstorm w/ Snow
▵↖↘	Thunderstorm w/ Hail
⌇→	Duststorm / Sandstorm
⫲	Tornado

Table 9.1. Some Common Present Weather Symbols and Their Meanings

From *The Teacher's Weather Sourcebook*. © 1999 Frank T. Konvicka. Teacher Ideas Press. (800) 237-6124

Besides data plotting, another aspect of the surface chart is a meteorological analysis of the data. In the analysis procedure, areas of high pressure and low pressure are located and noted on the chart with an "H" and an "L," respectively. Surface fronts are also analyzed, employing the conventions outlined in chapter 8. In short, weather maps are a fixture in the weather office.

The processes of plotting and analyzing data are so closely related that "weather forecasting" is probably more accurately known as "weather analysis and forecasting."

The Elements of a Public Weather Forecast

Although there are many different types of weather forecasts, the one we hear most often through the media is called a "public" weather forecast. It is intended for general use by the public who have no need for great detail or do not require highly specialized information. The public weather forecast contains several basic items. The expected maximum and minimum temperatures are used to decide how to dress for work and school. Forecasts involving extremes of temperature are vital for protection of life and property. Forecasts of precipitation probability and type allow the public to plan outdoor events. Windspeed and direction are important to farmers who are planning spraying operations for pesticides. Last, sky condition is included in all public weather forecasts.

Types of Weather Forecasts

The type of weather forecast either refers to the time period for which it is valid or to the specialized use of such information. Thus, there are two basic types of weather forecasts: time period and specialized.

Time Period Forecasts

Time period forecasts usually involve one of the following: nowcast, short-range, medium-range, and longer-range. The nowcast is a relatively new term that refers to a forecast valid for a few minutes to a few hours in advance. The short-range forecast is valid for time periods from 12 to 48 hours in advance. The information contained in the nowcast and the short-range forecast is accurate and of considerable value to users. The medium-range forecast covers the time frame of 3 to 5 days into the future; this is commonly called the "extended" forecast. Information in the 3- to 5-day forecast is not as detailed or as accurate as that contained in the short-range. Hence, its "trust factor" is not as high. For longer time periods such as 6 to 10 days, 30 days, and 90 days, the word *forecast* is not used because it implies a high degree of accuracy. Instead, the term *outlook* is used. These longer-range outlooks usually contain only very general information and have limited accuracy and utility.

The general question of atmospheric predictability is an intriguing topic. How far in advance can the weather be predicted accurately? It is generally accepted that there is an 8- to 16-day limit on atmospheric predictability. This limit is probably valid no matter what future technological advancements may bring. The reason for the inherent unpredictability of the atmosphere is scale interaction—the complex interplay of various motion systems that escape detection.

Specialized Forecasts

Many users of meteorological information require more detail than the public forecast provides. In addition, this information must be tailored to suit the needs of the user. Thus, a large array of specialized uses for weather forecasts is evident. These include retail, agriculture, electric and gas utilities, transportation, recreation, and others.

The Scientific Basis for Weather Forecasting

One of the greatest desires of scientists is to predict accurately the behavior of that which they are investigating. It may be an airplane in flight, a population of biological organisms, or, in our case, the behavior of the atmosphere. In meteorology, as in all the sciences, an intimate relationship exists between comprehension and the ability to predict. As our understanding of the atmosphere grows, so does our power to forecast its behavior. One of the main goals of chapter 5 is to understand the motion of the atmosphere in such a way that prediction would be possible. That basis for weather forecasting is presented here.

The physical concept underpinning weather forecasting is that the large-scale flow of the atmosphere will always tend to remain in equilibrium by striving to balance the physical forces acting on a parcel of air with the Coriolis Force caused by Earth's rotation.

Weather forecasting is an initial-value problem. This means that, for any given physical system, if the initial state is known and the laws governing its behavior are also known, then the future state of that system can be predicted. In the atmosphere none of these prerequisites is fully satisfied. Although the general laws that control the behavior of the atmosphere are well established, two formidable difficulties arise. First, the equations that govern atmospheric flow are so complex that no solution to them is either known or anticipated, and they can be simplified only through the use of certain assumptions. The second major difficulty is the lack of adequate observations. Although the number of observation points may seem high to the nonprofessional, in reality the current number of observations from around the world is inadequate to achieve the level of skill that meteorologists desire and that users expect. The lack of observations is especially problematic over the oceans, polar regions, the tropics, and in non-WMO member countries.

The Process of Modern Scientific Weather Forecasting

In order to successfully tackle a substantial problem like weather forecasting, an organized approach must be taken by the forecaster; this approach is illustrated in figure 9.2. The process consists of six steps and represents the mind-set of the forecaster. It is sometimes referred to as the "endless loop," because the process, like the weather, never ends. The first step in the diagnostic process may well be the most sweeping of all, for it contains the essence of the individual forecasters. In one way or another, the forecaster brings his or her personality to the process. This is why weather forecasting is more than a scientific endeavor, as it also involves subjectivity on the part of the person. The forecasting methodology begins with the total person.

In order to meet the supreme intellectual challenge that weather forecasting presents, the forecaster must be equipped with a reservoir of knowledge pertaining to atmospheric processes and behavior. In short, the person must understand "how the weather works." But we can safely state that the best forecasters need more than their formal education; they also need practical experience of "how weather works." It is in this way, with a combination of formal education and practical experience, that the person achieves the best forecast that is humanly possible.

The second step in the modern forecasting process is the analysis of all available data by the forecaster. As mentioned earlier, the volume of information is massive. For the most part, the data is presented to the forecaster as pictures, charts, or in alphanumeric form (a combination of letters and numbers that is either coded or descriptive). Picture data is derived from satellite and radar. Charts and alphanumeric data can come from any source such as wind profilers, lightning detection networks, rawindsonde, and reports from pilots, ships, offshore installations, and oceanic data buoys.

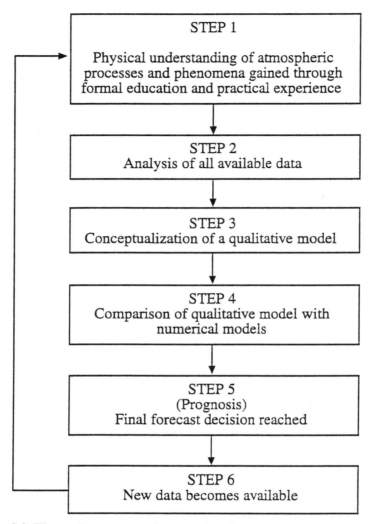

Fig. 9.2. The modern approach to weather forecasting as practiced by humans.

What does the meteorologist do with all of the information? Step 3 of the diagnostic process is the answer. Here, the forecaster develops a qualitative model of the atmosphere appropriate for the situation at hand. In formulating the model, the forecaster takes the huge amount of available information and produces a mental picture of the atmosphere and moves it forward in time. The qualitative model is nonmathematical and at its heart is pattern recognition. Not all forecasters are equally adept at the task of pattern recognition. The most gifted forecasters can simply capture the truth of the weather situation with nothing more than a glance at a few data sources, while others labor to achieve results.

After the forecaster develops the qualitative model, he or she must then compare that model to the solution offered by numerical simulation. This fourth step of weather forecasting represents a decision point for the meteorologist. The options are to completely accept the numerical solution, to accept the qualitative model, or, as is most often the case, to modify both the computer solution and the qualitative model.

After comparing the qualitative model with numerical output, the forecaster arrives at the final forecast decision. The fifth step in the process is called prognosis. Therefore, prognosis is considered part of the diagnostic process. At this time subjectivity can enter into a decision—the forecaster may even include a "gut feeling," an opinion borne out by many years of experience in one geographical region. It's possible that the best weather forecaster in the world is not a professional meteorologist, but an elderly person who has lived in the same geographical region for many years and has developed keen insight into the mysteries of weather and how it changes, a "sixth sense" about what's likely to occur next. Professional forecasters use this type of subjectivity when facing the prognostic decision. Although that may seem to remove some of the "science" from the process, it's what makes the process uniquely human, and it's the main reason why computers will never replace humans in the forecasting process.

The forecasting process is finally finished, right? Wrong! While evaluating incoming data and formulating a qualitative model, new data has arrived for the forecaster to consider. This new data must be evaluated in light of the current qualitative model. If the new information runs contrary to what the forecaster thought would happen, then the process starts over. Even if the current forecast is on target, the new data still must be considered in case "fine-tuning" of the forecast is required. In this light, the NWS once estimated that in the contiguous United States, some 10,000 significant weather variations are occurring at any one instant. Herein lies the reason that the diagnostic process never ends.

Numerical Weather Prediction

The most common modern prognostic technique used by meteorologists is numerical weather prediction. The era of computer-generated weather forecasts began around 1950, when the first research prototypes were developed. These gangly masses of hardware required 36 hours to complete a 24-hour forecast! Despite this problem the efforts were deemed successful and the development of numerical methods continued. In 1954, the Joint Numerical Weather Forecasting Unit was formed in Washington, D.C., to develop versions of the earlier research models that could be used in the Weather Bureau. The first of these operational (meaning government-sponsored) numerical models was introduced to government weather forecasters in 1958. Significant advances, both in hardware and in software, occurred in 1962, 1966, 1971, and 1980. Near-quantum advances continued through the 1980s and the 1990s, and at least four different types of short-range computer model output are available to forecasters. Several more experimental models are under design.

In order to simulate a particular atmospheric circulation using a numerical method, relevant factors such as differential solar heating, transformations of energy involving the water substance, and interactions between scales of atmospheric flow must be considered. This dictates that modern realistic numerical models of the atmosphere are complex programs developed to run on the largest, most expensive, and fastest supercomputers in the world. This complexity is necessary if the model is to reproduce realistically the physical processes controlling the motion of the atmosphere. Numerical modeling has two aims: to increase our knowledge of the physical processes governing our atmosphere and to provide reliable guidance to forecasters.

More than realistic physics is necessary for a reliable simulation of atmospheric motion. Like the human forecasting process, the Numerical Weather Prediction (NWP) process follows a series of interrelated and logical steps. Figure 9.3 outlines the NWP process.

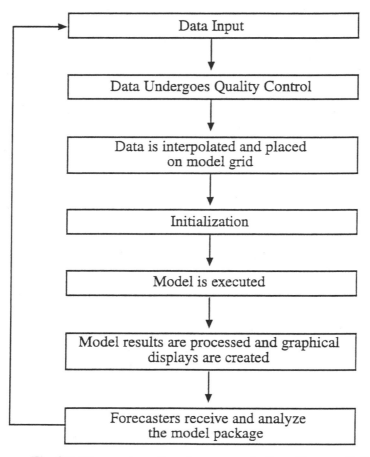

Fig. 9.3. The process of modern numerical weather prediction.

The first step in the NWP process is data input. The quantity of information is massive and represents all observations around the Northern Hemisphere from all available sources. The data is coded and placed into various software modules, where it awaits the next step in the process.

All data must undergo quality control to ensure that no erroneous information finds its way into the model. Errors due to coding, transmission, and equipment are all common faults that must be eliminated in the quality control process. Human mistakes also must be edited from the input process. Quality control is vital, because if the computer model forecast is based on contaminated data, then the forecast is likely to be inaccurate.

Following quality control all data is interpolated and placed on the appropriate grid used by the model. This is done because most models use a smaller grid size than what is available with observations, so any missing data points must be estimated, or interpolated. The procedure gives meteorologists the ability to statistically blend data sources of different types in time and space.

The fourth step in the NWP process is initialization. At this stage all data is prepared and coded for use by the model equations. This involves transforming the data into language the computer can understand. Common programming languages in meteorology are BASIC and FORTRAN.

After proper initialization the model is executed. Forecasters in the United States receive several packages of output twice daily. These models are executed on supercomputers at the NCEP in the early morning and the evening. Model output is processed and graphical displays of the information are created, generally in chart form. All of the model output must be put in a suitable form for interpretation by forecasters. The model package normally arrives to forecasters within two hours of execution. Of course, the computer-generated forecast is analyzed by forecasters (at the point, we're actually in step 4 of the human process).

The Process of Scientific Thought

Activity #1

Title: Observing, Recording, and Forecasting Your Own Weather

Objective: To apply observations to forecasting

At this point students should be well acquainted with observing their own weather conditions using the school weather station. They should also be well versed in recording their observations using the cloud chart and their observation form from chapter 6.

Use the Magic Weather Forecast Chart (table 9.2) provided to make weather forecasts based on data from the school weather station. Keep track of weather forecasts from a professional source as well.

SEA LEVEL PRESSURE	PRESSURE TENDENCY	SURFACE WIND DIRECTION	SKY CONDITION	FORECAST!
Higher than 30.20	Rising, Steady or Falling	Any Direction	Clear, High Clouds, Cumulus	1, 8
30.20 to 30.00	Rising or Steady	SW, W, NW, N	Clear High Clouds, Cumulus	1, 8
	Falling	S or SE	Clear, High Clouds	3, 10
			Middle or Low Clouds	4, 10
		E or NE	Clear or High Clouds	3, 8
			Middle or Low Clouds	4, 8
29.99 to 29.80	Rising	SW, W, NW, N	Clear	1, 8
			Partly Cloudy	2, 9
			Cloudy	2, 9
	Falling	Any Direction	Clear	1, 8
		SW, S, SE	High Clouds	3, 10, 4
			Middle or Low Clouds	4
		E or NE	Middle or Low Clouds	4, 7
		SE, E, NE	Cloudy	4
		S, or SE	Cloudy	6
Below 29.80	Rising	SW, W, NW, N	Clear	1, 7
			Partly Cloudy	2, 7, 9
			Cloudy	6, 7, 9
		NE	Cloudy	7, 9
			Clear	3, 9, 7
		SW, S, SE	Clear	3, 7, 4
			Cloudy	4, 7
	Falling	SW, S, SE	Cloudy	5, 7
		N	Cloudy	7, 9
		E or NE	Cloudy	5, 9

WEATHER FORECAST CODES:

1 = Clear to Partly Cloudy
2 = Clearing
3 = Increasing Clouds
4 = Precipitation Possible Within 24 Hours
5 = Unsettled, Heavy Rain or Snow Possible Within 24 Hours

6 = Precipitation Ending Within 24 Hours
7 = Windy
8 = Little Temperature Change
9 = Turning Colder
10 = Turning Warmer

Table 9.2. The Magic Weather Forecast Chart

From *The Teacher's Weather Sourcebook.* © 1999 Frank T. Konvicka. Teacher Ideas Press. (800) 237-6124

Elementary

- Let the students describe the weather verbally in addition to recording it. Also, they could write a poem about the day's weather.

- Draw graphs of temperature, dewpoint (or relative humidity), and pressure.

- Make "weather lists," outlining the three highest and lowest of the following: temperature, windspeed, pressure, dewpoint (or RH). Make a list of the three most common wind directions (or use the wind rose idea from chapter 6, pages 85 and 86).

- Be sure to discuss frontal passages, type of air mass present, and the sequence of weather conditions associated with the frontal passage.

- It will be very instructive to compare your weather forecasts with those issued by a professional. Use the forecast given by one of the TV stations in your market. Which forecast is more accurate? Why?

Secondary

- Compare the forecast given by several different sources with your forecast. How do they compare? Why are there differences between the professional forecasts? (Answer: Many broadcast meteorologists use the NWS forecast, but some use their own, independent of the NWS.) Which forecast is the most accurate?

- Modify the Magic Weather Forecast Chart (table 9.2) to better suit your local area.

Activity #2

Title: Weather Maps Everywhere

Objective: To gain practical experience using simple weather maps

Materials Needed: Maps 1, 2, and 3 in this chapter

Procedure: Look at maps 1, 2, and 3 and follow the directions given on each map. Map 1 asks the students to decode the plotted weather observations given. Table 9.1 and figure 9.1 may be referred to for help.

     Map 2 is designed to help students better understand the concepts of air masses and fronts and to show them how these ideas are represented on a weather map.

     Map 3 will help students use a weather map to issue forecasts. The plotted station model serves as a hint of weather to come.

Activity #3

Title: Special Forecasts

Objective: To learn about the many uses of weather forecasts

Materials Needed: time, patience, outside resources

Procedure: No academic topic is worth much unless its subject matter can be applied for the benefit of society. This activity focuses on applied meteorology and, specifically, on the many different uses for weather forecasts.

Elementary and Secondary

Have students get into groups of two or three and let them choose one of the following weather-sensitive operations: ski resort, shopping mall, a specific retailer (different groups can choose another retailer), agriculture (again, different components of the agricultural industry can be used), commodity traders, gardeners, the construction industry, timber/forestry, electric utility, gas utility, legal or forensic, transportation (rail, trucks, or river), and insurance.

Talk with a knowledgeable person involved in one of the above industries. Each group of students should be expected to give a report, both written and oral, regarding their findings. They should answer the following questions: How does weather affect the business or industry? How do those in the industry apply weather information to their own unique situations? What sources do they use? (If they use professional consulting services, contact them too.) What are ideal weather conditions? What weather conditions affect their business negatively? (For these last two questions, try to get them to remember a specific occurrence.) How accurate and useful do they feel the weather information they receive is?

Ideas for Science Fair Projects

1. Activity #3 can be used as a science fair idea.

2. In activity #1, students compared their forecast with professional sources. A focus on that can make a good science fair project, especially if the "magic" forecast is better than the local professional source (if it is, then the professional source is not very accurate). Cite differences and the reasons for those differences. An especially good aspect would be to modify the "magic" chart to better suit the local area.

3. Trace the historical development of weather forecasting using some of the information from the early part of this chapter and from other sources.

4. Center a project on the NWS reorganization effort.

5. Develop a project that answers the question. What factors determine if it rains or not? Using the class weather log, research times when it rained. What common elements are present? Look at times when precipitation did not occur. What common elements are present? What factors best foretell precipitation? Be sure you can explain why each factor is important.

6. Compare and contrast the approaches to weather forecasting taken by humans and by computers. Outline the process followed by each. What are advantages and disadvantages?

7. Prospective title: "How Accurate Are Professional Weather Forecasts?" Keep a record of information given in forecasts by a particular local source. Keep track of high temperature, low temperature, and precipitation. What was their accuracy percentage for precipitation forecasts? (Many claim an accuracy rate of 85%.) How close did they come to the actual high and low temperatures that were observed? In what aspect of the forecast was their accuracy rate the highest? The lowest?

8. Another title: "How Accurate Is the Almanac?" Obtain a copy of a commercial almanac and keep a record for one month of its forecast. Compare it to what actually happened. What is its accuracy rate?

School's Out!

1.   On a blank piece of paper, draw 10 station models.

2.   Visit a professional.

3.   Practice your weather observing skills.

4.   Fine-tune your forecasting skills.

5.   Collect weather maps.

6.   Make a poster of the weather.

7.   Practice drawing fronts on a U.S. map.

8.   Draw fronts on a map of another continent.

9.   Talk with elders about some of the old weather sayings they believe.

10.   Ask a professional for some old weather maps. You can do lots of useful things with these maps: practice writing numbers and letters, draw pictures, color, trade, or make a mobile.

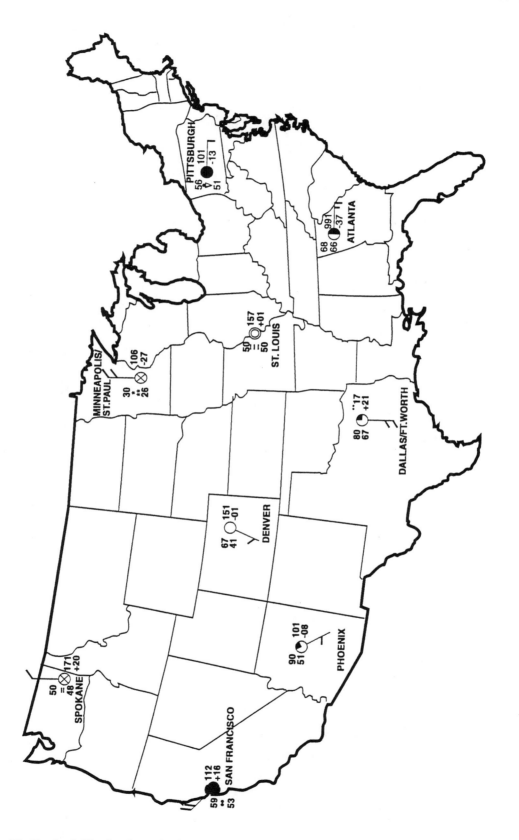

Map 1—Use table 9.1 and figure 9.1 to decode the weather for each location given on this map.

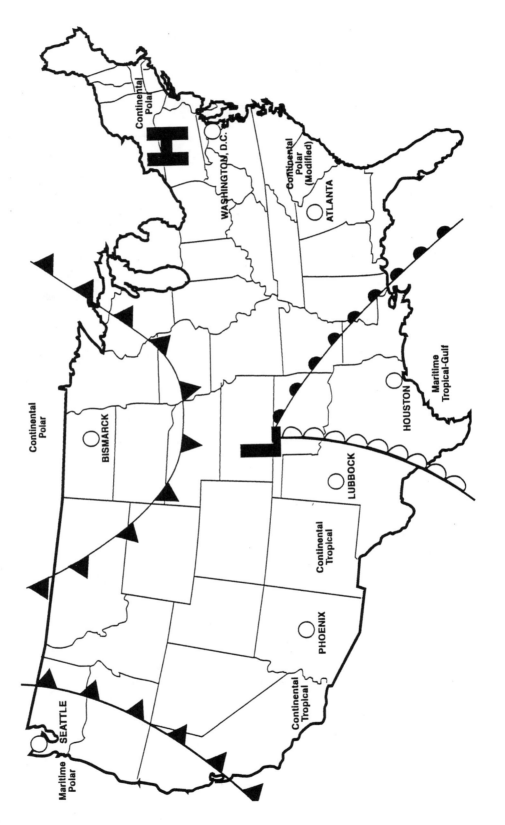

Map 2—Based on the above scenario, plot station models where indicated.

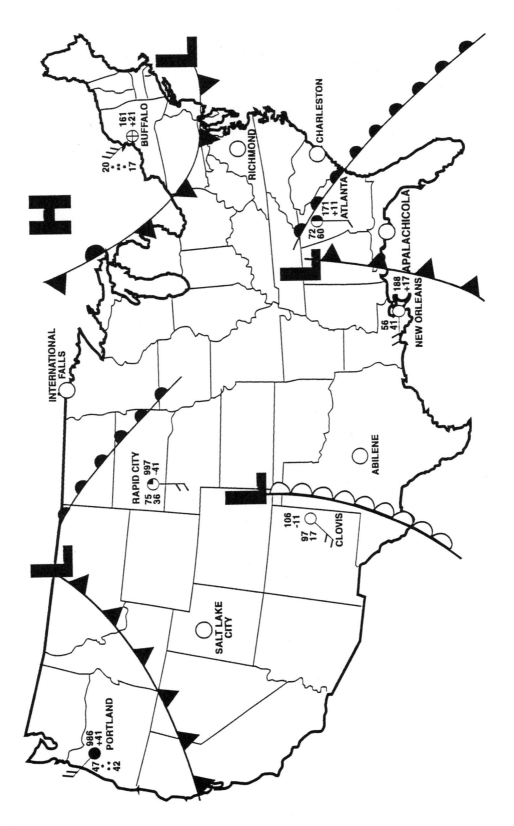

Map 3—Draw station models based on what your forecast will be for: Salt Lake City, International Falls, Abilene, Apalachicola, Charleston, and Richmond. Be sure to use the given station models for help.

Chapter 10

Weather Sights and Sounds

Everything is worthy of notice, for everything can be interpreted.
Herman Hesse

Who can deny the singular beauty of a rainbow? We stand in amazement as the aurora dances across the clearest of skies or we may be startled momentarily by a sonic boom.

Weather Sights

Among the best-known weather sights are sky color, rainbows, haloes, coronas, mirages, and the aurora. Before beginning our discussion of these topics, however, we must consider two important concepts from the science of optics, namely *refraction* and *reflection*.

Reflection and Refraction

During reflection, light is "turned back" by its encounter with a substance. The best-known example of reflection is the glass mirror. In the mirror, light is reflected and an image appears. But glass isn't the only substance that reflects light. In the atmosphere, raindrops and ice crystals reflect light.

Refraction is a change in the path of light brought about by a change in medium through which the light passes. Atmospheric contents also refract light and, when combined with reflection, they display the common optical phenomena that are evident.

Sky Color

What color is the sky? Everyone takes for granted that the clear daytime sky is blue, but go about 20 miles above Earth's surface, and the sky is nearly black. It turns out that sky color depends on the composition of the atmosphere. Apparently, no other planet in the solar system has a blue sky like Earth's.

Colors in the sky are created by the preferential scattering (the general term for reflection and refraction) of sunlight by air molecules. Sunlight is actually made up of many colors, each of which has its own wavelength. The human eye, however, is nearly blind to all of the color in the solar spectrum, as it only sees what is termed the "visible" portion. The shorter wavelengths of color (blue) are scattered much more than the longer wavelengths (red). To an observer it appears that the blue light dominates the other colors and causes the sky to become blue. Thus, during the day, when the orb of the sun is high, the sky is primarily blue. As sunset approaches and the sun angle lowers, light must pass through a thicker layer of atmosphere to reach an observer. The longer pathlength traveled by the sunlight causes most of the blue to be scattered out, leaving orange and red as the dominant colors. At night, when there is no sunlight to scatter, the sky becomes black, an excellent canopy to view the sights of the heavens.

Figure 10.1 illustrates the physical processes that contribute to the color of our sky. Reddish sunsets are occasionally enhanced by excessive dust in the atmosphere, such as particles from recent volcanic eruptions. A milky white is caused by haze, atmospheric condensation nuclei that are wetted at relative humidities as low as 70%. Finally, clouds are normally colored white because the water and ice scatter all wavelengths equally. A dark cloud base, however, occurs because it is shielded from sunlight by the cloud mass itself.

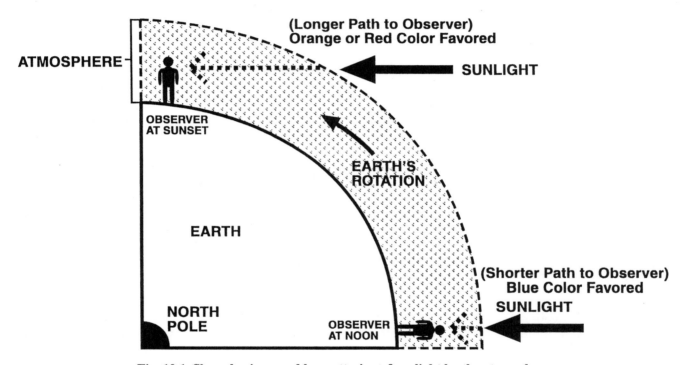

Fig. 10.1. Sky color is caused by scattering of sunlight by the atmosphere.

Rainbows

Stated simply, rainbows are caused by the scattering of sunlight by raindrops. They scatter light more strongly in some directions than in others and, in any given direction, they scatter light of some wavelengths more than others. Let's look at figure 10.2.

Our discussion begins with what happens for a single raindrop. The process of rainbow formation can be outlined in three steps. First, sunlight hits the surface of the drop and the initial refraction occurs. An important aspect of this initial refraction is that the separation of colors begins. This "first refraction" is analogous to the well-known separation of colors by using a glass prism.

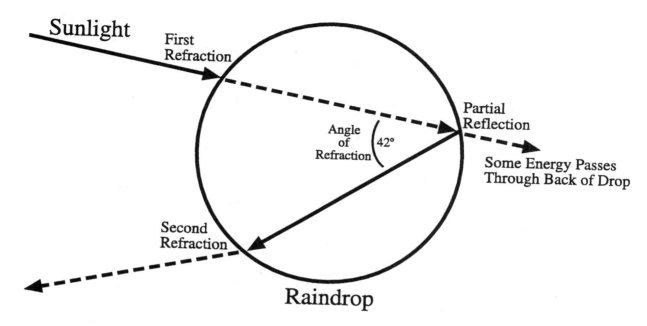

Fig. 10.2. An example of how sunlight is scattered by a single raindrop.

Following the first refraction the light waves hit the back of the drop and are partially reflected, which means only a small percentage of the light energy is reflected and travels back through the drop. Most of this energy actually passes through the back of the drop. As these reflected waves leave the drop, they are refracted again. This is referred to as the second refraction. The angle between the incoming light from the sun and the outgoing light in the second refraction is close to 42° for all colors.

The color of the light that reaches an observer's eyes depends on the angle made by the sun's rays and the position of the observer. Each of the raindrops in the shower separates the sunlight into its various colors, ranging from red to yellow to violet, but as illustrated in figure 10.3, the observer sees red from drops located at the highest altitudes, yellow from drops that are next highest, blue from still lower drops, and violet from the lowest drops. As a result, red appears on the outside of the bow and the colors progress to orange, yellow, green, blue, and violet.

A rainbow always appears in the opposite side of the sky from the sun. Thus, an observer must be positioned between the sun and the shower to see a rainbow. Because of the geometry involved, rainbows appear as semicircles when viewed from ground level.

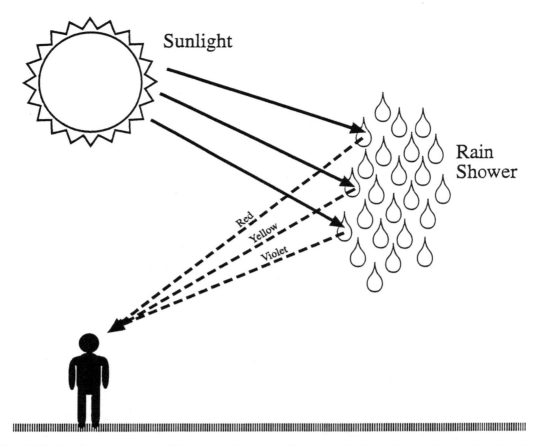

Fig. 10.3. Rainbows are caused by scattering of sunlight by raindrops located at various heights.

Supernumerary Rainbows

In some cases more than one rainbow is visible. Depending on the size of the rain shower and the position of the sun, a secondary rainbow may be seen. The idea of multiple rainbows being simultaneously visible to an observer was first explained in 1803 by Thomas Young.

When the sun's orb in the sky is located at an angle greater than 42° above the horizon, the primary bow is not seen. If the sun's orb is located at an angle greater than 51° above the horizon, then the secondary bows are not seen. In those special cases when the sun is located between 42° and 51° above the horizon, we are treated to seeing two rainbows, the primary and secondary. An interesting statement is that an almost infinite number of rainbows is produced by any given rain shower! This explains the very rare instance of three rainbows being visible from the same rain shower, a sight observed by the author on only one occasion.

The secondary rainbows result from additional reflections from the back of the raindrops. The arrangement of colors in secondary bows is reversed from that seen in the primary bow. The red is on the inside, and the violet is on the outside. Secondary rainbows are weaker (because the energy is shared by multiple reflections) than primary bows.

Haloes and Coronas

In addition to rainbows, haloes and coronas are common sights in the atmosphere. Rene Descartes ascribed their formation to the effect of ice crystals, an idea further pursued by Henry Cavendish, Thomas Young, J. G. Galle, and A. Bravais. It was Bravais who showed the general validity of the theory in 1847.

A halo appears as a colored or whitish ring or arc around the sun or the moon. The halo is produced by the light from the sun or moon passing through clouds composed of ice crystals. Normally, the cloud type responsible for haloes is cirrostratus. The halo appears because the light is refracted as it passes through ice crystals in the shape of hexagonal prisms. When a thin, uniform cirrostratus canopy containing such crystals covers the sky, a halo forms. The halo may be in the form of a complete circle or a segment.

Sun Pillars and Iridescent Clouds

Sun pillars and iridescent clouds are two more examples of atmospheric optical magic. Sun pillars are most common near sunrise and sunset. A sun pillar is a luminous streak of light located above and below the sun as light is scattered from the bottoms and tops of ice crystals that are in the form of plates.

Occasionally high, thin clouds exhibit patches of color of the purest blue, green, and red. They

Mirages

We've all heard it: "Don't believe everything you see." One reason for some merit of this trite expression is visual illusions created by mirages, a refraction phenomenon wherein the image of a distant object appears distorted and displaced from its true position. The mirage arises when the temperature profile near the ground is characterized by unusually large variations.

There are two categories of mirages: inferior and superior. The appearance of the mirage depends, respectively, on whether the spurious image appears below or above its true position. Inferior mirages are the most common, usually discernible whenever the air near the ground is extremely hot, when cool air moves over warm water, or when the sun heats streets or sidewalks. Figure 10.4 illustrates the paths taken by rays of

A corona is a series of colored or whitish rings around the sun or the moon. This sounds like a halo but the principle of formation is different. This also must be distinguished from the corona discharge associated with the lightning process.

Instead of resulting from refraction by ice crystals, the corona is caused by scattering of sunlight or moonlight by a tenuous collection of water droplets, all of which are nearly the same size. Like the rainbow, the corona is a mosaic; each part of it is contributed to by different drops. The cloud types most often responsible for a corona are altostratus or thin, low stratus.

may appear when the sun is either low or high in the sky. Such clouds, called iridescent clouds, are observed near the orb of the sun as the sun's rays are deflected around patches of uniform water droplets or ice crystals, and the light waves interfere with one another in such a way as to separate the various components of color. Iridescent clouds form no regular pattern; they are merely bits and pieces of coronas or just incomplete coronas.

light in the case of an inferior mirage. A wave of light moving on a downward path in the direction of an observer is refracted upward. As a result, objects are displaced downward. Rays of blue light from the sky appear to an observer to be coming off the surface, which makes it look like a body of water is present. In some inferior mirages, the image appears displaced downward and distorted, but not inverted. Superior mirages are associated with temperature inversions close to the ground. In this case, refraction leads to a downward bending of light rays. As a result, objects appear above their true positions. Depending on the variation of temperature with height, the images may be inverted and may appear to be smaller, or the same size as the original object. Figure 10.5 illustrates how a superior mirage operates.

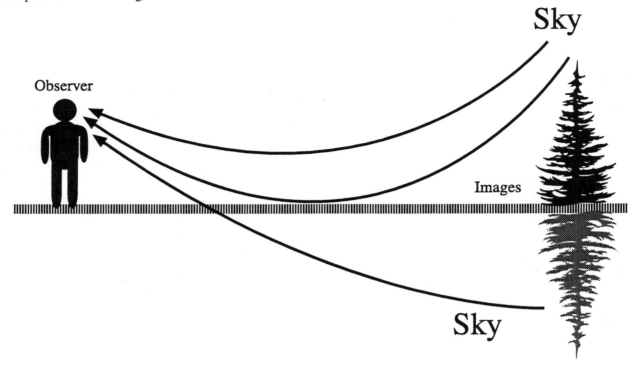

Fig. 10.4. In an inferior mirage, the image is displaced downward.

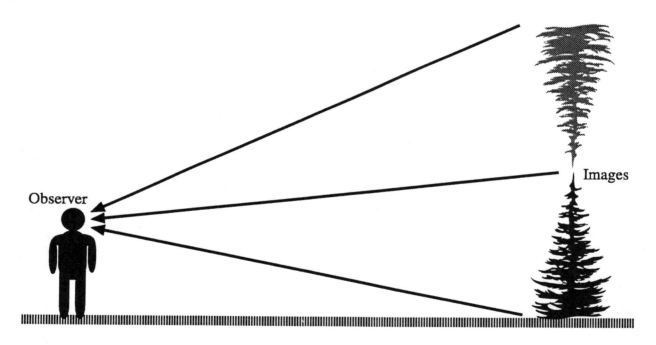

Fig. 10.5. Objects appear above their true height in a superior mirage.

In extreme cases, the rays of light emitted by an object are refracted by varying amounts depending on how the temperature changes with height. The result can be a fascinating, complex combination of inferior and superior mirages that causes objects such as boats and buildings to appear as towers of exaggerated vertical extent. Such a phenomenon is called *fata morgana*, after the Italian name of King Arthur's storybook sister Morgan le Fay, who could magically build castles out of air.

The Aurora

As one approaches polar latitudes, the frequency of a visually stunning phenomenon increases. This high-altitude light show is called the aurora. In the Northern Hemisphere it is known as the aurora borealis, the aurora polaris, or simply the "northern lights." In the Southern Hemisphere, it is called the aurora australis or the "southern lights." Auroras generally occur at altitudes of about 60 to 80 miles, a fact investigated some 200 years ago by Henry Cavendish. The aurora takes many shapes but the most common are arcs, bands, rays, and massive curtains. It's been estimated that the aurora may be visible as many as 200 times per year north of the Arctic Circle and south of the Antarctic Circle. In middle latitudes the aurora is less common, being visible once per year. In lower latitudes viewers are treated to this spectacle only once per decade.

The aurora represents a sporadic radiant emission from the upper atmosphere. Particles emitted by solar flares are electrically charged and are deflected toward the North and South Poles by Earth's magnetic field. When these high-speed particles collide with air molecules, they cause electrons to be freed. When these electrons recombine with the air molecules, energy in the form of light (mostly green and red) is emitted. This process can occur simultaneously over vast regions. Figure 10.6 is a sketch depicting the process of aurora formation.

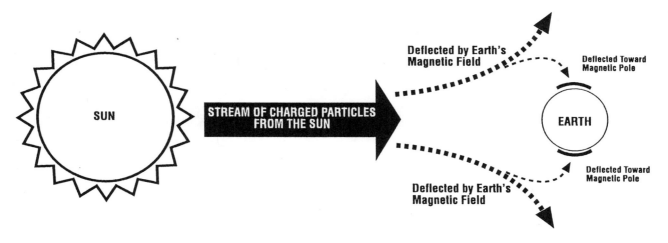

Fig. 10.6. The aurora phenomenon.

Weather Sounds

Sounds in the atmosphere range from the explosive crash of thunder to the soft dirge of a pine tree when its needles are set in vibration by the wind; in unison they produce faint aeolian tones. Most sounds of the weather result from electrical fields, wind, rapid temperature changes, and falling precipitation.

Thunder

Thunder is one of the most noticeable sounds of the weather. It can range from an ear-splitting crash to a distant rumble. Whatever its characteristics, thunder is caused by lightning; the intense heat of the lightning discharge literally causes the air to explode. Sound waves move from the lightning channel and eventually reach our ears as thunder.

The duration of thunder is due mainly to the characteristics of the lightning discharge that caused it. Thunder produced by a single stroke of lightning would reach our ears as a single boom. Along a crooked lightning channel, the timing of the sound is offset. For example, a multiple-stroked lightning discharge that is 5 miles long would cause thunder to rumble for 24 seconds. Frequent lightning flashes in a thunderstorm cause overlapping thunder.

When multiple strokes of lightning follow the same path (you see a "flicker"), the sound waves are amplified, thus resulting in louder and irregular thunder. Reflection of the sounds waves is also a factor. Mountains or hills may prolong the duration of thunder. A heavy curtain of rain is known to lessen the intensity of thunder, as the sound waves are reflected partially from the audible observer.

Thunder can be heard up to 20 miles under ideal circumstances. It is true that one can estimate the distance to a lightning discharge by counting the number of seconds between the lightning flash and the time when thunder is first heard and dividing by five. Thus, thunder heard 10 seconds after seeing the lightning is about 2 miles away. Frequent lightning makes application of this technique difficult, since it's hard to know which peal of thunder resulted from which lightning discharge.

Other Common Sounds

When the electric field strength at the ground becomes large, often just before a lightning strike, there is sometimes a sizzling or a crackling sound. Cloud-to-ground lightning discharges have, on rare occasions, been described as sounding like fabric being torn. A "clicking" noise sometimes occurs near the strike point of lightning, either just before it strikes or after the strike.

Sounds caused by the wind are often best heard away from the noises of urban areas. In forests, when the leaves have fallen, the wind sets millions of small twigs into vibration, producing a constantly changing murmur. In mountainous regions, the sounds generated by oscillating twigs and pine needles can be focused to produce what has been called the "roar of the mountains." In a forest the murmurs are occasionally joined by a high-pitched screech caused by the rubbing of the trunks when a dead tree falls into a fork of another tree that is blown back and forth by the wind.

Strong winds cause power lines and fences to hum or to whistle. The vibrations of power lines or a fence are transmitted to the supporting poles that serve as sounding boards. The same type of winds blowing over gables, around chimneys, and around corners of a house can cause howling sounds. Very high winds, such as those associated with tornadoes and downbursts, can be especially noisy and terrifying, resembling the loud roar of jet airplanes or trains. Tornadic winds have also been described as sounding like a "million bees" by firsthand observers.

Temperature changes bring about sounds. Exposed objects may cool or heat rapidly, and the resulting change in volume causes sounds. Most substances contract when cooled and expand when heated. The onset of bitter cold can cause explosive bursting of trees as frozen outer shells shrink more than the interior cores. The freezing and breaking of ice as it expands and contracts on rivers and lakes can send out booming sounds. In houses, especially older frame homes with poor insulation, one hears crackles and pops as the rafters, joints, and other sections contract or expand by varying amounts under the influence of temperature changes.

Sounds of the weather are associated with falling precipitation. The drumming of rain, particularly on a wooden or a metal roof, resembles the output of percussion instruments. The hammer or thump of large hail is a most unwelcome and scary sound. In severe hailstorms the noise can reach deafening proportions and can be made worse by high winds that propel hailstones against the house. The sound is also made worse when hail breaks windows, skylights, and roof tiles.

The Sonic Boom

Contrary to popular opinion, sonic booms are not produced by atmospheric processes. They actually result from the physical properties of the air itself, namely the compressibility and fluidlike characteristics. Sonic booms are caused by aircraft flying at "supersonic" speeds (above the speed of sound). This is taken as 760 mph at sea level. An airplane flying lower than this value only produces engine noises that propagate equally in all directions faster than the speed of the plane. Once the plane moves faster than the sound waves, the air ahead of it is forced to move abruptly and to "pile up," causing a narrow zone of compressed air in the form of a shock wave. The sudden changes associated with this process produce sonic booms in much the same way that explosions do.

Sonic booms move along the surface at the same speed as the aircraft. A large plane, flying at a height of 60,000 feet, can produce sonic booms along a track 50 miles wide, being most intense just under the plane and decreasing outward. Boom intensity depends on the speed, size, and flight level of the plane. A typical sonic boom produces a noise level about 1 million times greater than that of ordinary conversation. Rarely, sonic booms are strong enough to break windows or crack plaster. During the past 20 years, however, efforts to reduce the frequency and the intensity of sonic booms have been successful. Primarily, these ventures center on improved aircraft design and more careful selection of flight routes. Despite the best efforts, though, sonic booms cannot be eliminated as long as supersonic flight speeds are necessary.

The Process of Scientific Thought

Activity #1

Title: School-Made Rainbow

Objective: To make a rainbow

Materials Needed: garden hose, sunny day

Procedure: On a sunny day stand with your back to the sun and spray water from a hose (a fine spray of small droplets works best). The best time of day is early morning or late afternoon. You will see a rainbow. An even better rainbow can be seen if a dark background (a row of trees) is present.

Elementary

- Draw a picture of the rainbow. Be sure to name the colors.

- Write a poem or a story about the rainbow.

- Students should be able to explain briefly how the rainbow forms.

- Vary the output of the hose from large drops to a fine spray. Which gives the best rainbow? (Answer: the fine spray.)

Secondary

- Repeat the activity by standing on a stool or a ladder. How does this affect what you see? (Answer: The rainbow is almost a complete circle, broken only by your shadow.)

Activity #2

Title: The Feather Spectrum

Objective: To show refraction using a feather

Materials Needed: bird feather, candle

Procedure: Hold a large bird feather in front of one eye and look through the feather at a burning candle about 3 feet away. The flame seems to be multiplied in an X-shape arrangement and shimmers in the spectral colors.

Elementary

- Make a sketch of what is seen.

- Write a story or poem about a feather.

- Explain briefly what's happening. (Answer: The appearance is produced by the bending of light at the slits in the feather. The light from the candle is refracted and separated into the spectral colors as it passes through the slits. Because you see through several slits at the same time, the flame appears several times.)

Secondary

- Repeat using different feathers. Does this change the results?

• Optics is a branch of physics dealing with the laws of refraction and reflection. Explore this important topic in more detail and learn how optics is applied in everyday life. Talk to an optometrist or an ophthalmologist about how they use optics to correct vision problems.

Activity #3

Title: The Comb Light-Bender

Objective: To understand reflection

Materials Needed: comb, piece of white cardboard, small mirror

Procedure: Place a piece of white cardboard in a sun-drenched location. Hold a comb upright with the teeth resting on the cardboard. Tilt the cardboard so that the beams of light are 2 or 3 inches long. Place a small mirror diagonally in their path. The mirror will reflect the beams of light.

Elementary

• Draw a picture of the light beams. Be sure to show how they change direction.

• How are the light beams that strike the mirror reflected? (Answer: They are reflected at the same angle that they strike the mirror.)

• Turn the mirror and observe how the reflected light beams move.

Secondary

• Repeat using combs with various sizes of teeth. Does this affect the results?

Activity #4

Title: The Laws of Reflection

Objective: To understand reflection

Materials Needed: piece of paper, ruler, small mirror, protractor, pencil

Procedure: Draw a dotted line on a piece of paper with a ruler. Next, draw a straight line from it at any angle. Set a small mirror upright at the point where the two lines meet. Turn the mirror until the reflection of the dotted line is aligned with the dotted line. Now look into the mirror and line up one edge of the ruler with the reflection of the straight line.

Elementary

• Draw a picture. Be sure to draw the lines accurately.

• Briefly explain what reflection is.

Secondary

• Draw lines with your pencil and measure the angles on each side of the broken line with a protractor.

• Make a table. Label one column "angle of incidence" and the other column "angle of reflection." How do they compare? (Answer: They should be equal.)

Ideas for Science Fair Projects

1. Explore the laws of reflection in detail. Be sure to include the following in the project: State the laws, illustrate them by using a demonstration, and list applications.

2. Explore the laws of refraction. State the laws, demonstrate them, and list applications.

3. Trace the historical development of the rainbow through myth, folklore, superstition, and the Bible. Then focus a project on how rainbows form.

4. Do a project entitled "Why Is the Sky Blue?"

5. Separate the colors of the solar spectrum by using a prism. Explain the solar spectrum.

6. Center a project on supernumerary rainbows. What are they? When are they visible?

7. Include haloes, coronas, sun pillars, and iridescent clouds in a project entitled "Sights of the Sky."

8. "Different Skies" investigates the sky color of other planets in the solar system. For example, the Martian sky is pink because of iron particles in its thin atmosphere.

9. "Don't Believe Everything You See" focuses on mirages. Tell what a mirage is, the two types, and how they occur.

10. The aurora makes an appropriate topic for a science fair project. Include definition, altitude they occur at, shapes, frequency at various latitudes, and the cause.

11. The sonic boom is another idea that's appropriate for a science fair project. Include definition, factors affecting intensity, the cause, and modern efforts to alleviate the problem.

School's Out!

1. If you wear corrective lenses for vision, figure out how the laws of optics apply to your prescription. Do you have a concave or convex lens? How does this affect the refraction of light?

2. Talk to older people about weather sayings. Start a list of weather sayings that you hear and share them with the class. The class can then discuss their validity.

3. Read a book about the sky or rainbows to a younger child.

4. Record sights of the weather in a notebook.

PART II

SPECIAL TOPICS IN ATMOSPHERIC SCIENCE

Chapter 11

Earth's Climate System

Is there in the world a climate more uncertain than our own?
William Cosgrove

Climate is an active ingredient in the physical environment of all life-forms. Like Earth's biosphere, climate is diverse, the uncertainty of which leads to a resounding "yes" to the above statement.

Chapter 11 is strategically placed at the beginning of part II, for climate synthesizes much of the material contained in part I. Climate is best treated as an interdisciplinary subject.

Essential Definitions

Climate has been defined in many different ways. An appropriate starting point is the Greek scholar Eratosthenes, who lived a few hundred years before Christ. Eratosthenes noticed the great influence insolation had on temperature. In this vein, the term *climate* may have originated from the Greek word *klima*, referring to the inclination of the sun's rays, varying as the orb of the sun moves across the sky on its seasonal march.

In more modern times, climate has been defined as the composite of meteorological conditions that is observed over a significant time span, usually taken to be 30 years.

Climatology is the science that seeks to describe and explain climate, why it differs from place to place, and how it relates to other elements of the natural environment and to humanity. A climatologist is a professional who is qualified by education (usually a meteorology or a geography background) and experience in climatology. Chapter 1 noted that climatology is a subfield of atmospheric science, but climatology extends meteorology to a global or a regional scale for time periods as long as observations or scientific inference will permit.

The Concept of a Global Climate System

A proper perspective on climate includes all aspects of the total world environment; an integrated set of phenomena is called Earth's climate system.

Systems are classified as either open or closed. In an open system, inputs of energy and matter flow into the system and outputs flow from the system. In the case of Earth, energy from the sun pours through Earth's atmosphere, penetrating all terrestrial systems and transforming into various other energy forms. Ultimately, Earth radiates this back into space in an amount essentially equal to that which entered the system.

Earth also operates as a closed system that is self-contained. All natural resources such as water, minerals, precious metals, and air were either created with the planet or were the result of natural processes acting over very long time frames. The implication of this fact is staggering, for it issues a strong challenge to humanity to be good stewards of Planet Earth.

As it operates, the system's continuing performance is generated in the energy output and it's returned via pathways called feedback loops. Feedback can cause changes that guide further system operation. If elements amplify or encourage response in the system, that is positive feedback. If the infor-mation slows or discourages response in a system, that is negative feedback.

Earth's open climate system has inputs, outputs, and transformations as illustrated in figure 11.1. Earth's climate system is a complex mixture of components. Insolation, the intricate interaction between the oceans, air, ice, soil, and life-forms, influences the climate system through feedback loops. Another vital link in Earth's climate system originates with humankind. The influences on climate from civilization affect the chemical composition of Earth's atmosphere, thereby resulting in human-driven changes within the system.

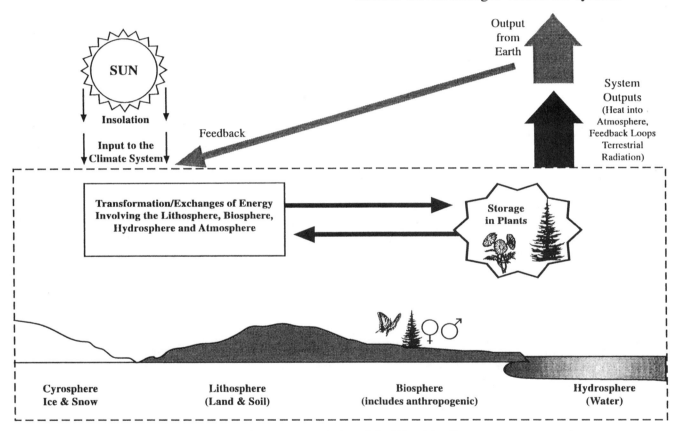

Fig. 11.1. A simplified conceptual model of Earth's climate system.

The primary storage component in Earth's energy system is plants, which supply the energy for all higher life-forms. Thus, plants are at the bottom of what is called the "food chain." Plants create their own tissues directly from sunlight, absorb part of the energy available through insolation, and, through chemical reactions of photosynthesis, store it in the form of sugars, fats, oils, and starches.

Herbivores, animals that eat only plants, sustain themselves by the energy contained in the plants they consume. Carnivores, animals that eat herbivores and other carnivores, ultimately feed on plant material. Humans are considered omnivores, meaning that they feed at all levels of the food chain. In this way, energy from the sun that is stored in plants is transferred through the food chain.

We often fail to notice the plants that surround us—the grass on our lawn, the moss on a rock, the algae in a pond, or the big oak that shades our backyard. Plants make up most of the mass of the biosphere, an astounding 90% according to some estimates! Hence, plants are a critical link between life and solar energy. Ultimately, the fate of Earth's biosphere rests on the success of plants and their ability to capture sunlight.

Factors That Control Climate

The combination of latitude, altitude, and the distribution and pattern of land and water are largely responsible for observed climate. The quality of insolation received is the single most important influence on the climate of a location. That quality is influenced by clouds, aerosol concentrations, and moisture content, but the angle of the sun's rays is the most important factor. Latitude is responsible for the amount of sunlight received at any point on Earth's surface.

Because air temperature decreases with increasing elevation by approximately 3.5° F per 1,000 feet, altitude also influences the climate found in a region. As a result, mountainous regions worldwide experience lower temperatures than do lowlands.

A third factor in climate control is continentality, the pattern of land/water distribution. In short, a location can be landlocked or seaside. The irregular arrangement of continents and oceans on Earth contributes to the overall climate of a region. In general, more moderate temperature patterns are associated with seaside locations and more severe patterns are observed for landlocked locations.

Mechanisms of Climate Change

Few natural phenomena attract the attention of so many scientific fields or elicit so many hypotheses as climate change. It is widely acknowledged by scientists that any single hypothesis cannot account for the climatic changes that have been observed over the history of Earth. The fact that different causes are active at different time scales adds to the challenge.

Solar Variability

In view of the fundamental role of insolation in the energy processes that produce climate, it is understandable that the possible effects of alterations in Earth's energy budget have been considered as a mechanism for climate change. One of the hypotheses holds that the sun is a variable star and that changes in its radiated output influence energy processes on Earth. Investigations have proven that the radiant output of the sun is not constant, but in fact, the sun actually "flickers." Small variations, on the order of a few tenths of 1%, affect Earth's climate system. Proponents of this idea say the increased solar radiation would warm Earth and account for such events as the melting of glaciers. Opponents believe that solar variability is too small to affect climate.

Sunspot Activity and Cycles

Closely aligned with the solar variability hypothesis is the possible influence of sunspot activity and cycles. An examination of the number of sunspots during a 200-year period reveals a cycle of about 11.3 years, but the period varies from 9 to 16 years. A 22-year multiple cycle is also evident. In 1977, the well-known American climatologist J. Murray Mitchell and his associates reported evidence relating sunspot frequency to drought occurrences in the United States. The droughts of the 1930s and 1950s fit nicely into this scheme.

Recently, it has been suggested that variations of solar radiation accompanying a sunspot cycle having a 90-year period, known as the Gleissberg sunspot cycle, can account for fluctuations of climate over such a time frame. According to this view the global temperature maximum around 1940 may have been the result of this particular sunspot cycle.

During certain lengthy periods sunspots virtually disappear from the face of the sun. For example, sunspots were practically nonexistent from 1645 to 1715. This 70-year period, known as the Maunder minimum in honor of the British scientist E. W. Maunder who first attracted attention to it, occurred near the middle of the Little Ice Age.

Earth's Magnetic Field

Earth's iron core produces a magnetic field, but the most intriguing feature is that the magnetic field sometimes fades to zero and then returns to full strength with north and south magnetic poles reversed. These magnetic reversals have taken place nine times during the past 4 million years and hundreds of times over Earth's history. The average period of a magnetic reversal is 500,000 years, with occurrences as short as several thousand years.

Continental Drift and Plate Tectonics

Climatic change, over periods of 100,000 to a few billion years, can be explained in terms of continental drift and plate tectonics. The continents are composed of relatively low-density materials, in the form of huge plates, floating on materials of higher density. A helpful analogy is to visualize a large bowl of water containing several ice cubes. The ice cubes are less dense than the liquid so they float. In like manner, Earth's continents move, or float, with respect to one another. This movement occurs at a very slow rate but lasts for very long time periods. For example, Los Angeles and San Francisco are located on different continental plates and are moving toward each other at the rate of about 2 inches per year. In 10 million years they will pass each other!

Earth's Orbit and Tilt

Peculiarities exist in Earth's orbit and tilt. Over time periods of 10,000 to 100,000 years, these certainly represent mechanisms of climate change. Around 1930, a Serbian geophysicist named Milutin Milankovitch developed a theory showing how certain orbital parameters of Earth vary with

In conclusion, there is still no acceptable explanation of how sunspots or related solar events can influence the circulation of Earth's atmosphere. Until more conclusive research is conducted, it is premature to claim that such events cause significant climatic fluctuations.

Paleoclimatologists have searched for a correlation between Earth's magnetism and climate changes, especially those associated with ice ages and the extinction of species in the fossil record. So far, proof is elusive, but one vital component of magnetic reversals is that they cause Earth to be vulnerable to the solar wind and UV bombardment, thereby increasing the danger to Earth's biosphere.

The proof of continental drift is also evident in the shapes of continents. It seems reasonable to imagine that Africa and South America were once connected. A comparison of the east coast of South America and the west coast of Africa indicates how they could be fitted together like pieces of a puzzle. The refinement of plate tectonics by geophysicists since the 1950s has given support to explanations of climatic change based on crustal movements. Continental drift during the past geologic epochs could account for climatic changes of major proportions as landmasses changed shape, position, and elevation. These changes have undoubtedly altered the general circulation of the atmosphere and the global climate.

periods of 23,000 years, 41,000 years, and 93,000 years. He proposed that these three cyclical processes, acting simultaneously, served as agents of climatic variability. His motivation was to explain the expansion/contraction of the Pleistocene ice sheets. The Milankovitch theory includes the following three principles.

1. Precession of the axis is a cyclic change in the orientation of Earth's axis that resembles the wobbling of a spinning top. Thus, we can visualize that as Earth rotates, there is a slight wobble. The length of this cycle is 23,000 years. Because of precession, in about 12,500 years, the Northern Hemisphere summer solstice will begin in December and the winter solstice will begin in June. Hence, precession brings a reversal of the seasons every 23,000 years. The most recent research on this fascinating topic was done by David Thomson of AT&T Bell Laboratories. Thomson scrutinized 340 years of temperature data available in the instrumental record and found that, because of precession, the onset of the seasons has shifted forward over time. According to Thomson's results, winter and summer begin 1.4 days later per century.

2. Variation of Earth's tilt is the second factor in the Milankovitch theory. At present, the tilt of Earth's axis is 23.5°. Over a period of 41,000 years, the tilt angle varies from 22.5° to 24.5°. At a tilt angle of 22.5°, there is less seasonal variation in the amount of solar radiation falling on each hemisphere. This scenario would lead to milder winters and cooler summers than exist at present. When the tilt reaches 24.5°, as it did 9,000 years ago, the distribution of solar radiation over Earth makes the winters colder and the summers hotter.

3. The shape of Earth's orbit is the third component of the Milankovitch theory. Over a cycle of 93,000 years, the shape of Earth's orbit varies from nearly circular to more elliptical, as it is today. The more elliptical the shape of Earth's orbit, the greater the differences in insolation between summer and winter. At present, Earth's orbit is about halfway between these two extremes and is advancing toward maximum ellipticity about 40,000 years in the future. Proxy data shows glacial episodes at intervals of approximately 90,000 years, thus supporting the validity of this principle.

Volcanism

It has been proposed that volcanism might account for climate changes. A single massive eruption could affect Earth's climate system on a time scale of 1 to 10 years. Multiple eruptions over much longer time periods would have increasingly significant effects. Volcanic eruptions introduce huge quantities of particulate matter and sulfur dioxide into the atmosphere. Sulfate particles can lie suspended in the stratosphere for several years and reduce the quality of insolation. Such stratospheric particles can lead to reductions in surface temperature of a few degrees. Ash layers in Antarctic ice cores show a period of intense volcanic activity from about 30,000 to 17,000 years ago, during which time global temperatures dropped by over 5° F. The latter portion of this volcanic maximum coincided with the maximum extent of the last Pleistocene glaciation event. In modern times, the eruption of Mount Tambora on the Indonesian island of Sumbawa in 1815 was followed by the "year without a summer" in 1816 in the eastern United States and Europe. The eruption of Krakatoa in the Strait of Sunda in 1883 produced red sunsets for many months and may have contributed to the severe winters that followed in the Northern Hemisphere.

Massive eruptions of the 20th century include Katmai (1912), Agung (1963), Taal (1965), Mayon and Fernandina (1968), El Chicon (1982), and Mount Pinatubo (1991). Measurements and estimates of direct solar radiation indicate a reduction by 10% to 20% for several months following the Katmai eruption and an accompanying decrease in surface temperature. Observed temperatures in the tropical stratosphere increased by 11° F during 1964 following the Agung eruption, whereas surface temperatures decreased by 1° F. Detectable cooling followed the eruptions of El Chicon in Mexico and Mount Pinatubo in the Philippines.

Foreign Body Impacts

Although it sounds like material from a science fiction novel, the fact is that Earth's climate has been drastically altered following collision with a large foreign object such as an asteroid or a comet. In the vastness of space, many asteroids and comets exist whose movement will bring them to a collision with Earth at some future time. Thus far, 140 impact sites have been documented. Where are the others? The evidence has been masked by oceans, vegetation, and geologic processes. The moon, however, remains striking testimony to the reality of foreign body impacts. One only has to look at its cratered face to gain an appreciation for the large numbers of impacts. Fortunately, many would-be invaders burn up in Earth's atmosphere. Others produce no effect on the global climate system, although their effect on local regions can be devastating. A recent example of this occurred on June 30, 1908, in a remote region of Siberia. At that time, a meteoroid 180 to 200 feet in diameter exploded at 55,000 feet high. The energy in this detonation was estimated to have been 1,000 to 2,000 times stronger than the atomic bombs dropped on Nagasaki and Hiroshima in WWII. This blast devastated 700 square miles of forest. On the other hand, the El Chicxulub impact near present-day Yucatan caused the extinction of 70% of marine species and other species of animals, including the dinosaurs. These events remind us of our ultimate vulnerability and the sensitivity of Earth's climate system.

Anthropogenic Factors

Thus far, we have considered mechanisms of climate change that could be classified as naturally occurring. Another part of the climate change picture is anthropogenic changes, meaning they result either directly or indirectly from human activities. Many critical contemporary issues center on climate change brought about by the presence of humans on Earth. These controversial topics are covered later in the *Sourcebook*.

Perception of Climate

At one extreme, a climatic event is regarded as a supernatural act; at another extreme it is analyzed in mathematical terms as a system of physical processes. Climatic hazards evoke a broad spectrum of cultural perspectives that vary not only among individuals but also with time and distance. It is common for people to minimize the threat of predicted hazards and to resist procedures that might help avert the threat. Remoteness from an affected area also influences the level of concern.

In spite of the advances in technology, human societies have become more vulnerable to the hazards posed by long-term climatic change. Growing pressures on food supplies, energy resources, and living space are but a few of the factors contributing to modern humanity's vulnerability. In summary, our perception of Earth's climate system determines social, economic, and political decisions that are related to climate; we are all affected in one way or another.

The Process of Scientific Thought

Activity #1

Title: Different Sunlight

Objective: To understand how latitude affects climate

Materials Needed: globe, small thermometer, lamp

Procedure: Have a student hold a globe (or use a globe that's already mounted) while another student holds a small thermometer with its bulb resting on the equator. Position a heat lamp or a strong flashlight 6 inches directly above the bulb of the thermometer. Record the temperature after 30 seconds. Now move the thermometer (not the light source!) until the bulb rests on 45° N latitude. Wait 30 seconds and record the temperature again. Repeat with the bulb of the thermometer located at the North Pole.

Elementary

- Draw a picture of the globe and be sure to place the appropriate temperature at the equator at the right location.

- How does latitude affect climate? (Answer: Temperatures are normally lower owing to the less intense sunlight.)

- Look at appendix B or C and choose two cities that are located at least 10° of latitude apart. What do you find? (Answer: The city with the higher latitude likely has the lower average annual temperature.)

Secondary

- Repeat by taking temperature readings at 10° latitude intervals. Record the data in a table. Look up the average annual temperatures of a city near these latitudes from appendix B or C. How do the results of this experiment compare to the "real world?" (Answer: It would really be remarkable if it turned out exactly right. In truth, some of the data will not match the "real world." The moral? Latitude is not the only climatic control.)

Activity #2

Title: Seaside or Landlocked?

Objective: To illustrate how continentality affects climate

Materials Needed: two drinking glasses, two identical thermometers, water, soil, desk lamp

Procedure: Obtain two drinking glasses. Pour 4 inches of water into one glass and 4 inches of soil into another glass. Place one thermometer in the glass with water and another identical thermometer in the glass with soil. Be sure the bulb of each thermometer is covered. Compare the temperatures. If they are not the same, adjust the temperature of the water until it is the same temperature as the soil. Now that the water and the soil are the same temperature, position a desk lamp so that the light is evenly distributed over both glasses. After one hour read each thermometer. Turn the light off and note the temperature after another hour.

Elementary

- Draw a picture of both glasses with the light on. Place the temperature of each on the correct glass. Do the same when the lights are off.

- Explain the results briefly. (Answer: The soil heats and cools faster than the water.)

- Choose two cities from appendix B that are located at the same latitude. One city should be seaside and the other city should be landlocked. Compare their average annual temperature, the difference between the average January temperature and the average July temperature, and the extremes of record. What do you find? (Answer: The difference between a seaside location and a landlocked city will really be noticeable when one compares the difference between January and July as well as the all-time highest and lowest temperatures. The landlocked location will have a greater variation of both.)

Secondary

- Compare five pairs of cities from appendix B (United States) and appendix C (international cities). Be sure they are located near the same latitude. What do you find? (Answer: Basically, these other pairs of cities should exhibit the signature of continentality.)

Activity #3

Title: High and Low

Objective: To demonstrate how altitude affects climate

Materials Needed: heat source, thermometer

Procedure: Obtain a heat source (a hot plate or a desk lamp turned so that the light points upward) and place a thermometer at various heights above the heat source; note the temperature at each height.

Elementary

- Draw a picture of the heat coming from the hot plate or lamp. Place the temperature readings noted at various heights on the picture.

- Is the temperature higher or lower close to the heat source? (Answer: higher.) Is the temperature higher or lower farther away from the heat source? (Answer: lower.)

- Briefly explain how this applies to climate. (Answer: As altitude increases, temperature decreases. It works this way because the atmosphere is heated from below.)

- Choose two cities that are located near each other but have significantly different elevations. What do you find? (Answer: The station at the higher elevation will likely have a lower annual temperature.)

Secondary

- Choose two cities located near each other but that have a significant elevation difference. Calculate the difference between their average annual temperatures. Now compare that difference to the moist adiabatic lapse rate (3.3° F per 1,000 feet) and the dry adiabatic lapse rate (5.5° F per 1,000 feet). Which is closer? Why? (Answer: It's unlikely that the agreement will be very good because there are many other atmospheric processes that affect these temperatures.)

Activity #4

Title: Climate Investigator

Objective: To develop a climatological profile of your location

Materials Needed: brainpower, patience, outside resources

Procedure: See below.

Elementary and Secondary

The purpose of this activity is to develop a climatological profile of your city (or a nearby city). This type of study provides valuable information to industry when it considers where to build a new plant or to relocate an existing plant. In fact, when you finish this activity, take the results to your local chamber of commerce. They may already have some of the information on file, but it's likely you will be providing them with some they do not have. If they do not have any of this data, let them use this climatological profile—it may help attract business and industry to your town!

Your climatological profile should include the following information: average annual temperature, average annual precipitation, average temperatures for January and July, average relative humidity, prevailing wind direction, average windspeed, amount of snowfall, hours or percentage of sunshine per year, number of times the minimum temperature is at freezing or below, number of times the maximum temperature is 90° F or above, the all-time record high and low temperatures, the number of days with thunderstorms.

Assign one or two students to gather one bit of the above information. Possible resources are the NWS, a local TV station, the library, the Internet, and appendixes A, B, and C.

Activity #5

Title: Climate Comparisons

Objective: To understand why climate differs

Materials Needed: brainpower, patience, outside resources

Procedure: See below.

Elementary and Secondary

- Choose any two cities in the United States and research their climates. Make comparisons and contrasts. Give a written or oral report explaining how their climates are similar, how their climates differ, and the reasons for similarities and differences.

- Repeat using any two cities in the world.

Activity #6

Title: Climate and Culture

Objective: To link climate with culture

Materials Needed: brainpower, patience, library

Procedure: See below.

Elementary and Secondary

- Choose two cities in the United States that are far apart. Research the climate and culture. Deliver a written and/or an oral report explaining: how the climate affects the types of business and industry that are located in each city, their dress, diet, recreation, and the physical characteristics of the people.

- Repeat using two cities of the world from different continents.

Activity #7

Title: Baggy Climate

Objective: To demonstrate Earth's climate system

Materials Needed: gallon-size plastic bag, hole punch, open tap

Procedure: Punch two holes in a gallon-size plastic bag with a hole punch. Fill the bag with water from an open tap until it appears the water level in the bag is remaining nearly constant.

Elementary

- Draw a picture showing the tap water flowing into the top of the bag and small water jets coming from the two holes in the bag.

- Does this represent an open or a closed system? (Answer: open.)

- What does the open tap represent? (Answer: the sun, the source of energy for Earth's climate system.)

- What do the two jets of water represent? (Answer: outputs from Earth's climate system.)

Secondary

- Increase the flow rate from the tap. What happens? (Answer: Water overflows from the top of the bag.) What is your interpretation? (Answer: The system gets overloaded and responds by chaotic and uncontrollable behavior.) How would you apply this analogy to Earth's climate system? (Answer: If the sun suddenly increased its output by a significant amount, then Earth's climate system would be overwhelmed and the system operation would jump to a new level, perhaps one that is not favorable for life.)

- Decrease the flow rate from the tap. What happens? (Answer: More water flows out of the jets than is replaced by the tap.) What is your interpretation? (Answer: The system is underloaded and responds by operating at a very low ebb.) How would you apply this analogy to Earth's climate system? (Answer: If the sun suddenly decreased its output of energy by a significant amount, then Earth's climate system would seek a level of operation that would be very low compared to what existed before. Again, this situation probably would not be favorable for life.)

- What does this activity suggest about the Earth-sun relationship? (Answer: It's balanced; not too much energy to Earth and not too little.)

- Empty the bag and punch a third hole in the bag. What happens? (Answer: The output from the other two jets decreases.) What is your interpretation and application? (Answer: A new output pathway, called a feedback mechanism, develops and affects the climate system.)

Ideas for Science Fair Projects

1. All of the activities in this chapter are appropriate for science fair presentation.

2. "Country vs. City." Compare urban climates to nonurban climates. This is best done by comparing two nearby locations, one located in town and the other located in the country. The information included in this chapter is a beginning point.

3. Study the mesoclimate of your area using data from the state climatological publication, available from a local professional or the NWS. Discuss why there are differences.

4. Develop a project that describes Earth as a closed system. Define what a closed system is, how it applies to Earth, and the consequences for humanity.

5. Develop a project that describes Earth as an open system. Define what an open system is, how it applies to Earth, and its application to human activities.

6. Study the albedo of various surfaces. Apply what you learn to developing an idea: "Earth: The Bright Blue Planet." Include pictures and comments from astronauts.

7. Research the "food chain" mentioned near the beginning of the chapter. What is it? Describe its organization and the role climate plays in maintaining the food chain.

8. "Climates of the World." How are the various climates of earth classified? See pages 163 and 164.

9. Center a project on the urban climate. Note characteristics and how a major population center impacts the natural environment.

10. The United States has several features that affect climate. In "The United States: A Unique Geographical Laboratory" you can outline these important features and tell why and how they dictate the basic climate of the nation. Mention the Rockies, Gulf of Mexico, Pacific and Atlantic Oceans, Great Lakes, and the Appalachian Mountains.

11. "Regional Winds of the United States" is an appropriate topic. Include the Santa Ana Wind, the Chinook, and the "Norther" of Texas.

12. Choose any topographic feature and discuss how it affects climate.

13. "The Winds of Europe" will include a discussion of the mistral or bora, the sirocco, and the jugo.

14. Research specific ocean currents and their effect on climate. The United States has the Gulf Stream and the Pacific Current, Africa has the Canaries Current and the Benguela Current, and South America has the Humboldt Current.

15. Research past climates. Include evidence, methods, and a brief paleoclimatic calendar.

16. Develop a project that focuses on any of the mechanisms of climate change.

17. How has climate impacted the characteristics of humanity? The answers make for an intriguing project.

18. Center a project on the applications of climatology.

19. Research climate and its impact on business and industry.

20. Concentrate on how climate relates to human health and disease patterns. Include mental health and physical health. Talk to a psychologist/psychiatrist and a medical doctor.

School's Out!

1. Read a book about climate to a younger child.

2. Take your science fair project to a local civic club.

3. Write a story or a poem about climate.

4. Keep a phenological journal.

5. Talk to older people about the differences they see in today's climate compared to when they were younger.

6. Check out a book at the library about any aspect of climate.

7. Talk to a climatologist.

Chapter 12

Thunderstorms

There is no such thing as bad weather, only different types of good weather.
John Ruskin

The manifestations of atmospheric processes can be as harmless as a gentle summer breeze or as malevolent as a tornado. Many would disagree with John Ruskin, the English essayist and reformer, especially those who have lost loved ones, property, or have suffered personal injury or hardship themselves. Yet the mind of the scientist seeks passionately to understand, and strives to reduce the impact of such fierce episodes of weather.

Thunderstorm Climatology

A thunderstorm is a storm accompanied by lightning and thunder. It is the presence of lightning (and the thunder that results from it) that separates a thunderstorm from all other atmospheric phenomena.

It has been estimated that about 100,000 thunderstorms occur annually in the 48 contiguous states, distributed as shown in figure 12.1. Thunderstorms are very common along the Gulf Coast from southeast Texas to Florida, where at least 60 thunderstorms per year are counted. The most active portion of this region is central Florida, where up to 100 thunderstorms can occur. Most Gulf Coast thunderstorms occur during the warm season, April through September, as daytime heating activates the moist, unstable Gulf air

mass. Frontal invasions are also a frequent cause of thunderstorms.

The second most active thunderstorm region in the United States is in southeastern Colorado and northeastern New Mexico. Here, thunderstorm frequency is augmented by the dryline and upslope associated with the Rocky Mountains. Activity is more seasonal than in the Gulf Coast, with the warm season accounting for 90% of all thunderstorms.

Thunder is heard only a few times each year across a broad area along the Pacific Coast. In this region, thunderstorm activity is suppressed by the cool, stable air associated with the Pacific Current offshore; thus, most rain falls as light to moderate. Thunderstorms along the West Coast are normally triggered by vigorous weather systems.

Fig. 12.1. The annual number and distribution of thunderstorms in the United States, based on National Weather Service records.

The Thunderstorm Life Cycle

Much of what modern scientists know about the thunderstorm life cycle is based on the 1940s research called the Thunderstorm Project, which was carried out in Ohio and Florida. The most important result was the discovery of the basic building block of the thunderstorm, the "cell," a region of relatively strong upward air motion called an updraft. Each cell has a distinct life cycle consisting of three logical and progressive stages.

Stage one, the towering cumulus stage, is a time of significant changes in the nature of the cloud. The updraft, at 20 to 25 mph, is strong enough to distinguish it from ordinary cumulus clouds, and its size separates it from smaller clouds. The cloud is typically 3 to 5 miles across at its base and reaches a vertical extent of nearly 20,000 feet, penetrating the freezing level in the atmosphere. The flow of air converges into the cloud from miles around. During the latter portion of the towering cumulus stage, precipitation-sized particles form and a radar echo is first detected. At this stage, lightning discharges are nonexistent, except in very rare circumstances. Figure 12.2 illustrates the towering cumulus stage.

In the mature stage both a substantial updraft and a significant downdraft occur within the same cell (see fig. 12.3). The formation of a storm-scale downdraft coincides roughly with the beginning of precipitation descent, which may require 5 to 12 minutes before reaching the surface. This stage is characterized by the greatest vigor of activity. The updraft and downdraft are at their maximum strengths, lightning is most frequent, and precipitation is heaviest. It is at this point that the maximum vertical extent of the cloud is reached and may vary from 25,000 to 70,000 feet. The cloud has grown to 5 to 10 miles in horizontal extent. The mature stage is brief, lasting only about 10 minutes on average.

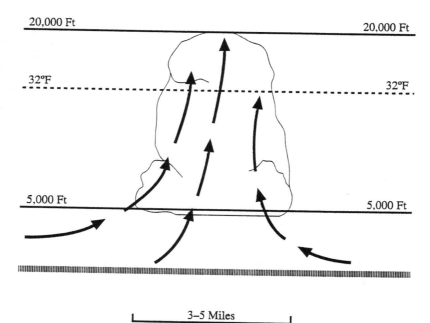

Fig. 12.2. The towering cumulus stage.

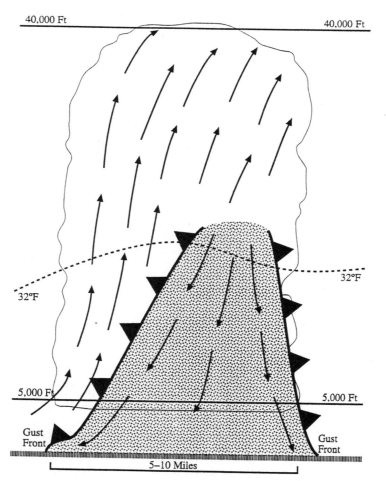

Fig. 12.3. The mature stage of a thunderstorm.

The thunderstorm downdraft arises from two processes: drag associated with falling precipitation and evaporation of smaller droplets. The gust front is the lateral spreading out on the surface of the downdraft and marks the surface boundary of the thunderstorm outflow.

In nonsevere, ordinary thunderstorms, the mature stage contains the seeds of its own demise, the downdraft. It spreads out on the ground, eliminating the convergence of warm, moist air into the cloud that had served as fuel. The downdraft undercuts the updraft and kills it. With the supply of energy gone, the cell quickly decays. Precipitation intensity decreases; lightning flashes decrease and end, and the cloud material evaporates. An anvil-shaped top is common and represents the only remnant of the once-mighty thunderstorm cell. The typical thunderstorm cell lasts 30 to 45 minutes. Figure 12.4 shows the important features of the dissipating stage.

A Classification Scheme for Thunderstorms

Recently, scientists have proposed a new classification scheme for thunderstorms that recognizes two distinct types of thunderstorms: the supercell and the nonsupercell. Although the updraft of both thunderstorm types may be large, strong, and persistent, the essential difference is that the supercell thunderstorm contains a rotating updraft called a mesocyclone.

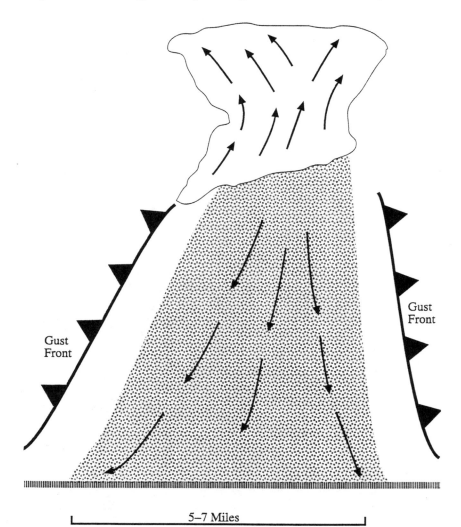

Gust Front

Gust Front

5–7 Miles

Fig. 12.4. The dissipating stage of a thunderstorm.

The Nonsupercell Thunderstorm

Nonsupercell thunderstorms include several different types of storms: multicell, squall line, and pulse. The multicell thunderstorm is essentially a stronger and better-organized ordinary thunderstorm. The distinguishing characteristic lies in the organization of individual cells, or elements. In the multicell case, there seems to be some type of larger-scale organizing process, possibly related to the way the convection interacts with its environment. Multicell thunderstorms can produce severe weather resulting in flash floods, tornadoes, hail, damaging wind, and frequent lightning.

A squall line thunderstorm is a lateral arrangement of connected cells. In this situation, airflow is convergent into the front of the line and the downdraft descends on the rear of the storm. The vast majority of squall line thunderstorms are nonsevere, although small hail, strong wind, and heavy rain can accompany them.

The pulse thunderstorm, recognized during the 1970s, closely resembles an ordinary single-cell thunderstorm but seems to have a much stronger updraft that "pulses" briefly. The pulse thunderstorm has a brief life span, and commonly develops in the states bordering the Gulf of Mexico during late spring through early fall. Although it rarely produces tornadoes, it can produce damaging nontornadic winds and hail. High rainfall rates, even over the brief life span of the storm, promote flash flooding, especially in urban areas.

The Supercell Thunderstorm

Supercell thunderstorms, the most dangerous type of storms, are associated with almost all major tornadoes, as well as the majority of "giant" hail-falls (hen-egg size or larger), and winds exceeding 70 mph.

Structurally, the supercell is a massive, 1,000-cubic-mile cloud formation that represents the "cancerous" growth of a normal cell. Highly organized, the storm can live for hours and travel 100 to 250 miles. The key element in the supercell's ability to outlive other thunderstorm types is the separation of the updraft and downdraft. Recall that the ordinary thunderstorm cell discussed earlier was short-lived because the downdraft stifled the inflow of energy to the cell. In the supercell, however, updraft and downdraft remain separate, allowing the storm to travel long distances.

The supercell is clearly larger as is evidenced by a radar identification in figure 12.5: the "hook echo." The hook, as it is commonly called, is the visible manifestation of the mesocyclone.

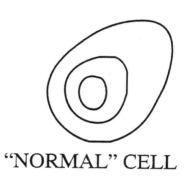

"NORMAL" CELL

"CANCEROUS" SUPERCELL

Fig. 12.5. A plan view of an ordinary and a supercell thunderstorm.

Supercell environments are highly unstable, capable of producing very strong updrafts. The vertical wind profile increases with height. It is common to see a surface wind from the south or southeast at 15 mph while, at 6,000 feet, the wind is from the southwest at 50 mph or higher, resulting in a spin. Hence, the updraft not only feeds the storm energy, but it ingests spinning air as well.

What Is a Severe Thunderstorm?

The National Weather Service determines whether a storm is severe, based on hail size, windspeed, and the existence of a tornado. If hail size exceeds 0.75 inch, or there is a windspeed of 50 knots (58 mph) or better, the storm is classified as severe. Of course, the presence of a tornado also earns a classification of severe.

About 10% of all thunderstorms produce any type of severe weather. Thus, the vast majority of thunderstorms are nonsevere, at least according to official definitions.

Lightning and Thunder

Lightning is a transient, high-current electric discharge with a path length measured in thousands of feet. Thunder is the audible result of the lightning. Lightning involves a tremendous current, measuring millions of volts. A typical lightning flash flows more electricity than could be produced by all U.S. power plants combined in that increment of time. Despite that fact, a lightning flash is not particularly energetic because the flash is so brief. In fact, the average lightning stroke is capable of powering a lightbulb for a few months. Virtually all of the energy associated with the lightning discharge is converted into light, sound (thunder), radio waves, and heat. The peak temperature of 55,000° F in the lightning channel lasts only a few millionths of a second (but it's five times hotter than the surface of the sun!).

Scientists, using data from lightning detection networks, estimate 50 million lightning strikes occur in the United States each year. But this is only the national average; there is a lot of variation because some parts of the United States experience more lightning than do other parts. The Pacific Northwest and West Coast have few lightning strikes (two or less per square mile). In contrast, central Florida receives about 40 to 45 hits per square mile. Worldwide, the estimate is that 2,000 thunderstorms are in progress at any instant and produce 80 to 100 lightning strikes per second.

Lightning flashes are divided into two distinct categories: cloud discharges, which do not contact Earth, and cloud-to-ground. Of these, cloud discharges are more frequent and can occur cloud-to-cloud, intracloud, or cloud-to-air.

The second primary type of lightning connects the cloud and Earth. Its common name is cloud-to-ground lightning. Although outnumbered significantly by cloud discharges, the cloud-to-ground flashes are by far the most important to humankind, because they are responsible for death and injury to humans and animals; damage to computers and power grids, communication systems, power lines, and transformers; and the ignition of forest fires. Table 12.1 presents the number of deaths and locations where lightning most often strikes.

In addition to the two major classes of lightning, there is a rare controversial form of lightning called "ball" lightning. Scientists have argued for many years about whether it actually exists. It appears as a luminous, usually red sphere near the strike point of a cloud-to-ground flash. The orange-to basketball-sized balls last a few seconds and move horizontally along solid objects, floating in the air, or bouncing on the ground. Hissing noises may emanate from such balls or they may explode or disappear without a sound. In addition to appearing outdoors, ball lightning has been reported to occur near or in electrical outlets in houses and inside all-metal airplanes, next to windows, and in chimneys.

LOCATION	# OF DEATHS	% OF DEATHS
Open Fields, Ball Parks Open Spaces	861	28%
Under Trees	545	17%
Boating, Fishing, and Other Water-Related	414	13%
Near Heavy Equipment	196	6%
Golf Courses	123	4%
Telephones	33	1%
Other/Unknown	953	30%

Table 12.1. A Summary of Lighting Deaths in the United States for the Period 1959-1992
(Source: National Weather Service)

Finally, what about a lightning discharge from a clear sky, the so-called bolt from the blue? Such an occurrence almost always refers to those times when a lightning discharge originates at the top of a parent cloud and strikes far away (sometimes 20 to 30 miles) from the cloud.

Cumulonimbus Electrification

How does a cumulonimbus actually become electrically charged to the point that lightning is produced? Many theories have been suggested and it is now clear there is probably no one unique charging mechanism. Consider the actual charge structure of a cumulonimbus as shown in figure 12.6.

Essentially, the upper cumulonimbus is positively charged while the middle and lower regions are negatively charged. A relatively small positive region is also associated with the precipitation cascade. A positive charge is induced on the ground due to the potent negative charge apparent in the lower region of the cloud. This area on the ground is sometimes called a "positive shadow." The negative charges are forced to scatter from the area located beneath the positive center in the lower portion of the cloud.

It is helpful to consider lightning in terms of being a process, following a well-defined sequence of steps. The total lightning process is called a *flash*, and has a duration of about one second or less. A flash is comprised of various discharge components, typically three or four high-current pulses called *strokes*, each lasting a tiny fraction of a second. Because of this, lightning often appears to "flicker."

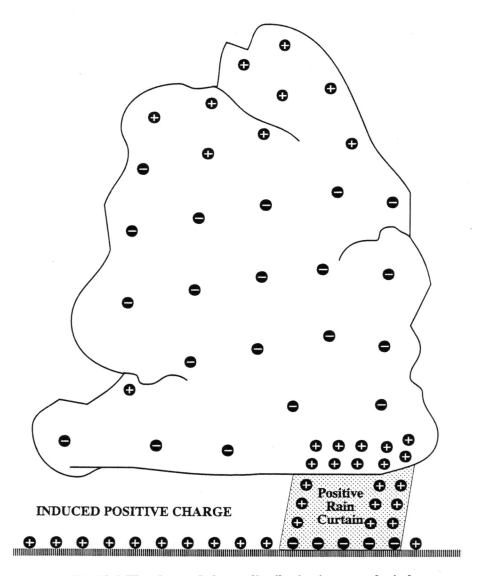

Fig. 12.6. The observed charge distribution in a cumulonimbus.

The Steps in the Lightning Process

Modern research indicates that the lightning process is a sequence of events: preliminary breakdown, stepped leader, attachment, and the return stroke.

The preliminary breakdown is indicated by the initial movement of electric current in the lower portion of the cumulonimbus. The detailed physics of preliminary breakdown are not understood but the concept is, basically, that static electricity builds in the lower portion of the cloud and negative electrons flow, triggering the preliminary breakdown. As the initial flow of electricity builds, it eventually descends from the base of the cloud.

The descending, growing current of electricity emerging from the cloud base is called a stepped leader, so named because this electric current descends in fits and jerks, or "steps," of about 150 feet in length. As the stepped leader moves at very high speeds toward the ground, it branches. Each "step" is completed in only a few microseconds, a phenomenon normally not seen by the human eye but believed to contain a channel 3 to 30 feet in width.

As the stepped leader continues its journey toward Earth, its electric field comes close enough to the ground so that any conducting object such as a hill, tree, utility pole, building, tower, or aircraft in flight will begin to emit an upward-seeking electric current called a streamer. The streamer is a positive electric current. When the negative stepped leader unites with the positive streamer, the "short circuit" between cloud and ground is completed, normally some 150 feet high. The attachment process has occurred. Figure 12.7 details the attachment process.

Immediately following attachment the return stroke becomes visible, the brightest part of the process, and lowers negative charges to Earth, often causing damage and even death. The return stroke is a brilliant surge of electric current, spreading in both directions from the point of attachment traveling at speeds greater than one-half the speed of light. Figure 12.8 illustrates the return stroke. Does lightning travel up or down? The return stroke travels in both directions from the point of attachment. Thus, the return stroke moves downward some 150 feet and upward the remaining length of the channel (usually a few thousand feet)

to cloud base. But since the distance to cloud base is so much greater than the short trek to the ground, the human eye only responds to that portion of the visible return stroke. Therefore, the return stroke appears to be initiated downward and lowers negative charges to the ground, but what we actually see is that part of the return stroke that moves up the length of the channel to cloud base. It appears to the human eye to move downward, but that is just an optical illusion.

It should be mentioned that most flashes contain multiple strokes and are called composite flashes. In this case, after the return stroke, the process would repeat. Another leader (called a dart leader to distinguish it from the stepped leader that occurred first) jumps down the same path, without stepping, of the first return stroke, because its ionized path offers least resistance. In this way, conditions favor the formation of a second return stroke. An important aspect of this process is that it debunks the myth that lightning does not strike the same place twice. In 20% to 40% of all cloud-to-ground flashes, the dart leader propagates down only a portion of the channel carved out by the initial return stroke and then forges a different path to the ground. In these instances, lightning actually is capable of striking two or more locations at or near the same time.

Effects of Lightning

Although the effects of lightning can be adverse, beneficial effects include maintenance of the fair weather electric field and a process called *nitrogen fixation*, which plants use in food-making. Nitrogen fixation is the process of converting nitrogen gas into nitrogen compounds by

bonding nitrogen to an atom of another element. This "fixed" nitrogen can then be used by plants as nourishment. Nitrogen fixation is accomplished in the lightning channel by the extremely high temperatures and the compounds are brought to the plants by precipitation.

Thunder

Thunder is the audible sound produced by a lightning flash. Because of this immense heat, the air along the lightning channel experiences rapid and violent expansion. This process occurs so

quickly and violently that the sound originates as an explosion. This explosive sound reaches our ears as thunder (see fig. 12.9).

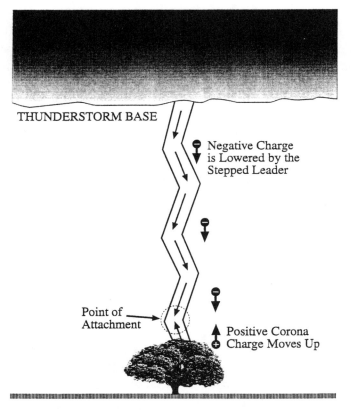

Fig. Figure 12.7. The attachment process for lightning.

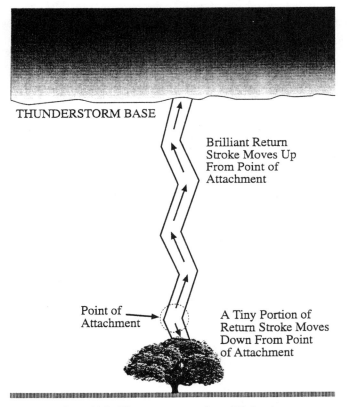

Fig. 12.8. The return stroke of lightning.

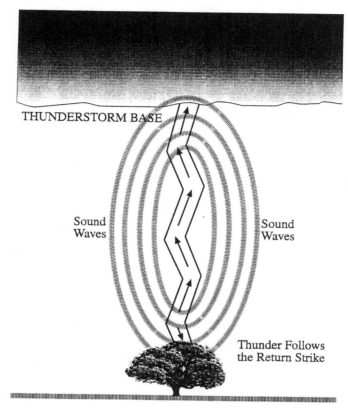

THUNDERSTORM BASE

Sound
Waves

Sound
Waves

Thunder Follows
the Return Strike

Fig. 12.9. Thunder results from a lightning discharge.

Safety Rules

Lightning kills more people than hurricanes and tornadoes combined; thus, it represents a formidable weather threat. Observance of these safety precautions may mean the difference between life and death:

- Stay indoors. If outdoors, seek shelter immediately in a nonmetal building of substantial dimensions.

- While inside stay away from open doors, windows, fireplaces, stoves, sinks, metal pipes, and plug-in electric appliances.

- Do not use plug-in electric appliances.

- Do not use the telephone; lightning can cause injury or death if it strikes nearby. An exception to this rule would be to report a tornado, wind damage, or a medical emergency.

- If you must remain outdoors, stay away from fences, power lines and utility poles, pipelines, and metal fabrication.

- Put down metal fishing poles and golf clubs.

- Get off heavy equipment.

- Get away from lakes, ponds, rivers, swimming pools, and water amusement parks.

- Leave ball fields, small boats, and golf courses.

- An automobile is generally safe from lightning. Seek refuge in an automobile if no substantial shelter is nearby.

- If you are caught outside with no substantial shelter and no vehicle nearby, lie flat or squat down in a ditch, cave, or ravine.

- In open country, do not be the highest object around; get low and stay low. Avoid hilltops and mountains.

- Never seek shelter under an isolated tree or a small clump of trees.

- Some claim they have "felt" an electrical charge before being hit by lightning or experiencing a near-hit. Evidence of this is a tingly feeling on skin or hair standing on end. If this appears to be happening, drop to the ground immediately and roll—it's better than being struck by lightning.

- One last bit of advice. Persons struck by lightning receive severe electric shock and they may be burned, but they carry no residual electric charge and can be handled safely. CPR techniques have been used to revive many people, and recovery is usually complete, although loss or impairment of sight and hearing may linger permanently. Other damage to the nervous system may also persist permanently.

Hail

Hail, like lightning, is a byproduct of thunderstorms. It has great destructive capacity, with annual crop and property losses from hail in the United States pushing the $1 billion mark. Despite its destructive ability, U.S. hailstorms normally do not turn deadly.

Hail is precipitation in the form of ice 5 millimeters or greater in diameter. The individual units of hail are called hailstones and are classified by size as seen in table 12.2. A hailstone is partially or totally opaque and has a layered, shell-like internal structure. Shapes are usually roughly spherical or conical, ellipsoidal, often with small lobes or knots, and spherical-irregular with protuberances, and they fall almost exclusively during intense thunderstorms.

The internal composition and structure of a typical hailstone, as shown in figure 12.10, have been known since 1806 when Alessandro Volta, an Italian, first investigated it. He described two characteristics considered fundamental to hail science. First, hail contains an alternating series of clear and opaque rings. Second, there is an opaque central nucleus, or what is now termed an embryo.

Hail has been known to contain a variety of substances. In addition to the nucleating particle encased by the embryo, most hailstones contain material scavenged out of the atmosphere within or below the cloud. Among the things found in hail are iron and chloride particles, fungi and bacteria, insects, frogs, fish, and even slight, nonharmful levels of radioactivity.

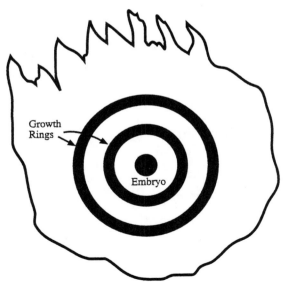

Fig. 12.10. Cross-section of a large hailstone.

SIZE (DIAMETER) OF HAILSTONE	EVERYDAY ASSOCIATION
1/4 inch	Pea
1/2 inch	Marble
3/4 inch	Penny or Dime
1 inch	Nickel or Quarter
1 1/4 inch	Half-Dollar
1 1/2 inch	Walnut
1 3/4 inch	Golfball
2 inches	Hen Egg
2 1/2 inches	Tennis Ball
2 3/4 inches	Baseball
4 inches	Small Grapefruit
4 1/2 inches	Softball
5 inches	Large Grapefruit

Table 12.2. Guidelines for Estimating Hail Size

Hail Climatology

Several regions of the world are known for frequent hail occurrence, some 3 to 10 times per year. These areas cover only a small portion of Earth's surface, but some of these "hail belts" are located in prime agricultural areas, and the frequency and severity of the hail season often determine success or failure for many farming operations. The two largest contiguous areas are in the Northern Hemisphere, one in the Great Plains of North America, extending some 2,000 miles from the Canadian provinces of Alberta and Saskatchewan southward across the Dakotas, Nebraska, Wyoming, Colorado, Kansas, Oklahoma, and Texas. Figure 12.11 shows the distribution of hail reports across the United States.

Hail shows a daytime peak and a nighttime minimum. Generally the afternoon peak runs from late afternoon through early evening, from 3:00 to 7:00 P.M. local time. A well-defined hail season extends from April through July.

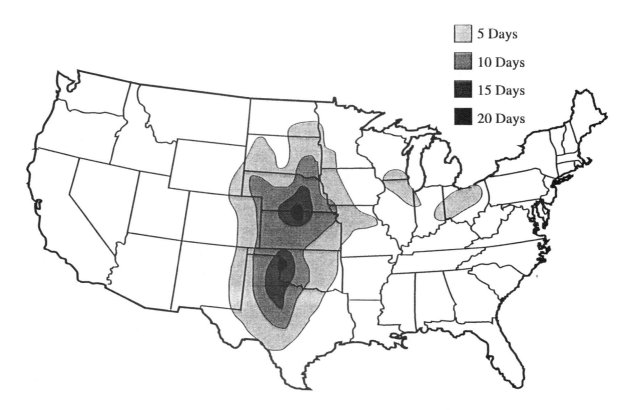

5 Days
10 Days
15 Days
20 Days

Fig. 12.11. Average number of days per year per 10,000-square-mile area with hail $\frac{3}{4}$-inch in diameter or larger, based on National Weather Service data.

The Physics of Hail Formation

The formation of hail occurs in the updraft of thunderstorms. In order for a hailstone to grow to a given size, an updraft speed roughly equivalent to or greater than the stone's terminal fall speed must be present.

A critical factor of hail formation involves the embryo. Although much research has been done, there seems to be little understanding of the embryo's origin. It is generally agreed that a hail embryo probably originates from either a graupel particle or a "frozen raindrop."

Hail formation takes place in a cloud of supercooled water droplets formed from the process of condensation or by several types of ice nucleation. Deposition of water vapor leads to the growth of ice crystals, which grow at the expense of minute cloud droplets. As the ice crystals grow they collide with cloud droplets that are essentially stationary and capture them. They freeze quickly, initiating the growth of graupel. Growth continues as supercooled water droplets are accreted on the surface of

the graupel particle. These growing hailstones can shed some of their liquid water skin in the form of large drops, especially when they rotate. As this conversion of cloud water into raindrops takes place at subfreezing temperatures, the newly formed larger drops can either freeze and form a new hailstone embryo or be captured by other hailstones. The alternating growth of a hailstone is the result of several passes through the updraft, until the stone finally becomes heavy enough to fall to the surface.

Although this "recycling" hypothesis of hail growth remains the explanation of choice for many nonspecialized authors, many meteorologists have called into question the necessity of up-and-down trips for a growing hailstone. In fact, some findings suggest that the concentric growth rings observed in the internal structure of hailstones are the result of changes in the growth manner of the stone. This growth can be "wet" or "dry."

As we have seen, hailstones grow by accreting supercooled water. Heat release associated with freezing this water is substantial. If the hailstone can dissipate all of this released heat, then dry growth occurs through deposition. If, however, all of the heat cannot be dissipated, the hailstone surface temperature remains at freezing and some accreted water remains unfrozen. This unfrozen water may either be shed or remain with the hailstone in cavities. It appears that variations in the position of the stone in the updraft, combined with local changes of the environmental factors superimposed on the basic updraft, are sufficient to produce alternating growth modes.

The Downdraft

Another important byproduct of a thunderstorm is the downdraft. We've all felt the refreshing wind from a nearby shower, yet there are times when a downdraft can become a deadly and destructive force.

Two factors are responsible for producing and maintaining a downdraft. The first is evaporative cooling. Tiny precipitation particles falling through the cloud are easily evaporated, producing a "chilling" effect. As the air becomes colder and heavier, the sinking of the air contributes to the downdraft.

The thunderstorm downdraft also arises through a "drag effect" associated with falling precipitation. A curtain of rain falling through the thunderstorm imparts some of its momentum to the surrounding air. Thus, the precipitation actually succeeds in "pulling" or "dragging" the air down with it.

The evaporative cooling and precipitation drag are not mutually exclusive; they operate in tandem to produce the thunderstorm downdraft. The relative importance of each mechanism will vary from one instance to another, but they work together in all thunderstorms.

Under certain environmental conditions the normal thunderstorm downdraft takes on destructive and potentially deadly proportions. A downburst is a concentrated thunderstorm downdraft and can be strong enough to cause property damage and threaten the safety of humans.

Those areas that experience the most hail are also at highest risk for damaging downbursts. Figure 12.12 shows the distribution of severe thunderstorm winds from the 1950s to the early 1980s. Those areas that experience damaging downbursts are generally located farther east than the hail belts.

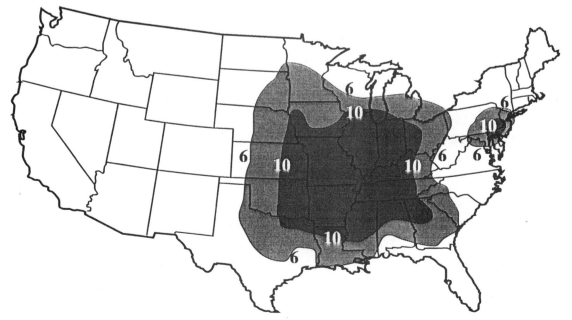

Fig. 12.12. Annual distribution of damaging wind reports per 10,000-square-mile area, based on National Weather Service data.

The Process of Scientific Thought

The first six activities are designed to illustrate how static electricity occurs. Try them!

Activity #1

Title: Static Electricity I

Materials Needed: smooth-soled shoes

Procedure: Rub both feet vigorously on a carpeted floor and then touch a metal object or another person. You will feel a minor "shock" and may even hear the discharge.

Activity #2

Title: Static Electricity II

Materials Needed: plastic comb, plastic or metal pen, puffed rice

Procedure: Rub each object vigorously on a piece of fur, flannel, or wool. Place near the puffed rice and watch the puffed rice move.

Activity #3

Title: Static Electricity III

Materials Needed: fluorescent lightbulb, piece of cloth

Procedure: Darken the room and rub a fluorescent lightbulb briskly with a piece of fur, flannel, or wool. You will see light from the static electricity.

Activity #4

Title: Static Electricity IV

Materials Needed: plastic spoon, woolen cloth

Procedure: Turn tap water on low so that a fine stream of water is produced. Rub a plastic spoon vigorously and place it near the stream. The water stream moves toward the spoon.

Activity #5

Title: Static Electricity V

Materials Needed: metal baking tray, drinking glass, balloon, cloth

Procedure: Darken the room and place a flat baking tray on a dry drinking glass. Blow up a balloon and rub it briskly on a piece of flannel, wool, or fur cloth. Place the balloon on the tray. Put your index finger close to the edge of the tray. An electric shock jumps between the plate and your fingers.

Activity #6

Title: Static Electricity VI

Materials Needed: cloth, plastic spoon, salt and pepper

Procedure: Sprinkle a mixture of salt and pepper on a table. Rub a plastic spoon briskly on a piece of cloth and slowly move the spoon toward the salt and pepper. The pepper responds first because it is lighter. Put the spoon closer and the salt responds too.

> The following apply to all of the above activities.

Elementary

- Have students draw a picture.

- Briefly explain what happened. (Answer: Electrons are rubbed off, thereby causing an electric charge.)

- How is this similar to natural lightning? (Answer: Both involve charge separation and both are a flow of electrons, or electricity.)

Secondary

- Devise other experiments that demonstrate static electricity.

- Research the possibility of harnessing lightning as an energy source for commercial or residential use.

- Explore the nature of electricity in more detail.

Activity #7

Title: Dancing with Electricity

Objective: To demonstrate how a cumulonimbus induces electric charge on the ground

Materials Needed: flat metal plate or sheet of aluminum foil, tissue paper, pane of glass, piece of cloth, two books each about 2 inches thick

Procedure: Lay a pane of glass between two books with a flat metal plate or sheet of aluminum foil underneath. Cut out from tissue paper figurines that are about an inch tall. Rub the top of the glass pane vigorously with a piece of fur, flannel, wool, or soft leather. The figures will dance!

Elementary

- Draw a picture. Label those materials that experience an electric charge (plate or foil, glass pane, figurines).

- What does rubbing the glass with the cloth do? (Answer: It strips away electrons, thus giving the cloth an electric charge.)

- Why do the figurines move? (Answer: The charge that exists on the glass attracts the figures and charges them by inducement.)

- Describe how this concept applies to a real thunderstorm. (Answer: The thundercloud induces, or forces, a charge on the ground, just like rubbing the glass induced a charge on the figurines.)

Secondary

- Repeat using different materials. How did this affect the results? (Answer: You might notice different levels of activity from the figurines.)

- How does this apply to real thunderstorms? (Answer: Different thunderstorms produce varying amounts of lightning.)

- What factor(s) do you think determine how much lightning a thunderstorm produces? (Answer: The updraft is the storm's energy source. In general, larger and stronger updrafts tend to produce the most electrically active storms.)

Activity #8

Title: Bang!

Objective: To demonstrate the sound we call thunder

Materials Needed: paper bag

Procedure: Fill the bag with air by blowing into it. Twist the open end and hold it closed. Hit the bag hard with your free hand. The bag will break and a loud noise will be heard.

Elementary

- Draw a picture of the sound waves coming from the exploded bag.

- Explain how this is like thunder. (Answer: Hitting the bag causes the air inside to compress so quickly that the pressure breaks the bag. The air rushing out of the broken bag pushes the air outside the bag away. This sets up a wavelike movement of air away from the bag. This is sound. Thunder results from violent expansion of air along the channel of a lightning discharge. Sound waves are produced and reach our ears as thunder.)

- Have students discuss orally the different types of sounds thunder makes.

Secondary

- Look into the nature of sound. Explain how sound travels through air, liquids, and solids.

- The intensity of sound is measured in decibels. Find out how many decibels there are in each of the following: rocket engine (180), jet at takeoff (150), clap of thunder (120), car horn at 3 feet (110), lawn mower (90), hair dryer (80), vacuum cleaner (70), ordinary conversation (60), whisper (30), leaves rustling (10).

- The speed of sound waves depends on the density of the substance through which they pass and the temperature of the substance. Have students find out the speed sound travels in air, water, brass, granite, and steel. (Answers: At 72° F sound waves travel at 1,126 ft/sec in air, 4,820 ft/sec in water, 11,500 ft/sec in brass, 12,960 ft/sec for granite, and 16,800 ft/sec in steel.) Convert these speeds to miles per hour.

Activity #9

Title: Updraft

Objective: To illustrate the thunderstorm updraft and its role in hail production

Materials Needed: source of compressed air, funnel, Ping-Pong ball

Procedure: Attach a funnel to a source of compressed air such as a vacuum cleaner. Turn on the vacuum and balance a Ping-Pong ball with the airstream.

Elementary

- Draw a picture of the airstream and illustrate how it holds the Ping-Pong ball up.

- What does the airstream represent? (Answer: The thunderstorm updraft.)

- What does the Ping-Pong ball represent? (Answer: A hailstone.)

- What does this experiment show about the thunderstorm updraft and its role in hail production? (Answer: The updraft holds the hailstone aloft.)

- Try to repeat using airstreams of different strengths and other balls besides Ping-Pong balls. What is your fundamental conclusion about the relationship between the updraft and hail? (Answer: You should find that stronger updrafts will support larger and heavier hailstones.)

- Have students discuss their personal experiences with hail.

Secondary

- As a class, research and present information on five hailstorms that affected your state in the past.

- There is a relationship between the speed of the thunderstorm updraft and the size of a hailstone that it will support. For example, a 0.5-inch-diameter hailstone can be supported by an updraft of 35 mph, a 1.5-inch hailstone requires an updraft of 68 mph, and a 2.5-inch stone requires an updraft of 81 mph. Draw a graph of updraft speed vs. expected hail size. What updraft speeds would be necessary to support the truly giant hail of softball or grapefruit size? (Answer: more than 100 mph!)

Activity #10

Title: Downdraft

Objective: To demonstrate one way that thunderstorm downdrafts originate

Materials Needed: large rectangular dish several inches deep, large drinking glass that is half full of water, small candle

Procedure: Obtain a large rectangular dish that is several inches deep. Place a small lighted candle in one end. In the other end, quickly pour out the glass of water. The candle flame will flicker.

Elementary

- Draw a picture of the pouring water and illustrate how it causes the candle flame to flicker.

- In nature, what does pouring out the water in the drinking glass represent? (Answer: The cascade of precipitation from a thunderstorm or a shower.)

- Why does the candle flicker? (Answer: The water falling into the other end of the dish causes the air to move. This air movement disturbs the candle flame.)

- Explain how this activity is like a real thunderstorm. (Answer: This activity demonstrates one of the primary causes of thunderstorm downdrafts—a "drag effect" created by the cascade of falling precipitation. This physical movement imparts momentum to surrounding air molecules, causing them to move. This force is initiated downward, thus the air is forced to move down. We know this downward-moving mass of air from a thunderstorm to be the downdraft.)

Secondary

- Repeat the activity with the glass containing just barely enough water to cover the bottom. How does this affect the results? (Answer: Should see less movement of the candle flame.)

- Repeat with the glass full. How does this affect the results? (Answer: Should see more movement of the candle flame.)

- State a generality that appears true from these results. (Answer: The more water that is dumped out, the more disturbed the candle flame becomes.)

- Apply this to real thunderstorms. (Answer: High wind frequently occurs when a large cascade of precipitation falls.)

- Which storm type does this typify? (Answer: The HPE supercell.)

Ideas for Science Fair Projects

1. "Society Responds to a Storm." Address the social context of thunderstorms. Mention their impact on life and property, financial considerations, displacement of population, impact on public events, impact on public services, and the effort to prepare and educate the public.

2. Any of the activities are suitable for presentation at a science fair.

3. Center a project on the life cycle of a thunderstorm. Follow the presentation given earlier in this chapter.

4. Outline the types of storms. Follow the presentation earlier in this chapter.

5. "The Super Storm." Enough information is given in this chapter to develop a project that focuses on the supercell thunderstorm only.

6. Consider the historical heritage of lightning. The information in this chapter will be a starting point.

7. Discuss the various types and forms of lightning. Be sure to include clear air discharges and ball lightning. Photos would be very helpful.

8. Center a project on Earth's fair weather electric field. How does it work? Why does it exist? Is it important? Include a sketch. Make sure you mention the role of thunderstorms as mechanisms that maintain the fair weather electric field.

9. Focus a project on how a cumulonimbus cloud becomes electrified. Include a sketch.

10. The lightning process makes a good science fair topic.

11. Outline the process of hail formation. Be sure to explain how hail gets big, the embryo, and the concentric growth rings. Include table 12.2.

12. "Hail Belts." Discuss when and where hail occurs in the world. Be sure you can explain the existence of hail belts.

13. Discuss the thunderstorm downdraft and how it develops; mention downbursts and microbursts, and include figure 12.12.

14. Try to find enough information for a project on lightning occurrences on other planets.

School's Out!

1. Help formulate a plan for storm preparedness at home.

2. Keep a log of thunderstorm occurrences at home for a year.

3. Try to observe the entire life cycle of a single thunderstorm.

4. Take your science fair project to a local service organization.

5. Observe thunderstorms visually and try to figure out which type you are seeing.

6. Try to estimate the windspeed associated with thunderstorms at home or school. Use the Beaufort Wind Chart (table 6.1).

7. Estimate hail size and preserve the stone.

8. Observe lightning and try to decide which type you see.

9. Read a book about storms to a younger child.

10. Write a poem about storms, hail, wind, lightning, or thunder.

11. Write a story where a storm affects a character or is a central element to the plot.

12. Look into lightning on other planets by reading at the library.

13. Cut open a hailstone and see if you can find the embryo and concentric rings.

14. Talk to an older adult about some of the storms experienced in his or her lifetime.

Chapter 13

Tornadoes

*So the whirlwind . . . moves things by the wind in the direction in which it is blowing . . .
and forcibly snatches up whatever it meets.*
Aristotle, *Meteorologica*

In the above text Aristotle presents his observation of the "whirlwind." Some biblical references from the Old Testament undoubtedly predate Aristotle. For as long as humans have lived on Earth, encounters with tornadoes have frightened and fascinated us. There is an aesthetic quality to tornadoes that is actually appealing, an ironic beauty that masks their deadly potential.

A tornado is a violently rotating column of air that descends from a parent cloud structure and is in contact with the ground. The word "violent" is used in order to separate the tornado from weaker vortices. It is also an appropriate adjective because tornadoes represent the most concentrated example of power that the atmosphere produces naturally. A tornado contains both horizontal and vertical components of wind.

Small-Scale Atmospheric Vortices

A tornado is but one example of an atmospheric vortex, a small-scale circulation system characterized by a swirling, convergent flow pattern of air motion. Four common, naturally occurring atmospheric vortices on a small scale are waterspouts, dust whirls, gustnadoes, and firewhirls.

A *waterspout* is simply a tornado over water. True waterspouts normally form under growing cumulus clouds that produce showers and grow because of convergence and shear zones at the water's surface. They tend to form over warm, shallow bodies of water and dissipate if they move over land. A second type, called tornadic waterspouts, is spawned by severe thunderstorms and will not dissipate upon moving over land. Both types are generally smaller and weaker than tornadoes

Dust whirls, also called "dust devils" and whirlwinds, are small-scale natural vortices that do not descend from a parent cloud structure. They usually form on hot days with strong sunshine, few or no clouds, and light winds. Under direct sunlight, as the ground becomes extremely hot, excess heat surges upward in a buoyant plume of air. If a slight gust of wind encounters this thermal plume, then the rising air brings with it enough momentum to result in a rapid spin. Animals and people can trigger small dust whirls as they disturb the superheated thermal plume with small air movements. Windspeeds are normally on the order of 20 to 40 mph with 50 to 60 mph possible in stronger ones. Occasionally, windspeeds up to 80 mph may occur.

The *gustnado* is a rotating column of air occurring at the leading edge of a thunderstorm downdraft, a site known as a gust front by meteorologists. They are weak and usually last less than one minute.

Firewhirls are triggered by large fires, and have been known to grow to truly tornadic proportions, extending over a mile high and producing winds over 100 mph. The physical mechanism that produces firewhirls is the extreme heat associated with a large fire, commonly resulting from forest fires or oil well fires.

Tornadoes

Although tornadoes occur in many areas of the world, the United States has more tornadoes than any other country, with an estimated 30% to 50% of the world's total. Canada is in second place with 100 to 200 tornadoes per year. Tornadoes in the United States tend to be more violent than those in other countries, owing to the clash of air masses east of the Rockies.

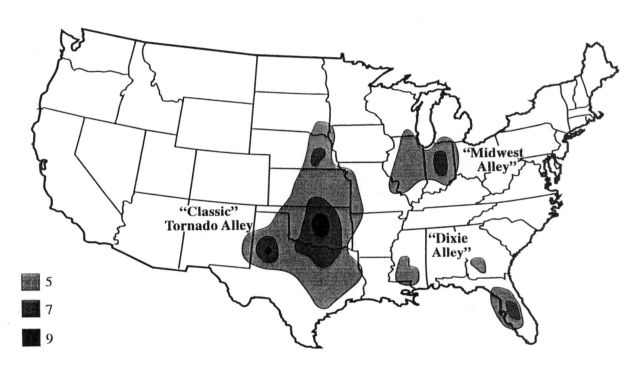

Fig. 13.1. Average annual tornado occurrence per 10,000 square miles, based on National Weather Service data.

Figure 13.1 shows evidence of three "tornado alleys," or regions of maximum tornado occurrence. The most obvious tornado alley extends from the plains of northwest Texas eastward into north Texas and then northward across Oklahoma, Kansas, and eastern Nebraska. A second tornado alley, called Midwest Alley, is located over most of Illinois and Indiana. Finally, Dixie Alley stretches eastward from Arkansas, Louisiana, and Texas through Mississippi, Alabama, and Georgia. Dixie Alley also extends southward into Florida.

Tornadoes occur mostly during the afternoon and early evening hours, from 2:00 P.M. until 7:00 P.M. local time as shown in figure 13.2. The most active time period of the entire day is from 5:00 P.M. to 6:00 P.M. It should be noted that some tornadoes do occur at night or during the early morning, especially in Dixie Alley.

Figure 13.3 shows the national tornado season is clearly from April through July; however, tornado season in the United States never really begins or ends but is ongoing.

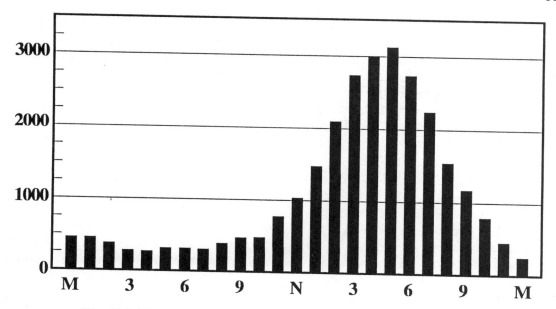

Fig. 13.2. Hourly tornado distribution in the United States for 1950-1995, adapted from National Weather Service data.

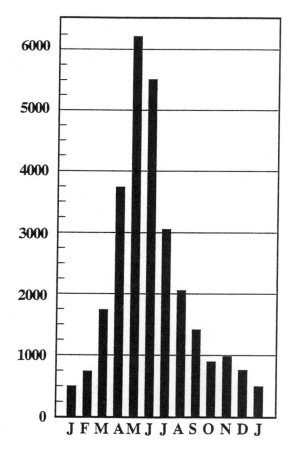

Fig. 13.3. Monthly tornado distribution in the United States for 1950-1995, adapted from National Weather Service data.

Thus, tornado frequency changes from the values that are considered normal. Tornado incidence increases in Dixie Alley in February. During the spring, tornadoes become more common farther west and north, extending into Texas and the Tennessee Valley. By May and June, tornado frequency increases in the plains of Texas, Oklahoma, Kansas, and Nebraska. In July, tornado frequency shifts to the Dakotas, the Upper Midwest, and the Great Lakes region while decreasing to a minimum in Dixie Alley. An interesting secondary peak is evident in November, particularly in Dixie Alley. Landfalling hurricanes also change the "normal" tornado patterns.

Classification of Tornadoes

Over 800 tornadoes were documented annually from 1953 to 1995. The 1990s have been especially active, with an average of nearly 1,200 tornadoes yearly. An average of 22 become "killers," claiming lives. The typical tornado travels 1 mile at speeds of 35 to 40 mph, is 50 yards wide, has windspeeds less than 110 mph, and usually moves from southwest to northeast (59%). Other common directions are from west to east, northwest to southeast, and north to south.

Tornadoes are classified according to intensity, path length, and path width. A workable and simple method of tornado classification was completed in the early 1970s by researchers at the University of Chicago. This system, called the Fujita Scale after T. T. Fujita, the University of Chicago meteorology professor who devised it, relates observed property damage with tornado strength, defined as a range of windspeed capable of causing the observed damage. Fujita scale rating numbers range from 0 to 5, with 0 being the weakest rating and 5 the highest rating. Tornadoes in the 0 and 1 categories (denoted as F0 and F1) are considered weak, strong tornadoes are rated as 2 or 3 (denoted as F2 or F3), and violent tornadoes are rated as 4 or 5 (denoted as F4 or F5).

Table 13.1 summarizes tornado intensity ratings, the percentage of tornadoes that fall into each category, the percentage of deaths, and some of the damage. It is important to note that 68% of all tornadoes produce windspeeds of 112 mph or less. These relatively weak tornadoes claim few lives, and only 1% of tornado-related fatalities can be attributed to them. A striking fact is that 2% of tornadoes are responsible for 68% of the deaths, demonstrating that only a few tornadoes are responsible for the majority of deaths, injuries, and property damage. All tornadoes should be respected, but it is these powerful tornadoes that concern the meteorological community in respect to public safety and preparedness.

Tornado Types

Two types of tornadoes exist. One results from a nonsupercell thunderstorm and is called a *nonsupercell tornado*. Some scientists call the nonsupercell tornado a landspout. The other type, spawned by a supercell thunderstorm, is called a *supercell tornado*.

The nonsupercell tornado forms during the early stages of thunderstorm development and is most common along ocean coasts and east of the Front Range of the Rockies in Colorado. These tornadoes are usually weaker than their supercell counterparts and do not travel as far. A few strong tornadoes are nonsupercell, but it is highly unlikely that any of the violent tornadoes are of nonsupercell origin.

By contrast, the supercell tornado is the most dangerous because it lasts longer and is more intense than its nonsupercell cousins. Nearly all strong tornadoes and all of the violent tornadoes are of supercell origin.

Tornado Category	Ground Level Windspeed	% Tornadoes	% Deaths	Damage Characteristics
WEAK	112 mph or less	62%	2%	Some damage to chimneys or TV antennas, sign boards damaged, windows broken, mobile homes pushed or overturned.
STRONG	113-206 mph	36%	30%	Roofs torn off frame houses, weak structures demolished, trains overturned, most trees severely damaged.
VIOLENT	207-318 mph	2%	68%	Trees completely debarked, entire frame houses hurled from foundations, steel-reinforced concrete structures badly damaged, trains hurled some distance. Incredible phenomena can occur.

Table 13.1. Tornado Strength as Related to Death and Destruction

The Tornado Life Cycle

The cycle described here is limited to supercell tornadoes. Nonsupercell tornadoes generally fit into this sequence but never progress into that part of the life cycle that is characteristic of the stronger supercell variety. Current data allows us to compile a four-stage process of tornado evolution: the organizing stage, the mature stage, the shrinking stage, and the decaying stage.

Early in the organizing stage, the first sign of a developing tornado may well be dust or other debris swirling upward from the ground. A short, pendant-shaped cloud may also extend from the cloud base at this time. Although the circulation is continuous from the cloud base to the ground, the "condensation funnel" (the visible funnel-shaped cloud feature) has not yet formed due to the weakness of the circulation. Damage, if any, in this part of the tornado life cycle is light. Late in the organizing stage, a "wall cloud" may form, marked by an abrupt lowering of the thunderstorm cloud base. The wall cloud is also frequently seen to rotate. In these cases, the rotation of the wall cloud is persistent and unmistakable. The presence of a wall cloud means that the mature stage will occur in an hour or less.

Many tornadoes never progress beyond the late organizing stage, but of those that do make it to maturity, the condensation funnel becomes better defined and expands, and the windspeed increases. The tornado attains its maximum width and intensity and may become enveloped with dust and debris. It is common to see the most severe damage at this point. During the mature stage, the tornado can become as unique as a fingerprint of a strand of DNA with different sizes, shapes, and colors.

The tornado enters the shrinking stage when its path width decreases. At this point the tornado may appear to "lift," although continuing to produce damage, thus indicating that the tornado is still in progress. The tornado may tilt and the wall cloud disappears. Despite being narrower, the tornado in the shrinking stage is still capable of producing significant damage and, of course, is considered dangerous.

From *The Teacher's Weather Sourcebook.* © 1999 Frank T. Konvicka. Teacher Ideas Press. (800) 237-6124

Finally, the tornado enters the decaying stage. The main characteristic of this is a ropelike form that disintegrates, and surface debris and damage are no longer produced. In some supercell thunderstorms the production of tornadoes is cyclic, in which case another wall cloud develops and the process repeats itself. Cyclic tornadic supercells sometimes produce up to six tornadoes over a distance of several hundred miles.

Theories of Tornadogenesis

Nonsupercell tornado formation appears to be related to the convergence of air occurring underneath a developing cumulonimbus cloud. The spin generated by this swirling flow is then tilted upward by the thunderstorm updraft and produces short-lived tornadoes.

Supercell tornadogenesis is a four-step process.

Step 1. Dry air flowing into the parent thunderstorm from a westerly direction begins to evaporate tiny, falling precipitation particles, resulting in the chilling of a large volume of air that cascades downward. This special downdraft is called the "rear-flank downdraft," or RFD. The RFD develops because the mesocyclone acts like a barrier to the environmental flow, so the natural tendency is for the RFD to be initiated downward as shown in figure 13.4. In this process, the mesocyclone now exists as part updraft and downdraft. Remember, in the supercell thunderstorm the updraft and the forward-flank downdraft remain divorced. Thus, it is the RFD that is the seed of destruction for a supercell thunderstorm. For an ordinary thunderstorm, death is marked by only a downdraft, but with the supercell, death is marked by a tornado.

Tornadogenesis typically begins at around 15,000 feet high during the collapsing phase of the supercell and is commonly "seen" by Doppler radar.

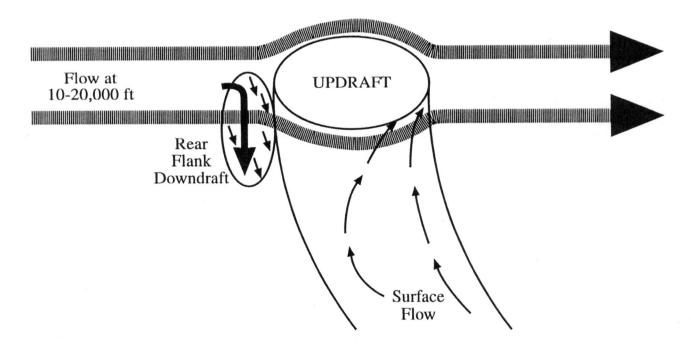

Fig. 13.4. Step 1 involves the mid-level flow intersecting with the thunderstorm updraft.
(Adapted from sketches by C. A. Doswell III, L. Lemon, K. Browning, and from supercomputer simulation.)

Step 2. At this point the RFD reaches the surface and the embryonic tornado develops along the interface of the RFD and the mesocyclone. Figure 13.5 illustrates what is happening.

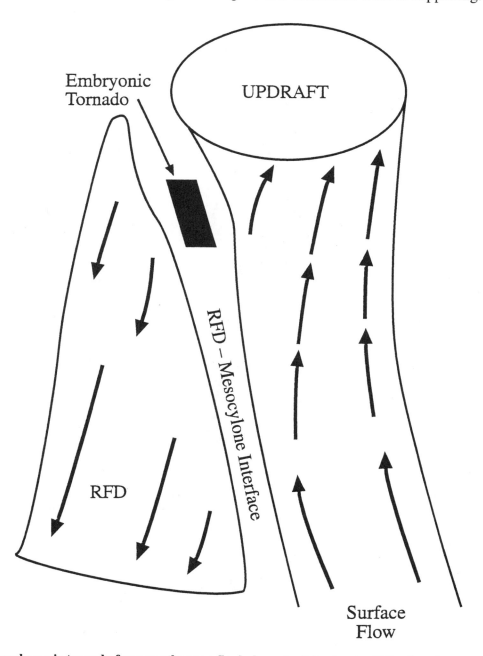

Fig. 13.5. An embryonic tornado forms as the rear-flank downdraft "eats away" the thunderstorm updraft. (Adapted from sketches by C. A. Doswell III, L. Lemon, K. Browning, and from supercomputer simulation.)

Step 3. The stage is now set for the production of a significant tornado. The creation of wall-like boundaries between the mesocyclone and the RFD is not unlike the boundaries of the bathtub wall that enhance the formation of the drain vortex. In the supercell situation the boundary is created by the strong rotation of the mesocyclone. The second boundary is associated with the RFD. In this type of environment, the tornado begins to stretch upward and downward in a "dynamic pipe" effect. Airflow through the sides is restrained and the air must flow into the vortex through the bottom and out through the top. This causes the tornado to lengthen in both directions. This aspect of tornado birth may surprise some, as it's natural to concentrate on the part of the tornado that stretches downward. When the tornado has stretched to the point where it actually makes contact with the surface, the ground prevents air from flowing easily into the bottom of the vortex. The pressure drops and the air is drawn into the base and lower edges of the vortex with drastically increased speed, thus giving rise to windspeeds of tornadic proportions. Figure 13.6 depicts step 3 of the supercell tornado development.

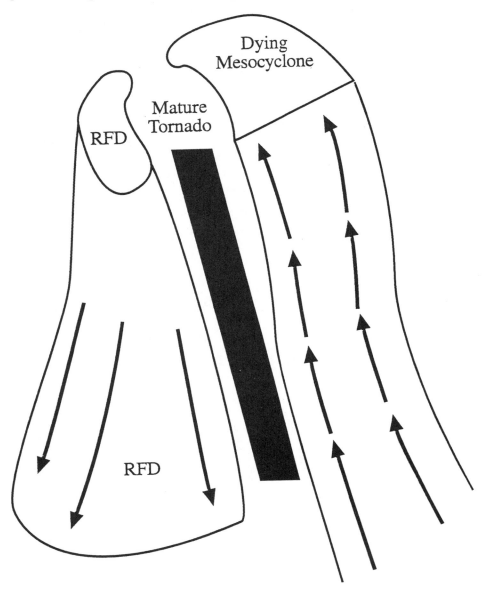

Fig. 13.6. A mature tornado develops as the mesocyclone dies and the rear-flank downdraft intensifies. (Adapted from sketches by C. A. Doswell III, L. Lemon, K. Browning, and from supercomputer simulation.)

Step 4. The tornado passes its mature stage and eventually dissipates, along with its parent supercell. In a cyclic supercell, a new mesocyclone would form at this time on the right side (east or southeast) of the supercell and the process would begin all over again, perhaps to be repeated two to six times over a distance of 100 to 300 miles and a time frame of one to six hours.

Tornado Structure

The airflow pattern in a tornado is complex and highly convergent. Also, an important component of a tornado's airflow is upward. This upward motion is responsible for the condensation funnel, the visible portion shaped like a funnel or pendant. Sometimes, however, the condensation funnel does not form due to the weakness of the tornado circulation or because of the lack of moisture in the surrounding environment.

Stronger tornadoes take on a multiple-vortex pattern. These subvortices spin along the edge of the main tornado and are a breakdown of the unstable vortex flow into smaller, more stable units of rotation. Windspeeds are highest in these subvortices, and intense tornadoes may have three to seven subvortices. Evidence of the existence of these subvortices is seen in the damage pattern of tornadoes and was discovered during the 1970s by film footage taken from tornado intercept missions. This explains some of the "strange" phenomena often associated with tornadoes, such as why one house may be destroyed yet leave the house next door or across the street undamaged. The answer lies in the concept of subvortices.

One important fact about tornado structure seen from figure 13.7 is that, contrary to popular belief, the highest windspeeds are not found in the center of the tornado. At point B, the center of the tornado, the windspeed is equal to the traveling speed of the tornado, or 50 mph. At points C and D the calculation of the windspeed presents an interesting case. For tornadoes that rotate counterclockwise (only one tornado in 800 spins clockwise in the Northern Hemisphere), the highest windspeeds are found on the righthand side of the tornado, where the circulation of the vortex itself (100 mph) is added to the travel speed of the tornado (50 mph). Thus, at point D, the windspeed is 150 mph. At point C, on the lefthand side of the tornado, the speed of movement is subtracted from the vortex wind since they are working in opposite directions. So the windspeed at point C is only 50 mph. Studies reveal that the most severe damage in counterclockwise-rotating tornadoes is on the righthand side, where the speed of movement and the component of vortex flow complement each other.

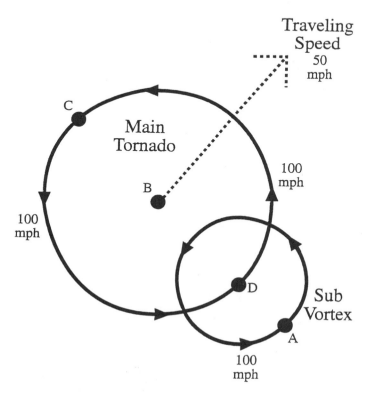

Fig. 13.7. A simplified example of how different windspeeds in tornadoes arise.

What happens in a multiple-vortex tornado? According to theory, the highest windspeeds would be found on the righthand side of the tornado where a subvortex is located. If the subvortex is spinning at 100 mph, then the windspeed on the righthand side, at point A, adds up to an incredible 250 mph! This is because all three components of motion complement each other at that point. This observed variation of windspeeds is probably sufficient to explain the sometimes chaotic and surprising damage patterns left by major tornadoes.

Safety Rules

When a tornado approaches, a person's immediate action may mean life or death. Two terms to know are *tornado watch* and *tornado warning*. A tornado watch is less serious, and means that atmospheric conditions are favorable for tornadoes, or that there exists potential for tornadoes. During a tornado watch, one should not become unduly alarmed and should continue normal activities, but be aware of approaching thunderstorms. A tornado warning means that a tornado has actually been sighted by a reliable witness or indicated by radar. If a tornado warning is issued for your local area, be prepared to observe the following safety rules.

In Homes. The basement offers the greatest protection. In homes without basements, take cover near the center of the house, on the lowest floor, in a small room such as a closet, bathroom, or interior hallway. If danger is particularly imminent and you do not have time to think about what to do, then seek refuge under a sturdy piece of furniture. Get away from windows, doors, and outside walls. Do not go outside and do not attempt to outrun the tornado in a vehicle.

In Schools. You should follow advance plans to take cover in an interior hallway on the lowest floor. It is also important that this hallway not be open to the south or west because it could become a dangerous wind tunnel. Avoid auditoriums, gymnasiums, and cafeterias. Again, stay away from windows and doors.

In Office Buildings. You should go to a small room or an interior hallway on the lowest floor, or to a previously designated shelter. Do not go to your car to drive home. Do not use the elevator to get to the lowest floor; electric power may be lost and you would be stranded. Use the stairs.

In Factories. Follow advance plans. If your factory does not have a plan, consult the NWS and have them help develop a plan.

In Shopping Centers and Malls. You should go to a previously designated shelter area. Again, do not go to your parked car thinking you can outrun the tornado or that it will be safer at home.

In Mobile Homes. You should abandon them immediately. If there is no substantial reinforced building or designated shelter nearby, take cover in a ditch, culvert, or ravine if there is time to do so.

In an Apartment Complex. You should basically observe the same rules that apply to homes if you live on the ground floor. If you live on the second floor or higher, then make friends with someone who lives on the first floor and have an understanding that you might seek refuge in his or her apartment if severe weather threatens. Some apartment complexes have designated shelter areas; use them if there is time to go there.

In Open Country. Move away from the tornado at right angles, if possible. If danger is imminent, get out of the vehicle and lie flat in a ditch, culvert, or ravine, but be aware of floodwaters also. The girders underneath a bridge can afford protection. As far as the decision to "outrun" the tornado is concerned, this remains an individual judgment based on factors occurring at the time.

If you observe the preceding safety precautions, then you will be doing your part to further reduce the death toll that tornadoes take in the United States.

The Process of Scientific Thought

Activity #1

Title: My Pet Tornado

Objective: To make a simple model of a tornado

Materials Needed: 2-liter soft drink bottle with a flat bottom, dish soap, food coloring

Procedure: Fill a 2-liter soft drink bottle almost up to the neck with water. Be sure the bottle has a flat bottom, or the experiment will not work. Put one or two drops of red food coloring into the water. Then put one-half teaspoon of dish soap into the bottle. Place the cap on the bottle, hold upright, and spin vigorously with the bottle oriented vertically. A "tornado" will form in the middle of the bottle.

Elementary

- Draw a picture of the "tornado in a bottle."

- Experiment with different food colorings. Is red the best choice?

- Spin the bottle in different ways. Does this affect how the tornado looks? (Answer: It should. This is just like natural tornadoes; the environmental conditions determine the type of tornado that forms.)

Secondary

- Observe the tornado in the bottle closely. Then view a video about tornadoes. In what ways are real tornadoes similar to the demonstration model? (Answer: Tornadoes come in different sizes, shapes, and appearances.)

- Observe the tornado in the bottle closely. Many people mistakenly believe that the tornado "skips." This can be seen when the tornado enters the decaying stage. Is the tornado really skipping? (Answer: No, the tornado is still in contact with the surface; it's just weaker.)

- Look into more sophisticated models of tornadoes. These would include laboratory models and computer simulations.

Activity #2

Title: Up and Down

Objective: To illustrate the mesocyclone and the RFD

Materials Needed: candle, bottle, piece of cardboard

Procedure: Obtain a large milk or juice bottle. Cut a T-shaped piece of cardboard. Lower a lighted candle into the bottle (or, if you prefer, drop a piece of burning paper into the bottle). Place the piece of cardboard in the opening of the bottle. Observe the movement of the air currents.

Elementary

- Draw a picture of the air currents.

Elementary and Secondary

- What does the upward-moving air current represent? (Answer: The thunderstorm updraft, or mesocyclone.)

- What does the downward current of air represent? (Answer: The RFD.)

- What does the T-shaped piece of cardboard represent? (Answer: The mesocyclone/RFD interface, the favored location for tornadogenesis in the supercell thunderstorm.)

Ideas for Science Fair Projects

1. The two activities in this chapter are appropriate for science fair presentation.

2. Research question: Does El Niño affect the number of tornadoes in the United States?

3. Research question: Do sunspots affect the number of tornadoes in the United States?

4. Research question: Are tornado patterns changing?

5. Research question: Are tornado outbreaks less violent now than they were in the past?

    Note: Science fair ideas #2 through #5 will involve the help of a professional. The necessary information needed to answer the research question is available, it's just a matter of locating the correct source, and a professional can help here. The extra effort is worth it, however, because a good presentation on any of these topics is capable of winning at any level of competition.

6. "Tornado Cousins" are dust whirls, gustnadoes, and firewhirls. Use the title to develop a project.

7. Center a presentation on waterspouts. Be sure to include the two main types, the differences between tornadoes, and any photos that are available.

8. "Tornadoes—When and Where" could cover many aspects of U.S. tornado climatology. Include maps and illustrations similar to the ones used in this chapter.

9. "Tornadoes Around the World" would center on a global view of tornadoes. Be sure to include why tornadoes occur in other countries; photos of a few "foreign" tornadoes would help your chances of winning.

10. "Not All Tornadoes Are Created Equal" explores the differences between individual tornadoes in path length, path width, and intensity. It's very important that you include a visual potpourri of the different appearances, colors, sizes, and shapes that tornadoes can take.

11. Research question: How high can the wind get in a tornado? Include a discussion of the methods used to infer or measure tornado winds.

12. "Tornado Families" analyzes outbreaks of tornadoes. Mention outbreak types, their characteristics, and use historical examples from your state or from the United States.

13. Describe the larger-scale environment responsible for supercell storms. Mention how instability, wind shear, and the lifting mechanism combine to achieve tornado potential. Also mention the pattern as related to the extratropical weather system. Include a map.

14. Develop a project that focuses on the tornado life cycle. Photos of each stage are a must.

15. "Tornadoes: Can Anything Be Done?" Research tornado mitigation strategies and their validity. Discuss pros and cons and legal issues.

16. Research question: What actually happens to a building in a tornado? Include photos of various degrees of damage, include sketches showing the forces on a hypothetical structure, and be sure you can explain the damage in the photo in relation to the wind-speed experienced.

School's Out!

1. Help your family develop a plan for tornado preparedness at home.
2. Take your science fair project to a local service organization.
3. Read a book about tornadoes to a younger child.
4. Write a poem about tornadoes.
5. Write a story in which a tornado is the antagonist.
6. Talk to elders about tornadoes they have experienced.
7. Keep a log of the major tornadoes that strike the United States. Do their location, season, and time of day fit in with the information presented in this chapter?
8. Help develop a tornado awareness plan for your neighbors.
9. Rent or buy a video about tornadoes.

Chapter 14

Hurricanes

The tornado packs nature's most concentrated fury, but it is the hurricane that deserves the honor as nature's most awesome storm. During its life cycle the hurricane expends energy equivalent to 10,000 nuclear bombs, such as those dropped on Hiroshima and Nagasaki, Japan, at the close of WWII in 1945. With such great energy release it comes as no surprise that hurricanes account for some of the worst natural disasters in U.S. history. The compilation of the "Hurricane Hall of Fame" in tables 14.1 and 14.2 illustrates the great toll on life and property. No portion of the U.S. Gulf Coast or the Atlantic coastline is immune, as the recent Hurricane Mitch dealt a devastating blow to Central America.

Table 14.2 tells us that the most costly hurricanes in terms of economic losses are from the modern era. This does not mean that hurricanes have become stronger and more damaging; it simply means that there are now more damage targets than ever before. Also, inflation plays a major role; it costs more now to repair or replace damaged property.

Location	Year	# Deaths
1. Galveston, TX	1900	7200
2. Louisiana	1893	2000
3. Lake Okeechobee, FL	1928	1836
4. South Carolina	1893	1000-2000
5. FL Keys & S.TX	1919	600-900
6. GA & SC	1881	700
7. New England	1938	600
8. AUDREY, (LA)	1957	526
9. FL Keys	1935	408
10. Atlantic Coast	1944	390

Table 14.1. Ten Deadliest U.S. Hurricanes (1880-1998)

Hurricane	Year	$Billions (in 1990 dollars)
1. Andrew (FL, LA)	1992	26.4
2. Hugo (SC, NC)	1989	7.1
3. Betsy (LA, FL)	1965	6.5
4. Agnes (FL, NE U.S.)	1972	6.4
5. Camille (MS, LA)	1969	5.2
6. Georges (FL, MS, LA, AL)	1998	5.0
7. Frederick (MS, AL, FL)	1979	3.5
8. Fran (NC, VA, MD)	1996	3.1
9. Opal (FL, AL, GA)	1995	2.9
10. Alicia (TX)	1983	2.4
11. Iniki (HI)	1992	1.8

Table 14.2. Eleven Costliest U.S. Hurricanes (1965-1998)

The Hurricane Life Cycle

Hurricanes begin as tropical disturbances, or seedlings. These appear on photographs taken by weather satellites and are noted as areas of "disturbed weather." About 100 to 110 seedlings are identified each year; however, only six seedlings on average will develop into hurricanes.

Seedlings move in a westerly direction, steered by the easterly trade winds that blow in the tropics. Two conditions must be present for further development: warm water and a favorable vertical wind profile in the atmosphere. Research indicates that sea-surface temperatures in areas where seedlings strengthen are almost always warmer than 79° F.

In addition, the seedling must encounter a favorable atmosphere on its journey westward. By far the most important component of the atmosphere in this respect is the vertical wind profile. The seedling must move through a sizable region of the atmosphere that is devoid of significant wind shear as it will dislodge the organization of the system. Further, the seedling is helped if the flow is weakly divergent, allowing the waste products of the system to be "vented" away, thus not allowing detrimental interaction with the system itself.

Given the favorable oceanic and atmospheric conditions, the seedling cloud pattern becomes better organized, the surface wind exhibits a swirling pattern, and a center of low pressure is evident. In this stage it is called a *tropical depression*, defined as a nonfrontal tropical weather system with a center of low pressure and a rotary windflow pattern at the surface of 38 mph or less. Windspeed criteria for tropical systems are based on a 1-minute average, or what is called sustained windspeed.

As the seedling continues moving in a westerly direction, it either weakens, strengthens, or reaches a steady state, depending on the conditions it encounters. If sea-surface temperatures higher than 79° F and a favorable wind profile in the atmosphere are encountered, then the depression is likely to strengthen into a tropical storm. The cloud pattern of a tropical storm is better organized, a center of low pressure is evident, and the rotary windflow at the surface is between 39 and 73 mph. At this point the system is named. Continued strengthening and organization allow the surface pressure to fall rapidly, resulting in a quick increase in windspeed and a tighter circulation. If the sustained windspeed reaches 74 mph, a hurricane is born.

The energy needed to maintain these great storms comes from the heat released by the condensation of water vapor and external mechanical forces. When the hurricane makes landfall, it is dragged apart by friction and its supply of energy is cut off. Thus, the hurricane enters the decaying stage and eventually dies.

The Structure of a Hurricane

A hurricane is an atmospheric circulation system comprised of a cloud structure that is arranged in a more or less circular pattern. The swirling, circular hurricane cloud system generally ranges from 200 to 500 miles in diameter.

A plan view and a vertical cross-section of a typical hurricane are illustrated in figures 14.1 and 14.2.

In general, most hurricanes possess the following structural features: the eye, the eye wall, rain shield, rain bands, and the prehurricane squall line. When this hurricane structure is present, it dominates the ocean and the atmosphere for tens of thousands of square miles.

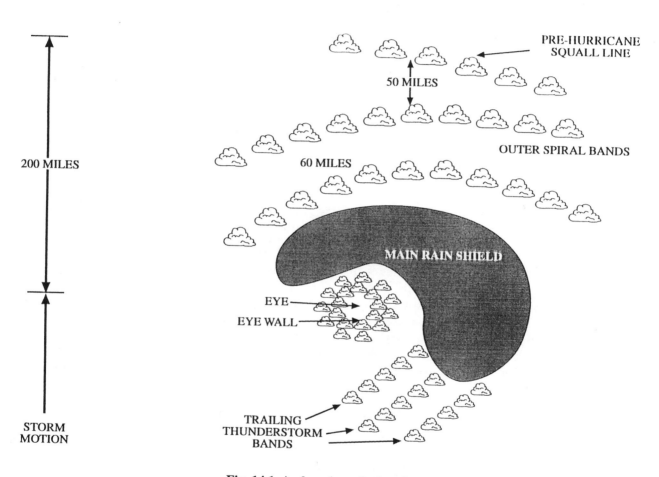

Fig. 14.1. A plan view of a hurricane.

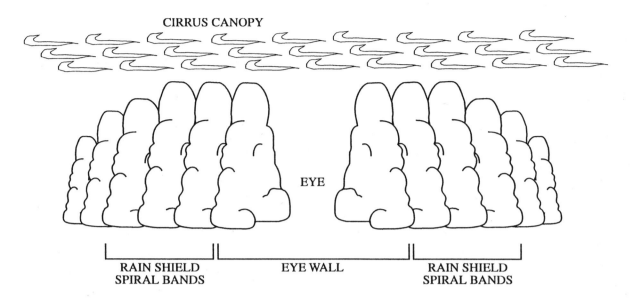

CIRRUS CANOPY

EYE

RAIN SHIELD
SPIRAL BANDS

EYE WALL

RAIN SHIELD
SPIRAL BANDS

Fig. 14.2. The vertical structure of a hurricane.

The Eye represents the pressure center of a hurricane, not necessarily the geometric center. The lowest atmospheric pressure, found in the eye, is an important measure of the hurricane's intensity, with the lower central pressure corresponding to the more intense hurricanes.

The Eye Wall represents the ring of intense convection immediately surrounding the eye. These are the largest and most violent thunderstorms of the entire hurricane system, producing the highest windspeeds and the heaviest rain. The overall health of the hurricane depends heavily on the vitality of the eye wall. A growing ring of convection surrounding the eye wall causes the central pressure to drop. This, in turn, causes the sustained windspeed to rise. A shrinking eye wall leads to a momentary lull in the intensification process. Thus, it is common for satellite pictures to show a pulsating intensification trend in hurricanes as the eye wall goes through alternating growing/shrinking cycles. Aircraft investigations have verified a link between this trend and hurricane intensity.

The Rain Shield/Rain (Spiral) Bands are another common element of the overall hurricane structure. The rain shield and rain bands normally surround the eye wall. In this area, the showers and thunderstorms produce more moderate rainfall rates and less wind, although high gusts are still possible. The rain shield is the entire precipitating part of the hurricane that is located outside the eye wall. The rain shield normally produces moderate to light rainfall rates and one-fourth the sustained windspeed of the eye wall. An exception is the rain bands, the banded features of convection located within the rain shield. The rain bands are capable of producing heavy bursts of rain and wind, perhaps one-half or two-thirds those of the eye wall.

The Prehurricane Squall Line is not evident in all hurricanes but is common enough to include in the discussion. This feature is usually seen well away from the eye, perhaps by several hundred miles. Except for the ocean swell and the advancing cirrus canopy, the prehurricane squall line is often one of the first signs of an impending hurricane. The prehurricane squall line produces heavy showers and thunderstorms with strong, gusty winds, perhaps up to one-third to one-half those of the eye wall.

The Naming Process

The word *hurricane* comes from an ancient tribe of aborigines in Central America known as the Tainos. For the Tainos, *Huracan* was a god of evil. Hurricanes are known by different names in different parts of the world. In the western Pacific (west of the International Dateline) and in Southeast Asia, hurricanes are known as *typhoons*. In Bangladesh, Pakistan, India, and the Indian Ocean they are known as *cyclones*. In the Philippines hurricanes are called *baguios*, and off the coast of Australia they are sometimes called *willy willys*.

A unique characteristic of hurricanes is that they are given names. Naming hurricanes is common around the world and is used to facilitate communications and warnings. For many years, hurricanes over the Caribbean were named in Spanish after the saints. Near the end of the 19th century, an Australian named Clement Wragge began giving female names to tropical storms, as well as naming a few after politicians whom he disliked. During WWII, meteorologists in the U.S. military picked up on the practice, naming storms after their wives or girlfriends. In 1950, the decision was made to name storms by using the phonetic alphabet (Able, Baker, Charlie, etc.). In 1953, the naming process became official, and the decision was made to use female names, with Alice and Barbara leading the way. The practice continued until 1979 when male names were added.

At present, the WMO uses a six-year rotating list of names, choosing names that are relatively easy to recall from three languages: English, French, and Spanish. These names are used by mutual agreement of the NWS and the WMO and reflect the different cultural origins of the lands they affect. One list of names is kept for the Atlantic Basin, another list is used for eastern Pacific storms, and others are used for central Pacific hurricanes and western Pacific typhoons. If a particular hurricane was especially destructive or deadly, then the name is "retired" and a new name is substituted. Some names that have been retired are Andrew, Betsy, Camille, Audrey, Hugo, Gilbert, Frederick, Alicia, Carla, and Agnes.

Hurricanes—A Global View

Each year approximately 25 to 40 hurricanes are born over the warm waters of Earth, with two-thirds occurring in the Northern Hemisphere. The North Atlantic Ocean, Caribbean Sea, and the Gulf of Mexico are the breeding grounds for hurricanes that cross the Gulf and Atlantic Coasts of the United States. Other regions include the eastern Pacific, western North Pacific, Indian Ocean, and South Pacific. No hurricanes form in the South Atlantic or eastern South Pacific, nor do they form within 4° to 5° of the equator. Only a few (about 13%) form poleward of 22°. The majority (65%) of hurricanes form between 10° and 20° on either side of the equator, indicating the importance and influence of Earth's rotation on the airflow of a hurricane.

The temporal distribution pattern shows that hurricanes peak in late summer and early autumn, although they can form in any month in the western North Pacific. For the Atlantic Basin, the official hurricane season begins June 1 of each year and continues through November 30, the most active season including the months of August, September, and October, when 84% of all hurricanes occur.

Effects of Hurricanes

Hurricanes are well known for widespread flooding causing contamination of freshwater supplies with saltwater intrusion, structural damage, significant erosion and damage to the aquaculture, destruction crops, and killing of livestock. Loss of communication systems and power is normally widespread, adding to the inconvenience and cost of repairs.

For all the detrimental effects, a hurricane does bring a few beneficial ones as well. One benefit is the rain a hurricane can bring to a drought-stricken area. A good example happened in 1955 when Hurricane Connie ended a 19-month drought in the eastern United States. A second benefit is the role it plays in recycling the nutrients in the oceans. This is accomplished through upwelling, a bodily "turning over" of the top layers of the ocean due to the action of wind. This upwelling mixes and helps redistribute nutrients, allowing them to rise to the surface from below. Marine life derives much benefit through the upwelling triggered by hurricanes. Upwelling also brings cooler water to the surface, which can actually limit the development of other tropical systems that may follow the hurricane over a period of several days.

Classification and Forecasting of Hurricanes

The development of a classification method of hurricanes followed, and was perhaps inspired by, the Fujita tornado classification. Hurricanes rated as Category III or above are considered major, and the damage potential increases exponentially with increasing category number. Table 14.3 details the modern scale used to rate hurricane intensity.

CATEGORY	CENTRAL PRESSURE (inches)	WIND SPEED (mph)	STORM ATTRIBUTES AND CHARACTER OF EXPECTED DAMAGE	HISTORICAL EXAMPLES
I	Higher than 28.94 in.	74-95	Damage primarily limited to trees, power lines, signs, and mobile homes. Little or no damage to well constructed buildings. Isolated tornadoes possible. Storm tide to 5 feet.	Agnes (1972) Juan (1985) Danny (1985)
II	28.50-28.93	96-110	Considerable damage to trees, power lines, signs, and mobile homes. Some damage to roofs and windows. Little or no damage to well constructed buildings. A few tornadoes likely. Storm tide to 8 feet.	Earl (1986)
III	27.91-28.49	111-130	Widespread, severe damage to trees, power lines, utility poles, signs, and mobile homes. Widespread power outages, damage to roofs, windows and doors. Some structural damage to well constructed buildings. High tornado potential. Storm tide to 12 feet.	Frederick (1979) Betsy (1965)
IV	27.17-27.90	131-155	Widespread, severe damage to trees, power lines, utility poles, signs, and mobile homes. Widespread power outages. Extensive damage to roofs, windows and doors. Considerable structural failures. Major beach erosion High tornado potential. Storm tide to 18 feet. Storm retains destructive winds well inland.	Galveston (1900) Audrey (1957) Hugo (1989)
V	Less than 27.17	156 or greater	Extreme damage to trees, power lines, utility poles, signs, and mobile homes. Widespread power outages. Many complete structural failures. Major beach erosion. High tornado potential, storm tide in excess of 18 feet. Storm retains destructive winds well inland.	Florida Keys (1935) Camille (1969) Gilbert (1988)

Table 14.3. The Hurricane Intensity Scale

From *The Teacher's Weather Sourcebook.* © 1999 Frank T. Konvicka. Teacher Ideas Press. (800) 237-6124

One major goal of hurricane research is improved predictions of strength and movement. An accurate forecast, with an optimum lead-time warning of 24 hours, can reduce the hurricane's impact. Several methods currently used are satellite pictures, radar, rawindsonde, and aircraft reconnaissance. In addition, ship reports and surface observations are used. Aircraft reconnaissance flights provide the most detailed information available and are thus vital to forecasting. The reconnaissance aircraft penetrate to the core of the hurricane and provide detailed measurements of the wind and pressure distribution, as well as an accurate location of the eye. These "Hurricane Hunter" missions are supported by specially modified aircraft of the U.S. Air Force (USAF) and the National Oceanic and Atmospheric Administration (NOAA).

Meteorological information obtained from reconnaissance is also obtained with instruments called dropsondes, which, dropped into a hurricane, continuously radio back measurements of pressure, temperature, wind direction, and windspeed. This data complements the information derived from other data sources.

Safety Rules

If you live in a hurricane-prone region, the following safety rules should prove helpful:

- Follow the progress of every tropical cyclone, even if it is far away or in a location that normally prevents it from coming to your area. You can do this using NOAA weather radio or commercial TV and radio weathercasts.

- Know the difference between a hurricane watch and a hurricane warning. A hurricane watch is issued by the NHC to state that hurricane conditions may occur in the watch area within the next 36 hours. A hurricane warning means hurricane conditions are likely during the next 24 hours.

- Prepare a videotape of your insured possessions and narrate it with pertinent information on each item such as cost, date purchased, and any applicable serial numbers. This will expedite the insurance claim process if damage occurs.

- Evacuate if asked to do so by local officials.

- If you live in a mobile home, leave and stay with friends or relatives.

- Know your evacuation route and plans in advance. Don't wait until the last minute to figure out what you're doing and where you're going.

- Store or secure any loose yard objects such as garbage cans, toys, signs, lawn furniture, and other light objects. These items could be blown away and become dangerous to others who live near you.

- Stock up on nonperishable food items and bottled drinking water.

- Check battery-powered equipment to be sure it is in proper working order.

- Keep your vehicle fueled. Service stations may lose power and become inoperative.

- If you own a boat, be sure that it is moored securely or moved to a designated safe area. Put the boat on a trailer in an enclosed garage or warehouse if possible. If these facilities are not available, securely tie down both the boat and the trailer.

- If you evacuate, pack the following: blankets, pillows, one change of clothing, an additional pair of shoes for each family member, medicine, and special items for the very young and the elderly.

- Eat a meal before you evacuate and prepare an additional meal to take with you.

- Go to the nearest designated shelter.

- Do not brings pets to the shelter.

- Be advised that shelters will not be as comfortable as your home, and a little extra patience is in order.

For those in shelters and those "riding out the storm" at home:

- Remain inside.
- Follow the safety rules for tornadoes, if possible. There are times when this may not be possible in a shelter.
- If the eye of the hurricane passes overhead, be advised that the fury of the storm will return shortly from the opposite direction.

After the storm passes and the "all clear" signal is given:

- Leave the shelter only after authorities say it is safe to do so.
- Don't sightsee.
- Stay out of disaster areas unless you are qualified to help.
- Avoid areas where power lines are down or areas where gas leaks occur.
- Enter a damaged residence with extreme care.
- Be aware of snakes, animals, and insects that have been deposited on your property by the storm.
- Notify your homeowner's insurance agent to get the claim process started.
- Make temporary repairs that will increase the safety of those in or near your residence.
- Take photographs of all damage before you repair anything.
- Make an inventory of damaged items in duplicate.
- Document any out-of-pocket costs associated with temporary repairs.

If you observe the preceding safety precautions, then you will be doing your part to alleviate the death toll that hurricanes take, and expedite your own recovery from financial loss.

The Process of Scientific Thought

Activity #1

Title: Pan Surge

Objective: To demonstrate the hurricane storm tide

Materials Needed: two aluminum pans (one round, one square or rectangular), drinking straw

Procedure: Fill each pan almost full of water. Blow through the straw at a constant rate across the water surface in each pan. Observe what happens.

Elementary

- Draw a picture of the wave action in each pan and the movement of the air over the surface.

- Explain why waves form in the pan. (Answer: The energy of the moving air is transferred to the water surface.)

- What does the air being blown through the straw represent? (Answer: The wind of a hurricane.)

- What do the edges of the pans represent? (Answer: The coastline.)

- What does the water moving against the edge of each pan represent? (Answer: The hurricane storm tide.)

- In which pan are the waves highest while breaking against the edge? (Answer: The square or rectangle-shaped pan.)

- What is the implication about coastlines and hurricane-generated waves? (Answer: The shape of the coastline affects the magnitude of the storm surge.)

- Repeat the activity but blow harder. What happens? (Answer: The waves are higher.) What is the implication? (Answer: Higher storm surges are associated with stronger hurricanes.)

Secondary

- Can you think of any other factors that affect the hurricane storm surge? (Answer: Speed of movement, size, location relative to the center.)

- It is well known that bays and estuaries magnify storm surges. Try to simulate this by putting a crease in the edge of one of the pans.

Activity #2

Title: Hurricane in a Sink

Objective: To demonstrate the airflow of a hurricane

Materials Needed: a sink full of water, a tracer

Procedure: Plug the drain and fill a sink with water. Place a tracer element in the sink and pull the drain plug. Observe the sequence of motion the tracer shows.

Elementary

- Draw a picture of the tracer's movement and the water current.
- What does the sink full of water represent? (Answer: The environment around a hurricane.)
- What does the drain represent? (Answer: The pressure center, or eye.)
- What does the tracer represent? (Answer: The motion of a parcel of air).
- Briefly explain the application of this activity to a real hurricane. (Answer: In hurricanes the air motion is convergent toward the pressure center, or eye. As a parcel of air gets closer to the eye, its motion accelerates.)

Secondary

- Study the hurricane intensity chart (table 14.3). Come up with a relationship between the wind-speed and the central pressure. Feel free to use a computer.

Ideas for Science Fair Projects

1. Research question: Does El Niño affect the number of tropical storms and hurricanes in the Atlantic Basin? This idea will involve help from a professional who can obtain years of El Niño activity as well as the number of tropical storms and hurricanes that occur each year.

2. Research question: Do sunspots affect the number of tropical storms and hurricanes in the Atlantic Basin? Again, some professional help may be needed.

3. Research question: Are hurricane movement patterns different now than in the past? Professional help may be needed to locate the necessary information. It is well known by meteorologists that the answer to the research question is yes. For example, the 1950s were quite active for the Atlantic Coast and the early part of the 20th century was active for the Gulf Coast.

4. Any of the activities are appropriate for science fair presentation.

5. Trace the life cycle of a hurricane.

6. Present the structural components of a hurricane. Include sketches of the plan and cross-section view.

7. Develop a project on how the hurricane-naming process evolved. Include the names of hurricanes in other parts of the world and include the "Hall of Fame" (tables 14.1 and 14.2).

8. Center a project on the classification of hurricanes. Include the Saffir/Simpson chart and historical examples.

9. Develop a project that considers the energy budget of a hurricane. Figure out how much energy a typical hurricane uses in: 1 second, 1 hour, 1 day, 1 week. Translate this into everyday terms. Hint to get started: Define a size for the hurricane and use 600 calories per gram for the latent heat of condensation.

10. Hurricane-induced tornadoes are an interesting and original topic. Follow the discussion presented in this chapter.

11. Another interesting topic is aircraft reconnaissance missions.

12. Develop your own method for forecasting hurricane movement based on historical data. You will need to enlist a professional for help in locating the data. Use a computer!

School's Out!

1. If you live in a hurricane-prone region, document the next hurricane strike. Document sequence of clouds, wind, precipitation, pressure, and eye passage.

2. Listen to the experiences of others who have been through a hurricane.

3. Read a book about hurricanes to a younger child.

4. Take your science fair project to a local service organization.

5. Write a story where the antagonist is a hurricane.

6. Help your family and your neighborhood develop a response plan.

7. Save newspaper clippings about hurricanes around the world.

Chapter 15

Other Inclement Weather

Floods, drought, blizzards, snowstorms, and temperature extremes all exact their toll on life and property annually in the United States. In many cases, the economic and personal loss is greater than the meteorological events themselves.

Floods

As a natural component of the Earth-atmosphere system, no portion of the United States is really immune to flooding. In fact, floods are among this nation's leading weather-related killers. Each year, several hundred thousand Americans are driven from their homes by floodwaters, more than 100 are killed, and several billion dollars' worth of property damage occurs.

A flood condition occurs when water overflows the natural or artificial confines of a streambed or other body of water, or accumulates by drainage in low-lying areas. Heavy rains associated with severe storms or unusually large seasonal rainfall totals typically cause most flooding. The nature of flood episodes varies. Some floods affecting large river systems or their larger tributaries build up on a cumulative basis, taking days, weeks, or months to evolve; this is known as a seasonal flood, a river flood, or a gradual flood. In contrast, flooding in urban areas and on smaller river systems and tributaries can develop in a matter of minutes or hours, thus the term *flash flood*.

Teacher's Extra

A Rainfall Records

The following are credible rainfall records for the time period given.

In 1 minute: 1.50 inches at Barst, Guadeloupe, on November 26, 1970
In 15 minutes: 8.00 inches at Plumb Point, Jamaica
In 42 minutes: 12.00 inches at Holt, Missouri
In 24 hours: 73.62 inches at Cilaos, La Réunion, on March 15-16, 1952
In 1 month: 366.14 inches at Cherrapunji, India, in July 1861
1 year (average): 463.4 inches, Tutunendo, Colombia
1 year (maximum): 1041.78 inches, Cherrapunji, India, August 1, 1860 to July 31, 1861
Most rainy days: Mt. Waialeale, Hawaii, with up to 350 days per year

Safety Rules

We begin by discussing two important terms: *flash flood watch* and *flash flood warning*. If a flash flood watch is issued, it means there is potential for flash flooding. Continue normal activities but be increasingly aware of nearby thunderstorms and the possibility of large rainfall rates. A flash flood warning means flooding has been observed or is imminent. The following safety rules provide for self-defense against floods and can mean the difference between life and death.

- You should have a general knowledge of the flooding characteristics of your area. If you do not, contact the NWS, 911, or other civil authority.

- If a flash flood watch is issued for your area, continue normal activities, but be aware of signs of heavy rainfall such as persistent lightning and thunder in one location.

- Realize that flash floods commonly occur with little or no warning.

- If you live in a flood-prone area, know your way out in advance and have a plan to get out before the flood strikes.

- Check your supply of nonperishable food-stuffs and battery-powered equipment.

- Farmers and ranchers will need to move live-stock and equipment away from flood-prone areas.

- Sportsmen will need to check on camps and leases.

- If camping, get away from streambeds and seek higher ground.

- Keep your vehicle fueled.

- Know that floods may interrupt water service and contaminate drinking water supplies.

- Do not attempt to wade through water that is above your knees—the force of rushing floodwaters is great.

- Never try to drive through streets that appear flooded or over a bridge where the road surface is not visible—the bridge may not be there!

- Be especially cautious at night.

- If you drive unexpectedly into high water and your vehicle stalls, abandon it immediately and seek higher ground. About 60% of all flood-related deaths are vehicle-related.

- After the flood, follow the rules for hurricanes (see pages 217-218).

Drought

Just as floods are an unpleasant surplus of water, a *drought* is a debilitating lack of moisture brought on by a period of abnormally dry weather, causing a significant hydrologic imbalance. The result can be crop damage, water supply shortages, and damage to ecosystems. The severity depends upon the degree of moisture deficiency, duration, and size of the affected region.

Definitions of drought vary from place to place. If yields of corn, wheat, or some other staple crop are significantly reduced, then it is said that a condition of drought exists. If cattle die from lack of drinking water, the same can be said. When residents of a city have to restrict lawn sprinkling and use of air conditioning, a drought is blamed. It can be argued that the criteria for a drought are as much nonmeteorological as they are meteorological. In some regions of the United States, the Gulf Coast for example, an annual rainfall of 35 inches would represent a serious rainfall deficit. In west Texas, however, it would be considered abnormally wet. The damage suffered by plants during a drought depends also on the species of the plant and the properties of the soil. Even within the same geographical region, a "drought" may harm some plant communities and not others. The time of year is another factor. In the summer when rain becomes more sporadic, one farm can be producing a bumper crop while the farm several miles away is suffering from lack of rainfall.

There are basically four types of drought. The first is caused by long-term climatological factors such as location or topographical features. Examples are the desert regions of Chile, the southwestern United States, and northern Africa. Drought is also a symptom of anomalous circulation patterns aloft. These regions are dominated by high pressure, general sinking motion, and lack of clouds. The recurrence of this pattern in the same region over a period of months or years leads to drought. A third type of drought occurs seasonally in certain climatic types. Several regions in the tropics and the subtropics have a distinct "wet season" and a well-defined "dry season" when little or no rain falls. Seasonal drought is commonly associated with the monsoon. The final type of drought is due to the spotty nature of convective rainfall. It is well known that in many locations, summer precipitation patterns are dominated by thunderstorms, which are normally not widespread in areal coverage. Over a period of weeks or months, this patchwork pattern brings ample rainfall to some points while others get very little. This situation can lead to huge differences in summer rainfall, with some locations receiving five times the rainfall of other locations.

Blizzards and Snowstorms

The beauty of snow is deceptive. A child's face beams as the snow flutters to the ground, but too much snow is dangerous; it can cripple cities and kill people and animals. Two terms are used for large-scale, significant snowfall events: *snowstorm* and *blizzard*. A snowstorm is a transient occurrence of snow, significant enough to be remembered. On the other hand, a blizzard combines strong wind, low temperatures, and blinding snow into a deadly and crippling weather phenomena. A blizzard is present when the sustained windspeed exceeds 30 mph, the temperature drops to 20° F or lower, and visibility is reduced to less than 500 feet either by falling snow, blowing snow, or both. A severe blizzard combines sustained winds of 45 mph, a temperature of 10° F or lower, and visibility near zero. If snow is not falling and the visibility is reduced by windblown snow, then a "ground blizzard" is taking place, meaning that the blizzard conditions are shallow, affecting only the near-ground levels of the atmosphere.

The socioeconomic impact of a blizzard depends on the frequency of similar events in a particular region. In the northern United States and most of Canada, blizzards occur several times each winter, and the populace is prepared for them. Familiarity with the dangers that result from loss of visual perception ("snow blindness") and exposure to extreme cold will lead experienced people to naturally seek substantial shelter quickly. The rare blizzard at lower latitudes tends to be more disruptive because people are not as familiar with the dangers and may fail to seek shelter until it is too late.

The Anatomy of a Blizzard

Several meteorological factors combine to produce blizzards and snowstorms, as shown in figure 15.1. The blizzard is but one manifestation of extratropical weather system evolution. The upper-level forces cold air to flow into the rear of the system while warm, moist air flows forward. The warm, moist air mass flowing into the system from the south provides part of the energy needed to fuel these massive weather systems. In addition, the temperature contrast associated with opposing air masses fuels the system. Strong winds arise because of the tight pressure gradient. The primary area affected by heavy snow is normally located to the north and west of the location of the surface low-pressure center.

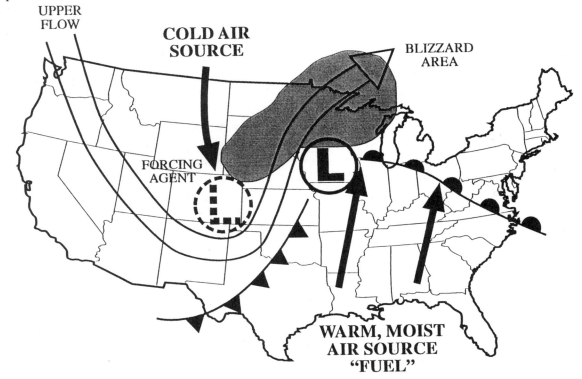

Fig. 15.1. The anatomy of a blizzard.

Teacher's Extra

No Two Alike?

The formation of snow begins when water vapor or a supercooled droplet of water forms an ice crystal, almost always hexagonal in shape, around a freezing nucleus that lies suspended in the atmosphere. From that moment on, the life of an ice crystal can be played out in many ways. The crystal may fall to the ground in its original form or, more frequently, the ice crystal grows through sublimation. Its shape will be determined by environmental conditions of temperature, moisture, and wind. As the crystals descend, they meet up with others, forming aggregates, otherwise known as snowflakes. The answer to the question No two alike? hinges on the unique environments in which snowflakes form and the complex manner in which they aggregate, or "stick together."

What snowflakes actually looked like was not widely known until the middle of the 19th century, when *Cloud Crystals*, with sketches by "A Lady," was published in the United States. The lady had caught snowflakes on a black surface and then observed them with a magnifying glass. In 1885 Wilson Alwyn Bentley, of Jericho, Vermont, took photographs of snowflakes through a microscope. Thousands of Bentley's photographs were analyzed and it was found that none of the snowflakes were identical, which is probably the basis for the idea that no two snowflakes are ever exactly the same. For two snowflakes to be identical, the environmental conditions in which the snowflake forms must be identical as well as the mechanics of its aggregation. Although the idea is unverifiable, it can, at the very least, be said that no material displays the bewildering complexities of snow.

Safety Rules

Since 1936, blizzards and snowstorms have accounted for some 100 deaths annually. Here are a few safety precautions to observe during blizzards and snowstorms.

- Farmers and ranchers will need to move livestock and farm animals to sheltered areas; extra feed will be needed.

- Use heaters in water tanks. Research indicates that, contrary to popular belief, cattle do not "freeze" to death during blizzards; they actually become dehydrated because their water supply freezes and they can't lick an adequate amount of water to survive.

- Check battery-powered equipment. Blizzards frequently bring power outages.

- Check your supply of heating fuel.

- Stock up on nonperishable food items. Blizzards can isolate you for days.

- Stay indoors during the storm.

- Dress appropriately if it is absolutely necessary to go outdoors. Dress in layers of clothing, not just in one big coat. The outermost garment should be hooded, tightly worn, and water-repellent.

- Be sure your vehicle is "winterized" with oil, wipers, heater, tires, electrical system, brakes, lights, antifreeze, and a full tank of gas.

- Carry a blizzard survival kit in your car. This includes blankets, sleeping bags, matches and candles, extra clothes, paper towels, facial tissue, nonperishable food items, compass, road map, knife, first-aid kit, flashlight and flares, tire chains, booster cable, shovel, ax, and special items for the very young and the elderly.

- If conditions test or exceed your expectations, seek refuge—do not try to drive through the storm.

- Plan primary and alternate routes in advance.

- Keep up with the latest weather information.

- Try not to travel alone; travel with two or three other persons.

- Travel in a convoy, if possible.

- Drive defensively.

- Find a way to stay active. Clap hands, move, or even get out of the vehicle and walk around (be sure not to get too far away). This will help you stay alert.

- Do not panic.

- Keep fresh air in your car by opening vents or downwind windows slightly.

- Run engine and heater sparingly.

- Leave dome lights on at night.

- Do not allow everyone in the vehicle to fall asleep at the same time. One person needs to stay awake.

Temperature Extremes

Extremes of temperature bring high death tolls and much suffering to plants, animals, and humans, as well as exacting tremendous economic losses.

Extremes of cold develop when there is a persistent southward displacement of the jetstream called a *trough*. In the United States this is commonly brought about by a southward displacement of the Hudson Bay Vortex, a semipermanent feature of Earth's general circulation, which behaves like a giant, spinning wheel of cold air. The counterclockwise flow around the Hudson Bay Vortex forces very cold air down from the far northern latitudes, allowing it to spill into the continental United States.

Extremes of heat develop when the jetstream flow is displaced northward into a feature called a *ridge*. The presence of high pressure aloft allows for a general, large-scale sinking motion in the atmosphere, leading to a nonfavorable environment for rainfall. Heat waves and drought commonly occur together.

Safety Rules

Survival during times of excessive heat requires common-sense preparation. This section outlines some of the most important self-defense points to remember when heat waves threaten your area (precautions for cold waves are the same for blizzards and snowstorms).

- Just slow down. Don't try to do too much.

- Heed the early signs of heat stress such as headache, dizziness, nausea, or weakness.

- Wear light-colored, loose-fitting, and light-weight clothing.

- Eat less.

- Drink plenty of nonalcoholic beverages; water is best.

- Step into the summer heat slowly, giving yourself time to become acclimated to the heat.

- Limit your time in the direct sunlight. This helps reduce sunburn and "sun poisoning."

- Know the symptoms of heat-related stress and the first-aid treatment for them.

- Learn about the Heat Index. Know your level of tolerance and do not exceed it.

- If you feel that you are starting to suffer from heat stress, stop what you are doing and rest in the shade for a while. Sip cool water.

The Process of Scientific Thought

Activity #1

Title: Self-Made Flood

Objective: To demonstrate why floods are dangerous

Materials Needed: large pan, several plastic model cars

Procedure: Obtain a large pan that will hold an inch or two of water. Place several plastic model vehicles in the bottom of the pan and begin pouring water into the pan slowly.

Elementary

- Draw a picture of the rising water and the model vehicles.
- What does the water in the pan represent? (Answer: Rising floodwaters.)
- What do the model vehicles represent? (Answer: Real vehicles that get trapped in rising floodwaters.)
- What happens when the water in the pan gets deep enough? (Answer: The model vehicles are moved.) Why? (Answer: The vehicles are moved by the force of the moving water.)
- How can this activity be applied to real-life situations? (Answer: Floodwaters can carry away cars and trucks; 60% of all flood-related deaths are automobile-related.)

Secondary

- Find out how much a square foot of water weighs. (Answer: About 16 pounds.) How much does a cubic foot of water weigh? (Answer: 62.4 pounds.)
- Floodwaters normally move at 6 to 12 mph. How much force is exerted on a vehicle by water 1 foot deep moving at 10 mph? (Answer: Lots! Choose the dimensions of one side of the vehicle and calculate it.)
- Buoyancy forces are even more important than horizontal forces. In effect, a car weighs 1,500 pounds less for each foot the water rises. How high must the water rise to carry away most vehicles? (Answer: Only 2 or 3 feet).
- Apply this to real-life situations. (Answer: Do not attempt to drive into flooded areas, especially when it is difficult to judge the water depth.)

Activity #2

Title: A Floating Flake

Objective: To demonstrate why snowflakes float

Materials Needed: two sheets of paper

Procedure: Obtain two sheets of paper. Crumple one into a ball. Hold the flat sheet in one hand and the crumpled sheet in the other hand. Be sure to hold them at the same level. Allow both sheets to fall at the same time. Observe which sheet strikes the floor first.

Elementary

- Draw a picture of the two sheets of paper falling toward the floor.

- Which sheet of paper hits the floor first? (Answer: The crumpled piece.)

- Is the force of gravity the same for each sheet? (Answer: Yes.)

- Why does the crumpled piece of paper fall to the floor sooner than the flat piece? (Answer: The shape of each sheet of paper is different and that becomes an important factor in their fall rates. The upward force of air is greater on the flat sheet because it covers a larger area than the crumpled piece.)

- How is the flat piece of paper like a snowflake? (Answer: It "floats" down to the floor just like a snowflake floats to Earth.)

Secondary

- A generally accepted approximation for snowflake fall speed is:

$$V = kD^n$$

where D is the melted diameter of the snowflake expressed in centimeters (cm), V is the fall speed given in cm/sec, n is equal to 0.3, and k is 160 for dendritic structures and 234 for columns and plates.

- Plug in some values for D. Present the data in the form of a table and a graph. Verify that the fall speed increases as the snowflake becomes wetter (meaning larger values of D).

- For the same-size particle, which falls faster, plates/columns or dendrites? (Answer: Plates and columns.) Why? (Answer: For the same reason that the crumpled piece of paper fell faster than the flat piece, i.e., the area covered by the dendritic structure is larger.)

Activity #3

Title: No Two Alike?

Objective: To demonstrate the many shapes of snowflakes

Materials Needed: white paper, scissors, pencil

Procedure: See below.

Elementary

- Have students draw as many different snowflakes as possible on a large sheet of construction paper. After they have finished, cut out the shapes and compare them. Are any two alike?

- If you live in an area where snow is frequent, catch some snowflakes on a black cloth and look at them with a magnifying glass. Are any two exactly alike?

Secondary

- The sheer number of individual snowflakes that reach the ground in a single snowstorm is astounding. Assume there are 14,400 snowflakes that fall per inch of accumulated snow. If a snowstorm leaves an average depth of 2 feet of snow over an area of 50,000 square miles, about how many snowflakes fell? (Answer: 4.5×10^{20}, or 45 quintillion!)

Activity #4

Title: Dangerous Heat

Objective: To illustrate the Heat Index

Materials Needed: the Heat Index Chart (table 15.1)

Procedure: Use the outlines given below to develop your own approach.

Elementary

- If the relative humidity (RH) is 50% and the temperature is 90°F, what is the Heat Index? (Answer: 96°F). Is this considered dangerous? (Answer: Not usually; it is well below the "danger threshold" of 105°F.)

- If the RH is 60% and the temperature is 95°F, what is the Heat Index? (Answer: 114°F.) Is this considered dangerous? (Answer: Yes, it is well above the danger level of 105°F.)

- If the RH is 15% and the temperature is 90°F, what is the Heat Index? (Answer: 86°F.) Why is the Heat Index lower than the actual temperature? (Answer: The air is very dry and allows for efficient operation of the body's cooling mechanism.)

Secondary

- If the RH is 55% and the temperature is 92°F, what is the Heat Index? (Answer: 103°F. You'll have to use a mathematical skill called "interpolation.")

- If the RH is 38% and the temperature is 98°F, what is the Heat Index? (Answer: 105°F, even more interpolation!)

- Are there other factors besides temperature and humidity that affect how hot a person feels? (Answer: Yes, there are several. The intensity of sunlight is one. If all other factors are the same, a person feels hotter on a sunny day than on a cloudy day. Another factor is wind. At air temperatures below body temperature, the wind exerts a cooling effect. At air temperatures above body temperature, however, the moving air actually adds heat. A third factor is acclimation. It will feel hotter if the onset of heat is sudden or if a person is not accustomed to it.)

Activity #5

Title: Dangerous Cold

Objective: To illustrate the windchill index

Materials Needed: The windchill chart (table 15.2)

Procedure: Use the outline below to demonstrate the idea of windchill and its significance.

Elementary

- If the temperature is 45°F and the windspeed is 20 mph, what is the windchill? (Answer: 26°F). Is this a life-threatening situation? (Answer: No, it's well above the danger level of -20°F).

- If the temperature is 25°F and the windspeed is 25 mph, what is the windchill? (Answer: -7°F). Is this a life-threatening situation? (Answer: Usually not, but frostbite on exposed skin is possible.)

• If the temperature is -5° F and the windspeed is 15 mph, what is the windchill? (Answer: -38° F.) Is this a life-threatening situation? (Answer: Yes.)

Secondary

• If the temperature is 32° F and the windspeed is 40 mph, what is the windchill? (Answer: -2° F.)

• If the temperature is -9° F and the windspeed is 23 mph, what is the windchill? (Answer: -54° F.)

• Are there other factors besides temperature and wind that affect how cold a person feels? (Answer: People feel colder on a cloudy day, if precipitation is falling, or if the onset of the cold is sudden or if they are not acclimated to it.)

Ideas for Science Fair Projects

1. Repeat activity #1. Be sure to mention how the force of floodwaters acts horizontally and vertically. It's also important to convey that floodwaters are underestimated by a naive public. Mention safety rules.

2. Research past floods that affected your city or state. Tell what caused them, their effects, and the type of meteorological event they were associated with. Did human intervention aggravate the problem or magnify the effects?

3. Look into snowflake shapes in detail. Your research question is "No Two Alike?"

4. Center a project on the Heat Index. Use table 15.1. Be sure to mention the adverse effect excessive heat has on health. Interview a health-care professional. Can you find the day with the highest Heat Index in your city during the last five years?

5. Center a project on the Windchill Index. Follow the same outline as given in #4 for the Heat Index.

6. Investigate the anatomy of a blizzard. What is it? How does it develop? Effects? Self-defense?

7. Develop a project on how temperature extremes affect businesses in your local area. Do they prosper or lose money? What preparations do they take when extreme heat or cold threatens? How do temperature extremes affect their employees?

8. Try to figure out return periods for excessive rainfall events in your area. How often can a 2-inch rainfall in 24 hours be expected? 4 inches, etc.?

9. Look into the past and investigate three droughts that affected your state, city, or the United States. What caused the drought? Effects?

School's Out!

1. Take your science fair project to a local service organization.

2. Maintain a record of snowfall at your house.

3. Review safety precautions for floods, blizzards, and temperature extremes with your family and neighbors.

4. Write a story where the antagonist is a flood, drought, blizzard, or excessive heat or cold.

Relative Humidity (%)

Air Temperature (°F)	0	5	10	15	20	25	30	35	40	45	50	55	60	65	70	75	80	85	90	95	100
140	125																				
135	120	126																			
130	117	122	131																		
125	111	116	123	131	141																
120	107	111	116	123	130	139	142														
115	103	107	111	115	120	127	135	143	151												
110	99	102	105	108	112	117	123	130	137	143	150										
105	95	97	100	102	105	109	113	118	123	129	135	142	149								
100	91	93	95	97	99	101	104	107	110	115	120	126	132	133	144						
95	87	88	90	91	93	94	96	98	101	104	107	110	114	119	124	130	136				
90	83	84	85	86	87	88	90	91	93	95	96	98	100	102	106	109	113	117	122		
85	76	79	80	81	82	83	84	85	86	87	88	89	90	91	93	95	97	99	102	105	108
80	73	74	75	76	77	77	78	79	79	80	81	81	82	83	85	85	86	87	88	89	91
75	69	69	70	71	72	72	73	73	74	74	75	75	76	76	77	77	78	78	79	79	80
70	64	64	65	65	66	66	67	67	68	68	69	69	70	70	70	70	71	71	71	71	72

Heat Index	Possible Heat Disorders for People in Higher-Risk Groups
130° or higher	Heatstroke or sunstroke highly likely with continued exposure
105° 130°	Sunstroke, heat cramps, or heat exhaustion likely, and heat-stroke possible with prolonged exposure or physical activity
90°-105°	Sunstroke, heat cramps, and heat exhaustion possible with prolonged exposure or physical activity
80°-90°	Fatigue possible with prolonged exposure or physical activity

Tables 15.1 Heat Index Chart

From *The Teacher's Weather Sourcebook*. © 1999 Frank T. Konvicka. Teacher Ideas Press. (800) 237-6124

Windspeed (mph)

	5	10	15	20	25	30	35	40
50°	48	39	34	31	29	27	26	25
45°	43	34	29	26	23	21	20	19
40°	37	28	23	19	16	13	12	11
35°	32	22	16	12	8	6	4	2
30°	27	16	9	4	1	-2	-4	-4
25°	22	10	2	-3	-7	-10	-12	-14
20°	16	3	-5	-10	-15	-18	-20	-22
15°	11	-3	-11	-17	-22	-25	-27	-29
10°	6	-9	-18	-24	-29	-33	-35	-36
5°	0	-15	-25	-31	-36	-41	-43	-45
0	-5	-22	-31	-39	-44	-49	-52	-54
-5	-10	-27	-38	-46	-51	-56	-58	-61
-10	-15	-34	-45	-51	-59	-64	-67	-69
-15	-21	-40	-51	-60	-66	-71	-74	-77
-20	-26	-46	-58	-67	-74	-79	-82	-86
-25	-31	-52	-65	-74	-81	-86	-89	-93
-30	-35	-58	-70	-81	-89	-94	-98	-101

Current Temperature (°F)

Arctic explorers and military experts have developed what is called the Windchill Index, which measures the combined effects of wind and temperature. In effect, the index describes the cooling power of the air on exposed flesh. To use the chart, just locate the current air temperature in the left column and then read across to the windspeed.

Example: If the outside air temperature is 20°F and the windspeed is 20 mph, it actually "feels" like -10°F outside.

Table 15.2. Windchill Chart

Chapter 16

Anthropogenic Air Pollution

What kind of planet will we leave for our descendants? This question squarely confronts us. Of central importance are several issues that fall under the scope of atmospheric science: global warming, ozone depletion, acid deposition, and air pollution. These issues are complex and controversial, involving political and ethical decisions on an international scale. An evenhanded treatment of these disputed matters is urgently needed; therefore, the *Sourcebook* will approach contemporary issues in the atmospheric sciences from the standpoint of "environmental realism," as opposed to ultraliberal and ultraconservative "environmental extremism."

Earth has two sources of air pollution: natural and man-made. A good example of natural air pollution is a volcano. On the other hand, the presence of humans on Earth has led to another, unnatural type of pollution termed *anthropogenic*. Anthropogenic air pollution is the inadvertent alteration of the chemical composition of Earth's atmosphere through human activities and processes.

A Historical Perspective

Human-driven air pollution is certainly not a new problem. It seems logical to state that the discovery of fire by early man was also the beginning of anthropogenic pollution of Earth's atmosphere. History records that the Romans, over 2,000 years ago, complained about the foul air of their cities. In London what was perhaps the first smoke abatement law was passed in 1273. At the end of Queen Elizabeth's reign during the latter half of the 16th century, the English Parliament attempted to alleviate the smoke problem by passing an edict whereby wood instead of coal was to be used for heating in London while Parliament was in session and the queen in residence. This was one of the earliest organized attempts by society at air pollution control.

The onset of the Industrial Revolution in England in the middle of the 19th century greatly aggravated the air pollution problem because of the massing of factories in already polluted cities such as London and Birmingham. The further concentration of industry to be near sources of raw materials, especially coal, fostered new urban areas. These efforts soon spread to continental Europe and to North America. With the drilling of the first successful oil well in the United States in Pennsylvania in 1859, and later the invention of the gasoline-powered engine, a new source of anthropogenic pollution—the burning of fossil fuels and automobile exhaust—would become the major pollutant source of the 20th century.

Air Pollution: The Modern Setting

Human-caused air pollution remains most prevalent in urbanized areas. Table 16.1 lists the names, chemical formulas, and principal sources of modern air pollutants. Seven of these (carbon monoxide, nitrogen oxides, hydrocarbons, ozone, peroxyacetal nitrates, sulfur oxides, and particulates) result from the combustion of fossil fuels in transportation and at stationary sources such as power plants and factories. Overall, automobiles contribute about 60% of the U.S. human-caused air pollution. Figure 16.1 identifies major human-caused pollutants and their sources in the United States. Some of these pollutants are described in more detail below.

POLLUTANT	SYMBOL	ANTHROPOGENIC SOURCE
Carbon dioxide	CO_2	Incomplete combustion of fossil fuels and wood
Carbon monoxide	CO	Incomplete combustion of fossil fuels
Exotics	—	Fission products, other toxics
Hydrocarbons	HC	Incomplete combustion of fuels
Methane	CH_4	Organic processes, combustion, natural-gas leaks
Nitrogen oxides	NO_x (NO, NO_2)	High-temperature combustion
Ozone (tropospheric)	O_3	Auto and industrial emissions; photochemical reactions
Particulates	—	Dust, dirt, soot, salt, metals, organics
Peroxyacetyl nitrates	PAN	Photochemical reactions
Sulfur oxides	SO_x (SO_2, SO_3)	Coal and oil combustion; smelting of ore
Watert Vapor	H_2	Combustion processes, steam

Table 16.1. A Summary of Modern Air Pollutants

Carbon Monoxide

Carbon monoxide (CO) is an odorless, colorless, and tasteless gas consisting of a combination of one atom of carbon and one atom of oxygen. The toxicity of CO is well known. Carbon monoxide is produced by incomplete combustion of fuels or other carbon-containing substances. Natural sources of CO, such as forest fires and the decomposition of organic matter, produce up to 90% of existing CO, whereas human sources, mainly transportation, produce the other 10%. Carbon monoxide did not become a problem until many fossil fuel-burning cars, trucks, and buses became concentrated in urban areas. Normal CO levels range from 10 to 30 parts per million (ppm) in metropolitan areas, but crowded freeways and parking garages can reach 80 ppm CO.

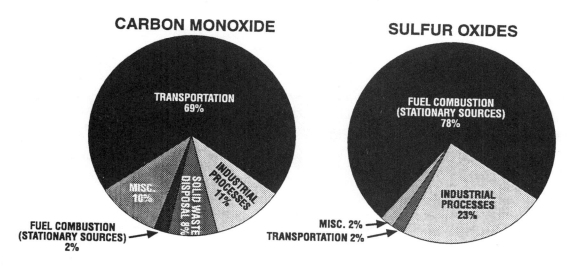

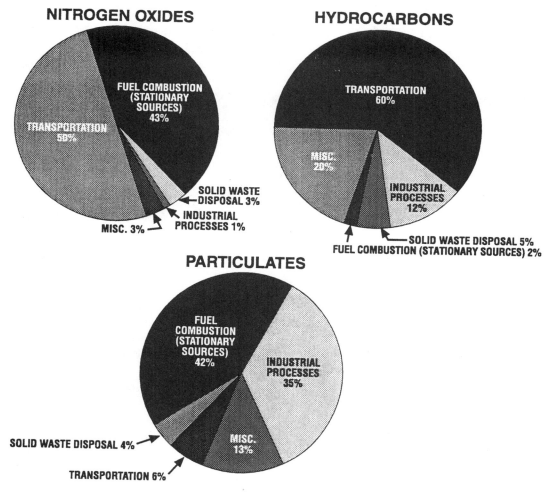

Fig. 16.1. Five principal types of human-caused pollution and their sources in the United States. (Compiled with information available through the Environmental Protection Agency.)

Photochemical Smog

Photochemical smog is another type of pollution evident in the modern setting, not generally experienced in the distant past but developed with the advent of the automobile. Today, it is a major component of anthropogenic air pollution. Photochemical smog results from the interaction between sunlight and the products of automobile exhaust. Although the term *smog* (a combination of the words "fog" and "smoke") is a misnomer, it is generally used to describe this phenomenon. Smog is responsible for the hazy sky conditions and reduced visibility in many large metropolitan areas.

The connection between automobile exhaust and smog was not determined until 1953, well after society had established its dependence upon individualized transportation. Despite this discovery, widespread mass transit has declined, the railroads have dwindled, and the automobile remains the preferred mode of transportation in the United States.

The higher temperatures in modern automobile engines react with fuels to produce nitrogen dioxide (NO_2). Nitrogen dioxide derived from automobiles, and to a lesser extent from power plants, is highly reactive with ultraviolet light. This reaction liberates atomic oxygen (O) and a nitric oxide (NO) molecule from the nitrogen dioxide (NO_2). The free oxygen atom then recombines with an oxygen molecule (O_2) to form ozone (O_3). Also, the nitric oxide (NO) molecule reacts with hydrocarbons (HC) to produce a whole family of chemicals generally called peroxyacetyl nitrates (PAN). These PAN products produce no known health effect in humans but are particularly damaging to plants, which provided the initial clue for discovery of these photochemical reactions.

Nitrogen dioxide (NO_2) is a reddish-brown gas that damages and inflames the human respiratory system, destroys lung tissue, and damages plants. Concentrations of 3 ppm are dangerous enough to require alerting parents to keep children indoors; a level of 5 ppm is very serious. Nitrogen dioxide interacts with water vapor to form nitric acid (HNO_3). Worldwide, the nitrogen dioxide problem is greatest in metropolitan areas. North American urban areas may have from 10 to 100 times higher NO_2 concentration than nonurban areas.

Industrial Smog and Sulfur Oxides

Over the past 300 years coal has slowly replaced wood as the basic fuel used by society. The Industrial Revolution required high-grade energy to run machines and to facilitate the conversion from animate energy (energy from living sources, such as animals powering farm equipment) to inanimate energy (energy from nonliving sources, such as coal, steam, and water). The air pollution associated with coal-burning industries is known as industrial smog, a term coined by a London physician at the turn of the 20th century. The combination of sulfur and moisture droplets forms a sulfuric acid mist that is dangerous in high concentrations.

Sulfur, an impurity that occurs to some degree in all fossil fuels, forms sulfur dioxide (SO_2) during combustion. Thus, sulfur dioxide is a problem wherever coal-fired power plants and heavy industry are common. Sulfur dioxide is colorless but can be detected by its pungent odor. Sulfur dioxide irritates the human respiratory system, especially in individuals with asthma, chronic bronchitis, and emphysema.

Once in the atmosphere, SO_2 reacts with oxygen to form sulfur trioxide (SO_3), which is highly reactive, and in the presence of water or water vapor, forms sulfuric acid (H_2SO_4). In the United States electric utilities and steel manufacturing are the main sources of sulfur dioxide.

Teacher's Extra

The "Other" Pollutions

Air and water pollution grab the headlines, but three other prevalent pollution problems are soil, light, and noise.

Soil pollution is a byproduct of water pollution, as the soil can become polluted by chemically contaminated water percolating down or through it. Soil can also become contaminated when pollutants, such as lead from auto emissions, settle into the soil from the air. One of the most common solutions for soil pollution is digging it up and carting it to a sealed area or landfill, but this process is expensive.

Light pollution is the excessive amount of light in the nighttime sky caused by streetlights and industrial and commercial lighting. It causes problems for nocturnal animals and plants. Birds that migrate at night are often confused by lights, especially in large cities; hatching sea turtles that depend on the natural ocean glow to find their way to the sea often move away from the sea and toward streetlights; and some plants can bloom prematurely if exposed to too much artificial light. Light pollution is also a problem for professional astronomers and amateur skywatchers, as the details of the nighttime sky are lost in the artificial glow.

Noise pollution, often a problem in cities, can be caused by traffic, airplanes, industry, commercial enterprises, and even human voices. It is thought that excessive noise can cause behavioral and chemical changes in the human body. Not much has been done to curtail noise pollution, but small steps are being made: Aircraft designers are trying to make quieter engines; automobile manufacturers are designing quieter cars (both inside and outside); and computer, air-conditioning, and heating-unit designers are working on developing quieter motors.

Effects of Air Pollution

It is now realized that air pollution is not merely a nuisance or an inconvenience, but that air quality has a great influence on the social aspects of human life. The flight of population from the urban centers during the last three decades in order to take advantage of cleaner air is a case in point. The quality of the air we breathe is becoming one of the most important factors in societal decision making.

Plant damage, especially in the vicinity of smelter complexes, is strikingly evident. In some cases, hillsides that are in the path of the prevailing wind from a smelting facility are almost completely denuded of vegetation. Among the pollutants considered to be most damaging are sulfur, fluorine, and the photochemical reactions between nitrogen and organic compounds. Pine trees are particularly susceptible to sulfur dioxide. The fluorine compounds, especially gaseous fluorides, can build up in forage crops, which may be eaten by cattle and sheep, causing fluorosis. The toxicity caused by the photochemical agents is particularly severe on salad crops such as spinach, lettuce, and celery.

The most important effect of air pollution on society is its relationship to human health. Table 16.2 provides a summary of the known and suspected effects of seven major pollutants on human health.

POLLUTANT	KNOWN OR SUSPECTED EFFECTS ON HUMAN HEALTH
Carbon monoxide	Reduces the oxygen-carrying capacity of the blood; low concentrations can impair mental abilities and high concentrations can cause death
Lead	Lead poisoning; impairs mental ability
Nitrogen oxides	Causes eye, throat and lung irritation
Ozone	Irritates the nose and throat; impairs lung function
Particulates	Causes breathing difficulties
Sulfur Oxides	Aggravates upper-respiratory disease and heart conditions; irritates eyes and throat
Toxins	Irritation of nose, throat and lungs; some forms are associated with cancer

Table 16.2. Known and Suspected Effects of Common Air Pollutants on Human Health

Prolonged exposure to pollutants commonly results in irritation of the eyes and the respiratory system. More serious effects may include a causal link with disease and cancer. With the concentration of pollutant sources in urbanized areas, it is inevitable that, under adverse meteorological conditions and favorable topographical conditions such as stagnant, stable air and confining valleys, pollution episodes occur that cause sickness and death. In the United States, perhaps the best-known example of this occurred in October 1948, in Donora, Pennsylvania, a factory town along the banks of the Monongahela River. A 4-day episode of air pollution killed 17 people with over 6,000 becoming ill. In London, a truly tragic pollution event occurred in December 1952, when a 5-day-long outbreak of air pollution killed more than 4,000 people.

The presence of polluted air poses a dilemma for society. On the one hand, we must continually breathe in air to sustain life. One the other hand, this same air may contain a wide variety of toxic substances that can be injurious to human health.

Solutions to the Problem

It is a fact that the distribution of human-produced carbon monoxide, nitrogen dioxide, ozone, PAN, and sulfur dioxide over North America, Europe, and Asia is tied to transportation and energy production. Implementation of solutions is important to individual health and agricultural productivity. Further, solutions to the growing air pollution problem pose no mystery: Technologies and legislation to eliminate or abate emissions are what's needed.

Technology

Because energy production is at the heart of the pollution problem, it stands to reason that conservation (using less energy) and efficiency (using energy with less waste) are key strategies. Less fundamental changes include cleaning stack emissions with precipitators, scrubbers, fillers, and separators. Car exhaust can be cleaned with more efficient carburation and emission controls. Automobile usage can be reduced with alternative transportation systems and actions as simple as carpooling.

Legislation

In the United States air-quality-control legislation was primarily the responsibility of local and state jurisdictions in the post-WWII decade. In 1955 the only federal law concerning air quality was the Air Pollutant and Technical Assistance Act, which provided federal research and development funds. By the 1960s there was increasing concern that the air-pollution problem transcended local and state jurisdictions. Consequently, in 1963, the U.S. Congress enacted the Clean Air Act.

The Air Quality Act of 1967 provided for establishing air-quality-control regions with state-set standards of air quality based on federally established criteria. The Clean Air Act Amendments of 1970 required the Environmental Protection Agency (EPA) to establish national air-quality standards to protect health and welfare, national standards for new facilities, and standards for facilities emitting hazardous substances. The 1970 piece of legislation also required states to develop implementation plans to bring their air quality to the levels set by national standards, and it required more stringent national emission standards for new automobiles.

The Clean Air Act Amendments of 1977 incorporated a requirement for preventing the significant deterioration of air quality in areas where air already is cleaner than required by the national ambient air-quality standards, and set new deadlines for achieving them in areas that do not meet the standards, but also required the review of those existing standards by the EPA.

The 800-page Clean Air Act Amendments of 1990 were adopted in large part to address the concerns put forth by environmentalists and government regulators that real improvements in air quality could not be achieved without a substantial revision of the 1970 and 1977 amendments. In effect, the 1990 act marks a fundamental and significant departure from traditional governmental approaches to environmental protection, as it is a product of unprecedented cooperation between the government and the private sector. Rather than relying on the traditional method of rule-making and regulation at the federal level, which often leads to expensive and time-consuming litigation, the EPA committed itself to achieving a consensus on air-quality standards at the outset of the process.

The 1990 amendments also encourage business to assume a leading role in environmental protection by providing incentives for companies to seek solutions to problems independent of government directives. Regulations in the 1990 Clean Air Act Amendments include urban pollution, motor vehicles, air toxins, acid rain, and ozone depletion. As of this writing, even more stringent amendments are being discussed.

The contemporary issue of anthropogenic air pollution confronts us, and the answer is clear: Action must be taken. Certainly, society cannot simply halt two centuries of industrialization; the resulting economic chaos would be devastating. Neither can society permit pollution to continue unabated, for harmful environmental feedback will result. People have been on Earth for such a short time, yet our present activities affect our future. In chapter 3 we learned that Earth likely evolved four atmospheres; we may now be contributing to the mix of the fifth atmosphere: the anthropogenic atmosphere.

The Process of Scientific Thought

Activity #1

Title: Make Your Own Smog

Objective: To illustrate how smog is produced

Materials Needed: milk or juice bottle, shallow pan of chilled water, warm dry cloth

Procedure: Cool the bottom of a milk or juice bottle by placing it in a shallow pan of chilled water. Introduce some smoke inside the bottle, replace the lid, and then warm the top of the bottle with a warm, dry cloth. After a few minutes, observe what happens to the smoke inside the bottle.

Elementary

- Draw a picture of the bottle and the pattern of smoke inside.
- What pattern does the smoke display? (Answer: It takes on a layered form, or stratification.)
- What is the coolest part of the bottle? (Answer: The bottom.)
- What is the warmest part of the bottle? (Answer: The top.)
- Explain why stratification occurs. (Answer: The cool bottom and the warm top make the air inside the bottle reflect the same pattern. The smoke stretches out along the boundary separating the cooler lower levels from the warmer upper levels.)
- How does this apply to the real atmosphere? (Answer: Essentially, a temperature inversion is created inside the bottle. An inversion is stable, meaning that it does not allow for efficient mixing of the air, thus causing the smoke to spread out along the top of the inversion. This is how smog forms.)

Secondary

- Construct a graph of temperature vs. height and plot the following data: ground level (50° F), 1,000 feet (52° F), 2,000 feet (55° F), 3,000 feet (56° F), 4,000 feet (58° F), 5,000 feet (55° F), 6,000 feet (52° F), 7,000 feet (45° F), 8,000 feet (40° F), 9,000 feet (35° F), and 10,000 feet (32° F). Label the portion of the graph that exhibits a temperature inversion. Mark where the stratification of pollutants would occur. (Answer: At the top of the inversion.)

Activity #2

Title: Index Card Pollution Detector

Objective: To determine if weather affects air pollution

Materials Needed: 3 x 5 index card, a dab of petroleum jelly, magnifying glass

Procedure: Draw a small circle in the center of an index card and put a dab of petroleum jelly inside the circle. Place the card outside at a certain location for one day. Collect the card the next day at the same time and count the number of foreign particles that stick to the petroleum jelly. Repeat on another day when a noticeable weather change has occurred (warmer, colder, windy). Be sure to note all weather conditions using your class weather log and cloud chart (see chapters 6 and 7).

Elementary

- Draw a picture. Put the number of particles that stuck to the jelly on the drawing.
- What weather conditions seem to be associated with the highest count?
- Does the weather affect air pollution?

Secondary

- Repeat using five cards. Place each one at a different location (one at the teacher's house and the other four at students' homes). Count the particles. Do this for several different types of weather.
- Organize your data in a table and draw a graph.
- State generalizations regarding the relationship between weather and air pollution.
- List the important weather-related factors that have the greatest impact on the count.

Ideas for Science Fair Projects

1. Study the history of air quality in your community over the past five years. Some possible data sources are newspapers and the NWS. Present the data in graphical form. Be sure to explain the observed trends.

2. Develop a project on the impact of air pollution on health. Select an urban area and determine periods of air pollution and correlate pollution episodes with information on health from hospitals or physicians. Show the data on a line graph. Study the characteristics of those most affected (elderly, very young, those with preexisting illness).

3. Both activities in this chapter are appropriate for science fair presentations.

4. Study photochemical smog in a selected urban area. Determine sources and concentrations of pollutants. Are they seasonal? Suggest solutions. Data sources are TV or newspaper reports, NWS, and government environmental agencies.

5. Suggested title: "Is *(put name of pollutant here)* a Threat to *(name your area here)*?" Measure the concentration of a selected pollutant in your area using available chemical and instrumental techniques. Be sure to measure at different times of the day. Offer explanations for the existence and behavior of this pollutant.

6. Prospective title: "The Levels of Carbon Monoxide in Our Lives." Trace the everyday sources of carbon monoxide such as automobiles. Locate sources for this toxic gas around the home and in your environment.

7. Look into the role of PCBs in pollution in a project entitled "PCBs: Toxic Avengers."

8. Center a project on any of the following "other" types of pollution: light, soil, or noise.

9. Develop a project covering the major aspects of water pollution.

School's Out

1. Go to the library and check out a book on air pollution.

2. Develop an increased awareness of chemistry.

3. Read a book about air pollution to a younger child.

4. Talk to a chemist or meteorologist about air pollution; prepare a list of questions.

5. Take your science fair project to a local service organization.

6. Take your science fair project to a local day care, Head Start, or early childhood enrichment program and teach the children about air pollution.

7. Visit the NWS or an environmental agency and learn how air-quality analysis is done. Report this to the class.

8. Make a mobile containing the various chemicals associated with air pollution.

9. Study the chemical formula and structure of a pollutant.

10. Photograph any damage that resulted from air pollution and share it with the class.

11. Find evidence of air pollution in your neighborhood.

12. Collect 1 square foot of snow, melt it, and filter it through fine wire mesh. Do you find any evidence of pollution?

13. Compare your air pollution problem with that of another city and share your results with the class.

Chapter 17

Global Warming

One possible manifestation of anthropogenic air pollution is *global warming*, defined as an increase in the average surface temperature of Earth.

This chapter explains why global warming is an important issue and outlines the physical framework of its operation.

Essentials

In chapter 3 we learned that Earth's atmosphere is a mixture of gases and aerosols. About 99% of Earth's atmosphere is composed of nitrogen and oxygen. The remaining 1% of the atmosphere is composed of "trace gases," meaning their concentration is minute compared to that of nitrogen and oxygen. Many of the trace gases function as "greenhouse" gases that promote global warming. In a greenhouse the glass is transparent to shortwave insolation, allowing light to pass through to the soil, plants, and articles inside. The absorbed energy is then radiated as infrared energy back toward the glass, but the glass effectively traps the infrared wavelengths and warms the air inside the greenhouse. Thus, the glass acts as a one-way filter, allowing the light to come in but not allowing the heat out. The same process is observed in a dwelling that has large windows or in a parked car in direct sunlight.

Figure 17.1 illustrates the operation of the greenhouse effect as it applies to Earth's atmosphere. Insolation penetrates the atmosphere and reaches Earth's surface, but a small portion of the infrared or terrestrial radiation is redirected back to Earth by the presence of greenhouse gases. This process simply results in a net warming of Earth's surface. In fact, Earth is about 60° F warmer than it would be if it did not have its atmospheric blanket of greenhouse gases.

In the past two decades or so the attention of the world has been drawn to the question of whether humankind is changing the global climate in a significant way through the greenhouse effect. The first quantitative calculation of the effects of adding carbon dioxide (CO_2) to the atmosphere by burning fossil fuels was done in 1896 by S. Arrhenius. Even prior to that, the greenhouse idea was well accepted; it has been studied carefully and successfully tested by observations of Earth's radiation budget. It has been affirmed through the study of the atmospheres of Venus and Mars, both of which contain CO_2. It remains one of the best-established theories in the field of atmospheric science.

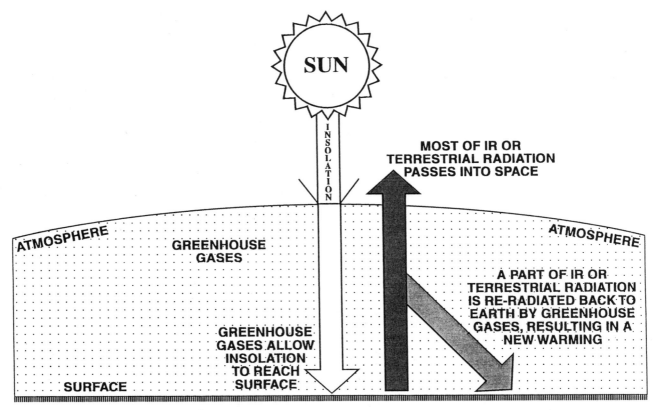

Fig. 17.1. The greenhouse effect: The mechanism of global warming.

The Lineup of Greenhouse Gases

Who are these important players in the greenhouse game and how do they act to bring about global warming? This section discusses many of the greenhouse gases. It turns out that about 50% of the greenhouse contribution is due to a group of at least 15 different gases, while the other 50% can be attributed to CO_2.

Carbon Dioxide

Carbon dioxide is generated by the burning of fossil fuels, with some 80% of atmospheric CO_2 due to the use of oil, coal, and natural gas. These petroleum-based energy sources first came into use with the burning of coal during the Industrial Revolution. During the past 100 years fossil fuel use has accelerated and, since 1945, petroleum consumption has increased dramatically, in large part because of increased usage of automobiles worldwide and the substitution of mechanized farm machinery for animal power.

Most scientists believe nearly one-half of the CO_2 being emitted each year remains in the atmosphere, while the rest is absorbed by trees and the oceans. The actual measurement of CO_2 levels was begun in 1958 by Charles Keeling of the Scripps Institute of Oceanography on Mauna Loa in Hawaii.

Methane

Methane (CH_4) is a significant greenhouse gas and a natural constituent of the atmosphere. Ice core samples dating back many thousands of years show that methane levels, like CO_2 levels, rise and fall with global temperature. In fact, methane is believed to be a much more efficient greenhouse gas than CO_2. Methane is formed by bacterial action in wet locations where oxygen is in short supply. These include swamps, garbage dumps, rice paddies, and the digestive systems of cattle, termites, and humans. The average methane molecule spends about 10 years in the troposphere (below 40,000 feet altitude) and is eventually destroyed by photochemical reactions with hydroxyl radicals (OH).

Methane is also produced by many industrial activities. Any leaks in gas transmission pipelines will add methane to the air because it is a principal ingredient in natural gas. Methane also leaks out of the ground when coal is mined. These industrial sources account for an estimated 20% of the total global amount of methane.

Chlorofluorocarbons (CFCs)

Chlorofluorocarbons, or CFCs, are synthetic gases produced in chemical factories. They are chemically very stable, at least until they enter the stratosphere, where they affect the ozone layer (more on this topic in chapter 18). CFCs are also powerful greenhouse gases. Some variants of CFC molecules have a greenhouse effect equal to 10,000 molecules of carbon dioxide. CFC gases have been added to the atmosphere since 1930, when they were first commercially produced for refrigerators. In the decades following their development, the use of CFCs grew rapidly.

CFCs are now used for refrigeration, air conditioning, fire extinguishers, cleaning solvents, and as blowing agents for rigid plastic foams. Although these gases have been around for a much shorter time period than other greenhouse gases, they have been added to the atmosphere at such a rapid rate that they now have an impact on the global warming issue. Estimates are that CFCs may contribute as much as 25% to the overall greenhouse effect.

Water Vapor

Water vapor is best known for serving in its role as the raw material for the precipitation process. But water vapor is also an important greenhouse gas. In the atmosphere, water vapor is transparent to insolation but is translucent to outgoing infrared radiation from Earth. Therefore, the presence of water vapor serves to produce a net warming. The thick cloud cover in the Venusian atmosphere is a prime reason why that planet is unbearably hot.

Additional Pieces of the Global Warming Puzzle

In addition to the greenhouse gases, there are several important pieces of the global warming puzzle, as shown in figure 17.2. In short, the presence of greenhouse gases in the atmosphere is not the only input to the global warming equation. In this section we consider four other components that impact global warming: the oceans, the biosphere, clouds, and aerosols and pollution haze.

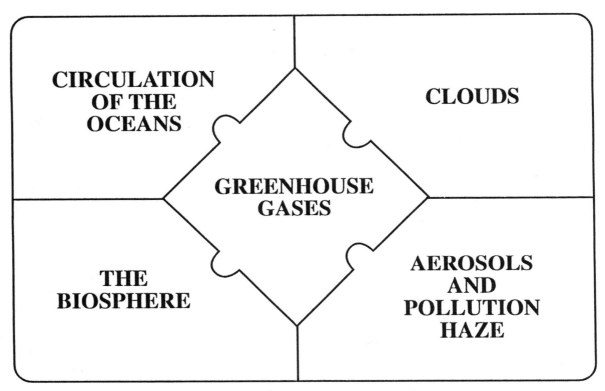

Fig. 17.2. Pieces of the global warming puzzle.

The Large-Scale Circulation of the Oceans

Probably the biggest piece of the global warming puzzle is the ocean's role in the situation. Certainly, the oceans hold the largest uncertainty in Earth's climate system. The initial problem is to determine how much heat-storage capacity the oceans have. It is logical to assume that the oceans have a tremendous heat-storage capacity because they occupy 72% of Earth's total surface area and because a certain mass of water can store more heat than an equivalent mass of most other common materials. Many scientists believe that the oceans may well delay the onset of global warming, making the detection of the "global warming signal" difficult until the phenomenon is well under way.

A second problem is understanding and modeling the movement of ocean currents. The behavior of these massive oceanic rivers influences Earth's climate system and will ultimately play a role in the global warming scene. Because of the powerful flow of ocean currents, large amounts of heat can be redistributed around the planet in ways that, at present, are poorly understood. The direction, depth, and strength of these currents are controlled by such factors as the amount of salt in the water, the temperature differences in various parts of the ocean basins, and the shape and depth of the ocean floor. Good measurements of these variables are simply not available at this time.

A final aspect involves the El Niño-Southern Oscillation (ENSO) phenomenon. Normally, the region off the west coast of South America is dominated by the northward-flowing Humboldt-Peru Current. These cold waters move toward the equator and join the westward movement of the south equatorial current. The Humboldt-Peru Current is part of the overall counterclockwise circulation that normally guides the winds and surface ocean currents around the subtropical high-pressure cell that dominates the eastern subtropical Pacific.

Occasionally, for unexplained reasons, pressure patterns alter and shift from their usual positions, thus affecting surface ocean currents and weather on both sides of the Pacific. Unusually high pressure develops in the western Pacific and lower pressure resides in the eastern Pacific. This regional change is an indication of large-scale ocean-atmosphere interactions. Trade winds normally moving from east to west weaken and can be replaced by a west-east flow. Sea-surface temperatures off South America then rise above normal, sometimes becoming more than 14° F higher, replacing the cold, upwelling, nutrient-rich water along Peru's coastline. Such ocean surface warming may extend westward to the International Dateline.

Fishermen working the waters off Peru expect a slight warming of the surface waters that lasts for a few weeks. Sometimes, however, the change in ocean temperature is more intense and is accompanied by strong changes of other environmental factors that may last for months or years. The fishermen use the name "El Niño" (Spanish for the "boy child") to refer to this phenomenon because these episodes periodically begin around the traditional December celebration time of Christ's birth, although it can occur earlier.

The shifting of atmospheric pressure and wind patterns across the Pacific is known as the Southern Oscillation and acts to initiate and support the El Niño. Scientists believe that at least a dozen significant ENSO episodes have occurred during the 20th century, with the strongest being the 1982-1983 event and the 1997-1998 event. The consensus among scientists is that the ENSO phenomenon contributes positively to global warming.

The Biosphere

A second key piece of the global warming puzzle is the biosphere. Specifically, the question capturing scientists' attention concerns the plant kingdom. Just as climate determines vegetative growth, the presence of plants also modifies climate. Plants inhale carbon dioxide and exhale water vapor and oxygen. When they die and rot, they release their stored carbon. If climate fluctuations bring about changes in the distribution or abundance of plants, they will also change the amount of carbon plants pull from the air and store in roots, trunks, and branches, and the amount of water vapor plants release from leaf pores. Major shifts in vegetation will also alter the amount of sunlight bouncing off the land and reflecting back into the atmosphere, as well as the movement of winds across Earth's surface. These changes will then feed back into the climate system to influence the severity and pace of further climate change.

At present, many scientists feel that the rapid destruction of tropical rainforests is a central element for adding plants to the global warming puzzle. When these forests are logged and burned, they release their stored carbon into the atmosphere. This process has the potential to raise or accelerate CO_2 levels, thus contributing to global warming.

The Role of Clouds

The consensus among climatologists is that one of the most challenging pieces of the global warming issue is the role clouds play in regulating global temperature. Computer simulations of global climate change differ substantially in the way they model the effect of clouds on global temperature—a problem scientists must solve if improved understanding of the global warming issue is to occur.

The central question is whether or not cloudiness cools or warms Earth. One prime aspect of this dilemma centers on how much insolation clouds reflect. The most recent research indicates that clouds likely reflect more insolation than previously thought. In addition, the type of clouds is important. Clouds associated with deep convection such as the cumulonimbus appear to have an overall warming effect in the atmosphere and would therefore contribute to global warming. On the other hand, cirrus and stratus tend to cool Earth. An important byproduct of cumulonimbus dissipation is cirrus. Thus, when all factors are considered, the opinion of most scientists is that clouds counteract global warming, perhaps by a greater amount than previously thought.

Aerosols and Pollution Haze

There is a growing body of evidence that aerosols affect the climate. In this case, sulfate aerosols, tiny droplets of sulfuric acid, are the most important. They contribute to acid precipitation and represent another path of the global warming maze.

The biggest natural source of sulfate aerosols is the ocean, where tiny phytoplankton produce dimethyl sulfide, or DMS. The DMS is converted to sulfate aerosols by chemical processes in the atmosphere. The largest man-made aerosol source is the combustion of fossil fuels. One estimate holds that human activity releases nearly 100 million tons each year.

Sulfur aerosols tug on the climate in two ways—one direct, the other more subtle. Aerosols exert their most obvious effect by reflecting insolation. They wield indirect climatic power by serving as nuclei around which water vapor can condense to form sunlight-reflecting cloud particles. In both cases, aerosol pollution acts as a giant shade, reducing the amount of light reaching Earth's surface. Preliminary estimates indicate that these aerosols may counteract global warming by 30% to 50%.

The Fingerprints of Global Warming

Recent heat waves and drought conditions in parts of the United States in 1980, 1986, and 1988 have prompted heightened concern about whether these are early signs of the global warming projected by the major climatic models. Other people, however, see the changes as completely natural. This brings us to one of the most perplexing questions concerning global warming: How can scientists distinguish an anthropogenic climate change signal against the background of natural climatic variability?

Data on several key variables indicates that the pattern of fingerprints of global warming when compared to recent climatic changes has both significant similarities and differences when compared with the pattern projected by climate models. Overall, the present state of the global climate appears to be at a critical juncture.

Fingerprint #1: A Rise in Global Temperature

In its most obvious sense, global warming will manifest itself through a rising trend in the average surface temperature of Earth. Look at figure 17.3. A clear upward trend is present, amounting to about 1° F. Perhaps the most striking bit of evidence, however, is that the 1980s and 1990s have produced the warmest years in the instrumental record. In fact, the eight warmest years on record are 1998, 1997, 1995, 1990, 1991, 1988, 1987, and 1983. Also, the warming since 1970 has been more rapid than during any comparable period in the instrumental record. Many researchers point out, however, that the temperature increases for these years are still no greater than the natural year-to-year and decade-to-decade variations.

Fingerprint #2: Cooling of the Stratosphere

In contrast to producing warming of the lower troposphere, global warming is almost certain to produce cooling of the stratosphere. Reduced upper-stratospheric ozone combined with increased stratospheric concentration of radioactive trace gases is projected to be responsible for the lower stratospheric temperatures.

The data on stratospheric cooling is mixed, with some evidence of recent cooling, but discrepancies between observation techniques have not yet been reconciled. Possible effects of volcanic events and solar cycles are not well understood. Also, the pattern of stratospheric cooling appears to be similar to that of stratospheric ozone depletion, and a cause-and-effect relationship is still unclear.

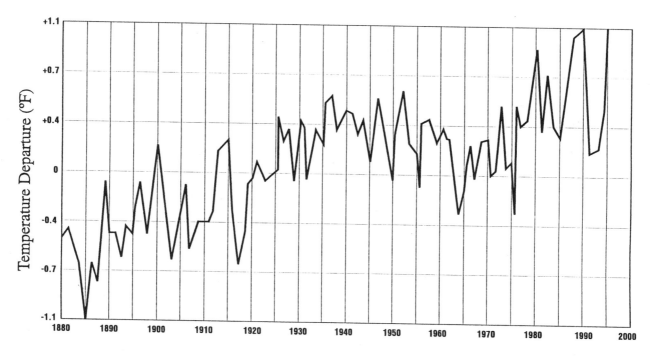

Fig. 17.3. Global temperature trends from 1880 to 1998. The 0 baseline represents the 1951-1980 global average temperature. Data courtesy of Dr. Reto Ruedy, Goddard Institute, National Aeronautics and Space Administration.

Fingerprint #3: Global Average Precipitation Increase

Global warming is expected to increase evaporation and therefore precipitation. Northern Hemisphere precipitation data over land does indicate a net upward trend, primarily in the mid to higher latitudes of 35° to 70° N, with a declining precipitation trend in lower latitudes. This appears to be consistent with the greenhouse warming expectation that increased moisture would be transported from the equatorial and tropical zones northward. Southern Hemisphere precipitation data indicates a net upward trend in both the low and mid to higher latitudes. It should be pointed out, however, that developing accurate global precipitation trends is very difficult because of lack of data for much of the oceans and remote land regions.

Fingerprint #4: Much Warmer Winters in Polar Regions

Global warming is expected to reduce polar ice volume, thereby greatly enhancing polar surface warming, perhaps by as much as three times the global average. Land-surface temperature data for the 1980s indicates that the global warming was driven by changes in the lower latitudes, not the higher latitudes as one would expect. Even temperature data since the 1950s indicates that the projected polar warming is not yet consistently evident. Recently, however, evidence to the contrary has surfaced. During the 1994-1995 southern summer, the Larsen Ice Sheet on the Antarctic Peninsula began to break up. The breakup set free an iceberg the size of Rhode Island. Although it is not known what mechanism is responsible, the average temperature on the Antarctic Peninsula has risen nearly 5° F over the past half-century. Some scientists point to this as proof of global warming, prompting speculation that global warming has begun to attack the fragile polar ice caps. Others, however, believe this warming is regional and not global.

Fingerprint #5: Summer Continental Dryness/Warming

In a greenhouse scenario the frequency of warm high-pressure cells aloft is expected to increase, thereby leading to a warmer and drier summer climatic regime in continental locations. This scenario will result in a significant reduction in midcontinent soil moisture during the summer. This projection has been related to recent drought episodes in 1980 and 1988 in the midcontinental United States. In contrast to this, we've already mentioned that precipitation in the United States has increased in the second half of the 20th century. For the most part, recent U.S. drought conditions tend to be consistent with global warming but are not as yet unprecedented and could be explained by natural variability alone.

Fingerprint #6: High-Latitude Precipitation Increase

In a greenhouse-driven climate the poleward penetration of warm, moist air masses is expected to increase. In addition, the melting of ice volume will serve as a second source of moisture. These two factors are expected to work together to increase the average precipitation amount in high-latitude regions. Current precipitation data appears to indicate an increasing trend over the last few decades at mid to high latitudes (35° to 70° N); in contrast, precipitation at lower latitudes (5° to 35°) has declined in some areas. In the Southern Hemisphere precipitation at lower latitudes (0° to 25° S) has increased, not decreased, and at a faster rate than at higher latitudes (25° to 60° S). Very limited data makes developing precipitation trends for the polar regions difficult.

Fingerprint #7: Glacial Retreat

A straightforward effect of global warming is the retreat of continental and mountain glaciers. Satellite observations provide conflicting indications. The NOAA data suggests no significant trend, while NASA data suggests a declining trend. Both sets of satellite data indicate no significant trend in North American or Eurasian snow cover. Data on mountain glaciers in Europe weakly supports a minor readvance from about 1960 to 1985. Granted, naturally driven changes in ice and snow cover show large annual variations. Also, ice responds to temperature and precipitation changes in complex and sometimes counterintuitive ways, thus possibly masking long-term shifts in the cyrosphere.

Fingerprint #8: A Rise in Average Sea Level

A rise in global average sea level is compatible with a global warming scenario. The rising sea level is caused by the thermal expansion of sea water and ice cap melting. Sea level has fluctuated by large amounts in the past. At the peak of the last Pleistocene glaciation 18,000 years ago, sea level was about 430 feet lower than it is today. Current indications are that sea level has risen 4 inches during the past 100 years. Estimates of future rises are conservatively put at 1 to 4 feet, with pessimistic estimates placed at 20 feet.

A Conclusion

Recent global warming of 1° F over the past 100 years is still within, although perhaps pushing, the upper limits of natural variability. Research suggests that distinguishing anthropogenic climate change from natural variability may be extremely difficult; therefore, a more complete and integrated approach to climate monitoring and reporting is needed to help scientists unravel the deeper complexities of Earth's climate system. In order to meet this need, the Earth Observation System (EOS), a series of four polar-orbiting satellites, is planned for the mid- to late 1990s. The EOS will usher in a new, more comprehensive approach to monitoring Earth's open energy system.

Global Circulation Models

Global Circulation Models, or GCMs, are the primary tool modern scientists use to help them unlock the mysteries of Earth's climate system. The GCMs are sophisticated computer software designed to simulate Earth's general circulation over long time periods. The GCMs are so intricate that only the supercomputers with the fastest execution time and the greatest memory capacity are practical for the task.

Future climate modeling research using GCMs is currently taking place at four or five major laboratories, including NASA's Goddard Institute for Space Studies, NOAA's Geophysical Fluid Dynamics Lab, and NOAA's National Center for Atmospheric Research (NCAR). To compare results among the different models scientists have developed a standard experiment that asks the question: How much will the average global temperature rise if the concentration of CO_2 in the atmosphere is doubled? Most current models show increases of between 3° F and 9° F. Some models will even generate additional results, such as maps of expected rainfall levels or soil moisture maps.

Much work continues to be done in the area of GCM development. As computing power increases and as the models themselves become more sophisticated, it is expected that a corresponding increase in accuracy will result. The amount of human and financial resources directed at GCM development and refinement will remain high in the foreseeable future.

The Consequences of Global Warming

Why are scientists concerned about global warming? The answer is, quite simply, that global warming carries with it some definite consequences. It will not be "business as usual" anymore on Planet Earth. This section will analyze several impacts on humankind that are expected to accompany a greenhouse scenario.

Consequence #1: Agricultural Changes

North America has long been known as the "breadbasket of the world." The primary reason for this distinction is a climate that allows high yields of grain such as wheat, barley, and corn. There is the likelihood that global warming will bring shifts in agricultural patterns, not only to North America but in other parts of the world as well. The combination of higher temperatures and reduced soil moisture may reduce agricultural productivity, perhaps to a critical level in the most severely affected areas. In the Northern Hemisphere the majority of GCMs predict most continental areas to have drier summer soils, due in part to earlier snowmelts in the spring and hotter, more cloudless summers. All of these factors would combine to raise the "water need" of crops. In the United States levels of soil moisture reduction are progged in the broad area from Pittsburgh to Omaha to Wichita and extending as far west as Spokane. These moisture losses will reduce crop yields in those areas.

One crop that is subject to extremely hot weather is corn. The EPA studied corn crop yields and found that the heat of the southern states, such as Georgia, Tennessee, and North Carolina, could cut corn harvests by more than 50% while states in the "grain belt," Kansas and Nebraska, could see 30% fewer yields. The EPA studies also indicate lower yields for soybeans. In fact, some scientists believe that the "corn belt" would eventually shift northward in response to global warming, possibly to the point where a majority of it resided in Canada.

Consequence #2: Lower Lake and River Levels

If the inland regions of the Northern Hemisphere are expected to receive less precipitation in a global warming scenario, then it follows that lake and river levels will decrease. Some predictions indicate the level of the Great Lakes will drop between 2 and 8 feet. River flows may be very vulnerable to increased temperature and decreased precipitation. A study by the Army Coastal Engineering Research Center indicates that a 3.6° F global temperature rise, coupled with only a 10% decrease in precipitation, would cut river flows by 40% to 76% for the Missouri, Rio Grande, Lower Colorado, and several California rivers. A decrease in lake levels and river flow volume affects several things. First, it may have implications for fresh drinking water supplies, as decreased levels in lakes used for drinking water sources would mean less fresh water to drink. Second, river commerce and traffic would be affected by lower river-flow levels. With less flow volume, it would take longer for transportation from one point to another. Thus, river commerce would not be as economically cost effective. Lower flow would also increase the incidence of vessels becoming stuck or running aground. Finally, hydroelectric power output would be lower with lower stream-flow volumes.

Consequence #3: A Rise in Average Sea Level

Perhaps the most talked about and feared consequence of a greenhouse Earth is a rise in global average sea level. With many of the world's cities located in coastal areas, this is a major concern.

One reason for the sea level increase is that extra water is produced when ice melts. Second, seawater naturally expands when it becomes warmer. The estimates of sea level change vary greatly from one GCM to another. This estimation problem is rooted in our lack of understanding of global ocean dynamics, with the added complications of understanding how various forms of ice are deposited, melted, and redistributed. The amount of ice melted and the corresponding thermal expansion are not the only factors contributing to sea level rise. Another aspect of the problem is that the elevation of various coastal land areas is rising and sinking because of geological factors. For example, the local sea level around Galveston, Texas, is rising much faster than the global average because of coastal subsidence.

Damage from rising sea levels takes many forms. Buildings and roads close to the water eventually will be flooded. These structures are also prone to damage from storms. As sea level rises, beach erosion will increase, and wetlands and fisheries will suffer. Another serious problem is the threat of saltwater intrusion into freshwater lakes and aquifers in coastal areas. Many cities depend on these for drinking water supplies. In a worst-case scenario, a rise of 20 feet in global sea level will flood 20% of Florida, inundate the Mississippi floodplain as far inland as St. Louis, flood the Pampas of Argentina, inundate Venice, and submerge the Bahamas, Netherlands, and Maldines.

Consequence #4: More Intense Hurricanes

Research at NCAR indicates that global warming may increase the number and severity of hurricanes. It is believed that the warmer air temperatures will result in warmer ocean temperatures, thereby suggesting a physical mechanism that would be responsible. It is thought that the occurrence of major hurricanes (Category III or above) would increase as well. Some scientists point to Hurricane Gilbert in 1988, Hugo in 1989, and Andrew in 1992 as suggestive of a greenhouse trend. True to form, two more costly major hurricanes, Opal in 1995 and Fran in 1996, affected the United States. In the future, damage inflicted by hurricanes to populated areas will be intensified as a result of higher sea levels.

Consequence #5: A Changed World Political Climate

If global warming brings shifts in world agricultural patterns, then it will also result in changes in the world political situation. In short, if climate dictates who eats and who starves, as it surely must, then changes in climate because of global warming must certainly shift the world political balance. Starvation is a powerful motivating factor for political action. In a global warming scenario the wealthy nations will be able to adapt more easily than their less developed counterparts. Some nations may lose their favorable climate and be forced to purchase food from others. Thus, a changed climatic regime in times of global warming may lead to increased stress and tension between nations.

Truly, a high degree of international cooperation will be necessary to prevent famine, strife, and perhaps even war.

Solutions to the Global Warming Puzzle

As with any problem, some solutions must exist. One obvious answer to the problem is education. In addition, international cooperation must take place. In the case of global warming, however, a final complicating factor is that implementation of solutions will involve sacrifice and costs. This section attempts to put the global warming jigsaw together by presenting these three ideas as solutions.

Education

Public awareness and education are a growing positive force on Earth. There is a strong belief that through education on a particular issue comes an important resource with which to confront the challenges and to implement solutions. One corollary to this is linkage of academic disciplines. A positive step in that direction is the "science without walls" approach, which involves an interdisciplinary method of problem solving. Exciting education of scientists and laypersons is being achieved toward an integrated understanding of Earth and the operation of its physical systems, with the approach being driven by our remote-sensing capabilities.

The wealthy and developed nations of the Northern Hemisphere have, for the most part, promised financial resources to accomplish Earth education through schools, workshops for teachers, the melding of industry and schools, colleges and universities, and professional scientists, most of whom reside in the Northern Hemisphere.

In the Southern Hemisphere, however, public education will not be so easy, although some nations of the North have promised to help. R. K. Pachauri, director of New Delhi's Tata Energy Research Institute, stated the southern stance well at the Earth Summit in 1992: "A person who is worrying about his next meal is not going to listen to lectures on protecting the environment."

The Need for International Cooperation

In modern times the world has already seen a dramatic example of environmental problem solving: the Limited Test Ban Treaty of 1962, which bans atmospheric testing of nuclear weapons. The International Geosphere-Biosphere Program (IGBP) represents another integrative effort; its goal is to improve understanding of the entire natural system and discern how many and varied subsystems interact.

In 1972, the shadows of nuclear war hung over the world, fueled by the Cold War between the East and West. In that year, however, 115 nations met in Stockholm, Sweden, at the first Earth Summit to discuss the perils of nuclear war to the environment. This was followed in 1992 by the second Earth Summit in Rio de Janeiro, Brazil. This Earth Summit was the largest and most complex conference ever held—bigger than the momentous meetings at Versailles, Malta, and Potsdam. A treaty to alleviate the unwanted consequences of climate change was the centerpiece of the summit.

In 1990, in Geneva, Switzerland, the Second World Climate Conference, sponsored by the UN's Intergovernmental Panel on Climate Change (the IPCC), was held. The major concern was lower CO_2 emissions. Europe's energy and environment ministers hammered out a joint goal to stabilize CO_2 at 1990 levels by the year 2000, as did Canada, Japan, Belgium, Ireland, Norway, and Switzerland.

These examples provide hope for the future. If humankind can come together to face an issue and walk away with tangible accomplishments, then the effort has been a success.

Sacrifice and Costs

At the heart of the global warming solution is sacrifice and costs. The nations of the world must abandon practices that are self-destructive, but there exists a societal structure in many countries that gives most of that nation's wealth to a tiny minority of the population. The disparities that mark individual countries are mirrored in the planet as a whole. Most of Earth's material wealth is concentrated in the Northern Hemisphere. From the South's point of view, it is the rich North's profligate consumption patterns of fossil fuels that are the problem. It comes down to a matter of cash; the North has it and the South needs it. And the changes that must be made will not occur unless some of that wealth finds its way from the North to the South. In fact, the tensions between North and South, and the financial conflicts that underlie them, run through the global warming issue. Here is where the cost and sacrifice come in. It is estimated that developed nations will need to contribute $125 billion annually to protect natural resources and clean up pollution. The developing countries will need to contribute an additional $500 billion per year. Can the North sacrifice some of its extravagant lifestyle? But, in a like manner, the South will need to take some responsibility for its own actions. In the issue of sacrifice and costs, the answer is compromise. Can the polarization of philosophy and material resources be narrowed? Only time will tell.

Concluding Remarks

Global warming is one of the most important environmental issues of our time. The only point scientists all agree on is this: Global warming is complex and controversial, representing a challenge to modern science. At one extreme of the issue are those who have already pronounced global warming as catastrophic by the middle of the 21st century, with coastal cities being inundated and significant alterations in agriculture, lifestyle, and politics. At the opposite end of the spectrum are scientists who say that global warming is not an important issue. The position taken in the *Sourcebook* is somewhere between these two diametrically opposed viewpoints: The faint fingerprints of global warming have appeared in the 1980s and 1990s. In keeping with that opinion, the IPCC in 1995 took an unprecedented stance when it stated that the warming of the past two decades is partially due to global warming. More research and observations are needed, however, before the signal becomes unmistakable. Also, some time needs to pass, to see what natural variability brings.

The Process of Scientific Thought

Activity #1

Title: Greenhouse Automobile

Objective: To demonstrate the concept of a greenhouse

Materials Needed: a closed car, a thermometer, a sunny day

Procedure: Read the thermometer you're using for the class weather station (call it thermometer A). Obtain another thermometer (call it B), read it, and place it in a parked car with all windows closed. Be sure to note both temperature readings on thermometers A and B. Place thermometer B somewhere in the car where it will not be exposed to direct sunlight. In 30 minutes, read both thermometers again and record the readings.

Elementary

- Which thermometer registered the highest temperature? (Answer: Thermometer B.)

- How do you explain the results? (Answer: Sunlight enters the car and heats the inside. However, that heat is not allowed to escape, thus it accumulates and the result is an increase in temperature.)

- How does this relate to the "greenhouse effect" of the atmosphere? (Answer: Sunlight passes into the car through the glass windows, just as insolation passes through the atmosphere and strikes Earth's surface. The presence of greenhouse gases, however, traps a portion of that heat, just as the closed car traps the heat inside of it. The net result in both cases is a temperature increase.)

Secondary

- Try the activity on a cloudy day. Are the results the same? (Answer: The temperature inside the car will not rise to the extreme levels that it does on a sunny day; nonetheless, some greenhouse effect is still present.)

- List other ways to illustrate the greenhouse effect.

Activity #2

Title: Earth Systems in a Bottle

Objective: To demonstrate the complexity of the global warming issue

Materials Needed: 2-liter soft drink bottle, open tap, something to punch holes with

Procedure: Obtain an empty 2-liter soft drink bottle and drill a vertical series of three holes in the bottle using a sharp ¼-inch drill bit. Place one hole near the bottom, another hole in the middle of the bottle, and the third hole between the first two. Try to arrange the holes in a spiral pattern so that they are not directly over one another. Place the bottle under the faucet with a steady moderate flow of water. Observe the water as it flows out the holes.

Elementary

- Draw a picture of the tap water flowing into the bottle and the jets of water shooting out from the holes.

- Does the bottle ever become full? (Answer: No, not if the same flow rate from the tap is maintained.)

- Do all of the water jets coming from the bottle look the same? (Answer: No, the bottom stream is under more pressure and produces a faster, straighter outflow.)

- Place a finger over one of the holes. What happens? (Answer: The water level inside the bottle rises and the outflow is increased in the other two jets.)

- How are the incoming and outgoing rates of water flow related? (Answer: They are equal when the water level inside the bottle is steady.)

- How are the incoming rates of water flow and the water level related? (Answer: They are directly related.)

- What effect would larger holes have? (Answer: Greater outflow, lower water level inside the bottle.)

- Explain how this experiment relates to global warming. (Answer: The inflow from the faucet represents the production of greenhouse gases, the outflow streams represent the destruction or use of greenhouse gases, and the water level inside the bottle represents the level of greenhouse gases.)

Secondary

- Place a piece of flexible tubing in one of the holes and allow the water to flow through it back into the bottle. What does this represent in the natural atmosphere? (Answer: A feedback loop.) How does it affect the results? (Answer: It leads to a higher water level in the bottle.) What is the implication? (Answer: Feedback can cause unexpected changes. In the analogy here, the feedback actually increased the level of greenhouse gases.)

- List ways in which humans interfere with global processes. Should humans interfere? To what extent should humans interfere? Does human intervention help or hinder natural processes? Research and find answers to these questions and then hold a class forum or debate.

Ideas for Science Fair Projects

1. Choose one or two of the greenhouse gases and show how they influence global warming. Give the chemical formula and structure and general information on why it is a player in the greenhouse game.

2. Both activities in this chapter are appropriate for presentation at science fairs.

3. Choose five cities in the United States. Obtain temperature and precipitation data for these cities through the NWS or the National Climatic Data Center. Try to get at least 30 years of data. Study the changes in average annual temperature and precipitation, seasonal and daily changes. Look closely at daily and seasonal temperature ranges—there is evidence that global warming manifests itself in a lower daily and seasonal temperature range. Is there more rain? Larger rainfall events?

4. Study the effect of global warming on plants. Recent research suggests a "greening" of the Northern Hemisphere by 8% to 15%.

5. Suggested title: "How does CO_2 contribute to global warming?"

6. Use a graphic display to show global temperature trends over the past 100 to 150 years (like figure 17.3). Show projections for the next 50 to 100 years.

7. Venus is well known for its "runaway" greenhouse effect. Develop a project that focuses on the greenhouse effect of Earth's sister planet. Compare and contrast Venus with Earth.

8. Mars also has a greenhouse effect. Develop a project that considers Mars as a greenhouse planet.

9. "How the Greenhouse Effect Affects Climate" is a prospective title for a project. Provide a review of the greenhouse theory. Then make use of SimEarth software to alter the amounts of greenhouse gases and to see the effects.

10. Relate tropical storms and hurricanes in the Atlantic Basin to global temperature. Use figure 17.3 for your data on temperature and obtain hurricane and tropical storm information from the National Climatic Data Center, the NHC, or the NWS.

11. Study the effect of global warming on the polar ice caps. Mention the anticipated rise in sea level and effects such as increased beach erosion, saltwater intrusion, and coastal inundation. Be sure you can state the two reasons why sea level would rise in a global warming scene.

12. Develop a project that focuses on how the ENSO phenomenon affects global warming. It's generally accepted that the ENSO amplifies the global warming signal. Be sure to state what ENSO is, where it develops, its far-reaching effects, and how it contributes to global warming.

13. Suggested title: "Is Global Warming Affecting *name your city?*" Obtain past records of temperature and precipitation and proceed as in #3 above.

14. Some scientists have correlated global lightning activity with global temperature. Basically, it seems that higher global temperatures result in increased planetary lightning. Check the resources in appendix E to see if there is any information on this idea. This would be a fascinating and original project.

15. Center a project on the carbon cycle.

16. How does Earth's biosphere affect global warming? Follow the discussion presented in this chapter and then search for other information from the library, a professional, or the resources listed in appendix D or on the Internet.

17. Center a project on the role clouds play in the global warming process. Follow the discussion presented in this chapter and search for additional information at the library, a professional, the resources in appendix D, or on the Internet.

18. Research question: "Are Aerosols and Pollution Haze Counteracting Global Warming?" The brief discussion in this chapter should help you to get started.

19. Possible title: "The Fingerprints of Global Warming." Follow the outline in this chapter and add pertinent information from the usual sources.

20. Possible title: "The Consequences of Global Warming." Follow the outline in this chapter and add other information from the usual sources.

21.   Find out all you can about GCMs and their application to simulating global climates and climate changes.

School's Out!

1.   Join or found an environmental club.

2.   Increase your awareness of the global warming issue by watching TV, reading the newspaper, or going to the library once in a while and looking at periodicals. Make a brief report to the class if you come across something interesting.

3.   Check out a book from the library on global warming and make a brief report to the class.

4.   Start a scrapbook of newspaper clippings pertaining to global warming.

5.   Take your science fair project to a local civic organization.

6.   Read a book about the environment to a younger child.

7.   Teach younger children at a day care, Head Start, or early childhood enrichment program about the global warming issue.

8.   Use a hanger to make a mobile that presents the lineup of greenhouse gases.

9.   Make a list of questions on global warming and seek answers from a professional.

Chapter 18

The Ozone Predicament

As we approach the 21st century, the issue of ozone depletion confronts humanity. Some scientists feel that it is a more pressing issue than global warming because the effects of ozone depletion on Earth's biosphere are obvious and detection of ozone loss is easier. In short, scientists have a better idea what they are up against. The pieces of the puzzle are not so intricate, and the fingerprints are not so faint. This chapter focuses on the current ozone predicament facing society.

The Ozone Layer

Ozone is a very important, highly variable constituent of the atmosphere. Ozone is found at high altitudes (called stratospheric ozone), but it is also found in urban localities having a great deal of industry, automotive traffic, and an ample supply of sunshine (called tropospheric ozone). Most stratospheric ozone occurs at altitudes of 12 to 25 miles. This region of highest ozone concentration in the atmosphere is called the *ozone layer*, or the *ozonosphere*.

The ozone layer was first discovered by S. Chapman in 1930, whose findings were later revised in the mid-1960s by J. Hampson. One of the most striking aspects of the ozone layer is that it is believed to have maintained a steady-state equilibrium for the past 500 million years. The high-altitude ozone layer is maintained by the following photochemical process. Molecules of oxygen gas (O_2) absorb UV solar radiation and are dissociated to form oxygen atoms (O). Collisions of oxygen molecules and the oxygen atoms (and other particles) lead to the formation of ozone (O_3). The process then repeats.

Functions of the Ozone Layer

The ozone layer performs two important functions. The first, and best known of the two, concerns the absorption of UV radiation in the stratosphere. In this process, the ozone layer reduces the amount of harmful UV radiation reaching Earth's surface. In effect, this thin and fragile veil of ozone acts as a massive protective shield to Earth's biosphere, gobbling up most of the harmful UV radiation from the sun. Without an ozone layer, the bulk of Earth's biosphere would perish. A thinning of the ozone shield allows Earth's biosphere to experience increased doses of UV radiation, leading to adverse reactions, including severe sunburns and increased risk of skin cancer in humans.

A second important facet of the ozonosphere is that ozone is thought to be an important factor in Earth's heat balance, which influences climate. The destruction of ozone in the stratosphere is believed to increase the greenhouse effect.

A Brief History of Ozone

Investigation and knowledge of ozone date back over 150 years. In 1840, a letter entitled "Research on the nature of the odor in certain chemical reactions" was presented by C. F. Shoenbein to the Académie des Sciences in Paris, France. Shoenbein was unable to determine the origin of the chemical species that he had found or to characterize its structure, but he named the mysterious, pungent-smelling molecule "ozone." A few years later, J. L. Soret identified the substance. The actual discovery of the ozone layer in the atmosphere followed some 30 years later. In 1879-1881, W. N. Hartley and A. Cornu measured the UV radiation reaching the surface of Earth and found a sharp cutoff, which they correctly attributed to ozone. These pioneering measurements also showed that the bulk of the ozone must be high in the atmosphere rather than near the ground. Hence, the discovery of the stratospheric ozone layer.

The first systematic measurements of the distribution and variability of the ozone layer were done in the late 1920s by G. M. B. Dobson and his colleagues. Dobson reasoned that stratospheric winds play an important role in transporting ozone around the planet. In fact, the concentration of ozone is measured in Dobson Units, a fitting recognition for this scientific pioneer.

The year 1957 was designated as the International Geophysical Year, or IGY. This marked a time when Earth awareness increased significantly and was highlighted by intense international research programs on Earth and the environment. A network of ground-based instruments for continuous monitoring of ozone using the technique pioneered by Dobson was established worldwide.

Another surge of interest in the ozone layer occurred in 1970 when the U.S. government considered major new investments in the design of a supersonic transport plane (SST). It was anticipated that it would fly at a cruising altitude of about 12.5 miles and at about three times the speed of sound. It was then realized that these planned flights would take place in the ozone layer. Certain scientists opposed the development of the SST airplanes on the grounds that nitrogen oxide gas emitted by the engines would react with and reduce ozone amounts. The discovery of this ozone-destroying catalytic cycle involving nitrogen compounds by P. Crutzen and H. S. Johnston in 1970-1971 revealed a previously undiscovered mechanism for rapid ozone loss. It also provided the first stimulus to public awareness regarding the importance and fragility of the ozone layer. Therefore, the SST controversy focused attention on the ozone layer as an environmental issue of importance and, as a result, a number of other important discoveries were made. In the early 1970s, various scientists noted that the nitrogen in certain heavily used fertilizers might, over a long period of time, represent a threat to ozone. Also, with the burden of the Cold War, it was found that the explosions from a nuclear war might destroy 30% to 70% of Earth's supply of ozone.

The Agents of Ozone Loss

Earlier, we outlined the natural process through which the ozone layer is replenished. Here, we detail how ozone is destroyed by human processes and activities.

The manufacture of ozone occurs mostly over the tropics and requires two ingredients: molecular oxygen (O_2) and sunlight. The sun's energy bombards the molecules of O_2, causing the two oxygen atoms to dissociate, or split apart. These oxygen atoms (O) quickly attach themselves to neighboring O_2, forming a new molecule called ozone (O_3). Although the sun breaks apart some of the ozone as soon as it's formed, air currents can move a significant portion of the ozone down into the stratosphere, where it is protected from intense radiation. These air currents are strongest in winter and eventually carry the ozone poleward. Ozone levels are variable, and therefore ozone is classified as a variable gaseous constituent of the atmosphere. But until recently, scientists believe, Earth ran a balanced ozone budget.

Now, however, industrial chemicals may be throwing the system out of whack. Chemists F. Sherwood Rowland and Mario Molina first detected a possible problem in 1974, arguing that the buildup of CFCs in the stratosphere could damage the ozone layer. CFCs, manufactured under the more familiar trade name Freon, are used as refrigerants and coolants. Rowland and Molina hypothesized that the very stable CFC molecules remained intact in the atmosphere, eventually migrating upward into the stratosphere. Being stable, CFCs do not dissolve in water and do not break down biologically. In the stratosphere, however, the increased UV light dissociates or splits the CFC molecules, releasing chlorine (Cl) atoms and forming chlorine oxide (ClO) molecules. This chlorine then acts as a catalyst, stimulating a complex chemical reaction that gobbles up ozone. In fact, a single chlorine atom can destroy up to 100,000 ozone molecules. The average residence time of these CFCs in the ozone layer is up to 100 years, and the possible long-term consequences will linger well into the 21st century.

Another agent responsible for ozone loss is a volcano. The volcano's chemical contribution to ozone loss generally is not chlorine-based, as the chlorine from volcanoes is soluble, which means that rain washes it away long before it ever reaches the stratosphere. It is thought that the important chemical agent in volcano-related ozone depletion is sulfur dioxide (SO_2). Once in the stratosphere, the SO_2 gradually decays into tiny droplets of sulfuric acid. These aerosols provide surfaces on which to activate chlorine. This process converts chlorine already in the stratosphere from CFCs into ClO at very high rates.

Record low levels of ozone were found in the Northern Hemisphere during 1992-1993. At that time, levels were 10% to 15% below normal. Scientists point to the eruption of Mount Pinatubo in the Philippines as the prime culprit. The volcano belched out a staggering 20 million tons of SO_2 into the atmosphere, 30 times the 1989 level of SO_2 aerosols. It is also possible that Pinatubo depressed worldwide ozone levels by changing circulation patterns. Ozone levels improved in 1993-1994, lending support to the Pinatubo hypothesis.

Global warming may also prove to be an agent for ozone loss. Carbon dioxide insulates Earth, heating the lower troposphere while cooling the stratosphere. This high-level cooling could serve to further accelerate ozone loss. Also, some scientists feel that global warming will increase evaporation from the oceans, thus increasing the amount of water vapor in the atmosphere that could contribute to the formation of clouds that provide surfaces for ozone-destroying chemical reactions.

Ozone itself may feed back and contribute indirectly to thinning of the ozone layer. The ozone layer absorbs energy from the sun and from Earth's surface and troposphere, which helps heat the stratosphere. Thus, removing more ozone may also cause the stratosphere to cool, providing a positive feedback mechanism that would lead to a more favorable environment for further ozone loss.

Last, sunspot activity has recently been suggested as a possible cause of ozone loss. There does seem to be a definite link between sunspot activity and UV output from the sun. Fewer sunspots are known to be associated with less UV radiation, and higher than normal sunspot activity is known to generate higher UV radiation. Therefore, a less active sunspot cycle would create less ozone because there would be less UV bombardment. A more active sunspot cycle would produce more UV bombardment, thus resulting in the creation of more ozone.

The Ozone "Hole"

The most important piece of evidence for stratospheric ozone depletion is the so-called ozone hole over Antarctica. But just what is this phenomenon? This section gives an overview.

The logical place to start is with remote-sensing capabilities. The Total Ozone Mapping Spectrometer (TOMS), on board NASA's Nimbus-7 weather satellite, has been observing ozone over Earth since 1978. Even prior to that, British scientists at Halley Bay had been watching ozone since 1970.

By the early 1980s, the ozone layer over Antarctica was showing signs of thinning, based on measurements by a British team of scientists working there. This data, not made public until 1985, led to NASA's discovery that the TOMS data had been detecting the same ozone loss since 1978, but the data was not being interpreted properly. With revised computer programs, full-color images documenting the formation of the now-famous "ozone hole" appeared.

In August and September 1987, NASA high-altitude aircraft flying through the ozone hole verified conclusively that chlorine monoxide, ClO, is present in high concentrations where the ozone was being destroyed. This was the final "ironclad" proof that CFCs were responsible in part for the ozone loss.

The size of the Antarctic ozone hole varies each year. In October 1985, the size was greater than the area of the continental United States. In 1987, the hole size hit record levels—larger than the entire Antarctic continent. The 1989 hole was equal in size to the record-setting 1987 hole. On October 6, 1991, however, the TOMS data received a new record low for ozone concentration. In each of these episodes, ozone loss amounted to about 50%. Following true to form, new record lows were set in 1992 and 1993.

The Antarctic "ozone hole," defined as the seasonal loss of a significant fraction of ozone concentration, requires very special conditions to form —conditions that are met only during the deep chill of the Antarctic spring. During other times of the year, most of the chlorine throughout the stratosphere is essentially out of commission: It's attached to nitrogen oxides and other chemicals, forming compounds that do not quickly destroy ozone. In the Antarctic winter, however, conditions change dramatically. Temperatures plunge and a roughly continentwide vortex forms, concentrating the frigid air. In short, the cold air sinks and begins to spin.

The vortex becomes so cold (about -108° F) that the nitrogen oxides condense into nitrogen solids; then, as temperatures fall even lower, ice particles also form. These ice particles and nitrogen compounds, which form what are known as polar stratospheric clouds (PSCs), are the key to ozone destruction.

One effect of the PSCs is the removal of nitrogen as a protector of ozone. Nitrogen gases in the stratosphere sequester chlorine, but nitrogen solids let it go free. The PSCs also foster ozone loss by providing surfaces for reactions that activate the chlorine into ClO, which gobbles up ozone with amazing efficiency. After the ClO buildup in winter, the Antarctic ozone hole is primed to make its annual appearance in the spring. By then, enough sunlight is available to trigger the chain of ozone-destroying reactions.

A central question facing researchers is, Will the Northern Hemisphere experience comparable losses? No one knows for sure at this point. Although CFCs lurk at both poles, conditions over the Arctic are much different. One key difference between the two regions is the distribution of land and sea. This creates more variable flow patterns in the atmosphere, creating a less stable Arctic vortex. The Arctic vortex does not get as cold, which is another factor that sets it apart from its southern counterpart. This is good news for the ozone layer and those who reside below it, because it means that fewer PSCs form. Often by the time the sun arrives in the spring, temperatures have risen enough to evaporate the PSCs.

Teacher's Extra

The "Forgotten" Ozone

Thus far, our discussion has centered on stratospheric ozone. But there is also an important minority of ozone that exists in the troposphere. The appearance of ozone in the troposphere seems to be a consequence of human pollution.

The study of tropospheric ozone dates back surprisingly far. From 1868 through 1893 Father Francesco Denza, an Italian monk and teacher, maintained records that are now helping scientists understand how the Industrial Revolution has contributed to ozone pollution in the troposphere. For 26 years the theologian and physics teacher took twice-daily readings of ground-level ozone at his college in Moncalieri, located at the foot of the Italian Alps. In Denza's time, researchers suspected that ozone might cause epidemic diseases. Today, scientists recognize tropospheric ozone as a greenhouse gas as well as an eye and lung irritant. A team of Italian scientists has converted Denza's data to a more modern scale in order to compare today's ozone levels with those of the early part of the Industrial Revolution. They report that the 19th-century data showed Moncalieri had one-third to one-half the tropospheric ozone present in a modern rural site. Exhaust from cars, power plants, and other sources creates ozone in the lower troposphere.

In conclusion, it's ironic that at one position in the atmosphere, ozone is deemed harmful (troposphere), while at another altitude it's a blessing of immense value (stratosphere).

The Implications of Ozone Loss

The loss of ozone from the stratosphere has far-reaching consequences for Earth's biosphere. One example of this occurs at the bottom of the oceanic food chain. Here, phytoplankton, tiny sea plants, serve as the primary food source for krill, the small shrimplike creatures that make up the next level of the food chain. The krill feeds whales, penguins, fish, squid, seals, and seabirds. Without healthy, abundant phytoplankton in the Southern Ocean, Antarctic marine life would cease. It appears that excess UV radiation caused by ozone depletion does in fact kill phytoplankton or seriously reduce their growth rates.

Humans, at the top of the food chain, are certainly not immune to the effects of ozone depletion. It has been estimated that a 1% decrease in stratospheric ozone will lead to a 2% to 5% increase in skin cancer. A United Nations panel concluded that a 10% decrease will cause 300,000 additional cases of skin cancer and 1.6 million additional cases of cataracts each year worldwide. Most affected are light-skinned persons who live at higher altitudes and those who work outdoors. Reduction in the effectiveness of certain body immune systems is possible, according to some researchers. Also, potential damage to crop yields is possible.

Solutions: An International Response

Like global warming, confronting the issue of ozone depletion demands an international response. Canada, Sweden, Norway, and the state of Oregon instituted bans on CFC propellants in aerosols between 1976 and 1979. The U.S. federal ban commenced in fall 1978. However, even with the U.S. ban, more than half of the country's production was not outlawed, including CFCs used as blowing agents in making polyurethane foam and as a refrigerant in commercial, residential, and automotive air-conditioning systems. Sales of CFCs initially dropped after the aerosol ban but increased again by 1981.

In 1985, an initial meeting of 31 nations produced an agreement on a short-term freeze of CFC production and a general consensus for a long-term phaseout. This led to the Montreal Protocol, an international treaty designed to control CFC emissions. The international community's environmental leaders met in London during summer 1990 to revive and strengthen the existing Montreal Protocol. At the London Revision meeting, held under the auspices of the United Nations Environmental Program (UNEP), the nations agreed to freeze production of CFCs at 1986 levels and to cut production 20% by mid-1993 and cut another 50% by mid-1998. The 12 nations of the European Community have committed themselves to total elimination of CFCs. Over 60 nations have ratified the Montreal Protocol. With new support from the United Nations, a fund is being set up to assist developing countries with the phaseout.

In addition to the UN efforts, scientists are mobilizing in a variety of studies, projects, and missions to better understand the chemistry and dynamics of ozone depletion. Because ozone destruction involves a number of interrelated chemical reactions occurring at various altitudes, locations, and times of the year, the research efforts are comprehensive. The United States is in the middle of its second Airborne Arctic Stratospheric Expedition, or AASE II. This involves two aircraft. The first is an ER-2 high-altitude plane, flying at up to 70,000 feet, based in Fairbanks, Alaska, and later at Bangor, Maine. The second jet, a specially instrumented DC-8, will fly over the North Pole from California to Norway, and return over Greenland and northern Canada. These planes will carry special air samplers and spectrometers. The aim of the mission will be to survey ozone trends in the Arctic region and the northern portion of the Northern Hemisphere.

In September 1991, the NASA space shuttle *Discovery* launched UARS: the Upper Atmospheric Research Satellite. UARS, the first satellite in NASA's "Mission to Planet Earth" program, will observe the chemistry, energy, and winds of the upper atmosphere during a 20-month observation period. This period will allow scientists to monitor one complete annual cycle of the Antarctic ozone hole formation, and two depletion cycles in the Arctic winter seasons. A spectrometer will be able to identify the concentrations of various chemicals at altitudes of 6 to 50 miles.

A massive project is the multination European Arctic Stratospheric Ozone Experiment (EASOE). Some 250 scientists, working in 60 research groups, began collecting ozone-related data in November 1991. They will use 20 ground sites, rockets, weather ships, and high-altitude balloons to collect atmospheric chemistry and ozone data. Almost all European countries are participating, as well as researchers from Japan, Russia, New Zealand, and the United States.

It's clear that an awareness of the ozone issue at the international level is occurring. The general depletion trend provides an early warning to civilization about the special implications of our ozone predicament.

The Process of Scientific Thought

Activity #1

Title: Monitoring Ozone from the Classroom

Objective: To determine when the "ozone hole" appears

Materials Needed: graph paper, data in table 18.1

Procedure: On a piece of graph paper, label the vertical axis "ozone concentration" (in Dobson Units, DU) and label the horizontal axis "month." Use the data in table 18.1 to construct a graph of the relationship between ozone concentration and the month of the year.

Month	January	February	March	April	May	June	July	August	September	October	November	December
Ozone Concentration in Dobson Units (DU)	251	241	214	213	222	223	222	208	162	124	158	235

Table 18.1. Average Monthly Concentration of Ozone for Latitudes 90° S to 30° S, 1987

Elementary

• Find out what a Dobson Unit is. (Answer: It's a measurement of the thickness of the ozone layer. One hundred Dobson Units equals 1 millimeter of pure ozone gas at normal temperature and pressure at sea level.)

• When is the ozone concentration lowest? (Answer: In October during the Southern Hemisphere spring.)

• When is the ozone concentration highest? (Answer: In January, during the Southern summer.)

• The average concentration of ozone at mid latitudes is 300 Dobson Units. Compare this to the monthly values from table 18.1. Express your answer in terms of a percentage.

• What does a low number of Dobson Units mean? (Answer: An area of low concentration of ozone molecules.) What does a high number of Dobson Units mean? (Answer: An area of high concentration of ozone molecules.)

• Would you describe this phenomenon as an "ozone hole?" (Answer: Not really; it is more correctly described as a low concentration or a "thinning" of ozone. A "hole" implies zero ozone.)

Secondary

• Explain why the ozone level begins to decrease when it does. (Answer: Ozone concentration is lowest in the austral spring, following the cold winter of perpetual darkness. Two things speed up the natural process of ozone destruction. First, the presence of pollutants such as oxides and CFCs. Second, the presence of PSCs that provide aerosol surfaces needed for certain chemical reactions. Also, sunlight and extremely low temperatures are needed. And finally, high-level winds create a stable vortex that concentrates the above parameters over the Antarctic continent.)

- Research ozone levels over the Arctic. What do you find? (Answer: Ozone levels are higher than those over the Antarctic.) Why? (Answer: Temperatures are warmer, there is a different distribution of land and water, and there is not a concentrated, stable vortex.)

- Find out about the instrument called a spectrometer.

Activity #2

Title: Plants and Ozone Depletion

Objective: To demonstrate the effect of increased UV light on plants

Materials Needed: a UV lamp, two groups of seeds, two beds of soil, some time

Procedure: This activity measures the effect of increased UV radiation on the germination and development of plants. Place several seeds on the surface of a bed of soil. Subject one group to an elevated level of UV radiation by using a UV lamp. Place the other seeds on a bed of soil that is exposed to ambient light. Monitor the progress of each group of seeds.

Elementary

- Draw a picture of each group of seeds.

- Determine the time it takes each group of seeds to germinate. How does this time compare to the germination of that seed under natural conditions?

- If the concentration of ozone in the atmosphere is decreased, will more or less UV radiation strike Earth's surface? (Answer: More.)

- Research how increased levels of UV light affect the plant kingdom in general.

Secondary

- Repeat the activity by using several lamps and varying the amount of UV light for different groups of seeds. Collect all of this data and construct tables and graphs.

- Research current examples of damage to the plant kingdom caused by ozone depletion.

- Try to find accounts of those scientists and explorers who have been in Antarctica and experienced the extremely high UV radiation.

Activity #3

Title: Microbes and Ozone Depletion

Objective: To demonstrate the effects of increased UV light on microorganisms

Materials Needed: a sample of pond water, microscope, UV lamp

Procedure: This activity measures the effect of increased UV radiation on microorganisms. Draw a sample of pond water. Examine the sample using a microscope. Subject the sample to an increased level of UV light by placing it under a UV lamp. Using a microscope, examine the distribution of the microorganisms in the sample before and after exposure.

Elementary

- See if you can draw a picture of what you saw in the microscope before and after exposure.
- Describe the changes that occur following exposure of the sample of UV light.
- What causes the observed changes?
- Research how increased levels of UV radiation affect the animal kingdom in general.

Secondary

- Repeat the activity by using several lamps and varying the amount of UV light for different samples of pond water.
- Research current examples of damage to the animal kingdom caused by ozone depletion.
- Research ozone measuring techniques prior to 1978.
- Hold a debate: Are the benefits of ozone-destroying chemicals worth the consequences of ozone depletion?

Ideas for Science Fair Projects

1. Any of the activities in this chapter are appropriate for science fair presentation.

2. Research question: Do the benefits of our use of ozone-destroying chemicals outweigh the consequences of ozone depletion? List the ozone-destroying chemicals and their use in society. Then list some of the consequences of global ozone loss. Be sure to explain why these chemicals affect ozone as they do. Do you have a solution to this dilemma?

3. Suggested title: "The Effects of Atmospheric Pollution on Stratospheric Ozone." Outline the chemicals responsible for ozone depletion. Be sure to explain the science behind their role as ozone-destroyers.

4. Look into the medical aspects of ozone loss and subsequent increased exposure to UV radiation. Talk to a dermatologist about the damage UV radiation can do to skin. Talk to a reconstructive surgeon about how to repair skin damage caused by UV light. Finally, interview an ophthalmologist about how UV light affects the eyes.

5. Center a project on ozone as a gas. Give a brief history and describe how it is formed and how it is destroyed. Give its chemical formula and structure. Include information on the ozone layer—its function and importance and where it resides in the atmosphere.

6. Center a project on the Antarctic ozone hole. Discuss why it occurs. Be sure to relate its cause to temperature, sunlight, PSCs, ozone-destroying chemicals, and the stable vortex flow over the continent. Also, explain why the "ozone hole" is not really a hole, but a "thinning" of ozone.

7. Develop a project that looks at ozone levels over the Northern Hemisphere. Compare and contrast with the Southern Hemisphere. What are the differences? How much difference is there? Why is ozone loss over the Northern Hemisphere considered more serious than ozone loss over Antarctica? (Answer: More people live in the Northern Hemisphere.)

8. Discuss solutions to the ozone predicament.

9. Obtain a portable, handheld UV meter and monitor the UV readings at your home or at school. Take readings three times daily; one at mid-morning, one at mid-afternoon, and one during the early evening. Present these daily findings. Also do this on a seasonal basis. Discuss the seasonal variation. Be sure you know the reasons for the trends you see.

School's Out!

1. Prepare a list of three questions about ozone to ask a professional chemist.

2. Take your science fair project to a local service organization.

3. Go to the library and check out a book about ozone, CFCs, or the environment.

4. Clip newspaper or magazine articles covering the latest discoveries on ozone depletion topics. Share this with the class.

5. Visit the local NWS office and learn how ozone is monitored and how ozone advisories are issued.

6. Teach younger children about the importance of ozone and the consequences of ozone depletion.

7. Keep track of your local ozone level through TV weather reports or the newspaper.

8. Keep up with local regulations for controlling ozone-destroying chemicals. Report to the class.

9. Visit with a person who works for an industry that manufactures synthetic chemicals. How does this person feel about the magnitude of the ozone problem? Are federal, state, and local regulations adequate? Are they biased?

10. Talk with an air-conditioning contractor about how this person feels concerning regulations for handling and disposing of Freon.

Chapter 19

Acid Deposition

The final contemporary issue confronting humankind is *acid deposition*, defined as the laying down of acidic material. Our discussion begins with the historical context of the problem followed by a survey of the chemical pH scale and the mechanics, effects, and solutions of the problem of acid deposition.

Historical Background

The content of rainwater intrigued philosophers and scientists as early as the 17th century. This, along with an emerging awareness that plants draw nourishment from the air and from the water in the soil, impelled scientists to search for these substances in rainwater. By the mid-18th century, these efforts led to the discovery of several impurities. Early studies focused largely on the identification of the impurities with the recognition of their nutrient value to plant growth; particular interest was directed toward the nitrogen content of precipitation.

One phenomenon that was noted early on was so-called acid rain. In an extraordinary account of studies in and around the industrial city of Manchester, an English chemist, Robert Angus Smith, in 1872 used his analyses of rain chemistry to infer the existence of acid rain. In 1911, investigators in and near the industrial city of Leeds, England, concluded that plant growth was impeded by acid deposition. Thus, evidence was becoming more abundant that the Industrial Revolution and all that it entailed had fundamentally changed the organic relationship of people and the environment.

The pH Scale

The acidity of precipitation, and of substances in general, is measured in terms of the *p*otential *H*ydrogen scale, or as it is more commonly designated, the *pH scale*. This scale expresses the relative abundance of free hydrogen ions in a solution. It is these free hydrogen ions in a solution that make an acid corrosive, for they easily combine with other ions. The pH scale is logarithmic and ranges from 0 to 14, with every unit change corresponding to a tenfold change in acidity. A pH of 7.0 is considered neutral, below 7.0 is increasingly acidic, and above 7.0 is increasingly basic or alkaline. Figure 19.1 is a diagram of the pH scale with several well-known substances placed on the scale for reference and comparison. Natural precipitation dissolves CO_2 from the atmosphere, a process that releases hydrogen ions and produces an average pH reading of 5.65, with a normal range for precipitation of 5.3 to 6.0. Therefore, natural precipitation is always slightly acidic.

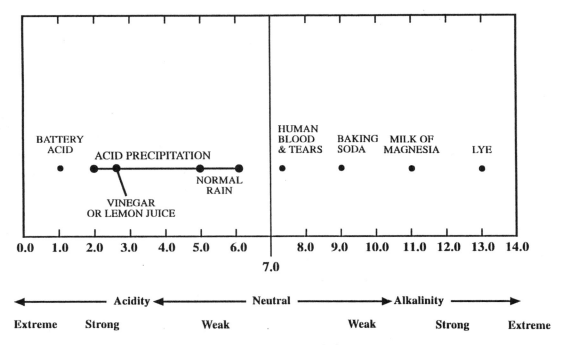

Fig. 19.1. The Chemical pH Scale

Mechanisms of Acid Deposition

Figure 19.2 illustrates the mechanisms of acid deposition. Gaseous and particulate matter can be removed from the atmosphere by either wet or dry deposition. In the dry form, large particles fall out of the air, small ones collide with land and water surfaces, and certain atmospheric gases are absorbed by material on Earth's surface. The term *wet deposition* refers to material carried out of the atmosphere principally by rain and snow. Much smaller amounts of wet acid deposition are thought to result from dew, frost, and even hail. In addition, winds carry the acid-producing chemicals many miles from their sources before they settle on the landscape, entering streams and lakes as runoff and groundwater flows.

Figure 19.3 depicts the wet deposition process associated with rain or snow. Certain anthropogenic gases are converted in the atmosphere into acids that are removed by either the wet or dry deposition process. Nitrogen oxides (NO_x) and sulfur oxides (SO_x) released in the combustion of fossil fuels can produce nitric acid (HNO_3) and sulfuric acid (H_2SO_4) in the atmosphere. The nitrogen oxides and the sulfur oxides are released into the air as waste products of fossil fuel burning

(coal, oil, and natural gas). Urban centers with heavy automobile traffic and lots of industry are the primary sources for NO_x and SO_x waste products. Now airborne, the NO_x and SO_x spread to downwind locations, driven by tropospheric flow patterns at the time. In the Northern Hemisphere, where acidic precipitation is a problem because of industry, this would mean that NO_x and SO_x waste is normally carried to the east, northeast, or southeast of the source site. Step 3 of the wet deposition process is a series of complex chemical reactions that occur as the airborne SO_x and NO_x substances interact with, and become involved with, the natural precipitation process. At this time in the process the SO_x produces sulfuric acid while the NO_x produces nitric acid. Last, the newly formed, acidic precipitation falls to Earth, landing on plants, man-made structures, and eventually running into lakes and rivers or percolating into groundwater. In figure 19.3, the oxidation of SO_x is much slower and affects long distances away from the source, usually hundreds of miles. The oxidation of NO_x is much faster and so it affects relatively short distances, generally from 10 to 100 miles.

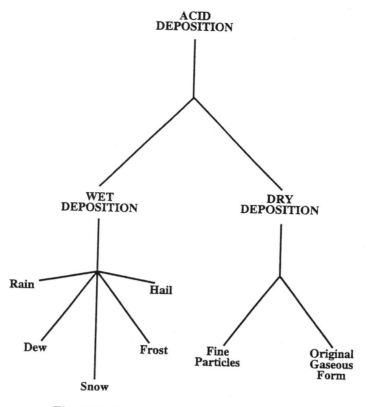

Fig. 19.2. The mechanisms of acid deposition.

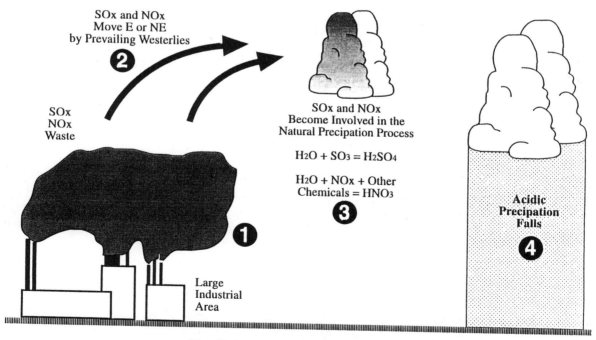

Fig. 19.3. The process of wet deposition.

Effects of Acid Deposition

The effects of acid deposition vary from time to time and from place to place. Figure 19.4 shows the annual average pH distribution of precipitation over North America. It is clear that the acidity of precipitation in North America generally increases from west to east, which is seen as evidence of transportation by tropospheric westerlies. At present, the most serious acid precipitation problem in North America is in the Ohio Valley, New England, the Tennessee Valley, and southeastern Canada. Acid precipitation is also a problem in other industrialized regions of the world such as Europe, Japan, Brazil, China, and South Africa. Dry deposition of dust or aerosols has even been found embedded in Arctic ice caps. Precipitation as acidic as pH 2.0 has fallen in the eastern United States, Scandinavia, and Europe. In comparison, lemon juice and vinegar have a pH near 3.0.

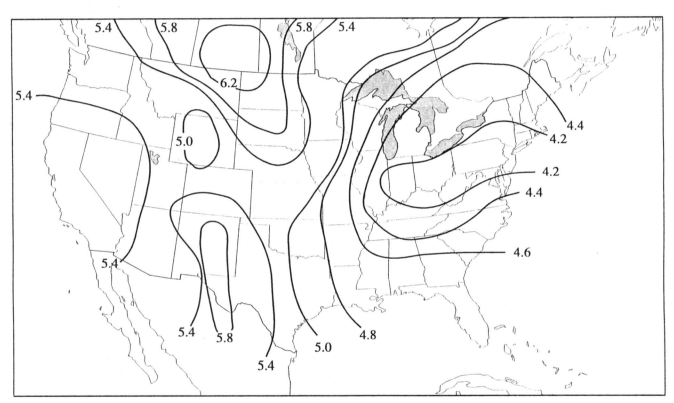

Fig. 19.4. Precipitation-weighed annual average pH distribution in North America.

Acid deposition is causally linked to declining fish populations and fish kills in the northeastern United States, southeastern Canada, Sweden, and Norway; to widespread forest damage in these same places and in Germany; and to damage to buildings, sculptures, and historical artifacts. More than 50,000 lakes and some 60,000 miles of streams in the United States and Canada are at a pH level below normal (pH 5.3), with several hundred lakes incapable of supporting any aquatic life. More than 90 lakes in the Adirondack Mountains in New York alone are fishless because acidic conditions have inhibited reproduction. A recent study of several hundred Norwegian lakes showed that at pH values of less than 4.5, more than 70% of the lakes were fishless. In addition to acidic lake water affecting fish directly, low-pH water frequently promotes the release of potentially toxic metals from the lakebed. Aluminum, for example, frequently found in high concentrations in fishless lakes, is released from soils at approximately pH 4.5. Rainfall runoff may carry aluminum from nearby soils into lakes, or into streams that empty into lakes, and thus magnify the problem. Also, relatively harmless mercury deposits in lake-bottom sediments are converted by acidified lake waters into highly toxic methyl mercury, which is deadly to aquaculture. In summary, the evidence points to the conclusion that reductions in the pH of water can lead to a decrease in the number and diversity of aquatic species.

Damage to forests results from the rear-rangement of soil nutrients, the death of soil microorganisms, and an aluminum-induced calcium deficiency. Europe is experiencing a more advanced impact on its forests than is apparent elsewhere, principally due to the burning of coal and dense industrial activity. In Germany, up to 50% of the forests are dead or dying; in Switzerland, 30% are afflicted. In the United States, trees at higher elevations in the Appalachians are being injured by acid-laden cloud cover and precipitation. In New England, some stands of spruce are as much as 75% affected, as evidenced by the analysis of tree growth rings. Another possible indicator of forest damage is the reduction by almost half of the annual production of U.S. and Canadian maple sugar.

Solutions to the Problem

The National Academy of Sciences (NAS) and the National Research Council have identified causal relationships between fossil fuel combustion and acid deposition, citing evidence that is "overwhelming." Despite this consensus, politics and special interests have halted preventive measures. The NAS stated that a reduction of 50% in combustion emissions would reduce acid deposition by 50%. Government estimates place damage in the United States and Canada at tens of billions of dollars and in western Europe at over $50 billion annually. Because wind and weather patterns cross political boundaries, efforts at reducing the impact of acid deposition must also be international.

The solution seems to lie in three areas: control of fossil fuel emissions, new technological advances, and more efficient equipment. Title IV of the 1990 Clean Air Act Amendments, which contain comprehensive provisions to control emissions that cause acid deposition, is the first legislation in U.S. history to directly address the problem of acid deposition. It calls for reductions in sulfur dioxide emissions from the burning of fossil fuels—the principal cause of acid deposition—and mandates significant reductions in nitrogen oxide and other toxic emissions. Title IV has been hailed around the world as a model of resourceful, inexpensive, and effective environmental policy.

Conclusion

Chapters 16 to 19 have addressed four of the most important issues in atmospheric science. These matters face humankind now and will confront future generations. A fitting conclusion is the following story. Let's pretend we have a black box. One side is labeled "global warming." Another side is labeled "acid deposition." The third side bears the words "air pollution," and on the fourth side "ozone depletion" is inscribed. On the top of the box in large, bold print is a warning: "DO NOT OPEN!" A little boy sees the box and, when no one is watching, he opens it. Immediately, an excruciating clanging noise begins. Slowly, a mechanical hand emerges from the box, closes it, and withdraws back inside. The awful clanging noise stops and things appear to be back to normal. In anthropogenic air pollution, and all that results from it, humankind has turned on the "black box." Will it stop without incident as it did in the analogy? Or will it continue unabated and feed back into something worse? Only time and human attitudes will dictate the answer.

The Process of Scientific Thought

Activity #1

Title: Acid Rain and Plants, Part I

Objective: To determine the effect of acid rain on seed germination

Materials Needed: two groups of bean seeds

Procedure: Plant two groups of bean seeds. Be sure to use the same type of soil, temperature, and lighting conditions. Water one group with an acidic solution; dilute nitric or sulfuric acid is appropriate. Water the other group with ordinary tap water. Observe the germination process of each group.

Elementary

- Which group took the longest time to germinate? Why?
- Repeat the activity with another type of seed. Are the results the same?
- Describe in general how acidic precipitation affects the germination process.

Secondary

- Expand the scope of the activity by using several groups of seeds and by varying the levels of acidity for each group. Record the results in a table and construct a graph.
- State generalizations evident from the number of trials attempted.
- Can you make predictions for future trials?

Activity #2

Title: Acid Rain and Plants, Part II

Objective: To determine the effect of acid rain on growing plants

Materials Needed: two identical plants

Procedure: Obtain two identical plants. Begin watering one with dilute sulfuric or nitric acid (spray it on the leaves also). Be sure to keep all other factors of the environment the same for both plants. Observe the health of each plant.

Elementary

- Draw a picture of each plant. Label which one was exposed to acidic solution.
- Describe what happened to the growth and health of the plant exposed to acidic solution.
- Repeat the experiment with another type of plant. Are the results the same?
- Describe, in general, how acidic precipitation affects the health of growing plants.

Secondary

- As before, expand the scope of the experiment by using several different types of plants and by varying the levels of acidity for each group. Monitor the growth and health of each plant. Record the results in a table and draw a graph.

- State generalizations evident from the number of trials attempted.

- Make predictions on other types of plants that are subjected to acid solution.

- Can you find evidence of damage to plants caused by acid precipitation in your local area?

Activity #3

Title: A Local pH Study

Objective: To determine the pH of local water

Materials Needed: a commercial pH test kit

Procedure: Obtain a commercial pH test kit and sample a body of water in your local area. Sample a lake, pond, or river. Be sure to sample at the same place each time over a period of several weeks. Collect and record data.

Elementary

- On a map, locate where you took your sample from.

- Draw a picture of the environment surrounding the sample site.

- Prepare graphs and tables in order to organize data.

- What does the data indicate about the pH of the test location? What trends are evident?

- Can you give reasons for the observed pH levels and for the observed trends?

Secondary

- Repeat the activity by using several sites. Locate each one on a map. You can also sample from different locations of the same river. Prepare tables and graphs of the data.

- State generalizations evident from the data.

- Explain observed pH levels and observed trends.

- Choose another test site. Try to make predictions in advance. How accurate are the predictions?

- Can you determine if there is any biological damage occurring at any of the test sites?

Activity #4

Title: Is My Precipitation Acidic?

Objective: To determine the acidity of local precipitation

Materials Needed: pH test kit

Procedure: Obtain a pH test kit and analyze the acidity of your local precipitation.

Elementary

- What is the pH value of your local precipitation? How does that compare to the pH level of "normal" precipitation?

- Is figure 19.4 accurate according to your results? Why or why not?

- Repeat the activity the next time precipitation occurs. How do these results compare to the previous results? Explain similarities and differences.

- Give reasons for the observed level of acidity of your local precipitation.

Secondary

- Expand the experiment by taking samples over an extended period of time (several months). Organize data in tables and graphs.

- State generalizations apparent from the data.

- Make a prediction about the pH level of the next sample. Then take the sample. How accurate is your prediction?

- Give reasons explaining the pH level of your local precipitation.

Ideas for Science Fair Projects

1. All four activities in this chapter are appropriate for science fair presentations.

2. Give an overview of the topic in a project entitled "Acid Deposition." Use figure 19.2, outline effects, include a brief history of the problem, and mention solutions.

3. Here's a variation of activity #4. Using your pH kit, take one test reading at the onset of precipitation and another reading at the end of the precipitation event. Are the pH levels different? Prepare attractive tables and graphs of the results. State a hypothesis that explains the results.

4. Suggested title: "Investigation of pH in Soil, Precipitation, and Surface Water." Take a pH reading for each location. Compare and contrast the results. Present data in eye-catching ways. Present conclusions.

5. Center a project on solutions to the acid deposition problem titled "Acid Deposition: Crisis with a Cure?"

6. Here's another suggested title: "Acid Precipitation and Its Ecological Consequences in *name your city or state*."

7. Research question: Does pH affect the growth of snow crystals? Construct a chamber to grow snow crystals at different pH levels. Evaluate the size, shape, and number of crystals.

8. Center a project on the effect of acid deposition on building materials. Cite examples from this chapter or other sources. Explain the chemical processes at work as the acidic precipitation interacts with different building materials. Interview a civil engineer or an architect.

9. Research question: Is acid deposition affecting crops in *name your city or state*?

10. "Acid Rain by Mail." Ask five friends or relatives from different states to send samples of their precipitation. Test these samples using a commercial pH test kit or litmus paper. Arrange them in order of acidity. Prepare attractive ways to represent the data. Develop a hypothesis.

11. Investigate whether the source direction of precipitation affects its acidity. Collect precipitation samples and record acidity levels with a pH test kit. Monitor atmospheric circulation patterns through TV weather reports, the newspaper, or ask a professional. Relate pH level to prevailing flow. State your hypothesis.

12. Center a project on how acid rain affects aquaculture.

School's Out!

1. Take photographs of damage caused by acid precipitation in your area. Bring them to class and discuss them with the teacher and classmates.

2. Read a book on acid rain or the environment.

3. Teach younger children about acid deposition.

4. Prepare a list of questions for a chemist.

5. Take your science fair project to a local civic club, day care, Head Start, or early childhood enrichment program.

6. Learn more about the pH scale. Verify the pH levels of some of the items in figure 19.1.

7. Experiment with acids and bases by using a chemistry set.

8. Maintain a record of pH levels of precipitation at your home.

Appendixes

Appendix A: State Record High Temperatures

State	Temp °F	Date	Location
Alabama	112	Sept. 5, 1925	Centerville
Alaska	100	June 27, 1915	Fort Yukon
Arizona	128	June 29, 1994	Lake Havasu
Arkansas	120	Aug. 10, 1936	Ozark
California	134	July 10, 1913	Greenland Ranch
Colorado	118	July 11, 1888	Bennett
Connecticut	105	July 21, 1991	Danbury
Delaware	110	July 21, 1930	Millsboro
District of Columbia	106	July 20, 1930	Washington
Florida	109	June 29, 1931	Monticello
Georgia	112	July 24, 1952	Louisville
Hawaii	100	April 27, 1931	Pahala
Idaho	118	July 28, 1934	Orofino
Illinois	117	July 14, 1954	East St. Louis
Indiana	116	July 14, 1936	Collegeville
Iowa	118	July 20, 1934	Keokuk
Kansas	121	July 24, 1936	Alton (near)
Kentucky	114	July 28, 1930	Greensburg
Louisiana	114	Aug. 10, 1936	Plain Dealing
Maine	105	July 10, 1911	North Bridgton
Maryland	109	July 10, 1936	Cumberland & Frederick
Massachusetts	107	Aug. 2, 1975	New Bedford & Chester
Michigan	112	July 13, 1936	Mio
Minnesota	114	July 6, 1936	Moorhead
Mississippi	115	July 29, 1930	Holly Springs
Missouri	118	July 14, 1954	Warsaw & Union
Montana	117	July 5, 1937	Medicine Lake
Nebraska	118	July 24, 1936	Minden
Nevada	125	June 29, 1994	Laughlin
New Hampshire	106	July 4, 1911	Nashua
New Jersey	110	July 10, 1936	Runyon
New Mexico	122	June 27, 1994	Lakewood
New York	108	July 22, 1926	Troy
North Carolina	110	Aug. 21, 1983	Fayetteville
North Dakota	121	July 6, 1936	Steele
Ohio	113	July 21, 1934	Gallipolis (near)
Oklahoma	120	June 29, 1994	Tipton
Oregon	119	Aug 10, 1898	Pendleton
Pennsylvania	111	July 10, 1936	Phoenixville
Rhode Island	104	Aug. 2, 1975	Providence
South Carolina	111	June 28, 1954	Camden
South Dakota	120	July 5, 1936	Gannvalley
Tennessee	113	Aug. 9, 1930	Perryville
Texas	120	Aug. 12, 1936	Seymour
Utah	117	July 5, 1985	St. George
Vermont	105	July 4, 1911	Vernon
Virginia	110	July 15, 1954	Balcony Falls
Washington	118	Aug. 5, 1961	Ice Harbor Dam
West Virginia	112	July 10, 1936	Martinsburg
Wisconsin	114	July 13, 1936	Wisconsin Dells
Wyoming	114	July 12, 1900	Basin

State Record Low Temperatures

State	Temp °F	Date	Location
Alabama	-27	Jan. 30, 1966	New Market
Alaska	-80	Jan. 23, 1971	Prospect Creek
Arizona	-40	Jan. 7, 1971	Hawley Lake
Arkansas	-29	Feb. 13, 1905	Pond
California	-45	Jan. 20, 1937	Boca
Colorado	-61	Feb. 1, 1985	Maybell
Connecticut	-32	Feb. 16, 1943	Falls Village
Delaware	-17	Jan. 17, 1893	Millsboro
District of Columbia	-15	Feb. 11, 1899	Washington
Florida	-2	Feb. 13, 1899	Tallahassee
Georgia	-17	Jan. 27, 1940	CCC Camp F-16
Hawaii	12	May 17, 1979	Mauna Kea
Idaho	-60	Jan. 18, 1943	Island Park Dam
Illinois	-35	Jan. 22, 1930	Mount Carroll
Indiana	-37	Jan. 19, 1994	New Whiteland
Iowa	-47	Jan. 12, 1912	Washta
Kansas	-40	Feb. 13, 1905	Lebanon
Kentucky	-34	Jan. 28, 1963	Cynthiana
Louisiana	-16	Feb. 13, 1899	Minden
Maine	-48	Jan. 19, 1925	Van Buren
Maryland	-40	Jan. 13, 1912	Oakland
Massachusetts	-35	Jan. 12, 1981	Chester
Michigan	-51	Feb. 9, 1934	Vanderbilt
Minnesota	-60	Feb. 2, 1996	Tower
Mississippi	-19	Jan. 30, 1966	Corinth
Missouri	-40	Feb. 13, 1905	Warsaw
Montana	-70	Jan. 20, 1954	Rogers Pass
Nebraska	-47	Feb. 12, 1899	Camp Clarke
Nevada	-50	Jan. 8, 1937	San Jacinto
New Hampshire	-46	Jan. 28, 1925	Pittsburg
New Jersey	-34	Jan. 5, 1904	River Vale
New Mexico	-50	Feb. 1, 1951	Gavilan
New York	-52	Feb. 18, 1979	Old Forge
North Carolina	-34	Jan. 21, 1985	Mt. Mitchell
North Dakota	-60	Feb. 15, 1936	Parshall
Ohio	-39	Feb. 10, 1899	Milligan
Oklahoma	-27	Jan. 18, 1930	Watts
Oregon	-54	Feb. 10, 1933	Seneca
Pennsylvania	-42	Jan. 5, 1904	Smethport
Rhode Island	-23	Jan. 11, 1942	Kingston
South Carolina	-19	Jan. 21, 1985	Ceasar's Head
South Dakota	-58	Feb. 17, 1936	McIntosh
Tennessee	-32	Dec. 30, 1917	Mountain City
Texas	-23	Feb. 8, 1933	Seminole
Utah	-69	Feb. 1, 1985	Peter's Sink
Vermont	-50	Dec. 30, 1933	Bloomfield
Virginia	-30	Jan. 22, 1985	Mountain Lake
Washington	-48	Dec. 30, 1968	Mazama & Winthrop
West Virginia	-37	Dec. 30, 1917	Lewisburg
Wisconsin	-54	Jan. 24, 1922	Danbury
Wyoming	-63	Feb. 9, 1933	Moran

Appendix B: Climatological Profiles for Selected U.S. Cities

Climatological Profiles for Selected U.S. Cities

State	Station	Latitude	Longitude	Ft. Altitude	Average Jan. Temp. °F	Average July Temp. °F	Aver. Temp. °F	Record Low	Record High	32° or Below	90° or Above	Snow In Inches	Average Wind Miles Per Hour	Average Relative Humidity %	Days with Thunderstorms	Days with Fog	Annual Rain In Inches
Alabama	Birmingham	33° 44N	86° 45'W	620	42	80	63	-10	107	57	85	1	8.2	68	57	159	54
	Mobile	30° 41N	88° 15'W	211	50	82	68	-1	104	23	76	T	9.0	72	79	150	66
Alaska	Anchorage	61° 10N	150° 01'W	114	15	57	36	-38	86	194	0	70	9.7	73	2	73	16
	Fairbanks	64° 49N	147° 52'W	436	-10	61	27	-66	99	225	1	67	7.2	72	7	78	11
	Juneau	58° 22N	134° 35'W	12	24	56	41	-22	90	141	*	99	8.3	78	*	21	53
Arizona	Flagstaff	35° 08N	111° 40'W	7,006	28	66	45	-30	97	209	3	100	6.6	57	51	11	21
	Phoenix	33° 26N	112° 01'W	1,110	54	94	73	16	122	10	167	T	6.3	37	23	6	7
	Tucson	32° 08N	110° 56'W	2,584	51	86	68	16	117	18	140	T	8.3	38	42	3	11
Arkansas	Little Rock	34° 44N	92° 14'W	257	39	82	62	-13	112	57	73	5	7.8	71	57	142	51
California	Los Angeles	33° 56N	118° 23'W	100	57	69	63	23	110	*	5	*	7.5	72	1	100	11
	Sacramento	38° 30N	121° 30'W	18	45	76	61	17	114	21	73	T	7.9	64	2	95	17
	San Diego	32° 44N	117° 10'W	13	57	71	64	25	111	*	4	0	6.9	69	5	97	9
	San Francisco	37° 46N	122° 26'W	75	49	63	57	27	103	*	2	*	10.6	73	2	N/A	20
Colorado	Denver	39° 46N	104° 52'W	5,286	30	74	50	-29	105	155	33	63	8.7	54	39	53	15
Connecticut	Hartford	41° 56N	72° 41'W	160	25	74	50	-26	102	135	18	46	8.4	64	20	165	44
Delaware	Wilmington	39° 40N	75° 36'W	79	31	76	54	-15	107	100	19	21	9.1	67	29	166	42
District of Columbia	Washington	38° 51N	77° 02'W	10	35	80	58	-15	106	71	34	18	9.4	63	30	127	40
Florida	Jacksonville	30° 30N	81° 42'W	26	52	82	68	7	105	16	83	*	8.0	72	65	175	52
	Miami	25° 48N	80° 18'W	12	67	83	76	30	98	*	55	0	9.3	73	74	39	57
	Tallahassee	30° 23N	84° 22'W	55	52	80	67	-2	104	31	86	T	8.3	71	83	202	63
	Tampa	27° 58N	82° 32'W	19	60	82	72	18	99	3	85	*	8.6	73	87	124	47
Georgia	Atlanta	33° 39N	84° 26'W	1,010	41	79	61	-9	105	49	38	2	9.1	69	48	148	53
Hawaii	Honolulu	21° 20N	157° 55'W	7	73	81	77	53	94	0	23	0	11.4	64	7	*	22
Idaho	Boise	43° 34N	116° 12'W	2,838	29	74	51	-25	111	124	44	22	8.8	56	15	51	12
Illinois	Chicago	41° 59N	87° 54'W	674	21	73	49	-27	104	132	17	39	10.3	70	38	124	35
	Springfield	39° 51N	89° 41'W	594	25	77	52	-24	112	118	30	24	12.9	70	50	134	35
Indiana	Indianapolis	39° 44N	86° 16'W	792	26	75	52	-27	107	119	19	25	9.6	73	43	162	40
Iowa	Des Moines	41° 32N	93° 39'W	938	19	77	50	-30	110	137	26	33	10.9	70	46	109	32
Kansas	Wichita	37° 39N	97° 26'W	1,321	30	81	56	-22	114	110	63	17	12.3	67	54	90	29
Kentucky	Louisville	38° 11N	85° 44'W	477	32	77	56	-22	107	90	35	17	8.4	70	45	142	44

State	Station	Latitude	Longitude	Ft. Altitude	Average Jan. Temp. °F	Average July Temp. °F	Aver. Temp. °F	Record Low	Record High	32° or Below	90° or Above	Snow in Inches	Average WindMiles Per Hour	Average Relative Humidity %	Days with Thunderstorms	Days with Fog	Annual Rain in Inches
Louisiana	New Orleans	29° 59'N	90° 15'W	4	51	82	68	7	102	13	70	*	8.2	75	69	175	61
	Shreveport	32° 28'N	93° 49'W	254	47	82	65	-5	110	36	90	2	9.9	69	57	107	46
Maine	Caribou	46° 52'N	68° 01'W	624	11	66	39	-41	96	187	2	110	11.2	69	20	27	37
Maryland	Baltimore	39° 11'N	76° 40'W	196	32	77	55	-7	105	97	31	21	9.2	66	27	146	41
Massachusetts	Boston	42° 21'N	71° 02'W	15	29	74	51	-18	104	98	13	40	12.5	65	19	23	44
Michigan	Detroit	42° 14'N	83° 20'W	633	23	72	49	-24	105	136	12	41	10.4	71	32	157	32
Minnesota	International Falls	48° 34'N	93° 23'W	1,179	1	66	36	-46	98	198	4	64	10.0	69	33	84	24
	Minneapolis/St. Paul	44° 53'N	93° 13'W	834	12	74	45	-34	108	156	16	52	10.6	69	37	96	27
Mississippi	Jackson	32° 19'N	90° 05'W	330	44	82	64	-5	107	50	84	1	7.4	74	68	195	55
Missouri	Kansas City	39° 19'N	94° 43'W	973	26	79	54	-23	113	110	39	21	10.8	70	51	124	38
	St. Louis	38° 45'N	90° 22'W	535	29	80	56	-22	115	100	43	20	9.7	71	46	141	37
Montana	Great Falls	47° 29'N	111° 23'W	3,663	21	68	45	-49	107	155	18	63	12.8	56	25	45	15
Nebraska	Omaha	41° 18'N	95° 54'W	980	21	77	51	-32	114	139	36	29	10.6	70	45	121	30
Nevada	Elko	40° 30'N	115° 47'W	5,075	24	70	45	-43	108	198	44	40	9.4	54	19	19	9
	Las Vegas	36° 05'N	115° 10'W	2,162	44	90	66	8	117	37	134	1	11.5	45	13	4	4
	Reno	39° 30'N	119° 47'W	4,404	33	72	51	-19	106	180	50	25	6.6	51	14	15	7
New Hampshire	Concord	43° 12'N	71° 30'W	346	19	70	45	-33	102	171	12	63	6.7	68	19	185	37
New Jersey	Atlantic City	39° 27'N	74° 34'W	138	31	75	53	-11	106	108	17	18	10.1	69	26	174	41
New Mexico	Albuquerque	35° 03'N	106° 37'W	5,326	34	79	56	-17	105	114	66	11	11.8	45	38	14	8
New York	Albany	42° 45'N	73° 48'W	275	21	72	47	-28	104	147	11	63	8.9	69	24	151	36
	Buffalo	42° 56'N	78° 44'W	705	24	71	48	-21	99	131	4	90	12.0	72	30	158	38
	New York City	40° 46'N	73° 54'W	11	32	77	55	-3	107	73	15	24	9.4	64	24	107	43
North Carolina	Charlotte	35° 13'N	80° 56'W	700	39	79	60	-5	104	65	44	6	7.5	69	41	162	43
	Raleigh	35° 52'N	78° 47'W	376	39	78	59	-9	105	77	39	8	7.8	70	42	181	42
North Dakota	Bismarck	46° 46'N	100° 46'W	1,647	9	70	42	-45	114	186	23	42	10.2	68	34	59	15
Ohio	Cincinnati	39° 04'N	84° 40'W	869	28	75	53	-25	109	107	23	23	9.1	70	39	160	41
	Cleveland	41° 25'N	81° 52'W	770	25	72	50	-20	104	123	12	55	10.6	71	34	146	37
	Columbus	40° 00'N	82° 53'W	812	26	73	51	-22	106	118	19	28	8.5	70	40	158	38
Oklahoma	Oklahoma City	35° 24'N	97° 36'W	1,280	36	82	60	-17	113	79	70	10	12.4	67	50	89	33
	Tulsa	36° 11'N	95° 54'W	668	36	82	60	-16	115	78	74	10	12.1	66	50	92	39
Oregon	Portland	45° 30'N	122° 36'W	21	40	68	54	3	107	42	11	7	7.9	73	7	33	37

State	Station	Latitude	Longitude	Ft. Altitude	Average Jan. Temp. °F	Average July Temp. °F	Aver. Temp. °F	Record Low	Record High	32° or Below	90° or Above	Snow in Inches	Average WindMiles Per Hour	Average Relative Humidity %	Days with Thunderstorms	Days with Fog	Annual Rain in Inches
Pennsylvania	Philadelphia	39° 54'N	75° 14'W	10	30	77	54	-11	106	94	23	22	9.5	66	27	163	41
	Pittsburgh	40° 30'N	80° 13'W	1,150	26	72	50	-22	103	121	8	43	9.1	67	35	178	37
Rhode Island	Providence	41° 44'N	71° 26'W	51	28	73	50	-13	104	117	10	36	10.6	65	21	167	45
South Carolina	Charleston	32° 54'W	80° 02'W	41	48	81	64	6	104	34	52	1	9.6	74	58	160	52
	Greenville Spartanburg	34° 54'N	82° 13'W	973	40	78	59	-6	103	66	35	6	6.9	69	44	151	51
South Dakota	Rapid City	44° 03'N	103° 04'W	3,162	21	73	47	-34	110	169	32	40	17.2	64	40	40	16
	Sioux Falls	43° 34'N	96° 44'W	1,418	14	74	46	-42	110	168	25	39	11.1	70	44	21	24
Tennessee	Knoxville	35° 48'N	84° 00'W	949	36	78	59	-24	104	73	33	13	8.6	69	47	172	47
	Memphis	35° 03'N	90° 00'W	258	40	83	62	-13	108	56	66	5	8.9	69	53	10	52
	Nashville	36° 07'N	86° 41'W	580	36	79	59	-17	107	76	51	11	8.0	70	54	147	47
	Dallas/Ft. Worth	32° 54'N	97° 02'W	551	43	85	65	-8	113	40	100	3	10.8	69	47	79	32
	El Paso	31° 48'N	106° 24'W	3,918	43	82	63	-8	112	61	105	6	8.9	42	34	9	8
Texas	Houston	29° 58'N	95° 21'W	96	50	83	68	5	107	21	96	*	7.9	75	62	193	47
	Lubbock	33° 39'N	101° 49'W	3,254	39	80	59	-17	110	93	80	10	12.8	60	47	57	18
	San Antonio	29° 32'N	98° 28'W	794	51	84	69	0	108	23	112	1	10.8	68	36	115	30
Utah	Salt Lake City	40° 47'N	111° 57'W	4,222	28	78	52	-30	107	128	56	63	8.9	55	38	42	16
Vermont	Burlington	44° 28'N	73° 09'W	332	16	71	45	-30	101	157	6	78	8.9	68	22	120	34
	Norfolk	36° 54'N	76° 12'W	22	39	78	59	-3	105	54	32	8	10.7	68	37	157	44
Virginia	Richmond	37° 30'N	77° 20'W	164	36	78	58	-17	107	79	41	13	7.7	68	43	138	43
	Roanoke	37° 19'N	79° 58'W	1,149	36	76	56	-11	105	90	31	24	11.2	67	35	122	41
Washington	Seattle/Tacoma	47° 27'N	122° 18'W	450	40	65	52	0	100	38	3	13	9.0	73	8	161	38
	Spokane	47° 38'N	117° 32'W	2,356	27	69	47	-30	108	140	18	51	8.9	65	11	101	17
West Virginia	Charleston	38° 22'N	81° 36'W	1,015	32	75	55	-17	108	100	22	32	6.3	70	45	236	43
Wisconsin	Milwaukee	42° 57'N	87° 54'W	672	19	71	46	-26	105	141	10	49	11.6	73	35	133	32
Wyoming	Cheyenne	41° 09'N	104° 49'W	6,120	27	68	46	-38	100	173	9	51	13.0	55	50	58	14

Appendix C: Climatological Profiles for Selected International Cities

North America (does not include the U.S.)										
Country	Station	Latitude	Longitude	Elevation (ft.)	Aver. °F Jan. Temp.	Aver. °F July Temp.	Average Temp.	Record Low	Record High	Annual Rain in Inches
Canada	Edmonton	53° 34'N	113° 31'W	2,219	7	62	37	-57	99	18
	Montreal	45° 30'N	73° 34'W	187	14	70	42	-35	97	41
	Regina	50° 26'N	104° 40'W	1,884	0	65	36	-56	110	15
	Resolute	74° 43'N	94° 59'W	220	-27	40	3	-61	61	6
	St. Johns	47° 32'N	52° 44'W	211	24	60	41	-21	93	53
	Toronto	43° 40'N	79° 24'W	379	23	69	45	-26	105	32
	Vancouver	49° 17'N	123° 05'W	127	37	64	50	2	92	57
Mexico	Acapulco	16° 50'N	99° 56'W	10	78	82	80	60	97	55
	Chihuahua	28° 42'N	105° 57'W	4,429	51	78	65	12	102	15
	Guadalajara	20° 41'N	103° 20'W	5,194	59	70	66	26	101	40
	La Paz	24° 07'N	110° 17'W	85	72	85	75	31	108	6
	Mazatlan	23° 11'N	106° 25'W	256	66	82	75	52	93	30
	Merida	20° 58'N	89° 38'W	72	73	83	79	51	106	37
	Mexico City	19° 26'N	99° 04'W	7,340	54	64	59	24	92	23
	Monterrey	25° 40'N	100° 18'W	1,732	58	81	71	25	107	23
	Tampico	22° 16'N	97° 51'W	78	67	82	76	34	104	45
Central America										
Belize	Belize City	17° 31'N	88° 11'W	17	74	81	79	49	97	74
Costa Rica	San Jose	9° 56'N	84° 08'W	3,760	67	70	71	49	92	71
El Salvador	San Salvador	13° 42'N	89° 13'W	2,238	75	77	77	45	105	70
Guatemala	Guatemala City	14° 37'N	90° 31'W	4,855	63	69	68	41	90	52
West Indies										
Barbados	Bridgetown	13° 08'N	59° 36'W	181	76	80	79	61	95	50
Bermuda	Hamilton	32° 17'N	64° 46'W	151	63	79	70	40	99	58
Cuba	Havana	23° 08'N	82° 21'W	80	72	82	77	43	104	48
Bahamas	Nassau	25° 05'N	77° 21'W	12	71	82	77	41	94	46
Haiti	Port-au-Prince	18° 33'N	72° 20'W	121	78	84	81	58	101	53
Jamaica	Kingston	17° 58N	76° 48'W	110	77	82	79	56	97	32
Puerto Rico	San Juan	18° 26'N	66° 00'W	13	74	81	78	60	94	64
Virgin Islands	St. Thomas	18° 20'N	64° 58'W	11	77	83	80	63	92	44
South America										
Argentina	Buenos Aires	34° 35'S	58° 29'W	89	74	50	61	22	104	37
	Mendoza	32° 53'S	68° 49'W	2,625	75	47	61	15	109	8
	Santa Cruz	50° 01'S	68° 32'W	39	59	35	48	1	94	5
	Santiago del Estero	27° 46'S	64° 18'W	653	83	57	71	19	116	20

South America (Continued)										
Country	Station	Latitude	Longitude	Elevation (ft.)	Aver. °F Jan. Temp.	Aver. °F July Temp.	Average Temp.	Record Low	Record High	Annual Rain in Inches
Bolivia	La Paz	16° 30'S	68° 08'W	12,001	53	48	51	26	80	23
Brazil	Belém	1° 27'S	48° 29'W	42	80	80	80	61	98	96
	Brasilia	15° 51'S	47° 56'W	3,481	73	65	71	46	93	54
	Manaus	3° 08'S	60° 01'W	144	82	82	82	63	101	71
	Rio de Janeiro	22° 55'S	43° 12'W	201	79	69	73	46	102	43
	Salvador	13° 00'S	38° 30'W	154	80	74	78	50	100	75
	São Paulo	23° 37'S	46° 39'W	2,628	70	60	65	32	100	57
	Sena Madureira	9° 04'S	68° 39'W	443	81	77	80	41	100	81
Chile	Arica	18° 28'S	70° 20'W	95	71	60	65	39	93	Trace
	Punta Arenas	53° 10'S	70° 54'W	26	52	36	44	11	86	14
	Santiago	33° 27'S	70° 42'W	1,706	69	48	59	24	99	14
Colombia	Bogota	4° 42'S	74° 08'W	8,355	58	57	58	30	75	42
Ecuador	Quito	0° 08'S	78° 29'W	9,222	57	53	58	25	86	44
Guyana	Georgetown	6° 50'N	58° 12'W	6	79	80	80	68	93	89
Paraguay	Asunción	25° 17'S	57° 30'W	456	83	64	75	29	110	52
Peru	Iquitos	3° 45'S	73° 13'W	384	81	78	79	54	100	108
	Lima	12° 05'S	77° 03'W	394	74	62	66	49	93	2
Venezuela	Caracas	10° 30'N	66° 56'W	3,418	66	70	69	45	91	33
Europe										
Austria	Vienna	48° 15'N	16° 22'E	664	30	67	50	-14	98	26
Bulgaria	Sofia	42° 42'N	23° 20'E	1,805	28	70	50	-17	99	25
Czech Republic	Prague	50° 05'N	14° 25'E	662	30	66	48	-16	98	19
Denmark	Copenhagen	55° 41'N	12° 33'E	43	33	64	48	-3	91	23
Finland	Helsinki	60° 10'N	24° 57'E	30	22	64	41	-23	89	28
France	Lyons	45° 42'N	4° 47'E	938	36	69	52	-13	105	29
	Marseille	43° 18'N	5° 23'E	246	46	68	57	9	101	23
	Paris	48° 49'N	2° 29'E	164	37	66	51	1	105	22
Germany	Berlin	52° 27'N	13° 18'E	187	31	65	47	-15	96	23
	Frankfurt	50° 07'N	8° 40'E	338	33	66	49	-7	100	24
	Hamburg	53° 33'N	9° 58'E	66	32	63	47	-4	92	29
Greece	Athens	37° 58'N	23° 43'E	351	48	81	64	20	109	16
Hungary	Budapest	47° 31N	19° 02'E	394	31	72	52	-10	103	24
Iceland	Reykjavik	64° 09'N	21° 56'W	92	32	63	41	4	74	34
Ireland	Dublin	53° 22'N	6° 21'W	155	41	59	49	8	86	30
Italy	Rome	41° 48'N	12° 36'E	377	47	76	61	20	104	30
	Venice	45° 26'N	12° 23'E	82	38	75	57	14	97	33
Netherlands	Amsterdam	52° 23'N	4° 55'E	5	37	64	50	3	95	26
Norway	Oslo	59° 56'N	10° 44'E	308	25	65	44	-21	93	27
Poland	Warsaw	52° 13'N	21° 02'E	294	26	66	46	-22	98	22

Europe (Continued)										
Country	Station	Latitude	Longitude	Elevation (ft.)	Aver. °F Jan. Temp.	Aver. °F July Temp.	Average Temp.	Record Low	Record High	Annual Rain in Inches
Portugal	Lisbon	38° 43'N	9° 08'W	313	51	71	61	29	103	27
Romania	Bucharest	44° 25'N	26° 06'E	269	27	74	52	-18	105	23
Spain	Barcelona	41° 24'N	2° 09'E	312	49	70	61	24	98	24
	Madrid	40° 25'N	3° 41'W	2,188	40	75	58	14	102	17
	Seville	37° 29'N	5° 49'W	98	50	82	65	27	117	23
Sweden	Stockholm	59° 21'N	18° 04'E	146	27	63	45	-26	97	22
Switzerland	Zurich	47° 23'N	8° 33'E	1,617	33	66	49	-12	98	41
Turkey	Istanbul	40° 58'N	28° 50'E	59	41	73	57	17	100	32
United Kingdom	Belfast (N. Ireland)	54° 35'N	5° 56'W	57	38	59	48	14	82	38
	Edinburgh (Scotland)	55° 55'N	3° 11'W	441	39	59	48	15	83	28
	London (England)	51° 29'N	00° 00'	149	40	64	52	9	99	23
Russia	Dnipropetrovsk	48° 27'N	35° 04'E	259	21	71	46	-25	101	19
	Kiev	50° 16'N	30° 39'E	596	21	68	45	N/A	N/A	24
	Moscow	55° 46'N	37° 40'E	505	15	66	39	-43	96	25
	Odessa	46° 29'N	30° 44'E	214	25	72	49	-13	99	14
	Verkhoyansk	67° 34'N	133° 51'E	328	-59	57	2	-90	98	5
Yugoslavia	Belgrade	44° 48'N	20° 28'E	453	32	73	54	-14	107	25
Africa										
Algeria	Algiers	36° 46'N	3° 03'E	194	54	76	65	32	107	30
	Tamanrasset	22° 42'N	5° 31'E	4,593	53	83	70	20	102	1.5
Angola	Luanda	8° 49'S	13° 13'E	194	79	70	76	58	98	13
Botswana	Francistown	21° 13'S	27° 30'E	3,294	77	58	70	24	107	18
Chad	Faya Largeau	18° 00'N	19° 10'E	837	69	93	84	37	121	0.7
Ethiopia	Addis Ababa	9° 20'N	38° 45'E	8,038	59	60	60	32	94	49
Guinea	Conarky	9° 31'N	13° 43'W	23	80	78	80	63	96	169
Ivory Coast	Abidjan	5° 19'N	4° 01'W	65	81	78	80	59	96	77
Kenya	Nairobi	1° 16'S	36° 48'E	5,971	66	60	64	41	87	38
Libya	Sabhah	27° 01'N	14° 26'E	1,457	53`	88	73	24	120	0.3
	Tripoli	32° 54'N	13° 11'E	72	54	78	67	33	114	15
Madagascar	Antananarivo	18° 55'S	47° 33'E	4,500	70	58	66	34	95	53
Mali	Gao	16° 16'N	00° 03'W	902	71	89	85	44	116	12
Mauritania	Atar	20° 31'N	13° 04'W	761	69	94	82	39	117	3
Morocco	Casablanca	33° 35'N	7° 39'W	164	54	72	63	31	110	16
Mozambique	Beira	19° 50'N	34° 51'W	28	82	69	77	48	109	60
Niger	Agades	16° 59'N	7° 59'E	1,706	68	90	82	40	115	7
Nigeria	Lagos	6° 27'N	3° 24E	10	81	79	81	60	104	72
	Maiduguri	11° 51'N	13° 05'E	1,162	72	82	81	43	112	25
Senegal	Dakar	14° 42'N	17° 29'W	131	72	82	77	53	109	21
Somalia	Mogadishu	2° 02'N	45° 21'E	39	80	78	80	59	97	17

Country	Station	Latitude	Longitude	Elevation (ft.)	Aver. °F Jan. Temp.	Aver. °F July Temp.	Average Temp.	Record Low	Record High	Annual Rain in Inches
Africa (Continued)										
South Africa	Capetown	33° 54'S	18° 33'E	56	69	54	62	28	103	20
	Pretoria	25° 45'S	28° 14'E	4,491	71	52	63	24	96	31
Namibia	Windhoek	22° 34'S	17° 06'E	5,669	74	56	67	25	97	14
Sudan	Khartoum	15° 37'N	32° 33'E	1,279	85	89	85	41	118	6
	Wadi Halfa	21° 55'N	31° 20'E	410	61	90	78	28	127	T
	Wau	7° 42'N	28° 03'E	1,443	80	79	81	50	115	43
Tanzania	Dar es Salaam	6° 50'S	39° 18'E	47	80	75	78	59	96	42
Tunisia	Tunis	36° 47'N	10° 12'E	217	51	79	65	30	118	17
Uganda	Kampala	0° 20'N	32° 36'E	4,304	74	70	72	53	97	46
Egypt	Alexandria	31° 12'N	29° 53'E	105	58	79	70	37	111	7
	Aswan	24° 02'N	32° 53'E	366	62	93	80	35	124	T
	Cairo	29° 52'N	31° 20'E	381	56	83	71	34	117	1.1
Zambia	Lusaka	15° 25'S	28° 19'E	4,191	71	61	69	39	100	33
Zimbabwe	Bulawayo	20° 09'S	28° 37'E	4,405	71	58	67	28	99	23
Asia - Far East										
China	Harbin	45° 45'N	126° 38'E	476	-4	75	39	-43	102	23
	Kunming	25° 02N	102° 43'E	6,211	49	70	61	22	91	41
	Shanghai	31° 12'N	121° 26'E	16	40	83	62	10	104	45
Hong Kong Island	Hong Kong	22° 18'N	114° 10'E	109	60	83	73	32	97	85
Japan	Nagasaki	32° 44'N	129° 53'E	436	43	79	61	22	98	76
	Tokyo	35° 41'N	139° 46'E	19	38	77	58	17	101	62
Mongolia	Ulan Bator	47° 54'N	106° 56'E	4,287	-15	61	27	-48	97	8
North Korea	Pyongyang	39° 01'N	125° 49'E	94	18	77	49	-19	100	36
South Korea	Seoul	37° 31'N	126° 55'E	34	24	77	52	-12	99	49
Taiwan	Taipei	25° 04'N	121° 32'E	21	60	84	72	32	101	73
Asia - Southeast										
Burma	Mandalay	21° 59'N	96° 06'E	252	69	86	81	44	111	33
Cambodia	Phnom Penh	11° 33'N	104° 51'E	39	80	83	82	55	105	55
Indonesia	Djakarta	6° 11'S	106° 50'E	26	79	80	80	66	98	71
	Manokwari	0° 53'S	134° 03'E	10	80	80	80	68	93	98
	Tarakan	3° 19'N	117° 33'E	20	79	81	80	67	94	152
Malaya	Singapore	1° 18'N	103° 50'E	33	80	82	81	66	97	95
Philippines	Manila	14° 31'N	121° 00'E	49	78	82	81	58	101	82
Thailand	Bangkok	13° 44'N	100° 30'E	53	78	83	82	50	104	58
Viet Nam	Ho Chi Minh City	10° 49'N	106° 39'E	33	80	82	82	57	104	78
Asia - Middle East										
Afghanistan	Kabul	34° 30'N	69° 13'E	5,955	27	77	54	-6	104	13

Asia - Middle East (Continued)										
Country	Station	Latitude	Longitude	Elevation (ft.)	Aver. °F Jan. Temp.	Aver. °F July Temp.	Average Temp.	Record Low	Record High	Annual Rain in inches
India	Bombay	19° 06'N	72° 51'E	27	75	82	81	46	110	71
	Calcutta	22° 32'N	88° 20E	21	68	85	80	44	111	63
	Delhi	28° 35'N	77° 12'E	695	57	88	76	31	115	25
	Madras	13° 04'N	80° 15'E	51	76	88	83	57	113	50
Iran	Tehran	35° 41'N	51° 19'E	3,937	36	86	62	-5	109	10
Iraq	Baghdad	33° 20'N	44° 24'E	111	50	93	73	18	121	6
Israel	Jerusalem	31° 47'N	35° 13'E	2,654	48	75	64	26	107	20
Jordan	Amman	31° 58'N	35° 59'E	2,547	47	77	63	21	109	11
Kuwait	Kuwait City	29° 21'N	48° 00'E	16	55	95	76	33	119	5
Lebanon	Beirut	33° 54'N	35° 28'E	111	57	80	69	30	107	35
Pakistan	Karachi	24° 48'N	66° 59'E	13	66	86	79	39	118	8
Saudi Arabia	Jidda	21° 28'N	39° 10'E	20	75	89	82	49	117	2.5
	Riyadh	24° 39'N	46° 42'E	1,938	58	93	76	19	120	3.2
Sri Lanka	Colombo	6° 54'N	79° 52'E	22	79	81	79	59	99	92
Syria	Damascus	33° 30'N	36° 20'E	2,362	45	80	64	21	113	9
Turkey	Ankara	39° 57'N	32 53'E	2,825	32	73	53	-13	104	14
	Izmir	38° 27'N	27° 15'E	92	47	81	63	12	108	26
Australia, New Zealand, Pacific Islands										
Australia	Adelaide	34° 57'S	138° 32'E	20	74	52	63	32	118	21
	Alice Springs	23° 48'S	133° 53'E	1,791	84	53	69	19	111	10
	Bourke	30° 05'S	145° 58'E	361	85	54	69	25	125	13
	Brisbane	27° 25'S	153° 05'E	17	77	59	69	35	110	45
	Broome	17° 57'S	122° 13'E	56	86	70	80	40	113	23
	Cloncurry	20° 40'S	140° 30'E	622	88	64	78	35	127	18
	Darwin	12° 25'S	130° 52'E	104	84	77	82	55	105	59
	Laverton	28° 40'S	122° 23'E	1,510	83	53	68	25	115	9
	Melbourne	37° 49'S	144° 58'E	115	68	49	58	27	114	26
	Perth	31° 56'S	115° 58'E	64	74	56	64	31	112	35
	Sydney	33° 52'S	151° 02'S	62	72	53	63	35	114	47
	Townsville	19° 15'S	146° 46'E	18	82	67	76	39	110	46
	Windorah	25° 26'S	142° 36'E	390	88	62	73	26	116	11
Tasmania	Hobart	42° 53'S	147° 20'E	177	62	46	55	28	105	24
New Zealand	Auckland (N. Island)	37° 00'S	174° 47'E	23	67	51	59	33	90	49
	Dunedin (S. Island)	45° 55'S	170° 12'E	4	58	43	51	23	94	37
Marianas Islands	Guam	13° 33'N	144° 50'E	361	78	80	79	54	95	89
Bonin Islands	Iwo Jima	24° 47'N	141° 19'E	353	68	82	76	46	95	53
Okinawa	Naha	26° 12'N	127° 39'E	96	62	83	72	41	96	83
Fiji	Suva	18° 18'S	178° 26'E	20	80	74	77	55	98	117

	Greenland and Antarctica									
Country	Station	Latitude	Longitude	Elevation (ft.)	Aver. °F Jan. Temp.	Aver. °F July Temp.	Average Temp.	Record Low	Record High	Annual Rain in Inches
Antarctica	Mirny	66° 33'S	93° 01'E	99	28	1	10	N/A	N/A	25
	Vostok	78° 28'S	106° 48'E	11,615	-27	-89	-69	-129	-6	Scanty
Greenland	Ammassalik	65° 36'N	37° 33'W	95	17	46	29	-26	77	31
	Eismitte	70° 53'N	40° 42'W	9,843	-43	10	-23	-85	27	4
	Ivigtut	61° 12'N	48° 10'W	98	18	50	33	-20	86	45
	Nord	81° 36'N	16° 40'W	118	-22	39	3	-60	61	9
	Thule	76° 31'N	68° 44'W	251	-11	42	12	-44	63	5
	Upernavik	72° 47'N	56° 07'W	59	-6	42	17	-44	69	9

Appendix D: Resources

Books

Battan, Louis J. *Fundamentals of Meteorology.* 2d ed. Upper Saddle River, N.J.: Prentice-Hall, 1984.

Bohren, Craig F. *Clouds in a Glass of Beer.* New York: Wiley, 1987.

Grazulis, Thomas P. *Significant Tornadoes.* St. Johnsbury, Vt.: Environmental Films, 1993.

Laskin, David. *Braving the Elements: A Stormy History of American Weather.* New York: Doubleday, 1996.

Ludlum, David M. *Field Guide to North American Weather.* New York: Knopf, 1991.

———. *The Weather Factor.* Boston: Houghton Mifflin, 1984.

Lutgens, Frederick K., and Edward J. Tarbuck. *The Atmosphere: An Introduction to Meteorology.* New York: Macmillan, 1995.

Moran, Joseph M., and Michael D. Morgan. *Essentials of Weather.* Upper Saddle River, N.J.: Prentice-Hall, 1995.

Williams, Jack. *The USA Today Weather Almanac.* New York: Vintage, 1995.

———. *The Weather Book.* New York: Vintage, 1992.

Wright, Nigel. *Environmental Science.* Upper Saddle River, N.J.: Prentice-Hall, 1993.

Periodicals

Adult/Secondary

Astronomy, P.O. Box 1612, Waukesha, WI 53187-1612; (800) 553-6644.

Discover, 114 Fifth Avenue, New York, NY 10011-5640; (212) 633-4400; http://www.discover.com.

E: The Environment Magazine, Earth Action Network, P.O. Box 5098, Westport, CT 06881-5098; (203) 854-5559.

Environment, 1319 18th Street NW, Washington, DC 20036-1802; (202) 296-6267; http://www.heldret.org.

National Geographic Magazine, 1145 17th Street NW, Washington, DC, 20036; (202) 857-7000; http://www.nationalgeographic.com.

Natural Hazards Observer, University of Colorado, Campus Box 482, Boulder, CO 80309-0482; (303) 492-6818; http://www.colorado.edu/hazards.

Natural History, Central Park West at 79th Street, New York, NY 10024; (212) 769-5500.

Newsweek, 251 West 57th Street, New York, NY 10019; (212) 445-4000.

Popular Science, 2 Park Avenue, New York, NY 10016; (212) 779-5000; http://www.popsci.com

Science, 1200 New York Avenue NW, Washington, DC, 20005; (202) 326-6400.

Scientific American, 415 Madison Avenue, New York, NY 10017; (212) 754-0550; http://www.sciam.com.

Sierra, 85 Second Street, San Francisco, CA 94105-3441; (415) 977-5656.

Sky and Telescope, P.O. Box 9111, Belmont, MA 02178; (617) 864-7360; http://www.skypub.com.

Smithsonian Magazine, 900 Jefferson Drive, Washington, DC 20560; http://www.smithsonianmag.si.edu.

Stormtrack, The Tornado Chaser's Magazine, c/o Tim Marshall, 4041 Bordeaux Circle, Flower Mound, TX 75022.

Time, Time-Life Building, Rockefeller Center, New York, NY 10020-1393; (212) 522-1212.

Weatherwise, Heldref Publications, 1319 18th Street NW, Washington, DC 20036-1802; (800) 365-9753; http://www.heldnet.org.

Juvenile

Cricket, Carus Publishing Company, P.O. Box 300, Peru, IL 61354-0300; (815) 224-6656.

Highlights for Children, 803 Church Street, Honesdale, PA 18431-1824; (717) 253-0179.

National Geographic World, National Geographic Society, 17th and M Streets NW, Washington, DC 20036; (202) 857-7000.

The World and I, News World Communications, Inc., 3600 New York Avenue NE, Washington, DC 20002; (202) 635-4000; http://www.worldandi.com.

Outside Kids, Mariah Media, Inc., Outside Plaza, 400 Market Street, Santa Fe, NM 87501; (505) 989-7100.

Owl Magazine, Owl Communications, 179 John Street, Suite 500, Toronto, ON MST 3G5 Canada; (416) 340-2700.

Ranger Rick, National Wildlife Federation, 8925 Leesburg Pike, Vienna, VA 22184; (703) 790-4274.

Government Agencies

Environmental Protection Agency (EPA), 401 M Street SW, Washington, DC 20460; (202) 260-2080.

National Aeronautics and Space Administration (NASA), NASA Headquarters, Washington, DC 20546; (202) 453-1000.

National Oceanic and Atmospheric Administration (NOAA), Environmental Research Laboratories, 325 Broadway, Boulder, CO 80303; (303) 497-3000.

National Science Foundation (NSF), 1800 G Street NW, Washington, DC 20550; (202) 357-9498.

United States Geological Survey (USGS), Department of the Interior, 12201 Sunrise Valley Drive, Reston, VA 22092; (703) 648-4460.

Scientific Organizations

American Association for the Advancement of Science (AAAS), 1200 New York Avenue NW, Washington, DC 20005; (202) 326-6400; http://www.aaas.org.

American Astronomical Society, 335 East 45th Street, New York, NY 10017; http://www.aas.org

American Geophysical Union (AGU), 2000 Florida Avenue NW, Suite 400, Washington, DC 20009; (202) 462-6900; (800) 966-2481; http:///www.agu.org.

American Meteorological Society (AMS), 45 Beacon Street, Boston, MA 02108; (617) 227-2425; http://www.ametsoc.org.

Geological Society of America, 3300 Penrose Place, P.O. Box 9140, Boulder, CO 80303; (303) 447-2020; http://www.geosociety.org.

National Geophysical Data Center, 325 Broadway, Boulder, CO, 80303; (303) 497-6826; http://www.ngdc.noaa.gov.

National Weather Association (NWA), 6704 Wolke Court, Montgomery, AL 36116-2134; (334) 213-0388; http://www.nwas.org.

NOAA Environmental Information Services, 1315 East-West Highway, Room 15400, Silver Spring, MD 20910; (301) 713-0575; http://www.esdim.noaa.gov.

U.S. Geological Survey, 807 National Center, Reston, VA 20192; (703) 648-4748; http://www.usgs.gov.

Science Equipment and Instruments

American Weather Enterprises. P.O. Box 1383, Media, PA 19063; (800) 293-2555.

Central Scientific Company, 11222 Melrose Avenue, Franklin Park, IL 60131; (312) 451-0150.

Davis Instruments, 3465 Diablo Avenue, Hayward, CA 94545; (800) 678-3669; fax: (510) 670-0589.

Edmund Scientific, Consumer Science Division, Dept. 16A1, C905 Edscap Bldg., Barrington, NJ 08007; (609) 547-8880; fax: (609) 573-6295; scientifics@edsci.com.

Fascinating Electronics, Inc., 31525 Canaan Road, Deer Island, OR 97054-9610; (800) 683-5487.

Fisher Scientific, 4901 West LeMoyne Street, Chicago, IL 60651; (800) 621-4769.

Frey Scientific, 905 Hickory Lane, Mansfield, OH 44905; (800) 225-FREY.

Hinds Instruments, 3175 NW Aloclek Drive, Hillsboro, OR 97124; (503) 690-2000; fax: (503) 690-3000.

Hubbard Scientific, P.O. Box 104, Northbrook, IL 60065; (800) 323-8368.

Lab-Aids, Inc., 130 Wilbur Place, P.O. Box 158, Bohemia, NY 11716; (516) 567-6120.

Maximum, Inc., 30 Barrett Boulevard, Suite F-06, New Bedford, MA 02745; (508) 995-2200; fax: (508) 998-5359.

Nasco Science, 1524 Princeton Avenue, Modesto, CA 95352; (800) 558-9595.

OHAUS Scale Corporation, 29 Hanover Street, Florham Park, NJ 07932; (201) 377-9000.

Peet Bros. Co., 1308-612E Doris Avenue, Ocean, NJ 07712; (800) USA-PEET; fax: (908) 517-0669; http://www.peetbros.com.

Qualimetrics, Inc., 1165 National Drive, Sacramento, CA 95834; (800) 824-5873 or (916) 928-1000; fax: (916) 928-1165.

Robert E. White Instruments, Inc., 34 Commercial Wharf, Boston, MA 02110; (800) 992-3045.

Science Kit, Inc., 777 East Park Drive, Tonawanda, NY 14150; (716) 874-6020.

Simerl Instruments, 528 Epping Forest Road, Annapolis, MD 21401; (410) 849-8667.

Texas Weather Instruments, Inc., 5942 Abrams Road #113, Dallas, TX 75231; (800) 284-0245 or (214) 368-7116; fax: (214) 234-1309.

Weather Bureau, P.O. Box 1045, Ann Arbor, MI 48106-1045; (313) 995-9000; fax: (313) 663-8888.

The Weather Company, Inc., P.O. Box 855, Skokie, IL 60076; (800) 803-8808.

Wind and Weather, P.O. Box 2320, Mendocino, CA 95460; (800) 922-9463 or (707) 937-0323.

Software

The World WeatherDisc CD-ROM contains a massive database of weather and climate information. Data is available for thousands of locations around the world, with some records dating back to the 1700s. These data sets encompass a large number of meteorological variables such as temperature, precipitation, heating/cooling degree days, freeze occurrences, wind, sunshine, lightning, tornadoes, tropical cyclones, and thunderstorms. The cost of the package is $195 (plus shipping) and is available from:

WeatherDisc Associates, Inc.
4584 NE 89th Street
Seattle, WA 98115
(206) 524-4314

Detailed information on every documented hurricane and tropical storm in the Atlantic Basin since 1886 is available. Data on windspeed, wind distribution, pressure, and other parameters is displayed on command on detailed maps. These maps are drawn to the county level and include major transportation routes and hydrology. The product comes in a professional version and a hobbyist version from:

PC Weather Products
P.O. Box 72723
Marietta, GA 30007-2723
(800) 605-2230; (404) 953-3506
http://www.wxperson@mindspring.com

Excellent CDs (for $39.95) on many aspects of Earth are available in the Small Blue Planet Series from:

Now What Software
500 Sansome Street, Suite 501
San Francisco, CA 94111
(800) 322-1954; (415) 885-1689

Earth science on a CD-ROM is available from the following two companies:

TASA Graphic Arts, Inc.
11930 Menual Boulevard. NE, Suite 107
Albuquerque, NM 87112-2461
(505) 293-2727; (505) 293-5757 (fax)
http://www.swcp.com/~tasa (Internet); tasagraph@aol.com (e-mail)

Wayzata Technology
2515 East Highway 2
Grand Rapids, MI 55744
(800) 735-7312
http://www.wayzatatech.com

The latest edition of the CD-ROM *Sourcebook for the Atmospheric, Oceanic, Earth, and Space Sciences* describes more than 500 CD-ROM titles that contain information on meteorology, astronomy, geology, oceanography, space, geography, ecology, hydrology, and many other topics. The publication identifies more than 100 sources for these CD-ROM titles. Contact:

MeteoQUEST
P.O. Box 10360
Bedford, NH 03110-0360
(603) 471-1802; (603) 471-1803 (fax)

Videos

- Beerger Productions, P.O. Box 935-W, Cannon Beach, OR 97110-0935; (503) 436-2559.

- *Chasing the Wind* and *The Chasers of Tornado Alley* are available from Prairie Pictures, P.O. Box 122020, Arlington, TX 76102.

- *The Storm Spotter's Video Field Guide* is available from: Dave Oliver, P.O. Box 3372, Amarillo, TX 79116.

- *Tornado Video Classics 1-3* are available from: The Tornado Project, Box 302E, St. Johnsbury, VT 05819; (802) 748-2505.

- *Tornado Warning I, II, and III* are available from: Texas Weather Devices, P.O. Box 309, Cresson, TX 76035.

- Several titles are available on tornadoes, hurricanes, lightning, and general interest from: The Weather Channel, 2600 Cumberland Parkway, Atlanta, GA 30339; (770) 434-6800.

- Several titles on hurricanes are available from: Richard Horodner, 10423 SW 153rd Street, Miami, FL 33157.

Other Resources

- Picturesque cloud charts are available from: Cloud Chart, Inc., P.O. Box 21298, Charleston, SC 29413; (803) 577-5268 and Viking Instruments, Inc., 524 Main Street, South Weymouth, MA 02190.

- Striking posters (24x36) of cloud-free Earth are available from: Satellite Visions, 2801 South 25th Avenue, Broadview, IL 60153-4589; (800) 275-4452; fax: (708) 343-0923.

- A set of 30 overhead transparencies about weather is available from: AMS Project ATMOSPHERE, 1701 K Street NW, Suite 300, Washington, DC 20006; (202) 466-5728; fax: (202) 466-5729.

- A document describing the most deadly and damaging tropical cyclones in the Atlantic Basin since 1492 is available from: National Technical Information Service (NTIS), 5285 Post Royal Road, Springfield, VA 22151. Ask for NOAA Technical Memorandum NWS NHC 47.

- A soft globe called Living Earth is produced from 10,000 Landsat 5 images with more than 1,000 names of countries, cities, and natural boundaries added. The polyester-cotton shell is filled with recycled new fiber and printed with nontoxic ink. It's 16 inches in diameter and costs $36.95. Contact: Hugg-a-Planet, 247 Rockingstone Avenue, Larchmart, NY 10538; (914) 833-0200; fax: (914) 833-0303.

- A set of stunning posters, part of a series called Face of the Earth, has been created by using data from global weather satellites and photographs taken from the space shuttle. All of this data was combined and clouds were deleted using special software. These posters are available from: ARC Science Simulations, Box 1955, Loveland, CO; (800) 759-1642; (970) 667-1168; fax: (970) 667-1105; Web page: http://www.arcinc.com/.

- Excellent poster maps for classroom use are available in 40x27 for the United States (cost $27.10) and in 35x27 (cost $18.85) for Asia, Africa, North America, South America, and Oce- ania. Contact: Gabelli U.S. Inc., 1300 Collins Avenue, Miami Beach, FL 33139; (305) 532-2633; fax: (305) 532-2740.

Appendix E: CyberWeather: A Guide to Weather Information on the Internet

The Internet, an array of interconnected computers, constitutes a massive online resource for teachers that can be used in the classroom and at home. The Internet greatly increases the amount of available material and adds to the pleasure of the learning process. Students also develop the necessary skill of computer literacy. The information provided in this appendix is not meant to be all-inclusive but is intended to whet the appetite.

- Two national professional organizations for meteorologists and students, the AMS and the NWA, can be accessed at: http://www.ametsoc.org/AMS and http://www.nwas.org, respectively.

- Access to The Weather Channel Website, which provides useful information, is available at: http://www.weather.com.

- Earthweek is a graphic chronicle of natural events throughout the world, including earthquakes, volcanic eruptions, hurricanes, forest fires, temperature extremes, and more. The address is: http://www.slip.net/~earthenv/.

- Information from the Total Ozone Mapping Spectrometer (TOMS) from NASA's Goddard Space Flight Center in Greenbelt, Maryland, is available. Students can learn about ozone monitoring, instrumentation, and documentation of changes in Earth's ozone layer. The homepage is located at: http://jwocky.gsfc.nasa.gov/.

- Information on the aurora phenomena is available at: http://www.geo.mtu.edu/weather/aurora/.

- The dynamic personality of Planet Earth can be seen with snazzy graphics from GOES satellites. The address is: http://www.ssec.wisc.edu/.

- The site of the U.S. Geological Survey contains information on geology, mapping, and water resources, as well as an extensive list of other Internet resources in the earth and environmental sciences. Here is the address: http://www.usgs.gov/.

- WeatherNet is an Internet site from the University of Michigan. It provides a gateway to some 100 other Websites at universities, federal laboratories, and TV stations. The various sources offer forecasts, maps, and satellite and radar images. The address is: http://cirrus.sprl.umich.edu/wxnet.

- Regional Climate Centers are a source of climatic expertise and maintain multifaceted interfaces with the public and private sectors. Each center manages the basic data for its region and delivers specialized products, conducts applied climate studies, and acquires and maintains regional data sets. Each center can be accessed through the other.

- The High Plains Regional Climate Center (http://hpccsun.unl.edu/) is located in Lincoln, Nebraska.

- The Midwestern Regional Climate Center is located in Champaign, Illinois.

- Cornell University in Ithaca, New York, houses the Northeast Regional Climate Center (http://met-www.cit.cornell.edu/nrcc_home.html).

- The Southeast Regional Climate Center (http://water.dnr.state.sc.us/climate/sercc/) is located in Columbia, South Carolina.

- Baton Rouge, Louisiana, is the home of the Southern Regional Climate Center (http://maestro.srcc.lsu.edu/srcc.html).

- Finally, the Western Regional Climate Center is located in Reno, Nevada.

World Weather Links are available through the following:

- World Meteorological Organization (WMO): http://www.wmo.ch
- Australia—Bureau of Meteorology: http://www.bom.gov.au
- Canada—Environment Canada: http://cmits02.dow.on.doe.ca
- France—Meteo-France: http://www.meteo.fr/e_index.html
- Netherlands—Royal Netherlands Meteorological Institute: http://www.knmi.nl/home/Home.html
- New Zealand—Met Service: http://metdg1.met.co.nz
- South Africa—Weather Bureau: http://cirrus.sawb.gov.za
- United Kingdom—Meteorology Office: http://www. meto.govt.uk

The U.S. government maintains a wealth of Internet sites:

- NOAA homepage: http://www.noaa.gov
- NWS homepage: http://www.nws.noaa.gov
- Interactive Weather Information Network (IWIN): http://iwin.nws.noaa.gov/iwin/main.html
- NWS Eastern Region: http://www.nws.noaa.gov/eastern.HTM
- NWS Southern Region: http://www.nws.noaa.gov/southern.HTM
- NWS Western Region: http://ssd.wrh.noaa.gov/index.html
- NWS Central Region: http://www.crhnwscr.noaa.gov
- NWS Pacific Region: http://www.nws.noaa.gov/pacific.shtm

The Global Learning and Observations to Benefit the Environment (GLOBE) Program (http://www.globe.gov) is a worldwide network of 2,700 schools in 32 countries that is made up of students, teachers, and scientists. The GLOBE program for kids (http://globe.fsl.noaa.gov) is a joint educational tool developed by NASA and NOAA. Students can formulate their own weather conditions and create a map or globe for instruction or entertainment.

The National Climatic Data Center (NCDC) is a depository for weather-related data from the United States and around the world. The address is: http://www.ncdc.noaa.gov

The latest information on El Niño is available via the Internet on the El Niño Theme Page. The information can be obtained at: http://www.pmel.noaa.gov/toga-tao/el-nino

Check out one of the 11 Environmental Research Laboratories of the federal government. The homepage is: http://www.erl.noaa.gov

The various National Centers for Environmental Prediction can be reached from the following address: http://www.ncep.noaa.gov

Interested in storms? Check out the following entries:

- Emergency Preparedness: http://www.fema.gov/fema/predis.html
- National Flood Insurance Program: http://www.fema.gov/fema/finifp.html
- Disaster Application Center: http://www.fema.gov/fema/dac.html
- Tropical Cyclone Watches: http://www.fema.gov/fema/trop.html
- National Hurricane Center: http://www.nhc.noaa.gov
- Colorado State University: http://tropical.atmos.colostate.edu
- Florida State University: http://thunder.met.fsu.edu
- University of Hawaii: http://lumahai.soest.hawaii.edu/Tropical_Weather/tropical.html
- Tropical Storms Worldwide: http://www.solar.ifa.hawaii.edu/Tropical
- University of Michigan: http://cirrus.sprl.umich.edu/wxnet/tropical.html
- Storm Prediction Center: http://www.nssl.noaa.gov/spc

- National Severe Storms Laboratory: http://www.nssl.ou.edu
- Weather Videos: http://iwin.nws.noaa.gov/iwin/videos.html

The Environmental Protection Agency homepage is http://www.epa.gov. A noteworthy component of the EPA Website is the Office of Air and Radiation, where you can obtain information on the ozone layer, acid deposition, indoor and outdoor air pollution, and more. The site contains lots of free publications and tips. Here is the Web address: (http://www.epa.gov/oar/oarhome.html).

The Sourcebook recommends teachers at all grade levels check out the Reinventing Schools page at: http://www.nap.edu/nap/online/techgap/welcome.html.

Available from NASA (homepage http://www.hq.nasa.gov) is an educational resource entitled "Amazing Facts" (http://pao.gsfc.nasa.gov/gsfc/earth/efacts/efacts.HTM). The George C. Mitchell Space Flight Center in Huntsville, Alabama, offers the following interesting site: Lightning Detection From Space (http://www.ghcc.msfc.nasa.gov/lisotd.html). Located at the Global Change Data Center, NASA Goddard Space Flight Center, Greenbelt, Maryland, the Global Change Master Directory is a comprehensive source of information about earth science, environmental, biosphere, climate, and global change data holdings available to the scientific community throughout the world. The site features links to hundreds of related resources. The address is: http://gcmd. gsfc.nasa.gov/.

The Council on Environmental Quality recommends environmental policy to the president and analyzes trends in the national environment (http://ceq.eh.doe.gov).

You can access satellite images from the following locations on the Internet:

- Africa:
  http://www.cnn.com/WEATHER/accu.data/afsat.gif
- Antarctica:
  http://www.ssec.wisc.edu/data/comp/latest_ant.gif
- Asia:
  http://lumahai.soest.hawaii.edu/gifs/gms_cur.gif
- Australia:
  http://www.cnn.com/WEATHER/accu.data/aussat.gif
- Canada:
  http://www.intellicast.com/weather/intl/cansat.gif
- Caribbean:
  http://www.intellicast.com/weather/intl/cbsat.gif
- Europe:
  http://www.meteo.fr/tpsreel/images/satt0.gihttpf
- Hawaii:
  http://lumahai.soest.hawaii.edu/gifs/hawaii_ir.gif
- Mideast:
  http://www.cnn.com/WEATHER/accu.data/Mideast.gif
- New Zealand:
  http://www.gphs.vuw.ac.n2/meteorology/pictures/ir1/latest.jpeg
- South America:
  http://www.cnn.com/WEATHER/accu.data/samersat.gif

Have you ever wondered what the weather looks like around the world? Select one of the links below to get a near real-time picture. These pictures, from remote cameras installed on towers, rooftops, and other locations, are maintained by TV stations, universities, and other entities.

- Huntsville, Alabama:
  http://www.whnt19.com/towercam/extra.jpg
- Phoenix, Arizona:
  http://www.azfms.com/Travel/camera.html
- St. George's, Bermuda:
  http://www.bbsr.edu/~norm/whatsup.gif
- Vancouver, British Columbia:
  http://www.multiactive.com/MFun/cam1.cgi
- Los Angeles, California:
  http://www.fountainhead.com/sniper.gif
- San Diego, California:
  http://www.live.net/sandiego
- San Francisco, California:
  http://www.kpix.com/live/

- Boulder, Colorado:
  http://www.ceram.com/cheyenne/chey.html
- Crested Butte, Colorado:
  http://www.rsn.com/~crested
- Vail, Colorado:
  http://www.rsn.com/~vail
- Cape Canaveral, Florida:
  http://www.fl-fishing.cam/menu/river.shtml
- Tampa, Florida:
  http://www.wtvt.com/skycam.htm
- Atlanta, Georgia:
  http://vista.homecom.com/cgi-bin/cam2
- Maui, Hawaii:
  http://www.maui.net/~sync/cam.html
- Oahu, Hawaii:
  http://planet-hawaii.com/ph/he.html
- Chicago, Illinois:
  http://www.habitat.com/cgi-bin/show_view
- Boston, Massachusetts: http://www-1.
  openmarket. com/boscam/boscam/
  boscambig.gif
- Bozeman, Montana:
  http://www.gomontana.com/skycam.jpg
- Lincoln, Nebraska:
  http://www.starcitymall.com/webcam/
- Wildcat Ski Area, New Hampshire:
  http://www.rsn.com/~wildcat/
- Empire State Building, New York:
  http://205.230.66.5/view.html
- Rockefeller Center, New York:
  http://www.ftna.com/cam.gif
- Toledo, Ohio:
  http://www.mco.edu/comp/camalli.shtml
- Tulsa, Oklahoma:
  http://kjrh.com/images/default3.gif
- Niagara Falls, Ontario:
  http://FallCam.niagara.com/FallsCam/Live/
  Movies/Falls.jpg
- Portland, Oregon:
  http://www.tek.com/PDX_Pictures/pictures.gif
- Pittsburgh, Pennsylvania:
  http://goober.graphics.cs.cmu.edu/~ajw/
  goober.gif
- Memphis, Tennessee:
  http://www.wmcstations.com/weather/
  high5m.shtml
- College Station, Texas:
  http://ENTCWEB.tamu.edu/camera.htm
- Salt Lake City, Utah:
  http://www.net.utah.edu/html/cameras.html
- Washington DC:
  http://wxnet4.nbc4.com/cgi-bin/showsScrCap
- Seattle, Washington:
  http://www.cac.washington.edu:1180/cambots/

Finally, here are a few miscellaneous items that might be of interest:

- What time is it? The most accurate clock in the world, the United States Naval Observatory Master Clock, can be accessed at http://tycho.usno.navy.mil/what.html.
- Congress:
  http://www.house.gov/whoswho.html
- Senate:
  http://www.senate.gov/senator/members.html
- President:
  http://www.whitehouse.gov/WH/EOP/html/
  couples.html

Happy Surfing!!

Index

Tom Konvicka is chief meteorologist at KALB-TV, the NBC affiliate in Alexandria, Louisiana. He is also an author and a consultant. Mr. Konvicka graduated from Texas Tech University in Lubbock, Texas, in 1981 with a degree in mathematics. He attended graduate school there in atmospheric science. Mr. Konvicka's main hobby is his profession.

from *Teacher Ideas Press*

THE WORLD'S REGIONS AND WEATHER: Linking Fiction to Nonfiction
Phyllis J. Perry

Use the power of fiction and the students' imagination to draw them into the world of climate and weather. Start students with high-quality fiction to peak their interest before moving them on to significant nonfiction endeavors. **Grades 5–9.**
Literature Bridges to Science Series
xvi, 157p. 8½x11 paper ISBN 1-56308-338-8

INTERMEDIATE SCIENCE THROUGH CHILDREN'S LITERATURE: Over Land and Sea
Carol M. Butzow and John W. Butzow

These hands-on and discovery activities use scientific concepts and span all disciplines of the middle school curriculum. Focusing on earth and environmental science themes, topics such as oceans, rivers, mountains, air, weather, deserts, fossils, plants, and environmental quality are covered. **Grades 4–7.**
xxv, 193p. 8½x11 paper ISBN 0-87287-946-1

A SENSE OF PLACE: Teaching Children About the Environment with Picture Books
Daniel A. Kriesberg

Introduce students to the wonders of nature in their own neighborhoods through simple activities and quality children's literature. Students will build a sense of place as they use their five senses to explore nature, human history, and our impacts on the environment. Easy-to-incorporate ideas enliven subject areas across the curriculum. **Grades K–6.**
xxvii, 145p. 8½x11 paper ISBN 1-56308-565-8

LEARNING FROM THE LAND: Teaching Ecology Through Stories and Activities
Brian "Fox" Ellis

Breathe life into the dry bones of geologic history! An integrative approach of hands-on science and creative writing lesson plans helps students explore ideas and hone a deeper understanding of ecological concepts. Step-by-step lesson plans give you the confidence and skills to take your classes outdoors. **All levels.**
xxviii, 145p. 8½x11 paper ISBN 1-56308-563-1

SOARING THROUGH THE UNIVERSE: Astronomy Through Children's Literature
Joanne C. Letwinch

Get students to reach for the stars—Teach the basics of astronomical and space science using quality children's literature. Chapters on the moon, sun, planets, stars, and flight offer reproducible activities and project ideas that combine stories and facts with multiple subject areas. Resources for further out-of-this-world research are included. **Grades 3–6.**
xvi, 191p. 8½x11 paper ISBN 1-56308-560-7

GRAVITY, THE GLUE OF THE UNIVERSE: History and Activities
Harry Gilbert and Diana Gilbert Smith

Take your students through a fascinating narrative on the evolution of scientific thought. Start before the discovery of gravity, move to Einstein's New Law of Gravity, and end with the discoveries of this century's Stephen Hawking. Twelve field-tested lesson plans follow. **Grades 5–8.**
xv, 209p. 8½x11 paper ISBN 1-56308-442-2

For a FREE catalog or to place an order, please contact:

Teacher Ideas Press
Dept. B999 · P.O. Box 6633 · Englewood, CO 80155-6633
1-800-237-6124, ext. 1 · Fax: 303-220-8843 · E-mail: lu-books@lu.com

Check out the TIP Web site!
www.lu.com/tip